American Aircraft Development of WWII

American Aircraft Development of WWII

Special Types, 1939-1945

Bill Norton

www.crecy.co.uk

Crécy Publishing Ltd

www.crecy.co.uk

First published in 2016 by Crécy Publishing

A CIP record for this book is available from the British Library

ISBN 9780859791885

Printed in Malta by Melita Press

Crécy Publishing Limited

1a Ringway Trading Estate, Shadowmoss Road, Manchester M22 5LH

www.crecy.co.uk

Front cover main Image: The Curtiss SC-1 was the Navy's move to create a floatplane with fighter like performance and armament. *National Museum of Naval Aviation*

Inset: The USAAF's cancelled Fleetwings PQ-12 drone program yielded nine airplanes that could serve to test the assault drone concept. *Air Force Test Center*

Back cover main image: Tactical vehicles were loaded into the Packet via wheel ramps between the interchangeable tail booms and vertical surfaces. *National Archives*

Inset clockwise from top:
This B-25D has been converted to an F-10 with the nose blisters encompassing the optical windows for its cameras. *National Museum of the United States Air Force*
One of eleven Beech JRB-1 drone control aircraft, 2543 models the 'cupola' added above the flight deck for the control operator and photographer. *San Diego Air & Space Museum*

An improved Platt-LePage machine was funded in the hope of resolving many of the more serious deficiencies. However, the XR-1A was beset by controllability issues and was therefore dropped. *National Archives*

A Grumman J2F-4 is captured on color film in 1940 at Pensacola. *Naval Aviation Archives*

The RB-1 was an imposing machine on the ground with its unusual slab sides and towering bulbous nose. *National Archives*

The earliest B-24s were not considered combat-worthy as the type was still maturing and adopting some of the required survivability features. *National Archives*

Front flap top: A Navy drone operator lands a TD2C-1 (PQ-14B), displaying the makeshift controller station mounted off the front bumper of the truck that contains a generator and transmitter. *Naval Aviation Archive*

Bottom: This Piper LBP-1 towed glider bomb is an example of a parallel class of weapons employing much the same technology as the assault drones. *National Archives*

Table of Contents

Acknowledgments

For their kind assistance, the author wishes to thank the following individuals and organizations, in alphabetical order: Gerald Balzer; Kasey Decker, Hayden Hamilton and Paul Minert of the American Aviation Historical Society; Bart Everett; Amy Heidrick, Dan Hagedorn and John Little at the Museum of Flight; Dennis Jenkins; Jay Miller and the people of the Jay Miller Collection; Alan Renga and the folks at the San Diego Air & Space Museum; Maurice Schechter; Dan Shumaker; Brett Stolle and the National Museum of the United States Air Force; Curtiss Utz and the staff of the Naval Aviation Archives; personnel at the National Museum of Naval Aviation archives; the late Ray Wagner; and the United States National Archives.

This Kingfisher floatplane is being hauled aboard the USS *Pittsburgh* (CA-72) on 16 May 45. As shown, aircrew, including the pilot, had an additional duty of clambering out onto the wing to snag the crane hook and attach it to the hoisting bridle. The sailors at the gun station are attempting to keep the aircraft stable and away from the unyielding steel hide of the vessel with fending poles. *Naval Aviation Archives*

Introduction

THIS IS THE FOURTH of a series of books presenting America's military aircraft development of the Second World War with emphasis on experimental and unproduced aircraft variants. The first volume addressed fighters (Specialty Press), the second bombers (Midland), and the third gliders (Schiffer). As the title of this book indicates, it encompasses special types that do not fall into the first three broad categories. Another is planned that will look at research and development together with experimental project aircraft.

I was motivated to undertake these projects by a desire to present a clear and concise examination of American accomplishments in aviation development during the war years. This would stand beside comparable texts on the work of other combatants. German subjects especially are covered in a generous number of books, some going far afield in examining projects that never progressed beyond conceptual sketches. By comparison, the scope of what the United States accomplished during the war was of considerably more breadth, technical success, and greater importance for the future.

These books discuss the technological maturation of US aviation weapons under the pressure of war with emphasis on experimental models and what was then high technology. The war years were particularly noted for rapid changes in aircraft design, with many remarkable aircraft coming and going in quick succession. The particular value of these works is their illumination of little-known or minimally documented projects that significantly advanced the science and technology of aeronautics, propulsion, aircraft systems, avionics and ordnance, but did not go into full-rate production and deployment, or only on a comparatively small scale.

Unlike the previous books, this volume is more 'episodic', each chapter introducing another class of aircraft, examining the state of the art at the beginning of the war, the standard aircraft or weapons (if any), and the advances during the conflict. This last is the vehicle to focus on the little-known experimental and prototype aircraft. These various classes are generally collected under the title 'special types'. These are less 'glamorous' than fighters and bombers, yet made their unique contribution to victory or aeronautical advancement.

Every weapon requires a period of development, test, optimization and production before it is introduced to combat forces where integration and training are required before employment against the enemy. Although truncated somewhat during the war, this meant two or more years of effort such that no major aeronautical system begun after the USA declared war on Japan made it into combat to any large measure. Yet the United States had been in a rearmament surge since the war began and was supplying warplanes to friendly powers. These endeavors reflect the nation's skill and will, and may be compared with other combatant nations of the period.

The text presupposes the reader has a fundamental understand of aircraft, how they fly, how aero engines work, and the basic course of the Second World War air war. A glossary plus list of acronyms and abbreviations is found at the back of the book for ready reference. The reader will find few references to actual combat experiences and associated personalities. Instead, the 'war stories' are those of military personnel, engineering teams and test pilots struggling against short schedules and tight resource constraints to develop new aircraft pushing the bounds of technology. These epic and sometimes life-threatening endeavors were as vital to the war effort as actual combat.

I welcome feedback and additional research material. Readers may contact me at williamnorton@earthlink.net.

Bill Norton
California City, 2014

The Douglas C-47 Skytrain was the most common American transport aircraft for the war and dominated the tactical missions. Yet, as these photos illustrate, being derived from a pre-war commercial airliner meant it was cumbersome to load and unload, especially with military equipment. Wartime projects to develop purpose-built tactical transports sought a level deck at truck bed height and loading of wheel cargo up a ramp along the longitudinal axis of the airplane. *National Archives*

CHAPTER ONE

Playing Catch-up

Technology chase

BETWEEN THE WARS, and especially in the economic crisis period of the 1920s and 1930s, the United States War Department bought few airplanes and struggled to foster aeronautical advancement. What meager dollars were available had to be focused on frontline combat types. Secondary and special types soldiered on with outmoded models. The aircraft and engine manufacturers suffered from lack of government contracts and constrained commercial sales – yet remained world class. The small community allowed close business relationships between service leaders and the principals in the major firms. This would pay dividends later when plain talk and considerable trust was required as everyone moved to a war footing. Creation of the National Advisory Committee for Aeronautics (NACA) in 1927 assisted technological progress, from which the military and commercial entities were able to benefit. The vision and talent for rapid innovation and prototyping was ready to be tapped and expanded. For specialized military applications the market fostered little advancement.

As fascist nations moved to determined military expansion and geographic influence, in America isolationism and resistance to foreign entanglements precluded immediate reaction. The armed forces watched potential adversaries acquire ever more advanced and capable warplanes. Knowledgeable individuals observed that the USA was falling behind in aeronautical sciences and advanced military

The US military and aircraft manufacturers worked with the National Advisory Committee for Aeronautics for fundamental research and to resolve developmental issues. The NACA frequently operated military aircraft in addition to its own fleet. This 6 June 1940 image shows a Lockheed 12A Electra Junior configured with a centerline fin for directional stability testing, added nose instrumentation probes, and wing leading edge thermal de-ice. *National Aeronautics and Space Administration*

applications. Should the Americans find themselves at war with the aggressive powers, it would be at a decided disadvantage. Only in 1939, with conflict in many parts of the world and the aggressors making marked gains, were some Americans moved to action. Backed by President Roosevelt, this propelled a progressive increase in investment and resource mobilization. Airpower was at the forefront of the build-up as the combat abroad, seen in the press and as reported by observers, emphasized the often decisive role of aircraft with an outsized advantage of technological superiority. Again, frontline combat aircraft were the primary beneficiaries of the growing largess, with only the most minor attention paid to the special types at the fringes of military capabilities.

Beginning in 1938, growing foreign orders for American arms were important in expanding plant capacity and personnel experience. This widened further with the passage of the Lend-Lease Act on 11 March 1941, which had government equipment provided to allies instead of via commercial sales, and so directly benefited the US military by ensuring immediate capacity should the US be drawn into the growing war. Pent-up demand was unleashed after Japan's 7 December 1941 attack on Pearl Harbor and American entry into the war. The US had a wealth of materials to draw upon and the nucleus of advanced combat types to take to high-rate production. Much expansion in plant capacity and personnel was still ahead as the country moved to a total-war footing. Yet the Americans were so far behind the other combatants in number of warplanes and combat capabilities that it would take considerable time before much new could be brought to the fight.

Even the best intentions, patriotism and money could accelerate aircraft development only so much, especially with all resources constrained by war prioritization. Entirely new designs required two to three years to reach combat readiness, with many thousands of engineering man-hours and hundreds or thousands of drawings, in addition to plant and production personnel preparation. Engine development and production ran longer still. Even new models of an existing design could be a year from concept to fielding, by which time the urgency could have eased or the anticipated advantage eliminated by enemy capability advancement.

Allocation of sometimes scarce resources had to favor frontline assets. Hence, some promising developments lagged to the point that they contributed nothing to the war. Alliance with Britain permitted a pooling of resources and efficient division of efforts. In some cases the Americans benefited from British work during the previous two years of war. Evolving tactics and doctrine, in response to enemy actions, national imperatives, or new weapon capabilities, were other forces driving shifts in aircraft programs.

Pre-war military aircraft acquisition began with a service need defined as a Request for Proposal to industry. Resulting submissions were evaluated, a detailed specification ('spec') written, and a contract issued to the winner for a prototype and static test article. A wooden mock-up would be built for service examination and comment. The static article represented the bare airframe and was subjected to maximum loads expected in operation, plus a safety margin. If engineering flight testing of the prototype proved favorable, service test examples would be ordered. These would be operated under representative field conditions for detailed data collection and suitability assessed. Only then would production be sought. While this process ensured fair and equitable contracting, with great care leading to an acceptable product before expending a good measure of the nation's wealth, it also guaranteed years before a warplane entered service.

An environment of total war made the pre-war acquisition system untenable. Laws permitting exceptions to the regulations were passed that included cost plus fixed-fee contracts replacing fixed-price. This could be hastened with a Letter of Intent to allow initial work to commence until a Letter Contract or final document was negotiated. Detailed assessment of military need was sometimes truncated to a service chief making a decision to pursue a program.

The Army Air Corps (USAAC) became the US Army Air Forces (USAAF) on 20 June 1941, with chief General Henry 'Hap' Arnold, as a semi-independent arm reflecting the priority airpower was receiving. Its principal aircraft development, test and program management facility was Materiel Division at Wright Field in Dayton, Ohio. In March 1942 this became Materiel Center, an element of Air Materiel Command (AMC) stationed in Washington, District of Columbia (D.C.). The titles morphed again in August 1944 with the merger of AMC and Air Service Command as Air Technical Service Command (ATSC). The US Navy's (USN) Bureau of Aeronautics (BuAer), also acquiring Marine Corps (USMC) aircraft, was based in Washington, D.C.. Testing was principally at Naval Air Station (NAS) Anacostia, Maryland, before moving south in late 1943 to Patuxent River.

Fundamental research was truncated to efforts likely to yield results directly applicable to weapons developed and fielded in the uncertain timescale of the war. General Arnold was particularly reluctant to undertake projects that were too technologically risky or not reasonable extensions of existing systems. The Navy was more guided by tradition and the limitations of its carrier-based infrastructure. However, both branches recognized that aviation advanced at a more rapid pace than other arms and were willing to take a technology step that appeared reasonably within reach and yielding a combat advantage. The NACA was the source for fundamental research and assistance in resolving development problems across multiple programs and services, while War Department laboratories performed more focused test and evaluation.

Moving from a position of deficiency, despite profound ambitions and motivation, was not certain to guarantee military success. The shocking Axis victories and Germany's vaunted aeronautical achievements were reasons for some inferiority fears. The Japanese were underestimated, with no small measure of racist dismissal. Rewards and failures followed, but determined progression yielded acceptable results supporting victory despite the usual missed opportunities, miscalculations, and general tendency towards chaos in complex human endeavors.

Underrated – floatplanes

The Navy went to war with a collection of lightly armed scout and observation class floatplanes (S and O type designations). These were catapult-launched from cruisers and battleships to serve as the 'eyes of the fleet'. At the time of Pearl Harbor the Navy had some fifty-two vessels equipped to launch and recover approximately 175 floatplanes of the SOC and OS2U types. By the end of the war there were eighty-six such ships capable of carrying 250 airplanes, to which had been added the SC type. Many hundreds more of the aircraft were employed as a reserve and for training or various shore-based duties. These numbers are comparatively small beside the tremendous growth of carrier-based aviation. Additionally, the importance of the capability diminished throughout the conflict as other classes of naval aviation emerged, matured, or grew and the likelihood of ship-to-ship gunfire combat diminished dramatically.

The US Navy began the war with a modest number of catapult-launched floatplanes for scouting and observation missions. The newest of these was the Vought OS2U-1, shown here in a 1940 image. These airplanes would be the embryo for a much larger force at the height of the conflict. *National Museum of Naval Aviation*

The catapult shot of a floatplane (the OS2U in 1943) was an abrupt event, going from 'zero to sixty' (literally) in about 3 seconds. The crewmen braced themselves and any items in the cockpit had to be secured or held. The canopy was kept open for the launch to permit rapid egress in the event of the airplane ending in the 'drink' for any reason. *National Museum of Naval Aviation*

Observation was ostensibly short range, remaining near the ship to adjust naval gunfire, while the scout went further and usually possessed greater engine horsepower. However, missions were mixed, with the first letter of the type designation indicating the emphasis. The versatile aircraft served whatever mission for which the crew was called.

The warships possessed one to four aircraft. The aviation units aboard surface combatants were oddballs that only got attention during launch and recovery operations.[1] They were appreciated when their work briefly aided the ship's mission, and cursed when complicating it with the hazard represented by the stored aviation fuel or dripping oil on a well-scrubbed deck. If the ship was at risk of being shelled or torpedoed, the aircraft were immediately launched to reduce the hazards. The mission consisted primarily of scouting targets, anti-submarine patrol, hunting mines, weather reconnaissance, and gun spotting (calling adjustments to shots via radio by observing impacts). They could also fly night missions to drop magnesium parachute flares illuminating enemy shipping for engagement. Other duties included personnel transport and air-sea rescue together with mail and message delivery, some of the latter by throwing a weighted sack containing the communication onto a deck as the airplane passed slowly overhead.

The photo gap

Aerial photographic reconnaissance was another aspect of military air operations that had been neglected by the US in the interwar years. During this period in the Army, photography was the domain of the lightly armed observation types designed to fly slowly at low to medium altitudes for long durations. Long range was not a priority because, in addition to calling adjustment to artillery fire, the missions were intended to support ground forces interested in the terrain and enemy dispositions within 50 miles (81km) of the frontlines. The observation aircraft were designed to carry a camera, albeit a limited model, and hand-held shooting was still practised. Photography was but one of the duties mixed with long looks and sketching targets on charts.

Observing the war in Europe made clear that awareness of enemy activities, target scouting, post-strike damage assessment, and photo-mapping in the absence of surveyed charts had taken on tremendous importance. British photo reconnaissance, known there as PR, came to be performed by fast fighter-type ships for short-range missions, and twin-engine airplanes, frequently modified medium bombers, for longer-range photography sorties. These examples were lightly armed or unarmed to permit the greatest fuel load for the initial portion of the flight, and speed for evasion at the mid-point.

The Americans were clearly deficient in PR capabilities. The existing observation aviation was exceptionally vulnerable. Such assets were wisely left behind when the Americans went to war, and the O designation retired as outmoded. In early fall 1940 the decision was made to use single-engine light airplanes for reconnaissance along the front, and medium twins for

At the beginning of the Second World War the US Army was operating a few hundred observation aircraft intended to directly support ground forces by scouting enemy dispositions, photograph routes, and spot artillery shot falls. The North American O-47 was one such, with the three crewmen shown and a belly station for the observer/photographer. This was typical of the airplanes the general staff felt the Air Corps should focus on as it directly supported the ground forces. *National Archives*

Another antiquated observation type in service at the start of the war was the Curtiss O-52 Owl, shown in a 24 February 1941 image. This was considered among the best of these aircraft with roomy crew space, plenty of transparencies for observation, and accommodations for a camera. Such an aircraft, intentionally designed to fly slowly, was quickly shown to be too vulnerable in the evolving air war realities, so remained at home. *Jay Miller Collection*

deeper penetration. By summer of the next year this policy was revamped to include high speed to reach and photograph specific objectives, then evade so as not to require escort. Apart from the light planes, the policy became to convert the top performing production aircraft for the photo role, type dependent on mission requirements.

At the beginning of the war this was how many of the combat aerial photographs were taken – a handheld camera muscled into the slipstream. Even in later years this was still done as an improvised means of taking urgently needed images or for documentary purposes. This staged ground demonstration shows a Navy photographer in the gun port of a PB4Y in close proximity to the gun, which would damage his hearing in the left ear if fired. *National Archives*

Clearly more suitable aircraft would be required if the Air Corps's ambitions of air interdiction and strategic bombing were to be fulfilled. However, Army staff kept the flyers under tight reins, fearing that they would neglect the ground forces and spend considerable budget on costly airplanes with narrow roles. Only the formation of the USAAF and further combat lessons would change these attitudes.

Conversion of production aircraft for the photographic mission was not trivial. It required sturdy camera mounts within the aero shell, with flat optical windows installed in front of lenses. Access for film magazine and camera replacement was mandatory but usually difficult. Common were systems changes for electrical, cooling, heating and window defog in support of the special gear, in addition to cockpit control heads for system operation. Some of the aircraft were adapted for high-altitude work requiring engine supercharging and pilot oxygen. The norm in America became a design often executed by an organization other than the aircraft manufacturer and the installation performed at a modification ('mod') center.

Cameras were various large-format still units built for the inflight environment. Vertical and oblique camera installations were necessary for suitable coverage – the oblique permitting some results without deeply penetrating heavily defended airspace. Two oblique cameras, with a third in between shooting vertically – the trimetrogon arrangement – could be tripped simultaneously to produce panoramic images, or at intervals for mapping along the flight path. Guns mounted nearby were usually removed to avoid the detrimental vibration from firing. A drift-meter might be installed to aid in dead reckoning navigation and ensure the flight over the objective with the desired ground track. Strike cameras added to many bombers also offered intelligence benefits.

Commonly ignored in all of this were the exceptional camera gear, photographic equipment shops, print labs, photographers, photo interpreters and intelligence distribution network. The missions themselves were not popular with aircrew as they often involved penetrating denied airspace, a long duration on oxygen in extreme cold, and occasionally going unarmed.

Transport dearth

Transport aircraft had been much neglected prior to the war. Even during 1940 and 1941 the Army felt it could get most of what it wanted 'off the shelf' by requisitioning civil aircraft and increasing their production rates. When war came, these civil models proved a mixed lot that created as many problems

as they solved, and in fewer numbers than required. Production rates for these existing designs were painfully slow to ramp up due to material shortages and continued low priority. After Pearl Harbor many of the commercial aircraft remained in airline service, although meeting war needs under government contract, until the Naval Air Transport Service (NATS) was created on 12 December 1941 and the Army's Air Transport Command (ATC) was activated on 20 June 1942.

Among the civilian passenger transports taken up by the military were the Douglas DC-3 and Curtiss CW-20 twins. These became the C-47 Skytrain (Navy/USMC R4D) and C-46 Commando (R5C). The Air Corps initially possessed just thirty-one DC-3s for its direct operation.[2] The C-47s and C-46s were conventional-gear aircraft with sloping decks when on the surface and the doors inconveniently far above the ground. Military models had to be developed with widened doors and reinforced floors containing tie-down fittings to accommodate cargo loading, in addition to more powerful engines. Yet they remained frustratingly difficult to load and unload. Wheeled cargo had to go up and down steep ramps with a turn at the top. Freight had to be packaged for manhandling, unless a lift or crane was at hand. New requirements were being formulated that included bulk freight, paratroop jumping, airdrop of parachute-recovered packages, and glider tow. Hence, the USAAF began a program to find more suitable aircraft for the tactical airlift mission.*

As the US prepared for a world-spanning war, the ability to move priority materiel and personnel across continental and oceanic distances was an obvious need. Twin-engine transports required frequent stops at sometimes small and remote stations with limited transient facilities. Such were few or non-existent in the early war years. A long-range airplane could avoid many of these intermediate stops.

* Terms like tactical and strategic airlifters were not common at the time, but are used in this text for association with current military terminology.

The earliest tactical transports were impressed commercial DC-3s while militarized examples were being built. They had understandable limitations as suggested by these paratroop jumps from the passenger door, tape apparently applied to hold padding within the narrow opening to prevent gear snagging. This image predates May 1942 and the configuration suggests it is a mobilized DC-3A labeled a C-47. *San Diego Air & Space Museum*

The acquisition of military transports as derivatives of commercial aircraft was always an exercise in compromise. The desire to rapidly load and unload by shoving equipment onto and off trucks, or rolling vehicles in over ramps, was never going to be possible without a dedicated design. This R3D-2 of 1940 (USMC 1904 derived from the Douglas DC-5, one of just seven) shows how cargo doors were added, but freight loading would still be a strenuous exercise using the supplemental hardware. *National Archives via Hayden Hamilton*

An example of the expropriated airliner assets operated by the US military is this Martin M-130 China Clipper, one of two, which had a capacity of just twelve passengers and cruised at 163mph up to 3,200 miles. Operated under the purview of the Navy, these airplanes never received a designation except for BuNo 48230/1. Often flown by civilian pilots under contract and virtual mobilization, they and their personnel worked for two to three years, bridging the gap before purpose-built long-range transports were available. *National Museum of the United States Air Force*

After entering the conflict and seeking to supply and reinforce deployed forces and allies, US shipping losses to submarines rose to shocking levels. The uninitiated naturally wondered why the Army and Navy didn't simply fly over these threats. The Senate waded in with hearings into apparent inadequate attention to the matter. A basic review made clear that there would never be enough aircraft of sufficient capacity – nor infrastructure to build and sustain them – to carry more than a few percent of the cargo moved by sea-going transport. While Liberty ships could float 10,000 tons, the largest aircraft then in existence could fly but a tiny fraction of this – the Martin XPB2M-1 Mars lifting 15 tons and the Douglas XB-19 9.4 tons. Yet there remained political pressure to advance heavy transports.

Short memories failed to recall that the armed forces had been starved of funds just a year or two previously and could little afford strategic transports, which some saw as encouraging military adventurism. Far from neglecting the matter, the run-up to war had seen the Army seize every airplane in the country of any practical value. Among the mobilized commercial assets were several four-engine, commercial flying boats and airliners. However, there were only sixteen aircraft capable of extended over-water flight.[3] The Navy already had large flying boats like the Martin PBM that had enormous range and were invaluable in communicating with far-flung outposts and allies. Some attention had to be given to diverting a portion of production as transports.

Large, four-engine airplanes were exceptionally complex machines and it could not be hoped that an entirely new aircraft program would meet needs within two years. However, the civil airline industry had been motivating aircraft manufacturers to develop such machines, and they were only just emerging as war strangled commercial opportunities. The projects were turned to meet military requirements while heavy bomber conversions were addressed as the timeliest solution. Yet with the tremendous mobilization of the nation

to equip the world's largest military force, some new programs were initiated to better meet the long-range movement of heavy equipment.

The airliners and the new heavy airlifters presented the most advanced aircraft with extensive safety features. Common were full-feathering constant-speed propellers, an extensive hydraulic and electrical system, radar in some, radio altimeter, autopilots, combustion heaters for the interior, control gust locks, and anti-ice and de-ice systems. Supercharged engines permitted flight above most significant weather, and cabin pressurization higher still. Flight engineers, sometimes with separate stations, were necessary. Such acquisitions placed an additional burden on the aviation industry that had to be weighed against development and delivery of combat types. The efforts required time to yield results, should progress of the war grant the time.

Rotorcraft emerge

The US Army and Navy had been interested in vertical flight since the formation of their flying elements. This would divorce the aircraft from runways and permit operations almost anywhere. During the 1920s the Army had funded several rotary-wing research programs and test aircraft. By the 1930s a reasonably practical rotorcraft had emerged on the civil market that provided a step towards vertical flight. This autogyro was worthy of military evaluation while helicopter development continued.[4]

With an autogyro, the rotor spin is initiated by the ground crew, and a short take-off run using the typical engine and propeller is required to get the rotor spinning fast enough to generate sufficient lift. A very steep climb-out at relatively slow speed is then possible. A slow landing approach ends with a flare and settling down almost vertically. A small window of airspeed and rotor rpm permits an aborted landing and fly-away. In the event of an engine failure, the rotor continues to turn at the glide airspeed and the forced landing is a much safer affair than in an airplane.

The autogyro presented the only production rotorcraft at the time of the Second World War. It had matured through the 1920s and 1930s to include collective and cyclic control, allowing wings to be eliminated. However, the aircraft (a US Army YG-1A is shown here) was still limited and only fed the desire for a true helicopter. *San Diego Air & Space Museum*

Apart from the common rotor articulation, autogyro innovations that had appeared included an accessory shaft from the engine to spin up the rotor to about 70 percent of flight autorotation speed before beginning the take-off roll, thus greatly shortening the take-off distance to a few body-lengths of the aircraft. Torque was reacted by weight-on-wheels and the power shaft declutched before brakes were released.

The near-vertical landing required a descent path clear of obstructions until the final plop onto the ground, usually tail-first from a very nose-high attitude as the rotor pitch was increased to maximum and rpm dropped. Inefficient control at such low airspeeds could allow the craft to drift with a wind gust from the side or rear, leading to touchdown in a manner that caused structural damage or an overturn. Additionally, at low rotor speed the centrifugal force that helped keep the blades up could be overcome by a side wind (gust or pilot change in heading) for unequal lift across the rotor disc. This could cause a blade to drop against its flapping stops, with the risk of blade droop allowing it to impact the fuselage or be struck by the propeller.

A safety solution to the low-speed control issue was to tilt the rotor head and direct the lift in any direction to permit attitude control without airplane surfaces. This 'direct-control' became common in the 1930s, and wings were eliminated. It contributed to reducing flight speed to below a then typical airplane stall. The empennage with rudder(s) was retained to permit tighter turns during lateral maneuvering, but also provided directional control at low airspeeds.

A drawback of the autogyro design was that at low rotor speeds, where it was not gyroscopically stabilized, the rotor was easily disturbed by out-of-balance forces, and this was fed back to the control column which thrashed about violently. It had to be mechanically locked during this period of spin-up and spin-down on the ground. Additionally, the undercarriage had to be designed to react to such disturbances, and this typically meant widely spaced main gear wheels. The spring reaction on the gear might also permit ground resonance.

The last major innovation of autogyros was vertical take-off, but still short of the more difficult helicopter hovering. A spin-up ('over-spin') with blades in flat pitch (feathered) to about 150 percent of typical rpm could be done before take-off. When the rotor was declutched from the engine, so as not to generate torque, the blade pitch was abruptly increased collectively beyond the typical few degrees, automatically or by the pilot. The craft would then leap abruptly into the air, but the rotor immediately resumed normal blade pitch and would begin to spin down naturally. During this brief period the engine was advanced to take-off power and the aircraft began moving forward, thus stabilizing rotor rpm as forward speed and translational rotor lift were built-up to fly away. The 'jump take-off' was typically only 5-15 feet (1.5-4.6 meters), so some clear area ahead was required to accelerate and climb out. This ability was typically marginal on a hot, calm day near maximum gross weight.

Prior to the war, significant progress had been made towards the goal of true vertical flight – hover, precision translation and straight up and down operations – that the autogyro could not perform. Such work built on the relative success of the autogyro and some experimental helicopters. The technical aspects of successful helicopter design were much explored in government and private research, with all possible rotor layouts and control methodology examined and most tested at least in the laboratory. International conferences and technical papers helped to share this progress. Numerous patents were awarded, which meant that licences were required to exploit some of the technology, at least up to the time of war.

The work up to the late 1930s had shown promise but was well short of goals. Countering rotor torque was a principal difference from the autogyro and approached by various methods. The autogyro had done much in pointing the way to successful collective and cyclic rotor control that appeared to be the most suitable flight control method.

Apart from countering powered rotor torque, there was also a requirement for an rpm step-down from the typical aero engine rotation speeds to that of a rotor, which required a heavy reduction gearbox. It also had to provide a disengagement feature (overrunning clutch) to permit emergency autorotation flight should the engine(s) quit. It was recognized that there would be an avoid region of altitudes (a few hundred feet) below which the aircraft, if hovering when the engine failed, would be unable to attain sufficient forward speed for a safe autorotation to a soft landing. In powered flight, the pilot or an automatic feature had to maintain speed above a predetermined rate to ensure the proper balance between the centrifugal forces keeping the blades straight out and the lift that tended to cause them to cone upwards towards destruction. It was still possible for the rotor to dip during slowing to a stop because of a relative wind, and possibly strike the airframe if the pilot did not keep the cyclic stick positioned properly.

Drones pursued

Work to develop an unmanned 'flying bomb' or 'aerial torpedo' airplane dated from the First World War in both the US Army and Navy. The first successful autonomous flight of an unmanned airplane in the world occurred in the US during March 1918, although automatic flight with a safety pilot aboard had been demonstrated previously. These aircraft were only minimally successful, most notably due to system unreliability, and were certainly not operationally practical.

The first successful naval target drone was the Curtiss N2C Fledgling primary trainer. In the late 1930s these aircraft were modified with wing flaps and tricycle undercarriage, together with the installation of radio control gear (right) for ship gunnery practice. Shown are several N2C-2 drones with Great Lakes TG-2 drone control aircraft and Grumman JF-2 utility amphibians at Guantanamo Bay, Cuba, during fleet exercises in January and February 1939. *National Soaring Museum, insert San Diego Air & Space Museum*

Development continued for a time after the war and explored remote radio control from a following aircraft, with successful unmanned flights of this kind in May 1922. Navy work culminated in another world first during September 1924 with a radio-controlled, automatically stabilized flight from take-off to landing, with a floatplane. Stability of such machines relied upon gyros for automatic corrections to uncommanded attitude or heading changes (although an electric compass was also employed for the latter), aided by natural aerodynamic stability via airframe design. Guidance control derived generally from electric servo motors for surfaces and powered by a wind-driven generator, barometric altitude control, and a timer device that paced automatic sequences. These efforts reached the stage of limited production for trials purposes.

The development showed that while automatic aircraft stabilization was generally practical, only radio control gave suitable guidance. For autonomous control, the best that could be achieved was flight at a pre-set altitude on a pre-set compass heading for a specific time before a timer-sequenced throttle cut and descent onto a target. Only an area target could be hit by such a weapon, and it would need to be beyond artillery range to be cost-effective. Radio control relied upon a nearby aircraft with a controller able to make small adjustments visually, but this defeated the value of the weapon. Error derived from the gyroscope mechanism and precession, and mechanical failure rate was high. The problem of getting the airplane safely to flying speed and climbing away from the ground proved a particular challenge. Conventional take-off under such control was difficult, and landing especially fraught. A lesson from this experience was to test the drone's electronic equipment in a pre-existing aircraft with a safety pilot aboard before going unmanned. Tests of a new drone aircraft type were best conducted in a manned configuration first (if practical) to prove out and optimize the design before attempting remote or autonomous flight.

The programs were revived in the mid-1930s but focused primarily on employing such technology for target drones to facilitate anti-aircraft gunnery training, with radio control favored. The radio-controlled target drone had been maturing, with guidance and control technology progressing apace. These machines would serve as the foundation for wing-borne and powered-flight attack assets. The wartime desire was to employ such machines to attack high-value, heavily defended, possibly point targets where conventional bombing had proven ineffective, or the risk to the attacking force was too great.

This outmoded Vought O3U-6 has been modified into a target drone during 1941. The normal main gear has been removed to permit installation of a tricycle undercarriage more stable and conducive to remote take-off and landing. Mock dive-bombing attacks during fleet anti-aircraft gunnery exercises brought forth the notion of such a drone delivering a weapon on a target vessel or shore installation. *Naval Aviation Archives*

CHAPTER TWO

Slingshot Floatplanes

Anatomy

NOT SURPRISINGLY, America's Second World War floatplanes were specialized aircraft designed and built to the environment and mission. They were commonly manned by a pilot and rear observer (variously observer/gunner or radioman/gunner). To be shot from a catapult and recovered at sea, the airplane had a centerline float and an outrigger float under each wingtip. For the catapult launch the aircraft commonly had wing high-lift devices such as leading-edge slats and trailing edge flaps. The stern of the centerline float had a water rudder that was connected to the pilot's rudder pedals. The water rudder was lowered after landing to permit directional control on the water. The flaps were also raised after landing to settle the aircraft quickly onto the surface and prevent damage from water spray impact. The aircraft were lightly armed, usually with a fixed .30 caliber (cal) Browning M-2 machine gun (MG) firing forward and a flexibly mounted gun for the observer in the rear*. The aft gun was on an articulated mount that also swung around a ring. Its field of fire was inhibited by the aircraft structure, especially to the rear. A small bomb or depth charge could be mounted under each wing. The wings were usually designed to be folded aft to reduce space occupied on a crowded deck. When the ship was in port the aircraft were flown off and the floats exchanged for a fixed undercarriage so that flight training could continue or shore-based operations conducted.

Even multi-engine flying boats avoided landing in the open ocean: an OS2U from the cruiser USS *Detroit* (CL-9) is shown here in 1943. Floatplanes typically only landed in the slick created by their ship, but could notionally set down anywhere if required. This could be stressful and hazardous for both the aircrew and airplane. *National Museum of Naval Aviation*

* Fighters employed ·50-cal MGs to knock down enemy aircraft, so the 0.30 'peashooter' had to be seen as mere discouragement to the adversary – or encouragement for the Navy aircrew.

The aircraft were designed for routine hoisting via a deck crane, to be lifted over the side or placed back on the catapult launch car. For the few ships with hangars, the folded-wing aircraft was lowered through a hatch to the crowded below-decks space. Lacking a hangar, the aircraft could be lowered via crane to a dolly on the deck. Maintenance was then carried out exposed to the elements. Jury struts attached the wings to the catapult during heavy seas, preventing damaging motion.

Flight was typically at an altitude of about 500-1,000 feet (152-305 meters) for the mission, and where wind (velocity,

This Naval Aircraft Factory N3N-1, photographed on 25 May 1941, was the initial trainer for pilots transitioning to floatplanes, with primary instruction at NAS Pensacola in Florida. It was rudimentary with an obsolescent 235hp Wright seven-cylinder R-760 Whirlwind 7 for a top speed of 112mph, and lacked water rudder or radio. Its yellow training colors earned it the moniker 'Yellow Peril' from the student pilots. *Naval Aviation Archives*

By the time of war the OS2U had already been in service for several years and the Navy was actively working to replace it with a higher performer. Yet production continued and examples were turned to advanced training. This OS2U-2 is engaged in this role, an instructor conversing with the student. *National Museum of Naval Aviation*

direction) could be determined by observing sea conditions. This was critical because the pilot used dead reckoning navigation since there was usually radio-silence discipline and no navigational aids apart from a compass and clock. The crewmen seldom donned their parachutes because of the low altitudes and the need to exit quickly if they went down. If arriving at the rendezvous point for their ship and finding nothing, the crew dropped a float light that produced smoke and flame for about 3 minutes to mark the spot. The pilot then zoom-climbed to a higher altitude to look around. Failing to locate their craft, the pilot flew an expanding square search pattern. If they exhausted their fuel, the crew landed in the sea and hoped for the best.

Flying such aircraft required skill to operate them safely and efficiently, especially in moderate sea states. Given the drag and suction of the water, achieving the ideal attitude and speed to lift off ('on the step') required judicious handling. The design of the float hull was vital to this, particularly the step about three-fifths of the way back from the bow. The varying wind and ground effect above the uneven surface made landings at sea a delicate task. The aircraft was flown on instead of with a full-stall landing to avoid unexpected jarring impacts with swells. Judging height over the water could be difficult, particularly at night, mandating a gingerly descent. Too high and the aircraft bounced with a sharp thud; too steep and the nose dug in and risked flipping the aircraft or causing a break-up. If the pilot misjudged swells and landed at too flat an angle the nose of the float could again dip. Too steep and the aft end of the float touched first and pitched the airplane forward with further potential for digging in. Swells of more than a few feet could be intolerable. Heavy swells might put the airplane back into the air and the pilot would need to add a bit of power to ease the next touchdown with sufficient control authority. Impacting such a wave at the wrong angle could open a seam in the float and flood the space, or catch a wing float to swing the aircraft violently ('water loop'). Floats were snapped off and other structure buckled as waves washed over the floatplane.

Flight off the water was possible after being lowered over the side, but only in relatively calm seas and with what could be a long take-off run. More common was catapult launch. The launcher, 68 feet (21 meters) long, was on a turntable to permit typically 180 degrees of rotation to fire into the wind. The vessels were typically equipped with two catapults, each firing off to one side, or one that could be swung to either side. The aircraft's center float was positioned on the cradle, where three fittings retrained the aircraft from side motion but permitted acceleration then separation at the end of the rail. The launch car was propelled by a piston hooked to the car via an arrangement of cables run through pulleys. The piston was pressurized explosively by gunpowder combustion from a casing, derived from the 5-inch naval shell, with a 36lb (16kg) charge.

To launch the aircraft into the wind, the ship steamed quartering the wind (15-30 degrees off the wind line) with the catapult aimed 30-45 degrees off the bow directly into the wind. The ideal was not always practical given the placement of other vessels in a formation or the available area of maneuver. All communications were non-verbal in the period of radio silence and the high-noise environment. Signals were via flags flown above the ship and a signal flag from the Catapult Officer. This man directed the pilot to start and check his engine. He also signaled for the Catapult Gunner to prepare the shot charge, and for the bolt restraining the car to be pulled. Next he signaled the pilot to prepare for launch by lowering flaps and running the engine up to full power. The pilot indicated ready. The Catapult Officer signaled for launch on a ship up-roll – firing the aircraft away from the ocean surface. A frangible metal link held back the car until the launch piston pressure built to maximum, at which point the link broke and the car accelerated.

The floatplane went off the end of the catapult at about 60-70mph (97-113km/h) in 3 seconds after a violent acceleration. The crew braced themselves and the pilot held the stick firmly to keep it from moving aft, while his other hand wedged the throttle full open. Everything in the cockpit had to be secured before launch. At the end of the catapult stroke the aircraft could

The floatplane catapult weighed approximately 35 tons; commonly two were installed on the deck of a surface combatant, as suggested here by the wingtip of a second OS2N-1. This vessel, the cruiser USS *Miami* (CL-89), photographed on 2 March 1945, is also equipped with a below-decks hangar as evidenced by the sliding deck hatches; this was of no use for the Kingfishers, which lacking folding wings. Note the servicing of the aircraft on the launch car, the boarding ladder, and the jury struts temporarily securing the aircraft to the catapult. *National Museum of Naval Aviation*

One of the USS *Detroit*'s OS2Us leaves the end of the port catapult in 1943. The system was fairly reliable but required a carefully choreographed series of events that was manpower intensive. The scouting and observation capabilities that these aircraft brought to the combat vessels were not always appreciated by the ship's company. *National Museum of Naval Aviation*

This Kingfisher is pictured on 16 May 1945 during 'Charlie' recovery operations. It has run up on the sea sled and is being towed by it while the gunner/observer hooks up the hoisting line. Sailors stand ready with fending poles to prevent the aircraft from crunching into the unyielding steel side of the ship. *Naval Aviation Archives*

A deck crane lifts the floatplane from the sea to place it on a deck cradle or back on the catapult, as demonstrated here by a Curtiss SC-1 Seahawk. In heavy seas or weather, this could be very difficult, requiring many men manning stabilizing ropes and possibly lying on the wings. The aircraft capability aboard a cruiser or battleship clearly demanded many resources and the ship had to accommodate the aircraft during flight operations. *Naval Aviation Archives*

be just a few miles per hour above stall. If the charge was inadequate or the aircraft lost power, the floatplane could skip off the water or the pilot had to abort the take-off and affect the best possible landing. If in a fleet, a plane guard (usually a destroyer) fell in behind the launch vessel to recover the airmen if the launch ended badly. Take-offs were made with the canopy open to allow rapid egress if the aircraft fell into the 'drink'.

Recovery of the floatplane was equally complex and fraught. The basic scheme was for the machine to land and be brought alongside the ship to be hoisted aboard via the deck crane. The landing itself was challenging in most sea states. The pilots generally sought to set down in the slick created on the inside of a 90-degree cross-wind turn executed by the ship, which eliminated waves but not swells. The aircraft landed into the wind on the windward side, then rapidly taxied alongside. Recovery needed to be expeditious as it disturbed the formation and made the vessel vulnerable to submarine attack. The recovery method was signaled with a flag on the ship's communications mast. The aircraft circled the ship, at which point the vessel began its turn 45 degrees across the wind line.

Four methods of recovery were practised. 'Able' and 'Baker' recoveries were for ships anchored, moored, or otherwise stopped. 'Able' had the aircraft taxi close, shut down, and be towed by a whale boat to under the hoist hook. 'Baker' recovery was the same except for taxiing alongside to hook up. 'Charlie', or 'cast recovery', had the ship perform the turn and the pilot taxied alongside to run up onto a sled towed in the sea, deployed from an over-side boom or crane, or the catapult. This recovery sled or sea trap was a yellow canvas rectangle with heavy cargo netting attached to a 6-foot (1.8-meter) wooden beam at the front. A smoke float might be attached at the front to aid the pilot in locating the sled, or with small red flags at the forward corners. A keel beneath the sled was angled to help steer it outboard of the ship as it trailed from the line, away from the waves washing high beside the hull. Upon taxiing onto the semi-submerged sled, the pilot reduced power and a hook on the forward bottom of the center float snagged the netting. The aircraft was then towed on the sled beside the ship for hoisting. The 'Dog' recovery was similar but the ship sailed in a straight line and aircraft landed in the wake slick directly behind; this was employed when the seas were relatively calm and also allowed recovery of two floatplanes simultaneously.

Once on the sled, the aircraft was reeled to the side, and sailors with long, padded fending poles shoved it back if it drifted too close to the side. For hoisting, the pilot cut the engine while the rear seat man clambered out to grab the dangling crane hook and insert it into the hoisting bridle pulled from an aircraft cavity. If the aircraft slipped off the sled the pilot had to quickly restart the engine. As this was commonly with a black powder cartridge with one shot, the engine was sometimes kept idling until hook-up was certain. Stay lines within the wings and connected at the tips were also pulled out and tossed overboard to be retrieved and held by deck crewmen. Hoisting the airplane from the sea and depositing it aboard required careful manipulation of the crane, stay lines and fending poles. One or more men might be required to lie on the wings to keep the aircraft level and steady.

Clearly, floatplane operations in the open sea were complex affairs requiring many personnel with proficient skills, and there was great potential for aircraft damage. Rough seas and foul weather made this activity all the more difficult and hazardous. Salt-water corrosion was a persistent menace addressed by frequent cleaning – a challenge aboard ship where fresh water was scarce. Some cargo vessels were converted to seaplane tenders as a mobile heavy maintenance shop. The aircraft could be sent ashore for depot maintenance or as part of a mission. Wheeled beaching gear would be attached with the aircraft in the surf and the machine then pulled up onto the beach or boat ramp. The gear might include brakes applied by the ground crew and a bar to turn the tail wheel.

Handling floatplanes at sea was manpower-intensive and hazardous, and the ship's aviation crew had to be able to perform repairs occasioned by rough seas or rough handling. This Grumman J2F-4 'Duck' has been lifted from the water in preparation for depositing on a deck for repairs to wing damage incurred during a bump against a ship's hull. *National Museum of Naval Aviation*

Slingshot floats

The main line (SOC, SON, OS2U, OS2N)

The Curtiss SOC Seagull (Model 71) entered service in the mid-1930s with the 600hp (447kW) Pratt & Whitney (P&W) R-1340-18 nine-cylinder Wasp radial engine.* It remained one of the few biplane types still in frontline service when the US entered the war. It featured what were then advanced top wing leading-edge slats, free to move according to the airload, and trailing edge flaps with small ailerons (larger ailerons on the bottom wing). The airplane was otherwise of typical fabric-covered metal construction. Each folding wing could carry 110lb (50kg) fragmentation bombs or a single 325lb (147kg) depth charge. An asymmetrical load required a higher workload from the pilot because the airplane lacked aileron trim tabs. Apart from a fixed ·30-cal MG in the nose with 500 rounds, the rear gunner had a ·30-cal and 600 rounds, with firing to the rear aided by collapsible aft decking.

Production through 1939 included 135 SOC-1s, forty SOC-2s with the improved R-1340-22s, and eighty-three minimally altered SOC-3s. The Naval Aircraft Factory (NAF), in Philadelphia, Pennsylvania, built forty-four of the SOC-3s as the SON-1.* As with many of the SC types to follow, all SOC/SON models had floats that could be removed and a fixed main gear and tail wheel fitted (officially 'convertible'). Initially with ground-adjustable propeller pitch, constant-speed models were retrofitted by the end of the war. In 1942 some models were given arresting hooks for operation (with wheeled landing gear) from the new escort aircraft carriers, and their designations were given the suffix A ('Arrester'). Three improved SOC-3s built for the US Coast Guard (USCG) were taken up by the Navy in 1942 and converted to SOC-3A standard.[1]

Some 275 Seagulls remained when the Americans joined the hostilities. This was reduced to about 145 when they were withdrawn in favor of the new SO3C (see later), but failure of that type led to seventy or so SOCs being restored to service in 1944. They remained active in all seas through to the end of hostilities.

---

* All horsepower ratings in this book are take-off at sea level values. Radial engines, indicated with an R prefix, are air-cooled.

* At the time, there was a law requiring the NAF to build 10 percent of any naval aircraft type as a check of manufacturing processes and cost. They also performed a good deal of aircraft modification work.

Curtiss-Wright SOC-1 Seagull characteristics
(floatplane configuration)

Span	36.0ft (11.0m)
Length	31.7ft (9.7m)
Height	14.1ft (4.3m)
Wing area	348ft² (32.3m²)
Fuel, max	170 gallons (644 liters)
Climb rate, initial	848fpm (258mpm)
Service ceiling	14,900ft (4,542m)
Weight, empty	3,508lb (1,591kg)
Weight, gross	5,153lb (2,337kg)
Overload	5,341lb (2,423kg)
Speed, max	157mph (253km/h)
Cruise speed	133mph (214km/h)
Range	846 miles (1,362km)

Sailors unfold the wings of an SOC-1 in the landplane configuration. The Navy sought for all its scout-observation floatplanes to be 'convertible', with floats able to be removed and replaced with landing gear. While this allowed operations when the parent ship was in port, it also enabled use on escort carriers when these were introduced and an arrester hook was added to the SOCs. *Jay Miller Collection*

The unrivalled workhorse of the US Navy's Second World War floatplane stable was the Vought OS2U.[2] Vought-Sikorsky submitted the VS-310 design against a 1937 requirement that led to a March 1937 contract for a prototype that flew a year later. In competition with two other types (biplanes), the XOS2U-1 was a two-seat monoplane. First flying in July 1938, it was powered by a nine-cylinder P&W R-985-4 Wasp Junior at 450hp (336kW). The airplane had the expected capability of swapping the floats for a fixed wheeled undercarriage, but lacked folding wings, as battleships had enough space on their

This Curtiss SOC-1 is tethered to the seaplane tender USS *Pines Island*, with engine still running to hold position in the current and wind, while the pilot prepares to grab the crane hook and attach it to the aircraft sling he has extracted from within the top wing. The SOC was the principal scout-observation type at the beginning of the war and was only phased out mid-war. It was resurrected to serve through to the end of hostilities (a rare biplane to do so) when its replacement did not meet expectations. *National Museum of Naval Aviation*

decks. When the double-slotted flaps were lowered, the ailerons drooped simultaneously for effective full-span flaps. Low-speed roll control was then assumed by spoilers with a small vent opening below the wing permitting air flow through the slot over the top of the ailerons. Construction of the XOS2U-1 featured the first use of spot-welding in aircraft manufacturing for a smooth exterior free of rivet heads. It was all metal apart from a fabric covering aft of the wing spar and on all control surfaces.

The Vought design found favor with the USN, which placed an order for fifty-four in May 1939, substituting the R-985-48 engine. There was a fixed ·30-cal MG in the nose with 500 rounds, and a flexibly mounted .30 in the rear with 600 rounds. Underwing stations could accommodate the usual 110lb bomb or 325lb depth charge. The observer had minimum essential flight controls and instruments.

Chance Vought handed over the OS2U-1s between May and December 1940, then moved on to 158 OS2U-2s ordered on 4 December 1939. These were externally nearly identical except for mission equipment and the R-985-50 engine of the same power rating. Internally, they added 253lb (115kg) of crew and oil tank armor. A 50-gallon (189-liter) fuel tank was added to each wing, but was reduced to a 96-gallon (363-liter) capacity with self-sealing, while the 144-gallon (545-liter) fuselage tank remained without this protection. The added fuel permitted up to 6 hours endurance. An especially advanced feature was purging of the ullage space in the tanks with carbon dioxide gas to prevent any build-up of explosive fumes. Although reflecting combat lessons from the war in Europe, the 493lb (224kg) empty weight increase cut the top speed by 7mph (11km/h).

Production then shifted to the OS2U-3 in summer 1941, following a 31 October 1940 contract that, with subsequent add-ons, amounted to a total of 1,306 airplanes. This easily made it the most numerous floatplane as the US moved to war. They were powered by the R-985-AN-2, also of 450hp, and were 198lb (90kg) heavier than their predecessors. First flying on 17 May 1941, the production line shifted to this model in

July and the Navy took on 368 on these airplanes that year. Seeking to free up production line space for F4U Corsair fighters, the last 300 on the Vought contract were cancelled, and on 30 January 1941 the NAF was ordered to produce these as OS2N-1s. They would use some of Vought's Stratford assets and subcontractor arrangements for full delivery in nine months. These airplanes were 400lb (181kg) lighter but otherwise identical. This arrangement was not without hurdles, and deliveries stretched over nearly a year, from 9 March 1942 through to the end of November. At the end of production Vought handed over enough excess parts for another 31 machines to be assembled by the Factory for a total of 1,306 of the -3 or equivalent model. The firm had also built a percentage of complete part sets, some of which were used by field units to build a handful of full-up aircraft lacking Bureau Numbers.[3]

The USCG operated fifty-three OS2U-3s/OS2N-1s between 1942 and 1944 for the usual convoy escort and coastal anti-submarine warfare (ASW) patrols. The British took 100 OS2U-3s as the Kingfisher I via Lend-Lease, which began to arrive there in spring 1942. Of the initial hundred, forty-five went to the British Isles, thirty-five to South Africa, and twenty to the West Indies. Other Lend-Lease customers included the Netherlands, with twenty-four bound for the Dutch East Indies; these were at Darwin when Japanese forces overran the colony. Australia assembled and operated eighteen, and the rest were never fully accounted for – likely taken up by local American forces. Other OS2U-3s customers were Chile with fifteen, six or nine to Argentina, Mexico took six, Uruguay six, and three to Cuba, originally destined for the Dominican Republic. The United Kingdom returned twenty OS2U-3s, most or all of which were passed to the Soviet Union together with two aboard a cruiser also loaned to the USSR. This brought to 162 or 165 the number of OS2U-3s supplied to foreign users.

The Kingfisher was well-established in service aboard surface combatants and shore patrols at the beginning of 1942. With 1,519 airframes produced, the Kingfisher was the most numerous of all floatplanes during the war, foreign or domestic. Not all the

The Vought OS2U was among the few floatplanes exported by the US during the war. The United Kingdom was the primary recipient; taking 100 of the machines and dubbing them the Kingfisher I. One of these Royal Navy aircraft is seen on the sea sled, flaps still down and spoilers evident, with the crew preparing to hook up the hoisting cable.
National Museum of Naval Aviation

Vought OS2U-3 Kingfisher characteristics (floatplane configuration)

Span	35.9ft (10.9m)
Length	33.8ft (10.3m)
Height	15.1ft (4.6m)
Wing area	262ft² (24m²)
Fuel, max	241 gallons (912 liters)
Climb rate, initial	413fpm (126mpm)
Service ceiling	13,000ft (3,962m)
Weight, empty	4,123lb (1,870kg)
Weight, loaded	5,600lb (2,540kg)
Weight, max	6,000lb (2,722kg)
Speed, max	164mph (264km/h)
Cruise speed	119mph (192km/h)
Range, typical, max	805 miles (1,296km)

An OS2U-3 of VS-70 on its wheeled undercarriage taxis at the Naval Air Auxiliary Field Cold Bay in the Aleutian Islands, Alaska, on 15 August 1944. The image illustrates the fixed wheeled undercarriage and the 110lb fragmentation bomb that could be carried under each wing. Hundreds of floatplanes were delivered with the landing gear and operated, like this one, in the patrol and anti-submarine role strictly from shore installations. *National Museum of Naval Aviation*

airplanes were delivered with floats, and the Kingfisher was never fitted with an arrester hook. These machines likely did as much or more shore duty on their wheeled undercarriage as on floats. While the operators could wish for more power from the OS2U – they nicknamed it affectionately as 'Old Slow & Ugly' – it got the job done handily. The exploits of this ubiquitous floatplane became legendary as it seemed to go anywhere and do anything. The rescue of personnel from the sea and materiel transport to remote installations endeared the Kingfisher to many. They disappeared almost entirely with the end of the war.

During the war the Kingfisher was used in tasks well beyond its original specification. This included communications with shoreline outposts during the Pacific Ocean struggle with Japan. These OS2Us have been drawn up on the beach in late 1943 (probably at Halavo Seaplane Base, Solomon Islands) for servicing and preparation for patrol missions, as carrier or runway-bound aviation was not consistently available. *National Museum of Naval Aviation*

The replacement (SO2U, SO3C, SOR)

The Navy had set out to develop a replacement for the SOC very early in the type's service because of the slow and underfunded acquisition process of the inter-war years. Both Curtiss-Wright and Vought-Sikorsky were invited to bid against the requirement for a two-place, mid-wing, all-metal floatplane of all-around improved performance. The mission dictated a weight not to exceed 6,350lb (2,880kg – the catapult capacity), a span of no more than 38 feet (11.6 meters), and 15 feet (4.6 meters) folded, a landing speed of no more than 56mph (90km/h), and stressed to 7.5g for dive-bombing. The service specified the experimental Ranger twelve-cylinder inverted-V XV-770 engine with supercharger because the inline design could reduce the cross-sectional area and it held hope for reduced fuel consumption. It was designed to be compact – engine and all accessories as a unit – easily accessed for maintenance, and quickly installed with four mounting bolts. Both firms were given prototype contracts in mid-1937. The testing of the two competitors continued through the first half of 1940 at Anacostia and Norfolk, Virginia.

The development and construction of Vought's prototype XSO2U-1 (VS-401 or V-167, BuNo 1440*) benefited from the ongoing OS2U work to include the adoption of the same spot-welding construction. Control surfaces remained fabric-covered. A .30 gun fired through the prop and another was flexibly mounted for the rear observer. Powered by the 500hp (373kW) XV-770-4 engine, a hardpoint under each wing accommodated depth charges.

The XSO2U-1 was first flown in July 1939 in landplane configuration, then on floats in December. It had many attributes superior to the Curtiss XSO3C counterpart; although 300lb (136kg) heavier, it was 3mph (5km/h) faster. Directional stability proved deficient and a large ventral surface joining the float and aft end of the fuselage was added. The same engine cooling problem that would plague the SO3C was experienced by Vought – the 520hp (388kW) XV-770-6 in a redesigned

cowling was substituted without success. However, the firm was fully occupied with other work and did not bemoan losing the production contract to Curtiss. The XSO2U-1 was retained until July 1942 when it was passed to Ranger to serve as a testbed for continued V-770 development until struck off charge on 6 July 1944 and eventually scrapped.[4]

The XSO3C-1 (Model 82, 1385) was built at Curtiss-Wright's Buffalo, New York, plant. The type was flown for the first time by Lloyd Childs on 6 October 1939 on the wheeled undercarriage and later on floats. It was initially powered by an XV-770-6 engine, and all models used a Hamilton Standard two-blade, constant-speed propeller. The wing had flaps and leading-edge slats. It had underwing hardpoints for two 325lb depth charges or 110lb bombs. A fixed ·30-cal gun in the nose with 500 rounds joined the observer/radio operator's flexibly

Vought XSO2U-1 characteristics (floatplane configuration)

Span	38.2ft (11.6m)
Length	36.1ft (11.0m)
Height	15.9ft (4.9m)
Wing area	299.8ft² (27.9m²)
Fuel, max	128 gallons (485 liters)
Climb rate, initial	890fpm (271mpm)
Service ceiling	22,200ft (6,767m)
Weight, empty	4,016lb (1,822kg)
Weight, gross	5,439lb (2,467kg)
Weight, max	5,634lb (2,556kg)
Speed, max	190mph (306km/h)
Cruise speed	127mph (204km/h)
Range, max	984 miles (1,584km)

Vought created the XSO2U-1 against the same requirement that led to the Curtiss SO3C-1. With the Navy's tight specifications, and dictating the engine to be employed, it is no surprise that these airplanes looked so similar and performed much the same. The Curtiss entry won the production nod while the SO2U-1 (seen here in Long Island Sound before the addition of the ventral strake) faded away, yet Vought went on to win many accolades for its aviation contribution to victory. *Naval Aviation Archives*

On its wheeled landing gear the XSO2U-1 (1440) looked particularly ungainly. Having lost the competition to the Curtiss SO3C, the Vought airplane was retained by the Navy until passed on to Ranger to serve as an engine test platform. The inline engine is tightly cowled, something Vought and Curtiss would both learn was intolerable for the Ranger, resisting proper cooling. *San Diego Air & Space Museum*

* The numbers in parenthesis are the Army serial number, with two-digit 19xx year ordered, and the Navy Bureau Number, or BuNo.

mounted MG with 600 rounds at the end of the long canopy enclosure. Fairings behind the rear cockpit folded down to increase the meager field of fire.

The SO3C-1 was trouble from start to finish. The cause lay mostly with the immature engine and its cooling challenges, which led to numerous cowling changes that transformed the airplane's nose. An engine failure on 21 July 1941 left the prototype sunk in shallow water. Rebuilt in Buffalo, the engine failed again in November, leading to a forced landing resulting in more damage. Navy-dictated design changes contributed to a weight increase of 463lb (210kg), which rendered the machine underpowered. Among these changes were wing fuel tanks for extended endurance and self-sealing tanks in the fuselage, together with 144lb (54kg) of crew armor. The wing fold line was moved outboard so that the floats would not also need to fold.

The airframe design was also partially to blame for the prolonged and only marginally successful development. Stability deficiencies were evident in both landplane and seaplane configurations. The wing dihedral was too low for the desired lateral stability, but altering this would require jig changes that were actively discouraged in the headlong rush to high-rate production. The XSO3C-1 was placed in the full-scale wind tunnel at the NACA's Langley Memorial Aeronautical Laboratory, Langley Field, Virginia, during September 1940, where solutions to the engine cooling and airframe stability problems were investigated. An imperfect solution to the lateral

axis shortcoming was found in 40-degree upturned wingtips. Directional stability issues on the float were initially answered with a deep strake under the aft fuselage. Eventually the vertical tail and rudder were greatly enlarged, the dorsal extension carrying forward onto the sliding canopy aft segment, and the end of the fuselage reshaped. The horizontal stabilizer was likewise expanded to improve longitudinal stability.

The Navy-mandated pedestal float mount suffered excessive structural flexure during operations on rough seas that could see the propeller slice the top of it. The expedient solution was to manufacture a groove in the float and fill it with balsa wood so that if the incident occurred no damage other than to the wood would result. A water take-off was not possible at full fuel load, 120-150 gallons (454-568 liters) having to be burned first or shorted in refueling to reduce the take-off angle of attack (AoA). Take-off runs remained long and the aircraft had to be pulled off the water to a startling attitude. The solution was an increase to the aft upsweep of the float that was dragging in the water at the excessive AoA, but the schedule could not support the production line changes. The wheeled undercarriage issued from the same attach point as the float. This relatively far aft placement caused the SO3C to sit exceptionally nose high and with a short wheel track that contributed to poor ground handling characteristics and challenging landings. The take-off and landings also presented less-than-desirable flying qualities.

The Curtiss XSO3C-1 competitor with the Vought SO2U was a clean design when it first emerged, lacking braces and wires in the floats or any struts under the tailplanes. The inline engine was neatly cowled and contributed to the slender fuselage. However, this 10 April 1940 photo shows evidence of work already under way to address deficiencies with the ventral fin ('scag') under the aft fuselage. *Naval Aviation Archives*

The SO3C-1 became notorious for being difficult to handle on the water and for its poor performance. The aircraft could not get off with a full fuel load and the center float was in need of a redesign, denied because of the urgency in moving to production. The machine (XSO3C-1 is shown) had to be pulled off the water at a steep angle. *San Diego Air & Space Museum*

Curtiss SO3C-2 characteristics
(on beaching gear)

Span	38.0ft (11.6m)
Length	35.7ft (10.6m)
Height (on beaching gear)	14.2ft (4.3m)
Wing area	293ft² (27m²)
Fuel, max	320 gallons (1,211 liters)
Climb rate, initial	380fpm (116mpm)
Service ceiling	16,500ft (5,029m)
Weight, empty	4,995lb (2,266kg)
Weight, gross	6,600lb (2,994kg)
Weight, max	7,000lb (3,175kg)
Speed, max	167mph (269km/h)
Cruise speed	117mph (188km/h)
Range, max	940 miles (1,513km)

Production design of the SO3C-1 (Model 82A) began under a 10 September 1940 contract for 300. While a Curtiss-Wright plant was built in Columbus, Ohio, parts construction began in nearby fairground cattle barns. Dedicated on 4 December 1941, the new factory team struggled with delays owing to the many design changes and continued flight testing of problem solutions. Edo Aircraft supplied the floats. The first SO3C-1 was flown on 4 March 1942 by 'Red' Hulse, and winter testing was performed at the Timm Aircraft facility in Van Nuys, California. Deliveries finally commenced in July 1942. Columbus turned out 141 of the Seagulls by the end of the year. By then the weight had increased by an additional 187lb (85kg).

The SO3C-1 first went to sea on 15 July 1942 for operational trials, and combat deployments followed into 1943. Some of the airplanes were fitted with ASV radar, as evidenced by the rotatable Yagi 'comb' antenna under the each wing outboard of the float. The shortcomings of the ugly floatplane were immediately evident and it was quickly and soundly rejected. To carry two depth charges – part of the lauded performance advantage over the SOC – the SO3C had to remove the pilot armor, the flex MG and its ammo and the fuselage fuel tank, and replace the self-sealing oil tank with a standard unit. The initial climb rate was excruciatingly slow. Only fifty-six of the type made it to sea aboard seventeen ships, but were returned after an average of just sixty days. The SOC was brought back from retirement to fill the catapults for the duration, or a lesser number of Kingfishers substituted – although without folding wings this aircraft had to be kept on the catapult instead of in the hangar.

A new plant was built in Columbus, Ohio, during 1941 to manufacture Curtiss-Wright warplanes. The SO3C was slow reaching serial production because of many changes requested by the Navy and demanded by deficiencies uncovered in flight tests. The SO3C-1 finally began to be delivered in the latter half of 1942, as suggested by this flightline image from the period. *San Diego Air & Space Museum*

Before the end of 1942 manufacturing had shifted to the SO3C-2, which kept the V-770-6 engine but sported arresting hook and catapult connection points added to the beefed-up wheeled undercarriage for carrier deck operations, the ability to carry a 500lb bomb on the centerline in this configuration, together with change to a 24-volt electrical system. It lost performance to another 105lb (48kg) weight gain. The first SO3C-2s emerged from Columbus during October 1942, and seven were handed over by the end of the year. Of the final 159 machines of the SO3C-1 order, 150 were to be completed as this model together with fifty more added to the books.

The UK negotiated a 21 October 1941 Lend-Lease contract for an additional 259 SO3C-1s as the -1B, but this was converted to SO3C-2s before delivery. Designated SO3C-2C for export, these aircraft featured the 550hp (410kW) V-770-8 engine, hydraulic brakes, and improved radio. The first was received by its new owners in December 1942. The Royal Navy took an immediate disliking to these Seamew Is and asked that deliveries be suspended with only about 100-150 taken up.[5] The airplanes were used solely for the training of aerial gunners and radio operators. In this role seventy or so were transferred to Canada and two were sent to Cuba. The balance of the order was picked up by the unhappy US Navy, which also adopted the British name as the SOCs had not faded away entirely.

Together with the UK examples, the SO3C-2s totaled 459. The -2 represented a move to turn the type into an escort carrier machine – albeit with a fixed undercarriage and miserable performance that endeared it to none. The USN first conducted carrier sea trials with the model on 22 June 1943. The aircraft was so underpowered that the rear canopy could not be opened for take-off, the usual safety practice, because of the added drag. It could do nothing better than existing types such as the Grumman TBF-1, and any routine deck-borne operations in the Atlantic proved very brief. The Coast Guard was given some of the wheeled SO3C-1s and -2s for land-based shore patrol duties.

With need for further changes to rescue the type, the SO3C-3 (Model 82C) derived from a weight reduction program, which included deleting equipment for carrier ops and resulted in all of 30lb (14kg) being cut from the airplane – essentially negligible. It also used the V-770-8 engine. The Navy placed a hopeful 699-aircraft order, and got its first in June 1943.

Above Left: Aircraft 4231, an SO3C-1, leaves the catapult of the cruiser USS *Biloxi* during Pacific Ocean operations in October 1943. Only a few dozen of the type ventured into the war zone, where they were roundly condemned and consequently withdrawn by the end of 1943. *Above:* is another -1 model Seagull a year earlier, showing finer details of the aircraft. *Naval Aviation Archives*

This photo shows one of hundreds of SO3C-2s that were shuffled across the country in search of useful work and contented operators. Little of either was found as the type was generally considered a miserable failure. Removal of the spinner on 4914 represents an effort to ease engine cooling, as is the opening of the cowl flaps. *National Museum of Naval Aviation*

As part of the vast Lend-Lease effort to supply friendly nations with war materiel, Great Britain received a large number of Curtiss SO3C-2Cs configured for deck operations (note the tail hook). Britain's experience with the Seamew Is, as the Curtisses were called, was not a happy one and they were relegated to training. The US Navy may have ended up with many of these machines as evidenced by this well-worn example in American markings. *San Diego Air & Space Museum*

The disappointing SO3C saga ended with the -3 model, just a few dozen of which were built before the waste was ended. This shot of one of the SO3C-3s shows the wing fold line well outboard. The censor has not removed the Yagi radar and weapons mount from this late-war image. *Naval Aviation Archives*

Ryan Aeronautical of San Diego, California, was setting up to produce the SO3C-1 as the SOR-1 under a 30 June 1942 order for 1,000 examples, added to seventy-two previously sought by a Letter of Intent from December 1941. The SOR incorporated design changes to improved flying qualities that would see the upturned wingtips eliminated as the wing was given the required dihedral and greater tapering from about mid-span. This effort was cancelled without a single aircraft being completed. Likewise, another variant for the UK, the SO3C-4B Seamew II, essentially a -3 dedicated to deck landings, was abandoned before any metal was cut. The SO3C-2 order was reduced to 200 on 21 September 1943 and production in Columbus was cut off entirely in January 1944, thirty-nine SO3C-3s having been completed, for a total 640 airplanes that all agreed were essentially worthless.

On 15 December 1943, as the end of production approached, the Navy reckoned that it would possess 118 SO3C-1s, 106 -2s, 49 -2Cs, and 196 -3s, for a total 469.[6] Plans were to retain thirty-seven -1s and -2s as trainers, while passing eighty-nine -3s to the Coast Guard (sixty new as delivered from the factory) while it would return all other SO3Cs it then possessed. Additionally, 182 machines would be converted to target drones as the SO3C-1K and -2K. Thirty drones were destined for the British (perhaps only eleven were transferred), who called them Queen Seamews. All other airplanes would serve as spares. Just a few short months

later, on 4 February 1944, with forty-one airplanes yet to be delivered from Curtiss, the type (then 411 machines) was withdrawn from all manned flight activities. The USCG, which had only forty-eight SO3C-1, -2, and -3s on force, was given Kingfishers instead. Apart from 250 planned for drone conversion in Oakland, California, the rest would be scrapped. Even the drone airplanes fell flat, with only a handful converted but little used. The SO3C disappeared entirely in March 1944.

The new guys (SC, S2E, OSE)

After Pearl Harbor the Navy was still seeking to replace the SOCs and OS2Us that were being steadily worn away by war tempo, but with an airplane possessing performance to hold its own in a fight if necessary, as the Japanese had done. A specification was issued in June 1942 for a higher-performance VS type, convertible as usual. The Curtiss Model 97 proposal, submitted on 1 August, quickly won favor, with a Letter of Intent on 30 October for a pair of prototypes and 500 production machines. The formal contract followed on 31 March 1943 and the production order came in June before the first XSC-1 had taken flight. That event was on 16 February 1944 under the control of Bill Webster. Deliveries of the SC-1 commenced in July 1944, with fleet deployment in October. Curtiss handed over the aircraft as landplanes while Edo was on separate contract for the floats. An arrester hook was only added as an experiment and never adopted.

The all-metal SC-1 Seahawk was intended to be a simple design, put into production and turned out quickly. Yet it was the largest, most advanced, powerful and heavily armed of any floatplane ever to enter Navy service. It was driven by the nine-cylinder turbosupercharged Wright R-1820-62 Cyclone of 1,350hp (1,007kW), which gave it remarkable performance. With a diameter of only 10.2 feet (3.1 meters), the four-blade Curtiss Electric propeller generated considerable noise at take-off power. When making a water take-off, the pilot had to begin the run 30 degrees off the wind direction because the powerful torque would pull that much before the airplane became airborne. The design had the requisite folding wings that featured automatic leading-edge slats and slotted flaps. These high-lift devices permitted a 75mph (120km/h) landing speed. Considerable difficulty was encountered in spin recovery, claiming one of the test aircraft in a crash. Production examples differed externally in the vertical tail dorsal extension (retrofitted to early deliveries) and a shallow strake under the aft fuselage, likely to address this issue. However, spins remained problematic.[7]

In the frustrating effort to find useful work for the SO3C, the Coast Guard was given many for anti-submarine patrols. The Curtiss was not well suited for this work either, and the Navy eventually pulled all of them back. This radar-equipped SO3C-1 is seen at USCG Air Station Port Los Angeles. *Jay Miller Collection*

Japan set the example of effectively placing fighters on floats. The Americans had encountered these aircraft and even evaluated some, such as this captured Kawanishi N1K1 Kyofu (Rex) examined by representatives from different design teams. The US Navy sought to create a similar capability. *via Dennis Jenkins*

The first five production SC-1s were employed as test assets. An urgent part of this work was solving an unsatisfactory spin recovery problem that led to this 18 February 1945 accident in Columbus with 35301 (the fourth production example). The wreck shows off the leading edge slats, inboard and outboard slotted flaps, and the lack of a full dorsal extension to the vertical tail that became one measure in addressing spins. *National Museum of Naval Aviation*

The Seahawk was armed with two ·50-cal guns and 400 rounds, each positioned outside the propeller arc in a wing. The usual two 325lb depth charges or 250lb bombs could be carried under the inboard wing segments. There was initially an option for two bomb cells in the center float, taking 100lb (45kg) weapons or 50-gallon (189-liter) auxiliary fuel cells. This feature had problems, so the float was eventually sealed with only a 95-gallon (365-litre) fuel cell fitted within. The 110lb (50kg) of armor included the seatback and forward bullet-proof glass. The main gear was a single unit attached at the same points as the center float with six hours of labor. The SC-2 also introduced the ASH radar to the mission, with an AN/APS-4 pod under the starboard hardpoint.

Curtiss-Wright SC-1 Seahawk characteristics (on beaching gear)

Span	41.0ft (12.5m)
Length	36.4ft (11.1m)
Height (on beaching gear)	16.0ft (4.9m)
Wing area	280ft² (26.0m²)
Fuel, max	215 gallons (814 liters)
Climb rate, max	2,350fpm (716mpm)
Service ceiling	37,300ft (11,369m)
Weight, empty	6,320lb (2,867kg)
Weight, gross	7,943lb (3,603kg)
Weight, max gross	9,000lb (4,082kg)
Speed, max	313mph (504km/h)
Speed, max level	243mph (391km/h)
Cruise speed	125mph (201km/h)
Range (125mph)	625 miles (1,006km)

The Curtiss SC-1 was the Navy's move to create a floatplane with fighter-like performance and armament. The powerful engine also had a turbosupercharger that lent it consider altitude capability, but did not benefit the mission. The single seat complicated sea rescues and left the pilot to prepare the sling after running up on the sea sled and after folding aside the antenna mast. *National Museum of Naval Aviation*

With only the pilot as crew (the only single-float, single-seat example in the Navy), a simple fighter-like canopy was possible. The aftmost canopy panes were not installed, to reduce buffeting during flight with the canopy open, and difficulty in opening otherwise. The pilot had to perform the sling hook-up himself after folding aside the antenna mast ahead of the canopy. There was a litter within the fuselage for a survivor to squeeze into, with the pilot on the wing pulling the seatback forward. However, sea rescue with the SC was fraught because it lacked ladder, rope or hand-holds, and had just the single crewman to assist. A folding ladder to be deployed by the pilot was added later. Hence the SC had a mixed reception due also to teething problems with its hasty introduction. Like the SO3C with the same pedestal mount float, a hard landing and rough seas could cause sufficient structural flexure for the prop to strike the top of the float. The autopilot would occasionally engage uncommanded during landing, making random and extreme inputs, resulting in several fatal mishaps. Subsequently, it was permanently disabled, leaving the pilot with a high workload and dangerous conditions if he also had to operate the radar that required him to bend over and peer into a hood over the scope. Nonetheless, the excellent performance was most welcome.

While the turbosupercharger gave tremendous altitude performance, the capability lent nothing to a mission that had little need to go above 5,000 feet (1,524 meters). The catapult-equipped ships required a scout, not a fighter, and the melding of the two did not mandate the turbine. It also proved unreliable, the impellers occasionally disintegrating and causing grave damage. Use of the feature was restricted until the turbos with intercoolers and other associated equipment were removed, later aircraft being delivered without the equipment, which required substitution of a longer engine mount. An SC-2 was developed to permanently eliminate the turbosupercharger and answer once and for all the unfortunate spin characteristics. The contract for 240 of these airplanes was let in May 1945.

The SC-1's landplane undercarriage was a neat single-piece construct replacing the center float at the same attachment point. The Curtiss airplane was equipped with radar via the APS-4 pod that could be installed on a dedicated starboard wing point (shown here on the inboard wing station before the outboard mount was adopted). Managing this gear while flying the powerful aircraft was a chore after the autopilot was permanently disabled following evidence of malfunction leading to fatal mishaps. *National Museum of Naval Aviation*

The SC-2 model had an enlarged vertical tail and rudder, the rudder extended below the bottom of the fuselage and with a deeper structure at this point to match. The horizontal stabilizers had strakes extending forward at the roots. The SC-2 featured the 1,425hp (1,063kW) R-1820-76 engine possessing a gear-driven single-stage supercharger in a new cowling. This required the forward fuselage and cowling to take on a circular rather than the original oval cross-section. A bubble canopy was adopted and a jump seat installed behind the pilot (beginning with the tenth example). This radio and rescue compartment was entered via a door in the starboard aft fuselage. The antenna mast was thankfully relocated aft. A dedicated starboard wing outboard mount was created for the APS-4 pod. Alternatively, a 90-gallon (41-liter) tank could be hung at the location, which moved to the centerline with the wheeled undercarriage installed.

A second contract for 450 additional SC-1s was truncated to sixty-six with the end of the war, giving a total of 566 from the Columbus plant. As many as 166 were stored when completed and never entered service.[8] Likewise, the order for the SC-2 was halted at just ten examples, apart from the prototype converted from an SC-1. Just twenty-two SC-1s were deployed in the Pacific war zone before the ceasefire.

Concurrent with the SC was another high-performance floatplane scout designed to use the Ranger inverted-V engine from the failed SO3C. The sleek inline engine allowed a narrow, lower-drag fuselage. However, this differed by adding a jet engine for sprint to intercept or evade. The Westinghouse 19 axial-flow turbojet engine of 1,000lbf thrust (4.45kN) was selected. Such composite designs with reciprocating engine and jet power unit (JPU) were also being pursued with the Ryan FR-1 and Curtiss F15C-1 fighters, as well as the Grumman TB3F-1 torpedo-bomber.

With all aircraft manufacturers large and small fully engaged on war programs, the Navy approached the Edo Aircraft Corporation on 13 August 1943 to develop the new VS airplane. Named after founder Earl Dodge Osborn and based at College Point, Long Island, Edo had long designed aviation equipment for the service, becoming America's most experience designer and manufacturer of aluminum floats. The company ultimately built 95 percent of the floats used by American seaplanes during the war. The company would design not only the floats for specific airplanes but also the structural changes allowing them to be fitted. The contract for its own airplane, the XS2E-1, followed on 11 January 1944. The ambitious project was undertaken with enthusiasm by Edo, which had previously had only a few such efforts.[9]

The design initially possessed a low-set wing with a two-seat layout. The turbojet was 19 inches (48cm) in diameter, and was installed within the aft fuselage, exhausting through the bottom. Ranger designed the recip engine installation including mount and cowling, choosing a two-blade Hamilton Standard constant-speed propeller with a 9-foot (2.7-meter) diameter. The Navy was pleased enough with the preliminary design to order ten more X-prototypes (75208/17) followed by an additional eight (75625/32).

The USN decided on 16 March 1944 to jettison the JPU, as the Westinghouse engine weighed 827lb (375kg) as initially

Only ten SC-2s were completed before production was halted after VJ-Day. Evident with 119529 is the lack of 'chin' in the cowling for the turbosupercharger, making for a circular cross-section. This image shows off the beaching gear, the wing hardpoints, and relatively small propeller diameter. *Ray Wagner collection*

With the fixed wheel gear, a 90-gallon drop tank could be fitted on the centerline of the SC-2 and a radar pod on an outboard starboard station. This image also shows off the empennage changes, the relocated antenna mast, the engine exhaust duct aft of the cowling, and the window in the fuselage behind the pilot for the jump seat occupant. The SC was the last 'slingshot warrior' in the Navy, ushering out an era when retired four years after the war. *Naval Aviation Archives*

run nearly a year before, and was unlikely to shed weight. Additionally, the powerplant was in demand for higher-priority projects, yet had initially flown only in January 1944 and production was lagging to a desperate extent. The loss of additional thrust meant the aircraft's weight and size would have to come down to retain the good performance sought and avoid a repetition of the design death spiral of weight and drag that doomed the SO3C. The second seat was eliminated and the wingspan limited to 38 feet (11.6 meters).

The design changes meant that the Navy was developing two nearly identical catapult seaplanes in the S2E and the SC. However, the S2E mission was also altered to observation-scout, although it meant that, like the SC, the pilot faced a considerable workload. Redesignated the XOSE-1, the wooden mock-up was inspected on 24 November 1944. Answering what was sure to be criticism from the operators, a two-place variant as the XOSE-2 (75214/5 to be so configured) was requested and two unarmed dual-controls trainers (75216/7) also ordered (later assuming the designation XTE-1). Radar was included in the design, with the observer as the operator. Aircraft 75208/9 were cancelled.

The airplane incorporated the 550hp (419kW) V-770-8 engine, but the installation benefited somewhat from the sordid history of its predecessors. Folding wings and an optional wheeled undercarriage were naturally required. The floatplane was armed with a .50 MG in each inboard wing segment, outboard of the prop disk, and hardpoints for two 350lb depth charges. The two-seat variant was to have only one gun, while the trainer was unarmed. Ease of maintenance was to be a hallmark, with many panels dropping down to serve as work platforms. The hydraulic wing-fold common with carrier airplanes was eliminated for a manual system. Leading-edge slats, flaps and drooped ailerons all helped keep speed down for landing. The flaps, with inboard segments and outboard beyond the fold line, were designed to automatically retract if struck by heavy sea spray, saving the structure from damage. Self-sealing fuel tanks and some 135lb (61kg) of armor offered combat protection. Drop tanks with a capacity of 50 gallons (189 liters) could replace the depth charges, or the radar pod take one station.

This airplane was nearing its first flight when the war was thankfully brought to a close. The flight occurred in December. It was a worthy effort by under-experienced Edo and held much promise. However, it did prove to have more than its share of problems as the flight test dragged on. The XOSE-2 eventually required an enlarged vertical tail and ventral strakes to cure directional stability issues prompted by the larger canopy, and

Edo XOSE-1 characteristics
(floatplane configuration)

Span	38.0ft (11.6m)
Length	31.2ft (9.5m)
Height (on beaching gear)	14.3ft (4.4m)
Wing area	237ft² (22.0m²)
Fuel, max	178 gallons (674 liters)
Climb rate, max	1,350fpm (412mpm)
Service ceiling	22,300ft (6,797m)
Weight, empty	3,973lb (1,802kg)
Weight, gross	5,434lb (2,465kg)
Weight, max	6,064lb (2,751kg)
Speed, max	205mph (330km/h)
Cruise speed	130mph (209km/h)
Range (111mph)	897 miles (1,444km)

there were engine difficulties with the -1s. By the time the problems were resolved the handwriting was on the wall, signaling the end of floatplanes as a combat asset. Only ten of the type were finished, including a pair each of the XOSE-2 and XTE-1 to join the six XOSE-1s.

The XOSE-1 was developed by Edo Aircraft, best known for its aluminum floats that equipped some 95 percent of all seaplanes used by the American armed forces. When challenged to build a fast but light observation-scout floatplane, the company responded with skill. Unfortunately, the worthy result flew only after the war concluded and never went into production. *Naval Aviation Archives/National Archives*

CHAPTER THREE

Floatplane Sidelines

WHILE THE ARMED FLOATPLANES, shot from warships, garnered a bit of limelight, there were others that shouldered their share of the military workload while attracting less attention. For the US Navy these included utility types dedicated to the roles that the 'slingshot warriors' were all too often called on to perform. There were also a handful of unique types sold solely to foreign air arms that displayed American aeronautical capabilities as the country moved into high gear supporting total war. In reaching that state, some 'short cuts' to high-performance floatplanes were examined in adopting landplanes or carrier-based types. No account of US wartime floatplanes would be complete without addressing these 'sideline' efforts.

High utility (J2F, JL)

The principal US Navy utility floatplane at the dawn of the war was the Grumman 'Duck' biplane amphibian. This design dated from the early 1930s as the JF, but harked back to even earlier designs featuring the center float integral with the fuselage, but still short of a flying boat hull. The main gear retracted into the float. The J2F was slightly larger and added a tail hook and deck catapult points, yet lacked the flaps or slats, and stalled at around 70mph (113km/h). These airplanes had the pilot and observer/radio operator under the canopy while below (accessed via a trap door in the rear cockpit) were seats for two or room for a stretcher. Although of metal

A Grumman J2F-4 is captured on color film in 1940 at Pensacola. This utility floatplane was in production at the start of the war but was followed by 474 later models. It proved a rugged and reliable mount, going just about everywhere from carrier decks, runways and unpaved surfaces to just taxiing up to shore or alongside a vessel at sea. *Naval Aviation Archives*

construction, all J2F aero surfaces were fabric-covered. By the time of the US entry into the war the USN and USMC possessed sixteen JFs and 168 J2Fs that were clearly obsolete. Yet the Navy did not want to divert resources from combat aircraft development and manufacturing to seek a replacement, so the Duck soldiered on but with expanded production.

The Grumman had already established a well-deserved standard and had continued in production at the dawn of war as thirty-two J2F-4s with the nine-cylinder, 790hp (589kW) R-1820-30 and three-blade constant-speed Hamilton Standard propeller. The aircraft was armed with a fixed forward-firing ·30-cal MG and a flex-mounted .30 at the rear, and a hardpoint in each wing for 110lb bombs. These were followed, after a pause of about a year, by an order for 144 J2F-5s, delivered in just eight months, with the 950hp (708kW) R-1820-50 and hardpoints beefed up to take 325lb (147kg) depth charges, but the forward gun deleted (and the rear gun seldom carried). At the urging of the Navy to free up space at Grumman's Bethpage plant for fighter assembly, Columbia Aircraft in Valley Stream, Long Island, was contracted in 1942 to take over J2F production. This firm delivered 330 J2F-6s from 1943 through to August 1945, additional examples being cancelled. Little altered, these were fitted with the R-1820-54 at 1,050hp (783 kW) but were heavier machines. Cowling changes accompanied each new engine installation.

Although ostensibly for utility duties (light cargo, personnel), the Duck saw use in target-towing, smoke-laying, air-sea rescue (ASR), medevac, observation and photography, as well as ASW, for which it carried depth charges. It operated from deck, land and sea alike. The Duck could be hoisted aboard a vessel equipped for floatplanes (though they were not fitted for catapult launch) and deposited on a fixture or its wheels on the boat deck. They seemed to go just about anywhere, and were rugged and reliable. These versatile machines were employed in all theaters by the USN and USMC as well as at home by the USCG.

Grumman (Columbia) J2F-6 characteristics

Span	39.0ft (11.9m)
Length	34.0ft (10.4m)
Height	12.4ft (3.8m)
Wing area	409ft² (38.0m²)
Fuel, max	190 gallons (719 liters)
Climb rate, max	1,330fpm (405mpm)
Service ceiling	26,700ft (8,138m)
Weight, empty	5,445lb (2,470kg)
Weight, normal	7,290lb (3,307kg)
Weight, max	7,765lb (2,367kg)
Speed, max	190mph (306km/h)
Cruise speed	155mph (249km/h)
Range, max (108mph)	850 miles (1,368km)

Grumman had begun working on a monoplane follow-on to the Duck in June 1939, but this G-42 design was sidetracked as war work took center stage. The effort continued at a slow pace with the Navy's concurrence regarding priority. Considerable progress was made during the latter half of 1942 and into 1943. At that point the decision was taken to have Columbia complete the detailed design. The USN ordered two XJL-1 prototypes (31399/400) and a static test article. The development still dragged on through to the end of the war, by which time the static test article had been completed and tested at Grumman, the first airplane was roughly two-thirds complete and the second half-finished. The contract was continued, but no production order was anticipated.

The JL retained the same 'flying shoehorn' layout of the Duck with an R-1820-56 at 1,350hp (1,007kW) in the nose above the float. There was a nose wheel in the float's nose and the main gear extended from the wing, all electrically actuated. The long-stroke main struts from the still high mid-wing required a system for compressing them before retraction. The crew of two were under the canopy while four to six passengers were accommodated below. The cargo/passenger area had an overhead trolley for moving heavy freight. Wing hardpoints accommodated weapons or an APS-4 radar pod. These were very large airplanes, with a wingspan of 50 feet (15.2 meters) (albeit with wing-fold), a height of 16 feet (4.9 meters), an empty weight of 7,250lb (3,289kg) rising to 13,000lb (5,897kg) loaded. Maximum airspeed was anticipated to be 200mph (322km/h), with a range at 119mph (192km/h) of 2,070 miles (3,332 km), and an initial rate of climb of 1,110fpm (338mpm).

Post-war, the JL-1 design proved sound yet had the usual share of developmental problems during testing. However, there was no military future for such equipment. The effort was terminated and Columbia soon liquidated.

A monoplane follow-on to the very successful Grumman Duck was on the drawing boards before the war, but the growing volume and pace of wartime work continually delayed completing the design. Finally, Columbia was tasked with doing the detail design and building two prototype XJL-1s, which remained uncompleted as the war concluded. This photo of the first example (31399) shows its great size, especially in comparison to the J2F beyond. *Naval Aviation Archives*

Foreign consignment (N-3PB, STM-S2)

The newest company created by Jack Northrop, Northrop Aircraft of Hawthorne, California, was approached in 1939 by the Norwegians to design a three-place float-mounted patrol bomber. The company was already designing a landplane attack aircraft, the N-3, based on its contribution to the Douglas 8-A. This also derived from its work on the Army A-17 attacker and BT-1 trainer, which had conceptual provisions for water operation. The design was altering to meet Norway's mission, with twin floats, and specifications were agreed to on 7 March 1940. An order for twenty-four N-3PBs (c/n 301-324) was placed on the 12th at $57,000 apiece for delivery within ten months.

This was not an easy affair as the Norwegians requested changes during development. The most significant of these was insisting on a clean cantilevered mounting of the floats to ensure underwing store points were clear of braces and wires. The original European guns had to be replaced with American MGs. Late delivery of floats and engines further compounded the schedule issues. Vance Breese took the airplane up for the maiden flight from Lake Elsinore, California, on 22 December. No significant changes were made as a result of testing and the first was handed over on 5 February 1941 at a final unit price of $60,168.94. The N-3PB was soon heralded as the fastest seaplane in the world.

The N-3PB was a three-place, all-metal aircraft powered by a 1,200hp (895kW) GR-1820-G205A turning a three-blade Hamilton Standard constant-speed prop. Selection of the engine was no doubt influenced by its use in other Norwegian warplane purchases. A pair of Edo floats supported the aircraft on the water, and beaching gear could be attached. The pilot and rear gunner-observer were under a greenhouse canopy with controls duplicated at both stations. A radioman-bombardier occupied a space in the fuselage to the rear of the cockpit. The machine had a pair of ·50-cals in each wing with 267 rounds per gun (rpg), a flex-mounted .30 adjacent to the aft seat, and another deployed through a hatch in the lower aft fuselage served by the radioman/bombardier (a total of 2,200 .30 rounds). The aircraft could carry a single 2,000lb (907kg) torpedo on the centerline or an equivalent weight of bombs, with two hardpoints inboard of the floats under each wing for a total of five.

Northrop N-3PB characteristics

Span	48.9ft (14.9m)
Length	38.0ft (11.6m)
Height	12.0ft (3.7m)
Wing area	376.8ft² (35.0m²)
Fuel, max	320 gallons (1,211 liters)
Climb rate, max	2,540fpm (774mpm)
Service ceiling	28,400ft (8,656m)
Weight, empty	6,560lb (2,976kg)
Weight, gross	10,639lb (4,092kg)
Weight, overload	11,213lb (5,086kg)
Speed, max	257mph (414km/h)
Cruise speed	215mph (346km/h)
Range	1,400 miles (2,253km)

The newly established Northrop Aircraft took on the ambitious project of designing and manufacturing twenty-four patrol bombers for Norway in just one year. Developed on the back of an existing design and adopting Edo floats, the N-3PB was born. The first example (301) is shown on Lake Elsinore, California, where testing and training were performed. *Gerald Balzer collection*

Even after Norway fell to the Germans, its air arms continued to fight under the RAF. The N-3PBs were based in Iceland under severe operating conditions, as suggested by this machine on beaching gear with servicing equipment awash in the chilly surf. However, the powerful floatplane (316 is shown) acquitted itself well in patrol and escort duties, among other tasks. *Gerald Balzer collection*

Soon after the contract was inked, Norway was overrun by Germany. The aircraft were subsequently supplied to the Free Norwegian Air Force operating as a squadron of the Royal Air Force (RAF). All aircraft were test-flown at Lake Elsinore, where Northrop also trained eighteen Norwegian pilots. The first six aircraft were ferried up the coast to Vancouver, where winter training was conducted. Two were lost there and the remaining four sent on to the permanent training base in Toronto, on Lake Ontario. The final machine was accepted on 27 March 1941. The balance of eighteen were shipped by rail to New York, then taken aboard a Norwegian freighter to cross the Atlantic. After another loss, the three Toronto birds were also sent across the water in March 1942.

Instead of the coastal patrol mission originally intended, the N-3PBs were dedicated to anti-submarine patrol and convoy escort tasks from three Icelandic bases. Other duties included photo-reconnaissance, casualty evacuation, air-sea rescue and general transport. 'Bases' is a generous word, as the floatplanes were simply drawn up onto the beach were all servicing and maintenance was performed in some of the harshest conditions of the war. Flight and water operations were also extremely challenging during most times of the year, and the small fleet (lacking de-icing equipment) was steadily worn away in nineteen months of this grueling exercise. None are known to have fallen to enemy action. Complaints about the Northrops were few, centering on a compass unsuited to operations at such high latitudes, magnesium elements that had to be routinely inspected and treated to prevent corrosion, and cracking of the float mounting bracket, which required a redesign.

Northrop found no other customers for its fine seaplane. It did not fit into the US Navy's operational schemes, and that would have been the avenue for Lend-Lease sales. The company moved onto other programs, none involving floats.

Another commercial-sale military floatplane for a foreign customer went to Ryan. The Dutch East Indies was trying to arm up for a likely confrontation with the expansionist Japanese Empire after the fall of the Netherlands to Germany in May 1940. Among the several aircraft orders for the Royal Netherlands Indies Army Air Division and Naval Air Forces from the Netherlands Government in Exile were 108 Ryans. The four contracts between 20 June and 7 October 1940 included forty-eight STM-2 trainers for the navy, an airplane that saw brisk sales overseas during the rearmament period. It was a spin-off from the popular STM all-metal monoplane trainer version (YPT-16 for the USAAC) of the civil S-T model. It was powered by the 150hp (112kW) Menasco C-4S Pirate four-cylinder inline inverted air-cooled, supercharged engine turning an 80-inch (203cm) two-blade fixed-pitch Sensenich wooden propeller. As a result of a request from the customer, Ryan also developed a twin-float variant called the STM-S2 (Sport Trainer Military-Sea) with single-step Edo Model 1965 hardware. A dozen of the Dutch airplanes (c/n 447 to 458, Dutch serials S-11 to S-22) were built as STM-S2s, together with twelve landplane undercarriage assemblies for conversion.[1]

The forty-eight Navy aircraft were built starting in November 1940 and shipped from Los Angeles; the last arrived in February 1941. Deliveries of the floatplanes to Surabaya, Java, commenced in January 1941, where they were operated from a naval base as primary, basic, advanced and instrument trainers – all in one. With the coming of war, they also conducted spotting, liaison, and harbor patrol duties. As the naval facilities came under Japanese attack, the airplanes were flown from flooded rice paddies. Eight or so of the machines had been lost in training accidents and others now to enemy action. As pressure mounted, the thirty-seven remaining naval STM aircraft (including eight STM-S2s, 450 and 452-58) were boxed up and left on 17 February 1942 aboard a ship bound for Australia.[2] There the floats were exchanged for wheeled undercarriages to serve Australian flight instruction.

Ryan STM-S2 characteristics

Span	29.9ft (9.1m)
Length	22.7ft (6.9m)
Height	7.4ft (2.3m)
Wing area	124ft² (12m²)
Fuel, max	24 gallons (91 liters)
Climb rate, max	700fpm (213mpm)
Service ceiling	12,250ft (3,734m)
Weight, empty	1,311lb (595kg)
Weight, gross	1,828lb (829kg)
Speed, max	122mph (196km/h)
Cruise speed	108mph (174km/h)
Range	247 miles (398km)

This pre-delivery photo shows the first Ryan STM-S2 (s/n 447) in flight from San Diego near the end of 1940. Destined for the Dutch East Indies, only a dozen of the STMs were placed on floats. The unarmed light airplane did all manner of duties after the Japanese moved into the area before the remainder were evacuated to Australia. *San Diego Air & Space Museum*

Naval expedient (XSB2U-3, TBD-1A, XSB2C-2, F4F-3S, F6F-3)

The Navy experimented with adding floats to existing fighters and naval bombers to permit operations in the absence of carriers or sufficient land bases. These were intended to equip a proposed sea-based USMC expeditionary force. Such aircraft, operating from sheltered waters like coral lagoons, could cover amphibious operations while airfields ashore were being built, should the carriers be forced to withdraw. The Japanese had been doing the same with some perceived success, fielding several models including putting the notorious Nakajima Zero on floats (the Nakajima A6M2-N 'Rufe'), first encountered in this guise in 1942.[3]

The Vought SB2U-1 Vindicator was adapted as a Marine Corps long-range scout-bomber mission, the SB2U-3. This included considerable increase in fuel capacity and an upgrade in the number and caliber of weapons. However, provision for a pair of floats was a major challenge. The prototype XSB2U-3 was wrought from the final production SB2U-1 (0779), which flew in the new configuration (sans floats) in February 1939 before going back to Stratford for the addition of the 27.8-foot (8.5-meter) floats. Emerging again in April, it went to Anacostia in May for further testing. The work soon uncovered the need for a ventral fin to add directional stability.*

After another trip back to Vought, the trials resumed on 9 August 1939 and at least one change in the Edo float design was found necessary. It also required larger water rudders.

---

* The added vertical surface area of floats, particularly if more is ahead of the aircraft center of mass, can be directionally destabilizing and so it is common to add a ventral fin area to aircraft modified with floats.

Flight testing demonstrated a discouraging speed loss of 36mph (58km/h) to 210mph (338km/h). Performance of the basic aircraft, 921lb (418kg) heavier than the SB2U-2, was already compromised. Consequently, the floats went no further. Only this prototype and the first production SB2U-3 (2044), delivered to Anacostia on 26 February 1941, were actually fitted with floats. Although fifty-seven SB2U-3s were built, no others had even provisions for floats.

Twin Edo floats were added by the NAF to the initial production Douglas TBD-1 Devastator (0268) between June and August 1939 to create the TBD-1A. There seemed no plans to make the aircraft convertible as the arrester hook and tail wheel were removed and their openings faired over. With a 2,000lb torpedo the Devastator was heavy for a floatplane, and the floats, 29 feet (8.8 meters) long, were the largest the Navy had so far attached to a single-engine airplane. First flying in this configuration on 28 September, the modified airplane was evaluated at Anacostia for a month before moving to NAS Gould Island, Newport, Rhode Island, for further testing. The airplane handled well in the air and on the water with no additional vertical surface area, and the floats slowed the airplane by only 20mph (32km/h). After an overhaul at the NAF in 1940, the TBD-1A went back to Gould Island to be operated by the Naval Torpedo Station, where it remained for the next four years as a general test aircraft and for torpedo trials. It played a role in helping resolve the Mk 13 torpedo issues that were affecting US offensive capability. It was struck off on 23 September 1943 and scrapped. The Netherlands was offered the configuration in 1939 as the basis for a coastal patrol bomber with enlarged rudder and the more powerful R-1820-G105A at 1,200hp (895kW), but the German occupation ended these plans.

The final production Vought SB2U-1 was modified as the prototype of the SB2U-3. This was intended as a long-range scout-bomber for the US Marines, and floats were seen as a beneficial addition. Testing during 1939 (the XSB2U-3 seen here was photographed on 7 September 1939) revealed the need for the ventral surface added under the tail. *Naval Aviation Archives*

Although the first production SB2U-3 was delivered with floats (photographed here on 9 May 1941), they were by then already eliminated from the design. The model, with added fuel cells and armament, was overweight and suffered performance loss. The ancillary mission as a floatplane was not worth adding to that deficiency. *Naval Aviation Archives*

The first production Douglas TBD Devastator was given floats (here also on the unique beaching gear) for evaluation of this TBD-1A configuration at NAS Gould Island in late 1939. It was surprisingly successful and considered as a coastal bomber design for the Netherlands. The unique asset was used for vital testing of torpedoes over four years before being salvaged. *San Diego Air & Space Museum*

Conversion of the Curtiss Helldiver with twin floats and ventral fin as the XSB2C-2 (Model 84C) was first considered for the Marines in January 1940, before the type first flew. These plans solidified to fitting new Edo floats to the XSB2C-1 prototype after essential baseline testing had been completed. However, it was March 1941 before Curtiss was instructed to plan for modification to this configuration, given the long and frustrating SB2C-1 development. Although the Navy was already looking forward to acquiring 294 of the seaplane variant, most as SB2C-1s converted on the line (Model 84D), the plans were set back by the loss of the prototype before the modification could begin. The 'mod' was then performed instead on an SB2C-1 (00005) in Columbus, and the aircraft ferried to Anacostia where the addition of the twin Edo floats and a ventral fin was completed on 28 October 1942.

The modification added 1,314lb (596kg) to the airplane, knocked 700 miles (1,127km) off the maximum range, and 35mph (56km/h) from the top speed. Rough water trials were performed at Hampton Roads beginning on 9 March 1943. Take-off runs were rather long for the heavy aircraft (nearly 15,000lb/6,804kg gross), but otherwise the configuration appeared acceptable. Nonetheless, production plans were dropped on 14 April 1944 as no longer required.

In October 1942 the service contracted with Grumman to pursue a seaplane modification to a Wildcat fighter. The initial intent was to convert the balance of the 100 F4F-7s on contract to this configuration, but in the event only a single prototype was completed via the modification of an F4F-3 (4038). Edo installed its single-step aluminum floats in the fall of 1942. The landing gear wells in the fuselage were faired over. Auxiliary rudders were attached to the tips of the airplane's horizontal tail, moving in concert with the primary rudder.

This F4F-3S 'Wildcatfish' first flew on 28 February 1943 with 'Hank' Kurt at the controls. A ventral fin was found necessary for suitable directional stability, and this was added in May. A take-off run on calm water required an astounding 34 seconds. The modification added 500lb (227kg) to the

The sole XSB2C-2 was photographed at NAS Anacostia on 29 September 1942. This type had a long and troubled development history, so it was late when the floatplane variant planned for the Marines was finally prototyped. Although it appeared practical, by the time production of this model could have commenced it was no longer required. *Jay Miller Collection*

aircraft's empty weight, but only 266mph (428km/h) was realized, or a loss of 60mph (97km/h), while the range dropped about 260 miles (418km) to 600 miles (966km). Given the agonizingly slow rate of Hellcat production, it was not prudent to divert F4F production to such marginal pursuits, and the Wildcatfish died.

Work began on fitting 29-ft (8.8-m) long Edo floats to the Grumman F6F-3 Hellcat per December 1942 Navy direction. Model tests in the wind tunnel and water tank were performed that year before the idea was shelved.[4] By the time testing on all similar concepts was yielding results, USN and USMC interest in such aircraft had waned. The astonishing rate of carrier and carrier aircraft production, combined with the Seabee construction battalions' successes in rapidly building beachhead runways, together with general improvement of the US strategic situation after the Battle of Midway, made further such efforts unnecessary.

The F3F-3S 'Wildcatfish' is shown on its beaching gear, emphasizing the large size of the connecting struts. The auxiliary rudders added near the tips of the horizontal tail moved in concert with the primary rudder. The ventral fin was added after the previous photo of the airplane on the water. *Naval Aviation Archives*

Converted from a Grumman F4F-3 (4038), the solitary floatplane version was tested in the first half of 1943 (seen here near NAS Norfolk). This was one of the least successful such creations, with a very long take-off run to become airborne. The floats and series of connecting struts severely impacted flight performance. *Naval Aviation Archives*

The performance of the Piper L-4, the lightest liaison type in the Army during the war, must have been significantly impacted by the addition of floats. Note the single individual aboard this example during a take-off run on a lake near Fort Sill, Oklahoma. It is likely to have been meant only for floatplane training. *US Army*

In the same manner and likely the same motivation, one or more Stinson L-5 light planes were placed on Wollam floats. The typical aft ventral surface was added. There is no evidence such aircraft were deployed. *National Archives*

Army afloat (AT-7A, L-1E, L-1F, L-4, L-5B, XC-47C, P-38E)

The Army Air Forces addressed early war fears similarly to the Navy. Transporting supplies to American forces on far-flung Pacific Islands and across the China-Burma-India (CBI) Theater as the US moved to the offensive was initially challenging owing to enemy action and thinly stretched resources. Airlift was a fine idea but limited by the distances and the number of available airfields and aircraft. Navy flying boats were just too few. The notion was hatched to place Army transport aircraft on floats to help meet the demand.

As a stateside seaplane trainer for these types, a few Piper L-4s were also put on plywood floats in 1944.[5] Piper Aircraft performed tests on the Susquehanna River at Lock Haven, Connecticut, in May and June 1944 with two float-equipped L-4Hs (43-30039 and 44-79629).[6] These probably derived from pre-war commercial designs. The L-4H aircraft appeared to have Edo floats while others had a different design. Likewise, at least one Stinson L-5 was modified with Wollam floats and a ventral surface addition. The L-5B Sentinel ambulance conversion was fitted with provisions for amphibious floats. Although 730 of these airplanes were built, it appears that installing the floats was a rarity. Rarer was a North American O-47A placed on Edo floats in late 1941 for unclear purposes.[7]

Meeting an explicit yet limited need was the conversion of a few Vultee L-1 Vigilant observation airplanes (formerly Stinson Model 74 and previously designated O-49) with floats to be used in Burma for medical evacuation via rivers. The two-place airplane was already blessed with outstanding short-field and slow-flight capability provided by wing leading-edge slats and slotted flaps plus drooped ailerons. Seven L-1s were fitted with two Edo Model 77 single-step floats, each with retractable nose and main wheels; the aircraft's tail wheel was removed. These machines had already been modified as ambulances with a fuselage hatch to admit a litter into the cabin. Adding the floats made them L-1Es. The same was done to an L-1A (already lengthened by 1.1 feet (0.3 meter) and previously modified as an ambulance) to become the L-1C and, with the addition of the floats, the L-1F. A further 113 L-1Cs were configured with floats but retained their original designation. Many of these aircraft were also sent to Burma, where they flew from 1943 to 1945. Some sources suggest there were seven L-1Es and five L-1Fs.

On a larger scale, six Noorduyn UC-64 Norseman aircraft were fitted with floats to support communications by the Army Corps of Engineers during construction of the Alaska Highway, but others were also so configured using a pre-war production option with Edo YD floats. Seven Beech AT-7A multi-engine trainers (among them 41-21156/61, 42-53522, 44-70536, and 45-41746) were also converted with Edo floats. This required the addition of a ventral fin under the aft fuselage. This effort

The first picture shows a Vultee O-49 Vigilant near Ladd Field, Alaska, and the other the same type redesignated L-1A at the Burmese Myogan Air Strip, both capturing the Vigilant on floats, making them L-1Fs. Note the lack of tail wheel and the amphibious gear. The aircraft's wing high lift devices and modification as an ambulance made it a valuable asset in the Burma campaign. *National Archives*

was likely undertaken to collect engineering data and to gain operational experience with the equipment on a twin while also meeting special utility needs.

The real work began to add floats to the Army's ubiquitous C-47 Skytrain cargo airplane to permit it to land just offshore to load and unload. Enormous Edo Model 78 floats – Edo's largest at 40 feet (12 meters) long – were attached by large struts, the aftmost with steps to reach the rear passenger doors. Each float had a 300-gallon (1,136-liter) fuel tank and a pair of retractable main wheels with brakes and possibly steerable nose wheels to make the airplane amphibious. The C-47's maximum gross weight was increased from 31,000 to 34,162lb (14,061 to 15,496kg) to accommodate this marked configuration change, making it among the heaviest floatplanes. The first of these aircraft was a C-47 (42-5671) modified by Edo as the XC-47C at the American Airlines facility at La Guardia Field, Long Island.[8] It flew there at the beginning of June 1943 and was then ferried to Wright Field on the 13th.

The months-long evaluation of the XC-47C found that the aircraft handled reasonably well in flight as well as on the water or ground. However, it was difficult to get the airplane to lift off from anything but smooth water, and it was very sensitive in crosswinds.[9] The brakes were overly sensitive, leading to rapid tire wear or blow-outs. The giant floats cut the top airspeed from 230 to 191mph (354 to 307km/h) in addition to 3,500-4,000lb (1,588-1,814kg) off the payload weight. Take-off performance left something to be desired, so tests were performed in July and August 1943 with Jet Assisted Take-Off (JATO) booster rockets installed under the belly. Center of gravity travel was also further constrained, making loading more challenging. The real trouble came in loading and unloading cargo, given the very high deck. Servicing was clearly also going to require higher stands. Just replacing tires would be frustrating as this required enormous jacks. The utility of the aircraft in supplying remote and spartan island facilities seemed minimal given these limitations.

This Noorduyn UC-64 Norseman has had Edo floats installed for operation on rivers and lakes in Canada and Alaska during construction of the famed Alaska Highway (ALCAN). As suggested by this 14 May 1943 image, the Norseman was a rugged airplane with a large interior for moving people and materials. The float installation was a pre-war production option and therefore readily exercised by the USAAF. *National Archives*

Among the various utility types that the USAAF placed on floats were a handful of Beech AT-7As. As was common, more vertical surface area was required at the aft end of the aircraft, the added ventral fin evident on 41-21161 (first such conversion, in 1942) in addition to an innovative ladder to the entrance door. The second image shows an example with a deeper ventral fin. *National Archives*

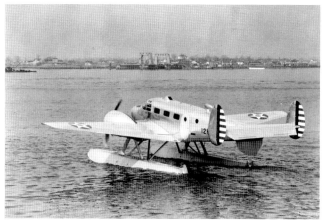

A fine idea of supplementing Navy flying boats in supplying remote island bases in the Pacific saw the largest floats Edo ever manufactured added to a C-47 to make this XC-47C; this angle emphasizing their enormous size. The prototype (42-5671) is shown in flight after the Edo modification.
San Diego Air & Space Museum

The floats of the C-47C contained addition fuel and retractable wheels to make the aircraft an amphibian. The main wheels, retracting just aft of the step, may have contributed to the poor take-off capability from anything but a smooth water surface. This aircraft (converted C-47A 42-92577) is one of just five fitted with the floats beyond the XC-47C, although Edo manufactured 150 pairs of floats and associated hardware. *San Diego Air & Space Museum*

The aircraft did well enough on paved surfaces except in crosswinds. Carrying the nose number 615, C-47C 42-92577 shows the attitude and very high stance of the airplane in the water, complicating what was already a frustrating cargo loading and unloading task. This and servicing challenges caused the idea to be set aside. *San Diego Air & Space Museum*

Any plans to create a fleet of C-47Cs were shelved. Yet Edo was given a contract for 150 sets of floats, and five Skytrains were modified in field shops to the configuration where they saw some use in Alaska and New Guinea without notable acclaim. Of these, only C-47As 42-92577 and 42-108868 were formally redesignated C-47C, while C-47s 41-18582 and 42-5671, together with C-47A 42-92699, retained their original designations.

The Army performed additional such work under the motivation of permitting fighter self-deployment to the distant theaters rather than having to rely on vulnerable and then scarce cargo ship transport that could carry other war materiel. A candidate for this was the Lockheed P-38 Lightning, which had the safety of two engines for long over-water ferrying. The twin floats, attached to the centersection hardpoints, would contain fuel for the long-range ferry. A range of 5,000 miles (8,047km) was proposed. The floats could be dropped or removed at the end of the route and the aircraft's normal landing gear employed. The standard Lightning was not suitable because the tail surfaces would be in spray from the floats, so the booms aft of the engine coolant radiators would have to be swept up while also adding area to ensure suitable directional control with the floats.

A P-38E (41-1986) was modified in spring 1942 with the upswept aft booms.[10] The initial design, first flown on 2 March 1942, had the booms lengthened by 2 feet (0.6 meter) and the horizontal tail raised 1.3 feet (0.4 meter). This was replaced by 2 December with a 'swoop' tail of normal length, but raising the horizontal by 2.8 feet (0.8 meter). The space aft of the pilot seat had radio gear removed and other gear displaced for an observer to squeeze in to record data.

The floats were never fitted to the Lightning Seaplane. The change in strategic situation precipitated by the Battle of Midway, and realization that adequate shipping would be available for aircraft delivery, was justification for abandoning such projects.

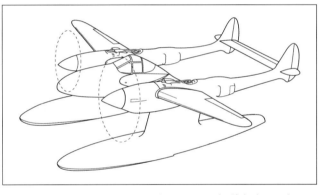

The Lightning Seaplane was conceived as a means of self-deploying the P-38 fighter across the sea to areas where it could operate without relying on runways that might be lacking. The floats would contain fuel tanks that could be drawn upon during the flight. This drawing was based on concept art that clearly did not benefit from engineering advice, as the cantilevered arrangement from the engine nacelles was unlikely to be adopted, and the tails do not reflect the up-sweep considered necessary. *Author*

Photographed on 2 December 1942, the greatly modified tail booms of this Lockheed P-38E are very evident, both raising the empennage away from the spray off the planned floats as well as adding ventral area. However, the improved American situation in the war made such measures unnecessary. *American Aviation Historical Society*

CHAPTER FOUR

Photo Recce Make-Do

Half measures

THE AMERICANS, struggling to launch a massive rearmament effort and build up combat forces, were not in a position to develop and manufacture dedicated PR types. Imperfect addition of cameras to existing types was considered sufficient. Photo reconnaissance continued to be underfunded, if not under-appreciated, as staff struggled against Army inertia and reluctance of ground force commanders to relinquish direct control of reconnaissance aircraft, as well as trying to acquire suitable recce aircraft. This state of affairs prevailed while the war abroad demonstrated it as ill-advised.

The USAAC did manage to have cameras installed in Beech 18s, C-45As and C-45Fs to become the sixty-nine F-2s, with several models featuring various camera arrangements including trimetrogon for mapping purposes.* For 'high-altitude' work, an oxygen supply was installed for the aircrew and the cabin door was fitted with a hatch in which a camera could be positioned. These airplanes were delivered between December 1939 and into 1943 but were kept clear of combat zones. At a typical 200mph (322km/h) and 700-mile (1,127km) range, the new war showed such types to be exceptionally vulnerable.

An effort to devote aircraft to photography saw Beech C-45 transports converted as F-2s to take cameras mounted in the floor of the baggage compartment for ground mapping. The cabin door had a hatch installed that, when removed, permitted an oblique camera to be positioned in the opening. This example, from Bolling Field in D.C., has a stencil by the door declaring that it was to be used for photographic purposes only. *National Archives*

As a half-measure towards something more like what the European combatants were employing, the first Douglas A-20 Havoc had two cameras mounted in tandem within the bomb bay, becoming the unsatisfactory XF-3. Two more A-20s were similarly converted later as pre-production YF-3s. The three were delivered in April 1943, but not deployed. Finally recognizing the severe deficiency, an astonishing 775 observation/reconnaissance variants of the A-20B were ordered as the O-53.[1] The Havoc had an advantage of about 100mph (161km/h) over the Beech but became vulnerable to fighters. However, the bomber role had to take precedence during the early years of production, when demand far exceeded output. The O-53 was cancelled before any were completed.

* The F-1 modification of the C-8 transport predated the war by a decade. The designation F was for 'Foto'.

The initial version of the Douglas A-20 looked much like this A-20A. Three of the early aircraft were converted with developmental camera installations as a XF-3 and a pair of YF-3s. Although an order for an O-53 variant of the A-20B was placed, the combat role took precedence during the period when production was ramping up. *National Museum of the United States Air Force*

Speedy shutters

In addressing the fast PR role, the twin-engine Lockheed P-38E and F were an early source for the high-speed photo recce as F-4s and F-5s. The aircraft's unobstructed nose was easily modified, after the guns were removed, with four cameras shooting straight down or obliquely out of windows. Some were blessed with an autopilot, and the F-4s were the first Lightnings to be equipped with underwing drop tanks. Initially with just two vertical cameras, the F-4A model introduced two oblique units for trimetrogon. Three F-4s were provided to the Royal Australian Air Force and Free French forces, the latter also operating several models of F-5.

By mid-1942 119 F-4s and F-4As were turned to training, while the F-5 became the large-scale production variant. It featured a standard five cameras, various numbers and combinations appearing, with several retaining a pair of .50 guns. The various models of F-5s were built from the later-model Lightning then in mass production, where some attention to the alterations could be accommodated at the manufacturer's plant. Throughout the war various models of the V-1710 engine were also fitted based on either ready availability or performance requirements, such as turbosuperchargers for high-altitude operation. Fuel drop tank capability and oxygen were also added as specified. Adjustments to F-5 camera installations were introduced as required until, near the end of the war, a longer nose, departing from the fighter profile, was introduced with the F-5G (P-38L). A total of some 1,215 to 1,400 Photo Lightnings were operated as camera ships. They were the most common and successful photo recce platform in the service and among the outstanding such assets of any nation during the war years.

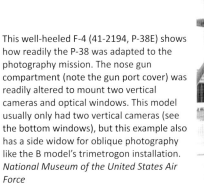

This well-heeled F-4 (41-2194, P-38E) shows how readily the P-38 was adapted to the photography mission. The nose gun compartment (note the gun port cover) was readily altered to mount two vertical cameras and optical windows. This model usually only had two vertical cameras (see the bottom windows), but this example also has a side widow for oblique photography like the B model's trimetrogon installation. *National Museum of the United States Air Force*

Above and left: The most numerous photo reconnaissance asset in the Army Air Forces was the F-5 derivative of the P-38 in several variants depending on base model (shown here is F-5B 42-67343 modified from a P-38J). The close-up (F-5A 42-12982, P-38G) shows one of the more common camera installations of the A and B models with two oblique and two vertical units. Note the long-range drop tank and the relative ease of camera access in the nose. *Top San Diego Air & Space Museum/ Left National Museum of the United States Air Force*

Below and right: An alternative external appearance for the F-5E (42-104081, P-38L, is shown) had a wider oblique window with an 'eyebrow' fairing. The nose accommodated improved trimetrogon units together with a fourth vertical camera. Although lacking cabin pressurization, the turbosuperchargers provided excellent high-altitude performance. *National Museum of the United States Air Force*

The F-5F introduced yet another camera configuration into the P-38 nose bay. At left shows a custom job, as evident by the fresh aluminum fairings for lens clearance, permitting an exceptionally large vertical camera noted as a 'split 40inch'. Noteworthy is the excellence of the installation workmanship. *San Diego Air & Space Museum/ National Museum of the United States Air Force*

A departure from the usual P-38 nose contour came with the F-5G (seen here is Free French Air Force 44-25828, P-38L). While retaining the side windows, an especially large round window on the bottom demanded an extended fairing. *San Diego Air & Space Museum*

The North American P-51 offered an armed, fast reconnaissance capability as shown here with bombs under the wings, which retained the internal guns. The camera ports are evident in the aft fuselage of this F-6D (44-14841, P-51D) where a vertical and an oblique unit could be mounted. Several hundred of the 'foto' Mustangs were created, this example being in a Pacific theater setting. *San Diego Air & Space Museum*

Below: The inconvenience of converted fighters as photography platforms is illustrated by these GIs servicing the cameras in an F-6 through the bottom and side access ports. It can be imagined how unpopular this was when the ground was wet and muddy. The image also suggests the non-trivial nature of a photo conversion with camera mounts, access openings, electrical connections, and likely heating and defog lines. *Air Force Test Center*

Some 482 F-6 modifications of the North American P-51 Mustang were also performed. Through several models, all carried a pair of cameras in the aft fuselage, and armament was unaffected, giving the aircraft an armed recce capability. Despite the weight of retained weapons and armor, the F-6 still had a speed advantage on the F-5. As with the Lightning variants, the camera installation was altered both as official configurations and as field modifications. The otherwise worthless Brewster Buffalo found some value as the F2A-2P photo ship. Such fighter adaptations could do around 350mph (563km/h) with a 600-mile (966km) range depending on the engine and fuel system.

Navy photo reconnaissance was a smaller-scale affair than that of the Army, and much of it was by necessity carrier-based. Most of the vessels had three or four camera ships, so the required number of available mounts had to increase as the number of carriers multiplied later in the war. The camera-equipped Douglas Dauntless dive-bombers comprised eight SBD-1Ps, fourteen SBD-2Ps, forty-three -3Ps and sixteen -4Ps. These likely located the camera vertically in the aft fuselage. This became the norm, with a small number of the latest model fitted with a camera mount for the ancillary mission. The exception saw the USN borrow four F-5B Lightnings (P-38L) as XFO-1s (010209/01212) to fill a gap during the North Africa campaign.

Some eighteen Grumman Wildcats were converted to F4F-3P and -3AP camera ships with a single camera aimed out of the port side of the aft fuselage. Contrary to mission needs, this displaced a reserve fuel tank, but the wing guns were retained. A dedicated platform as the F4F-7, it was unarmed and unarmored, with wing-fold deleted to add outboard fuel cells. An autopilot was fitted and the camera shot out of the bottom of the fuselage. With such a heavy fuel load, a dump feature was required to get the aircraft down to a suitable landing weight if it returned early – the gross rose to 10,328lb/4,685kg versus the usual 7,002lb/3,176kg. Valves and lines ran from the wing tanks aft to the aft fuselage opening under the rudder, where two pipes emerged, forcing relocation of the navigation light to the rudder trailing edge. Additional engine oil capacity was necessary as flight duration rose to 24 hours (exceeding the 'endurance' of most pilots) and the range to 3,700 miles (5,955 km). Only twenty-one were built (5263/83), to be operated by Marines. Another 100 F4F-7s were anticipated but did not come to fruition. Most were subsequently converted to F4F-4Ps, only one of which (03386) had previously existed.

The standard approach was taken with the Hellcat, a handful of F6F-5Ps being created with the same aft fuselage camera. Some Vought F4U-1 Corsairs had a camera mounted behind the cockpit to become -1Ps, as were eleven F4U-4Ps and forty -5Ps. The Grumman TBF Avenger also saw P camera variants. Even the Curtiss SC-1 catapult floatplane had provisions for reconnaissance camera gear. Likewise, the F7F-3P saw cameras fitted to the Grumman Tigercat. It appears that fifty-eight of these aircraft, both single-seat and dual, were delivered between 16 March and 31 August 1945, then ferried to the Lockheed Air Service Center, Van Nuys facility, for conversion. The first was re-delivered in April, and the Marine photo recce outfit arrived in Guam just as the war concluded. An oblique and vertical camera together with a trimetrogon trio were mounted in the aft fuselage with remote-controlled covers over the optical windows. The pilot was also provided with a vertical periscope sight.

The Americans had since March 1943 sought to take advantage of the British lead and get hold of some de Havilland Mosquito wooden reconnaissance twins. The volume of the aircraft permitted larger cameras to be carried compared with the F-4/5s, while the range and ceiling were superior at 30,000-35,000 feet (9,144-10,668 meters) cruising at about 236mph (380km/h) for 1,500 miles (2,414km). It would also permit P-38 fighter production to increase. The RAF resisted releasing any it possessed and planned to draw down local Mosquito production. Consequently, it was 1943 before the USAAF took up forty Canadian-built Mosquito B Mk VIIs and XXs, to be modified with cameras by Bell Aircraft in Buffalo, New York. These F-8s proved disappointing and, of the sixteen flown to Britain in the latter half of 1944, none were used operationally.[2] In-theater, the USAAF continued to seek Mosquitos until late 1944 and operated a few ex-RAF Mosquito PR.XVIs, beginning in February, for various tasks that included night photography.

The US Navy's combat photo reconnaissance capability was, by necessity, largely carrier-based and was therefore characterized by single-engine fighters. For the early war years that meant the Grumman Wildcat, with a handful of F4F-3s equipped with cameras. An exception was the F4F-7, with a fixed wing for extended fuel tanks, no guns, and fuel dump masts emerging from the aft fuselage, but this was produced in small numbers. *Grumman Historical Center*

Above: Like the earlier Navy fighters, the powerful Grumman F6F Hellcat was turned to photography when necessary. A small number of F6F-5Ps were produced and mixed into the carrier air wings. They would have looked like these F6F-5s, with a centerline fuel tank but with a vertical camera in the aft fuselage. *National Museum of Naval Aviation*

Right: This GI installs a camera into the aft fuselage of a F4U-1 somewhere in the South Pacific. The panel with the lens port and that it is replacing lies beneath. This demonstrates how photography was an ancillary mission for the fighter.
Vought Historical Archives

Below: If Vought Corsairs dominated a carrier's strike force, it was reasonable to have one or two configured for photo recon. Thus about fifty F4U-4P and F4U-5P aircraft come into being, looking much like this -4 model. Like all the other carrier-based camera ships, they remained armed and could accommodate only one vertically mounted camera in the aft fuselage. *Vought Historical Archives*

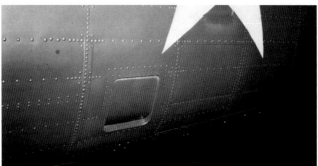

This Grumman F7F-3P reveals in the aft fuselage one of the trimetrogon camera side windows and the indentations of the two bottom windows. These were usually shielded behind translating covers. The Navy's first tricycle gear carrier aircraft, the Tigercat possessed the safety of two engines and outstanding range to lend greater capability to the naval photo recce mission than ever before, yet was too late to contribute to the war. *Grumman Historical Center*

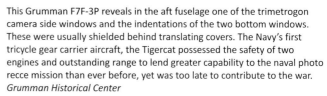

Another famous British mount obtained for fast recce was the Supermarine Spitfire. A number of Spitfire Vs were eventually replaced with twenty-one unarmed PR Mk XIs for flights from the UK. Such aircraft typically had a pair of vertical cameras in the aft fuselage and possibly oblique cameras in underwing fairings outboard of the main gear wells.

A very fast camera ship arose from the new Lockheed P-80 jet so late in the war that it did not see frontline service. Cruising at 410mph (660km/h), some of the Air Forces leadership saw this as the most vital mission for the new aircraft, although the high fuel demands of the early turbojet engines allowed a comparatively short 540-mile (869km) range. The second YP-80A (44-83024) was converted as the XF-14, a single vertical camera replacing the nose guns, the top of the nose rotating forward for ready access. When this was lost to a mishap in December 1944, two P-80As were given the same installations as XF-14As, soon renamed XFP-80A. Converging on a production design with an oblique camera added, thirty-eight P-80As were converted on the production line as F-14As, and 114 more were purpose-built, most delivered well after the war.

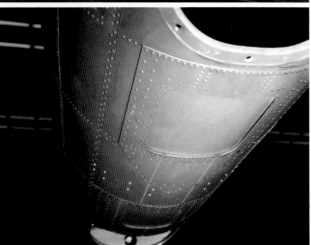

Left top, middle and bottom: This series of images shows the aft fuselage camera ports of the F7F-3P Tigercat. They show respectively the port-side window for the trimetrogon, the cover partially retracted, the starboard-side oblique port (covered), and the two bottom ports for vertical camera and the center component of the trimetrogon. Covering the costly optical windows when not in use protected them from thrown engine oil, residue from moist air condensation, and material kicked up by the landing gear, but the complexity meant that they were not commonly adopted during the war. *Grumman Historical Center*

This image of an F-8, taken at Bolling Field on 20 June 1944, shows one of the two camera ports in the bomb bay doors, with any other changes unclear. The plywood de Havilland Mosquito had gained acclaim in British service and was long-sought by the USAAF. However, when the service finally managed to acquire Canadian-built models and convert them as camera ships, they were disappointing and set aside in favor of RAF examples. *National Archives*

Another adopted foreign mount meeting an urgent need was the Supermarine Spitfire of RAF fame. Like many adapted fighters, this PR Mk XI has a vertically mounted camera installed in the aft fuselage. However, this example also has camera fairings outboard of the main landing gear, barely visible under the starboard wing. *National Museum of the United States Air Force*

America's first deployed jet fighter also promised very high-speed photo reconnaissance capability, albeit with a short range. Several prototype installations were made to early Lockheed P-80s during the last year of the war, leading to a production design like the F-14A (44-84998) shown here. None were completed during the span of the conflict. *San Diego Air & Space Museum*

Deviants

The photography mission left much room for innovation in meeting changing mission demands. Alterations could be introduced with a bit more ease than others, to include mounting different cameras. By 1944 the home industry had reached a high stage of experience and could respond quickly to requests for engineering and shop work. Servicemen in the field were skilled and usually had access to sufficient shop and materials resources to improvise an installation.

The one standout innovation of the F-5 'foto Lightnings' was the XF-5D (from F5A 42-12975, P-38G), built with a cramped cameraman/navigator station in an elongated nose possessing a vertical camera and two ·50-cals. A camera was also installed in each tail boom. Although the guns were welcome (except perhaps by the 'photog' who would have been deafened by them), the heavier installation reduced performance for the small benefit of the onboard operator, who probably could only change the film. A field modification of suspect utility was a large pod on a drop tank position on a P-38E with a clear nose for a prone photographer.

An even greater remolding of the Lightning nose was the sole XF-5D (the reworked F-5A 42-12975, P-38G). 'Bobbie', as the airplane was dubbed, provided an extended enclosure and transparency for a camera operator (note the seatback cushion suggesting a reclined seat and not the prone position many sources mention) and one large vertical camera supplemented by others in the tail booms. The design also allowed for two .50 guns, but was not adopted for production. *National Museum of the United States Air Force*

Above: This F-5E (P-38J) has an exceptionally large pod under the port wing, created from a 310-gal tank. Looking closely one sees a man holding a camera inside the transparent nose. The utility of this (almost certainly not officially ordained) for combat reconnaissance would be minimal and was only made to collect still and movie footage of a June 1945 Okinawa strike mission with a very willing photographer. *National Museum of the United States Air Force*

Depot or field modifications of whatever aircraft were at hand to provide PR capability were common – some officially sanctioned and others impromptu projects launched by local commanders unhappy with photo support.

Something that likely fell in between was a vertical and an oblique camera installed in the aft fuselage of the Bell Airacobra. Some 497 P-39s in various models were modified at Bell with cameras, yet never received the F designation. These were the first photo ships to go to war with the US Army, in North Africa. With the P-39 and A-20 (see later), it is not surprising that North African experience suggested an airplane more like the P-51 and B-25 would be more desirable.[3]

One P-40 (40-326) was fitted with a reconnaissance camera in the aft fuselage during March 1942 and designated a P-40A. This apparently derived from a directive issued by Arnold that the P-40 be examined for the reconnaissance role.[4] There are indications that the P-40 was considered for PR duties, but Lend-Lease and other demands on production made this impractical. Like the P-39, it was not a cutting-edge type, so promoting its use as a recognized PR type was contrary to the prevailing policy. This may be why the hundreds of camera-configured P-39s were not given an F designation; they were considered a stop-gap until F-5 production caught up with requirements. Several other one-off projects were

Left, below left and right: This pair of images shows an improvised camera installation in a Bell P-39L (42-4558). Few modifications to a fighter were trivial, and this shows good workmanship for the rework. An optical window was avoided; instead a fairing integral to the access panel protects the lenses from thrown engine oil and other debris. *Below National Museum of the United States Air Force/left San Diego Air & Space Museum*

A new mission for aerial photography was to shoot images of a radar screen aboard a reconnaissance aircraft, the images then helping to guide the bomber crews that followed to navigate and identify the target for bombing through overcast. This Mosquito PR XVI is fitted with an H2X radar in a heavily modified nose as a prototype of such an aircraft. These and other such aircraft saw good use in Europe during the bombing campaign against Germany. *National Museum of the United States Air Force*

Taking advantage of the fast recce bird for additional combat missions saw other field improvisations. This F-5E (43-29008, P-38J) has been modified to take a bulky chaff dispenser. Running ahead of a bomber formation, the aircraft would dispense the cloud of metallic foil strip 'window' to hide the bomber formation from radar tracking or decoy enemy interceptors. *National Museum of the United States Air Force*

fielded. Some of the P-47Bs were given camera installations, but this was not widely seen or employed operationally. The USN and Marines had similar experiences with field modifications to meet urgent needs.

An evolution of aerial reconnaissance photography saw such airplanes also employed in weather reconnaissance, target-marking or chaff-dropping. More in line with photography was the fitting of an onboard radar for the new role of radar scope photography. This provided images from the ground-mapping radar for bomber crews to compare with when using bombing-through-overcast radar.

The sport plane market was tapped to provide light observation types (renamed 'liaison' in April 1942, mostly as a morale measure) with small cameras or a cameraman carried aloft. This practice brought complaints of mission duplication from the PR crowd. However, the 'grasshoppers' continued to perform the traditional observation duties over friendly lines or where air superiority had been achieved, while PR across the line became the sole domain of high-performance types.

Long look

Bombers came to be employed wherever long range was called for. The Havoc was brought up again later in the war, with forty-six A-20Js and Ks converted for photo work as F-3As. These had a vertical camera replacing the generally worthless ventral gun in the aft fuselage, and a camera in the nose requiring the forward guns to be removed. Another camera and four photoflash bombs could be carried in the bomb bay. These were busy during 1944 and 1945 in both day and night work. There appear to have been earlier A-20s converted as camera ships, as the North Africa campaign saw such aircraft used between the F-3s being abandoned and the J/K models emerging.[5]

The forty-five North American F-10s were B-25Ds fitted with ground-mapping cameras. Two oblique cameras were fitting behind nose fairing and another shot vertically, while additional cameras could be installed in the aft fuselage. A photo tech joined the crew of four other men, which included a navigator. Appearing in 1943, these unarmed and unarmored machines carried long-range fuel tanks installed inside the bomb bay. They endured mapping missions of up to 10 hours, but not in combat zones. Such medium bombers did about

The F-3 photo design was resurrected in 1944 with the conversion of forty-six A-20J and K medium bombers. As well as the usual camera in the nose and aft fuselage, there was another in the bomb bay that could also accommodate photoflash bombs supporting night photography. This A-20K is reported to have been one of those converted to F-3A. *Ray Wagner collection*

250mph (402km/h) for around 700 miles (1,127km). For the Navy, a few Lockheed Ventura patrol airplanes were included, fitted as camera PV-1P ships. This spin-off of the civil Lodestar typically cruised at 170mph (274km/h) with a range of about 1,500 miles (2,414km).

For longer range at higher altitudes, conversion of four-engine bombers appeared the quickest solution. The USAAF began by converting 216 Consolidated B-24Ds, Hs, Js and two Ms to F-7s in several models with from six to eleven cameras in the nose, bomb bay and aft fuselage. The first foto Liberator was ordered in March and completed in summer 1943.[6] All defensive armament was retained and long-range tanks were installed in the forward bomb bay. Deliveries of the 216 aircraft ran over a year from August 1944. These included seven fitted with AN/APS-15 radar for scope photography as 'F-7 H2Xs'.[7] Marines operated the navalized B-24, the PB4Y, in long-range photographic missions. Some sixty-five of the PB4Y-1Ps were created, and they performed vital service photographing Japanese installations about which little had previously been known. The seventy-five F-9s in several models were derived from B-17Fs and Gs between 1942 and 1944. As usual, various camera installations were introduced. These heavies did roughly 280mph (451km/h) for approximately 1,000 miles (1,609km) but the ceiling of 25,000 feet (7,620 meters) made it vulnerable.

This B-25D has been converted to an F-10 with the nose blisters encompassing the optical windows for the cameras. The second image shows the modification to better advantage, except for the window at the base of the nose for a vertical camera. The medium bomber retained all but the nose armament, and an auxiliary fuel tank in the bomb bay permitted exceptionally long photo-mapping missions. *National Museum of the United States Air Force*

The B-24J below has been converted while retaining armament to an F-7B as evidenced by the optical window in the port aft bomb bay door. The 216 F-7s performed invaluable service in target reconnaissance and post-strike damage assessment. They commonly carried the cameras indicated in the accompanying period drawing, with the trimetrogon trio in the nose under the turret replacing the bombsight, and cameras in the aft bomb bay, while a long-range fuel tank filled the forward bay and the aft fuselage. *Above USAF/below Air Force Test Center*

A camera fitted to a Lockheed Ventura patrol bomber like this would make it a PV-1P. The camera likely shot out the sighting window in the bottom of the nose. Especially with the wing drop tanks, this aircraft had considerable range, albeit at slow speed, to provide a badly needed land-based photo reconnaissance capability for the US Navy. *National Museum of Naval Aviation*

Another long-range heavy employed in the foto business was the B-17, in several models as production moved along and armed because escort was rare. At least one extensive modification for a large collection of cameras is shown in this period illustration, with a B-17G shown in the second view. The unsatisfactory F-9s were created in smaller numbers between 1942 and 1944 as the strategic bombing campaign against Germany ramped up. *Above National Archives/right Ray Wagner collection.*

Facing daunting distances in the Asia-Pacific region as the USAAF moved to a concentrated bombing campaign against Japan, the service could not wait for special models to be developed. The United States found it had little intelligence upon which to build target lists for the Japanese islands. Despite the tremendous value of the Boeing B-29 Superfortress as a bomber, the very high altitude capabilities via cabin pressurization made it urgent that some of the aircraft be diverted to the reconnaissance role as a stopgap. Cameras installed in the B-29s and B-29As yielded 138 Boeing F-13s and F-13As. All normal armament was retained and the bombing capability not permanently disabled. Long-range fuel tanks filled the aft bomb bay, permitting a mission duration of up to 25 hours. The front bay could carry photo-flash bombs for night photography or additional cameras. The main camera gear was in the unpressurized space behind the aft compartment, with six to eight focusing out of windows installed in the lower hemisphere. Hand-held cameras could be sighted out of the gunner blister windows.

Some F-13s were on hand in June 1944 for training. The first arrived on Saipan on 13 October and immediately departed on the initial mission over Japan – the first American aircraft over Tokyo since the Doolittle raid in April 1942. At its high altitude it went unchallenged, as did most that followed. The prints were invaluable in planning the first bombing missions later that month. The Navy also expressed an interest in acquiring a few B-29s for high-altitude photography.[8] The aircraft had a large crew and high maintenance demands, so was a difficult choice for the photography mission.

Aiding the work over the home islands were to be three of the rare and unpressurized Consolidated B-32 Dominators (serials unknown) fitted at Wright Field with a suite of cameras, but the war's termination ended the project.[9]

Among what was certainly multiple camera installations for the F-9 were these nose fairings, the bay and aft fuselage cameras possibly retained. The above picture shows F-9C 43-37194 (B-17G) from 1 November 1944, and below a 30 May 1944 image of an F-9 converted from a B-17G. These was very likely intended to enclose the optical heads of a trimetrogon trio. *Top San Diego Air & Space Museum/bottom National Museum of the United States Air Force*

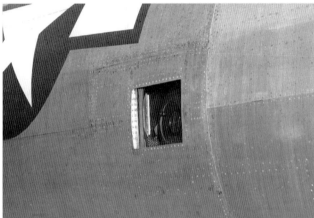

This F-13 was a conversion of the B-29 to the high-altitude, long-range photo role. The camera windows (left) are barely visible from a distance on the large airplane. All cameras were between the pressure bulkheads, so were inaccessible during high-altitude flight. *Top National Archives/ left National Museum of the United States Air Force*

Below: Details of the camera installation in the three Consolidated B-32s are lacking, but were likely similar to that in the F-13. This large bomber had been in contention with the B-29 before being redesigned as an unpressurized very heavy bomber that sacrificed much of its advantages. Seeking some utility for the short production run of airplanes, the model's long range and large internal volume lent itself to the photo-mapping mission. *National Archives*

The projects

Following the first Army combat experience in the Mediterranean there was a reorganization of the reconnaissance assets that eliminated observation aviation. Tactical reconnaissance could be entirely visual or with simple camera systems to provide short-term intelligence for rapid prosecution. Strategic reconnaissance was of broader objectives and far ahead of the battle front, and might include collecting data for mapping and aeronautical charting. For the strategic needs a dedicated high-speed, high-altitude photo reconnaissance platform was seen as highly desirable, but such requirements could not be met by conversion of heavy bombers. This clearly addressed a strategic need while most tactical requirements were satisfactorily met by conversion of fighter types.

Adapting existing types was imperfect and did not always meet the demands of the battlefield or air war. Urgent combat needs for escort fighters or to replace bomber losses would occasionally see conversions waylaid and recce airframes shorted. Advanced projects to develop dedicated American PR aircraft came late in the war, and only the Air Forces undertook such efforts. The very long ranges over enemy territory found in the European and especially Asia-Pacific theaters were challenging, only bombers providing the capability. Yet they were also slow and, except for the B-29, of inadequate ceiling owing to lack of pressurization. A high-speed, high-altitude aircraft optimized for camera work was clearly indicated by the field units and high-level reviews.

By January 1943 the pressure for such an aircraft had built to the point where formation of requirements could commence. Without much background, the recce team recommended consideration of the McDonnell XP-67. This was quickly dismissed as the single-place aircraft was far from flight and with many technologically risky features from a firm that had yet to place an airplane in series production.

Tentative characteristics, drafted in April, received scorn from aircraft development personnel. They called for two crewman, a 3,000-mile (4,828km) range, a speed of 400mph (644km/h) at 30,000 feet (9,144 meters), and a 60,000-foot (18,288-meter) ceiling.[10] Convincing senior officers of the advisability of this approach remained a challenge.

Formal military characteristics were issued on 15 October 1943 as a request for proposals, and spoke of such high-altitude operation as to be essentially invulnerable. They specified the minimum of 400mph (644km/h) and a range of 3,000 miles (4,828km), but dropped the altitude to 45,000 feet (13,716 meters). A relief pilot/navigator was required together with a photographer/engineer, and the airplane would be unarmed.[11] Very little armor was to be included, but all fuel cells were to be self-sealing. An on-board film processing lab was favored to speed delivery of the intelligence. Negatives if not prints could be ready on landing for immediate transfer to commands that could exploit the knowledge. There was a need for as many as 100 to 500 airplanes.[12]

It was pointed out by several people in the aircraft development branches that a previous attempt at developing a high-speed photo recce airplane had resulted in an asset falling short of evolving requirements by the time it flew. Of three prototype XB-28s (40-3056/8) ordered on 13 February 1940 from North American Aviation, it was decided soon after the award of the contract to finish the third as a reconnaissance/photo-mapping airplane. Fitted with P&W R-2800-27 Double Wasp twin-row 18-cylinder engines augmented with turbosuperchargers and counter-rotating props, the pressurized aircraft cruised at 255mph (410km/h) and could make high speed at 24,000 feet (7,315 meters). Cameras were in the aft fuselage, an unpressurized space. First flying on 24 April 1943, this XB-28A (40-3058) crashed on 4 August owing to vertical tail flutter. By this time the notion of a high-flying medium bomber had lost favor, and North American had more important work to do in its production programs. The airplane did not meet the performance goal for the new photo type and it was feared that the next development would suffer the same fate. While many in authority urged continuing the practice of modifying the best tactical aircraft for the photo role, the pressures to undertake a specific development were insurmountable and it was important to maintain harmony between the branches of the Army.

The XB-28 was developed as a high-speed, high-flying medium bomber. As such it had pressurization and met most of its requirements, but the desire for such a bombing platform had faded. A photo ship variant, the XB-28A, was explored but died when the aircraft crashed and the newly defined reconnaissance requirements stood well beyond the type's capabilities. *San Diego Air & Space Museum*

On 12 June 1943 Wright Field was reluctantly directed by the Chief of Materiel Division to move on an acquisition program for the new recce type. Brigadier General Chidlaw wrote, "Despite all efforts to continue utilizing aeronautical engineering resources of this country in a balanced way to improve existing and develop promising projects, it now becomes necessary to divert some effort to a specialized photographic airplane design study…"[13] Boeing's revised B-29, which also had the benefit of serving as a bomber, was apparently never considered before direction from Arnold came to proceed. Each of the bidders were granted a contract for their very different solutions.[14] With the prospect that these development efforts would be prolonged, yet the operational need immediate, the F-13 design and eventual conversions were set in motion in the latter half of 1943.

Hughes XF-11

The Hughes Aircraft Company's XA-37 (Model D-2 or DX-2) had a complex history leading to a disappointing test aircraft. Built of wood veneers via the Duramold process, the airplane was the subject of substantial design changes. The D-2 was a particular passion of company founder Howard R. Hughes Jr, who continued to lobby for some mission suiting the airplane (the reverse of common practice). A photo recce variant concept caught the attention of Hap Arnold on 27 June 1943, knowing that the Air Forces lacked adequate fast, high-altitude photo assets and aware of the continuing failure in obtaining the plywood Mosquito. When queried, Hughes revealed that the D-2 had flown, but an entirely new wing was being contemplated, the redesign identified as the D-5 (alternatively DX-5). The company offered the outline of a proposal for a two-place, unarmed reconnaissance D-5 of 36,400lb (16.511kg) gross with a 3,600-mile (5,794km) range and a maximum of 488mph (149km/h) at 30,000 feet (9,144 meters). This was still to be made of wood and had cameras in the nose and tail booms aft of the wing. Underwing fuel tanks could be carried between the center pod and the nacelles. Hughes stated the company would need $7,250,000 for capital investments, but would deliver the first production example in twelve months.

The AAF finally managed to examine the D-2 on 1 July, but all performance and flight characteristics were provided

by Howard Hughes, the only pilot to have flown the airplane. Wright Field judged the performance numbers optimistic. The extent of the changes required to produce a suitable testbed for the proposed recce bird appeared so extensive as to be impractical and cost-ineffective. Hughes continued to be evasive and an exasperated Materiel Command finally washed its hands of the effort on 21 August.

The Hughes design was then championed by Colonel Elliot Roosevelt, son of the American President, who was high up in the USAAF photo reconnaissance organization. He and other officers had embarked on a fact-finding mission in August 1943 to seek a suitable platform for the dedicated high-speed, high-altitude camera airplane. Hughes welcomed the men, wining and dining them as well as personally flying them out to see the D-2 at the remote Mojave Desert test site. Praising the aircraft, Roosevelt told Arnold that the D-5 was the only aircraft in development that met current PR needs. Curiously, the General considered this excessive praise of a non-existent airplane enough and send word on 31 August to set in motion the procuring of 100 D-5s. In a meeting with Hughes Aircraft and AAF officials on 8 October, Roosevelt went so far as to claim that obtaining sixteen of the airplanes in sixteen months would shorten the war by six to eight months.

Wright Field engineers remained wary of the Duramold material and the ability of the inexperienced Hughes to manufacture military aircraft.* Instead, they suggested that converting the Lockheed XP-58 to the PR role would likely produce better results sooner, as it was already in flight test and the manufacturer could more reliably move to production.[15] Regardless, a 6 October 1943 Authority to Purchase was promulgated for 100 D-5s (MX-575).[16] Much discussion ensued, with concern that the multiple issues associated with Hughes and the D-5 would bring trouble later, including Congressional scrutiny. Nonetheless, a letter contract was approved on 11 October for $50,497,200. The initial delivery schedule established on 27 January 1944 called for the first airplane to be delivered in October and peak production of ten airplanes per month by May 1945. The 3 September 1943 specification called for a cruise speed of 400mph (644km/h), a 450mph (724km/h) top speed, a 5,000-mile (8,047km) range, and a ceiling of 36,000 feet (10,973 meters) with a design GW of 36,400lb (16,511kg).

The Hughes development team encountered almost immediate difficulties that slowed progress to such a worrying extent that cancellation was threatened as early as February 1944. That month the delivery schedule was altered to the first aircraft in March 1945 and ten per month by September. The

Hughes Aircraft had developed the wooden D-2 bomber with its own money from the late 1930s through to 1943. Although periodically seeking an Army contract, and the airplane also identified as the XA-37, company owner Howard Hughes resented military oversight and proceeded in secret. Although flying briefly in spring 1943, it was a disappointment yet offered the basis for a fast photo reconnaissance aircraft. *National Archives*

* The Hughes Aircraft Division of the Hughes Tool Company had been established in 1936 and moved into new facilities with an adjacent grass runway in Culver City, California, during summer 1941. It had built one-off airplanes to meet its founder's aviation ambitions but had never placed an aircraft into series production.

Above: Lockheed had worked long on the XP-58 through many design and powerplant shifts until the prototype flew in June 1944. It had become an exceptionally heavy fighter for which no one evinced much interest. However, it was briefly considered as a short path to a dedicated photo reconnaissance platform instead of pursuing the Hughes Aircraft project. *Tony Landis collection*

formal specification was approved on 13 March, and the mock-up was inspected on 20 April. An adequate number of personnel was a persistent issue, but Hughes relayed an expectation that those working on the cancelled Hughes-Kaiser flying boat would be reassigned and that floor space consumed by that project would be freed up. This eliminated another impediment to the contract, but as it happened Hughes continued the flying boat project on his own.

The F-11 would have been ambitious in the absence of the design and manufacturing challenges faced by Hughes, in addition to labor disputes and arguments with the AAF over the specification. As Wright Field had anticipated, it was not just a matter of redesigning the D-2. The F-11 had the same twin-boom layout but was much enlarged with a 68 percent increase in span and a 50 percent greater loaded weight. Addressing some of the criticisms, a mix of aluminum and wood was proposed. The USAAF insisted on an all-aluminum structure to cope with the dramatic environmental changes throughout the flight envelope, avoiding high maintenance demands, and because plywood as an aircraft material had been proven questionable. Hughes acknowledged the change in January 1944.[17] Hughes also resisted the requirement for all tankage to be self-sealing, proposing to fill ullage in the unprotected tanks with carbon dioxide, but the Air Forces insisted. Hughes was able to argue

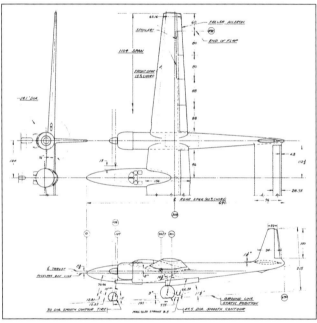

Above: This engineering three-view from 13 October 1943 shows the XF-11 at an early stage in development. A bubble canopy was ultimately adopted, and turbosupercharger exhausts emerged from the nacelles. Notable in the design was the high-aspect ratio wing supporting a high-altitude, long-endurance cruise. *National Archives*

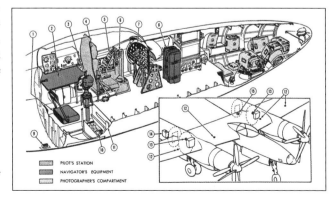

The final layout of the XF-11's pressurized cabin did not provide for a relief pilot or photo technician. A seat is provided for a navigator beside the driftmeter (3). The slender nose compartment shows a bevy of cameras that were likely never seriously considered given the cramped space. Note the outline of the large bubble canopy and also the contra-rotating propellers that became a source of program delays and safety issues for the program. *Jay Miller Collection*

Both high-altitude, high-speed photo reconnaissance aircraft projects used the most powerful piston aero engine in production. Shown here on a Hughes Aircraft test stand in an XF-11 cowling, the Pratt & Whitney R-4360 had four rows of seven cylinders for low frontal area. Matched with a pair of turbosuperchargers, this promised tremendous performance yet was still subject to development bugs as production ramped up under war-driven delivery pressures. *National Museum of the United States Air Force*

the maximum load factor down from 9g to 6. The center pod was reduced in cross-section while still accommodating the crew of two with an optional photo tech to process film.[18] Hughes was compelled by the performance requirements to change from the D-2's R-2800 to the 3,000hp (2,237kW) P&W R-4360-31 Wasp Major engines, the four-row twenty-eight-cylinder 'corncob' of low frontal area. As the most powerful engine in production, this was an easy choice. However, its dry weight alone was 3,500lb (1,588kg) and manufacturing was only just ramping up against high demand. Hughes chose two four-blade Hamilton Standard Super Hydromatic contra-rotating propellers, the rear disk having a diameter of 15.3 feet (4.7 meters) and the forward one 15.1 feet (4.6 meters), also featuring reversing.* These were developmental props that had not as yet passed any government qualifications.

The laminar flow wing was greatly expanded in aspect ratio for efficient high-altitude cruise. Small ailerons were employed for high-speed roll while spoilers augmented these for low-speed control. The ailerons lay within outboard flaps, the high lift surfaces running nearly full span. An A-20 was modified with the F-11's vertical tail to collect flight test data. The 700-gallon (2,650-liter) drop tanks were moved outboard of the nacelles.[19] Each engine was boosted by a pair of General Electric (GE) turbosuperchargers. During cruise, one of the turbos could be bypassed for greater efficiency. The cockpit was shielded with 350lb (159kg) of armor. Up to twelve cameras were to be accommodated, although details included only seven in the long, narrow nose and four in the port boom aft of the gear well. The boom camera window was normally covered by twin doors. The design was frozen on 15 February 1944. An attempt to introduce leading-edge hot air deicing was only permitted after the sixth production article.

Tough negotiations over many months ensued in working up the final contract, with much disquiet concerned the delay at high levels. The War Department wanted to move

production to Houston, near Hughes Tool Company facilities, where more and less costly labor would likely be found, but Howard Hughes successfully argued to keep the work in Culver City. There was also a dispute over reimbursement for the D-2 development.[20] After much back-and-forth, the contract was signed on 5 May 1944 for $70,274,666.86. It called for two XF-11s (44-70155/6), a static test airframe, and ninety-eight production examples (44-70157/254). The delivery schedule by then was first article in March 1945 and eleven per month by January 1946.

Development delays arose from multiple sources. The inexperience of the Hughes team was evident in late and inadequate work. As was his habit, Hughes made himself central to the design process while dividing his attention between numerous projects and disappearing for long periods. By 30 June 1944 the design was still only 45 percent complete after much of the work was thrown out as unsatisfactory and twenty-one engineers, including the project engineer, had quit. The design gross weight had grown 30 percent to 47,500lb (21,546kg). The USAAF became so concerned with the slow progress and lack of clear communications that it threatened cancellation unless Hughes hired an experienced production manager. Even after he did this, design and development continued to encounter organizational and quality difficulties brought on in no small part by the company's lack of experience. By 30 September 1944 production had slipped to a May 1945 initial delivery and fifty-four by the end of the year, the balance in 1946.

The wings and empennage had been subcontracted to Fleetwings in Bristol, Pennsylvania, which was to make its first delivery on 15 December 1944 but was well behind schedule. The AAF proposed west coast firms that could assume the work, but Hughes would not hear of it.[21] When reconsidered later it was determined to cost too much money and time. Fleetwings had encountered difficulty getting basic data from Hughes and balancing this work with its other projects. The company finally shipped the first XF-11 hardware on 9 April 1945. The engine and propeller were also

* Reversible pitch propellers were only just entering production, and contra-rotating propellers were also quite new. These represented more technological risk for the program.

well behind schedule. Pratt & Whitney saw its first shipment no sooner than February 1945, and Hamilton Standard (itself awaiting an engine for testing while also supporting other programs) did not expect delivery before August 1945. When the first engine arrived in March it was not flightworthy, sent for 'build-up purposes only'. As summer approached the propeller delivery remained on the distant horizon.

By April 1945 the XF-11's first flight would clearly not occur before August, with the production deliveries well beyond that. A review still found the Culver City plant ill-prepared to manufacture the airplane economically. The entire effort was very costly by comparison with similar projects. Despite the high priority given the program, it had to be concluded that there was little probability of the F-11 contributing anything to the war. On 3 May the decision was made to reduce production from ninety-eight to thirteen (including ten YF-11s), leaving open the potential for a larger order if the type proved successful.[22] By 18 May, after Germany's surrender, even this was considered excessive and reduction in the prototypes and static test article was being discussed. Consequently, cancellation of the much-delayed ninety-eight production airplanes was affected on 26 May 1945, with Hughes allowed $8,642,242 in termination settlement. The XF-11s and static article were continued for $13,000,000.

Priorities dropped after the war and more labor disputes were encountered. The first engine was not delivered until September 1945, yet still not approved for flight. Likewise, propellers delivered in the same period were time-limited and would not last to flight. The first airplane did not come together until spring 1946. Taxi runs and hops off the ground in April found issues that prompted a rework of the hydraulic system. The ground tests resumed in June and revealed high rudder forces that also required remedy.

The first XF-11 crashed on this maiden flight in July 1946, seriously injuring Hughes, who served as his own test pilot. One prop had gone into reverse following a seal failure from inadequate lubrication. Hughes resorted to standard 14.7-foot (4.5-meter) Curtiss Electric props and R-4360-37s for the second machine. This flew in April 1947 with Howard Hughes again at the controls. Performance fell behind its competitor and low-speed lateral control was deficient.

Although a fine and beautiful airplane, the XF-11 appeared to be just another fighter imperfectly adapted to the photo mission. There was one set of controls and instruments for the pilot and a navigator station, leaving no relief crew option for exceptionally long missions. There were no provisions for radar or for carrying photo-flash bombs supporting night photography. Camera access was difficult in the sleek nose – requiring the tech to crawl into the very confined space (with a widest outside diameter of 5.3 feet [1.6 meters]) from the cockpit since it lacked outside access. Removal and replacement of cameras was near to impossible. In any event, the military had decided that it could not afford such aircraft in the immediate post-war era. The advantage of altitude and speed quickly faded with the advent of jet interceptors. The Hughes aircraft was likely to cost approximately twice the F-12 competitor owing to the many non-standard elements (including something as basic as the tires), the considerable capital costs to establish production given the meager Hughes infrastructure, and the labor costs of building in California.

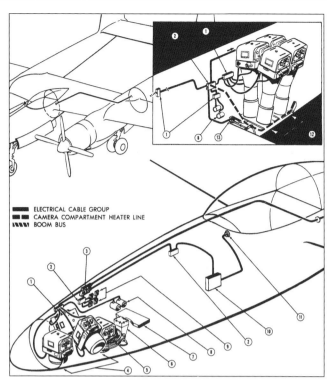

ELECTRICAL CABLE GROUP
CAMERA COMPARTMENT HEATER LINE
BOOM BUS

This drawing illustrates the camera installation for the XF-11 as it was ultimately realized. Even the small number of units in the narrow nose would be very difficult to access for servicing and replacement, something likely also true for the nacelle units. Although the drawing optimistically notes a photographer seat (7), who would actually have had to be prone, and a control panel (3) with viewfinder (6), these features were impractical. Ultimately the Hughes aircraft (this drawing showing the single-rotation props from the second prototype) appeared more like the converted fighters the entire effort had sought to replace with purpose-built airplanes. *National Archives*

Hughes XF-11 characteristics (estimated)

Span	101.3ft (30.9m)
Length	65.4ft (19.9m)
Height	23.2ft (7.1m)
Wing area	983ft² (91m²)
Fuel, built-in	2,650 gallons (10,031 liters)
Fuel, max	3,030 gallons (11,470 liters)
Climb rate, initial	2,025fpm (617mpm)
Service ceiling	48,000ft (14,630m)
Weight, empty	39,392lb (17,868kg)
Weight, gross	53,530lb (24,281kg)
Weight, ferry	58,315lb (26,451kg)
Speed, max (33,000ft)	450mph (724km/h)
Cruise speed	400mph (644km/h)
Range, normal	4,000 miles (6,437km)
Range, ferry	5,000 miles (8,047km)
Landing distance (over 50ft obstacle)	3,500ft (1,067m)

Republic XF-12

Republic Aviation had gotten word of the desire for a high-altitude, high-speed photographic airplane and came to Washington in June 1943 to present a conceptual design for a four-engine transport-type airplane it was proposing to develop for the new mission.[23] By the time characteristics were formalized and Wright Field set into motion, the development people felt the requirements had been influenced by the Republic design, which was actually aimed at the post-war airline market.[24] On 21 December they recommended slowing the process enough for Boeing to prepare a proposal. Nonetheless, on 6 January 1944 Materiel Division ordered the procurement to go forward.[25]

Republic's 11 January 1944 proposal with four R-4360-31 engines was given a go-ahead on the 29th. A letter contract for two machines was issued on 15 February calling for the first to be delivered a year hence and the second after another three months. The formal contract document on 4 August for the XF-12s (44-91002/3, MX-495) at $6,717,511.80 specified deliveries in March and November 1945. After protracted discussion, reimbursement for the design work prior to October was ultimately allowed. Mock-up inspection occurred on 26-28 June 1944 and again on 24-25 November. It was during the first inspection that the government increased the crew complement from four to six, added special radio and radar gear, altered the photographic equipment installation, and added carriage of nineteen photo-flash bombs.[26] The first aircraft was then to be delivered in September 1945 and the second in February of the following year.

The Farmingdale, Long Island, company's design of the XF-12 was principally the work of chief designer and Russian expatriate Alexander Kartveli. The airframe was especially clean aerodynamically for the best performance attainable. The fuselage and nacelles were of circular cross-section with as few scoops and protrusions as practical. Flush riveting was used throughout and the wing had a laminar flow airfoil. All gaps were sealed as best as could be achieved. Control surface balance weights were all internal and fabric sealed the leading edge of each surface and the interior of its cove. Consistent with most long-endurance aircraft of the period, an autopilot was included. The bay for eighteen AN/M-46 flash bombs and the five camera bays (two vertical and a trio for trimetrogon) all had doors that retracted into the bays.[27]

The control surfaces had spring-loaded balances for acceptable pilot control forces, and trim tab assist for light control forces instead of the weight and complexity of hydraulic boost. Small ailerons were used in high-speed flight, while retractable plug-type spoilers augmented the lateral control at low airspeed. Double-slotted Fowler flaps, three segments per side, extended across 57 percent of the span. Automatic speedbrakes of 7-inch (18cm) chord on the bottom of the wings near the leading edges helped ensure against over-speed. The wing thickness at the root was sufficient to enclose the very large single main gear wheels, 5.8 feet (1.8 meters) in diameter, when retracted.

Originally the two pilots were to sit line-abreast within the plexiglass ogive nose to provide the 180-degree vision called for in the requirement. However, the mock-up inspection board expressed concern with reflections and rain distortion such as experienced by B-29 pilots with their curved windscreens. To investigate the potential problems, Republic mounted a mocked-up nose with pilot seats on a truck at representative height to be run up and down a runway at night and in rain. The results of this, together with pressurization tests, compelled a redesign, directed on 4 October 1945, to make the nose cone unpressurized, the pressure vessel ending inside with a slanting bulkhead containing the cockpit flat forward windscreen. The two curved upper transparency panels of the nose slid down into the lower shell during take-off and landing for improved visibility – although it is unclear whether this feature was built into the prototypes.

The cabin pressurized volume ran unbroken from the cockpit to the aft fuselage. To eliminate a wing center box or carry-through structure impinging on the cabin interior, each wing's two spars were attached to heavy frames outside the fuselage. Wing leading edges featured hot-air deicing while the props had electric heaters. All fuel was stored in the wings with self-sealing tanks. For extended range, it was proposed that tanks in the outer wing panels need not be leak-proof provided they had a purge system for inerting the ullage.[28]

The crew of seven included two pilots with a navigator/camera operator and flight engineer on the flight deck and three camera technicians in the rear, one of which also served as a radio operator. The aircraft would not only carry many cameras, including enormous new models, but the techs could also process the film onboard for immediate delivery upon landing. While lacking such support as that from the President's son enjoyed by the famous aviator Howard Hughes, Republic was in touch with the leadership of Wright Field's Photographic Branch, Colonel George Goddard and Colonel Karl Polifka. These men favored a bomber-size airplane with an onboard photo lab. Such features and endorsement ensured the program's continuation when fighter pilots expressed more desire for the F-11 during a 10 August 1944 review that

This early concept drawing of the Republic XF-12 is interesting in revealing the initial intent to have the pilots inside the plex nose providing 180 degrees of lateral vision. While the flight-deck-in-nose concept was altered, retained were the drag-reducing clean lines with the wings attached to the middle of the circular cross-section fuselage and circular nacelles. Also eliminated were the contra-rotating propellers and scoop intakes under the nacelles, the cowl flaps were replaced with a translating ring, and a leading edge slot intake was added between the nacelles. *National Archives*

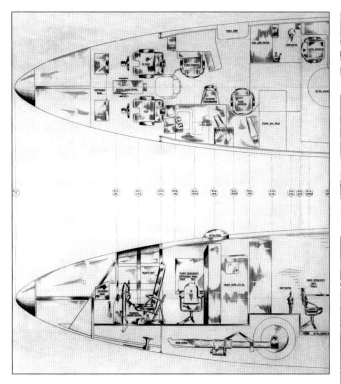

The image of the mocked-up flight deck looking out of the curved transparent nose (the inspection photo with markings associated with comment notes) reveals some distortion, at least from the plexiglass used in the mock-up. The drawing shows the slanted pressure bulkhead with the windscreen in front of the pilots, which was adopted in response to the suspected problems with reflections and distortions with curved transparencies. Note also the crew stations, which include a radar operator. *National Archives*

considered whether to continue both programs.[29] This had been called after some in Washington challenged the efficacy of the large, unarmed and under-armored airplane. The dispute went so far as canceling the military characteristics on 19 July 1944 in preparation for drafting them anew. Given that all had previously agreed to the requirements and two contracts had been let, both programs were permitted to proceed in the event that one failed.

The XF-12 was the USAAF photo reconnaissance team's dream come true. All cameras were readily accessible from within the cabin, with photo techs onboard to operate and service them (note the operator station in the mock-up photograph with inspection notation numbers), and even process the film in flight. The drawing shows five camera bays while the final design had just three. *National Archives*

The original concept had three-blade contra-rotating propellers for the R-4360 with Ham Standard units. Wright Field urged a change to Aeroproducts' dual-rotation props with electric deicing. Both of these, as well as an alternative Curtiss product, were complex and developmental props that appeared to pose a schedule if not technology risk. After wavering for more than a year, 16.2-foot (4.9-meter) four-blade Curtiss Electric propellers with reversing were adopted in January 1945 as a temporary measure, permitting flight testing to begin without delay despite some small anticipated performance shortfall. All propellers were automatically synchronized. By June 1945 it had become clear that meeting the schedule would mean production beginning with standard props.[30]

To ensure suitable engine cooling inside the very tight cowling, two variable-speed impeller fans inside the forward

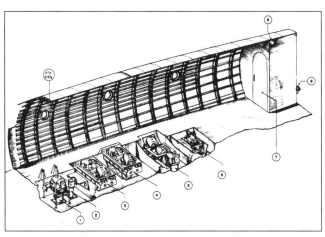

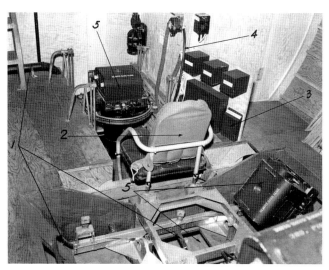

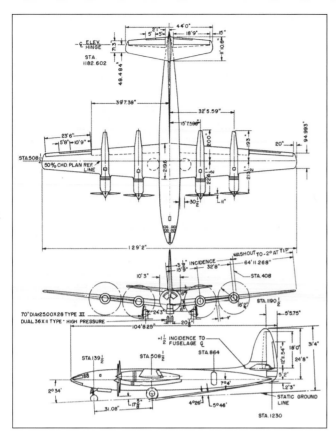

Above: This three-view drawing of the XF-12 shows the aircraft as it was eventually built. Notable are the single-rotation propellers and large main gear tires retracting into the wing to keep the nacelles as small as practical. The sleek lines bespeak the unusually high airspeed sought for the bomber-size aircraft. *National Archives*

face of the inlet ensured suitable cooling airflow. In place of cowl flaps there was a translating ring, flush in the nacelle aft of the engine, which controlled the flow of air through the cowling by sliding fore and aft to increase or decrease the exit area. There were also slot air intakes in the wing leading edge between the nacelles on each half-span to feed air to the turbosuperchargers, supercharger intercoolers, oil radiators and nacelles. The design of the slots, and obtaining suitable internal airflow from them through the nacelles, was so critical that a quarter-scale model of this hardware was built for wind tunnel data collection. Waste heated air was dumped out of slot nozzles in the bottom of the nacelles to extract some jet-effect thrust. Two GE turbosuperchargers in the aft portion of the long engine nacelles had their exhaust orientated to exit through an elliptical nozzle to generate jet thrust equating to 250-350hp (186-261kW) per engine, or 10 percent of the total at a 40,000-foot cruise. One of the turbos could be bypassed during cruise.

Construction of the first Rainbow, as Republic christened the airplane, was delayed until December 1944 by the redesigns as well as slips in the engine delivery schedule and issues with the turbosuperchargers. The airplane rolled out a year later. The redesign and other costs drove an overrun in excess of $2.5 million. An order for a service test quantity of thirteen YF-12 airplanes had been considered in July 1945 but

Below: Typical of the final generation of high-performance reciprocating-engine airplanes, the XF-12 required considerable air ducting for the turbosuperchargers and intercoolers. All were contained in the nacelles aft of the engines. Unusual was the annular cowl flap and the way that the turbosupercharger exhausts were directed to elliptical nozzles at the end of the nacelles to extract a jet thrust contribution. *National Archives*

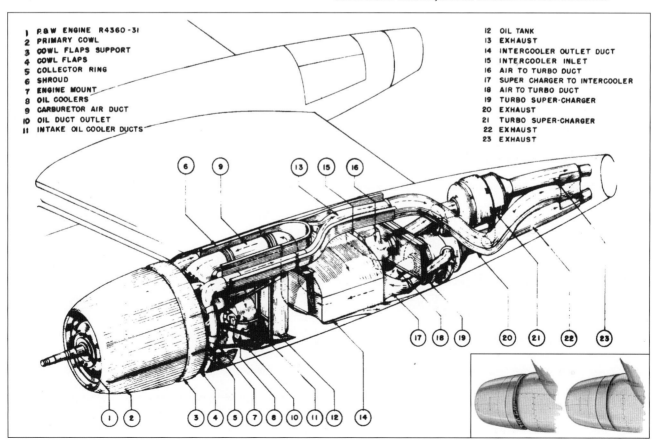

rejected because there was no urgent requirement and it was advisable to await flight testing results.

Lacking any mission systems, the airplane took flight in February 1946. The beautiful, technologically advanced machine did much as expected with astonishing performance, some claiming it was the fastest multi-engine (or four-engine) propeller-driven airplane ever built. Despite an order for six more, the program was cancelled before performance had been fully explored.

Republic XF-12 characteristics (estimated)

Span	129.2ft (39.4m)
Length	93.8ft (28.6m)
Height	28.3ft (8.6m)
Wing area	1,640ft² (152m²)
Fuel, design	4,350 gallons (16,467 liters)
Fuel, max	5,514 gallons (20,873 liters)
Climb rate, initial	1,600fpm (488mpm)
Service ceiling	45,000ft (13,716m)
Weight, empty	70,500lb (31,978kg)
Weight, gross	100,845lb (45,743kg)
Weight, ferry	108,435lb (49,185kg)
Speed, max	460mph (740km/h)
Cruise speed	348mph (560km/h)
Range	3,460 miles (5,568km)
Range, ferry	4,270 miles (6,872km)
Landing distance (over 50ft obstacle)	3,300ft (1,006m)

Northrop XF-15 Reporter

Even as the XF-11 and F-12 moved forward, another avenue was explored in November 1944 as possibly responding sooner with much less development.[31] The Northrop XP-61E was the prototype of a very-long-range fighter, itself derived from the P-61B night-fighter. The North American P-82 Twin Mustang was selected for the long-range fighter role, but the XP-61E remained an impressive performer. Another twin-boom aircraft, it appeared eminently suitable as a long-range, fast recon platform and production could be initiated quickly. The baseline design had two pilot stations under an enormous bubble canopy, permitting relief for the long-duration missions. Cameras would replace the guns in the nose.

Turning the Northrop design to this role was championed by Colonel Minton Kaye, on the air staff within the CBI Theater. He took the proposal to Washington and it won favor in the form of a June 1945 175-aircraft order (down from an initially proposed 320) for F-15As (45-59300/474, reassigned P-61E serials). Of the two XP-61E prototypes, initially flying on 3 January 1945, only one (42-39549) survived to be immediately modified as the XF-15. A pre-production XF-15A was derived from a P-61C (43-8335) with equal haste.

The XF-15 carried over the 2,000hp (1,491kW) R-2800-65 engines from the XP-61E. The XF-15A brought the P-61C's 2,100hp (1,566kW) R-2800-73 with turbosuperchargers and Curtiss Electric props of 12.7-foot (3.9-meter) diameter. The principal change was the nose redesign for the camera installation, which was subcontracted to Hughes. The nose was

The full-size mockup of the XF-12 reveals the stance on the ground while a man on the wing gives scale to the airplane. Flying six months after the war, it proved to be an outstanding design and among the fastest multi-engine prop aircraft ever built. It is unfortunate that the ambitions that fostered the development were acted on so late in the conflict. *National Archives*

shortened by 4 inches (10cm) while the production examples would be 8 inches (20cm) longer and with larger side windows. It featured a hinged top for easy access to the camera compartment, which could be configured per mission with up to twenty-four arrangements of six cameras of seventeen models. Armor was provided for the crew, whose seats could recline a bit for more comfortable long-endurance flights. Range was extended with drop tanks. The P-61C's wing speedbrakes were eliminated from the production design.

Aircraft 42-39549 flew as the XF-15 on 3 July 1945 with LA 'Slim' Parrett doing the honors. The XF-15A entered mod in Hawthorne on 10 August and flew in October. Ultimately only thirty-six F-15A Reporters were finished, all post-war.

Northrop XF-15 Reporter characteristics

Span	66.0ft (20.1m)
Length	49.6ft (15.1m)
Height	13.3ft (4.1m)
Wing area	662ft² (62m²)
Fuel, built-in	1,130 gallons (4,278 liters)
Fuel, max	2,370 gallons (8,971 liters)
Climb rate	2,000fpm (610mpm)
Service ceiling	41,000ft (12,497m)
Weight, empty	22,900lb (10,387kg)
Weight, gross	32,015lb (14,522kg)
Weight, ferry	40,365lb (18,309kg)
Speed, max	440mph (708km/h)
Cruise speed	315mph (517km/h)
Range	4,000 miles (6,437km)
Landing distance (over 50ft obstacle)	1,700ft (518m)

Northrop subcontracted the XF-15's nose design to Hughes, but the USAAF likely dictated the features. With a swing-up cover for ready camera access, the nose could be reconfigured to twenty-four arrangements with any of seventeen camera models. This photo shows such an arrangement with the electrical and air lines emphasizing how complex such an installation could become. *Gerald Balzer collection*

The Northrop XP-61E was a long-range fighter derivative of the P-61B night-fighter, which was converted again to the XF-15 fast photo reconnaissance bird. One of the two prototype XP-61Es is shown after the modification with the camera nose replacing the gun nose. It lacks the turbosupercharger scoop below the cowling that characterized the F-15As. *Gerald Balzer collection*

CHAPTER FIVE

Tactical Haulers

Improvising

OF TACTICAL TRANSPORTS, only the Douglas Aircraft C-47 Skytrain would be available to the Americans in great numbers in all theaters. The February 1940 specification for the military cargo variant of the commercial DC-3, aimed at carrying airborne task force assets, was for 170mph (274km/h) at 5,000 feet (1,524 meters) to a top speed of 200mph (322km/h) and a minimum range of 1,000 miles (1,609km) while operating from a 2,000-foot (610-meter) field surrounded by 50-foot (15-meter) obstacles. A contract for 147 of these Santa Monica, California, company airplanes came a full year later and the first was delivered just sixteen days after Pearl Harbor.

The airplane was powered by the twin-row fourteen-cylinder P&W R-1830 Twin Wasp* turning a three-blade, 11.6-foot (3.5-meter) Hamilton Standard prop. Skytrains would usually carry around 6,000lb (2,722kg) of cargo on a 30-foot (9.1-meter) loadable length of cargo floor, 6 feet (1.8 meters) wide at the door. Alternatively, it accommodated twenty-eight troops on benches, or eighteen stretcher cases.

A GI shows off the troop door within the large cargo door of a Curtiss C-46D, the angled line at the bottom of the doors marking what would be a level deck segment just inside when parked tail-down. Although the twin troop doors of the D were welcome by the paratroops, they still faced a horizontal stabilizer upon exiting, as on the C-47. The performance of the Commando was superior to the Douglas airplane but commenced production two years later and suffered a maturation period that discouraged some operators. *San Diego Air & Space Museum*

All models were conventional semi-monocoque metal structure with fabric-covered control surfaces and three-axis trim. The conventional gear and split flaps were common for the day. The main gear tires remained partially exposed when retracted. Most moving elements used hydraulics, but the airplane was reliable and with few vices when airborne. The standard crew was three including the radio operator, but could be augmented to include a navigator and flight engineer.

For combat operations the C-47 would be operated principally by Troop Carrier Command (TCC), organized at the same time as the ATC. As the Army developed airborne forces, this called for an aircraft capable of hauling 10,000lb

* Some 178,000 of this dependable radial were built, as the most numerous aero engine of the war.

69

(4,536kg) for 1,500 miles (2,414km) at 175mph (282km/h), requiring 1,000 feet (305 meters) to land on a grass field 2,000 feet (610 meters) long surrounded by 50-foot (15-meter) obstacles. Only the rugged C-47 came close to meeting these requirements and was at hand to be pushed to immediate high-rate production. Pressed into service as a paratroop platform, it acquiring an overhead static line cable. It was then called on to tow gliders, requiring aft fuselage strengthening and pilot control of the tow release mechanism. Facilities for a snatch block were added to ease cargo loading, but the aircraft remained an adaptation for such missions. For airborne replenishment of troops in the field, the Skytrain dropped up to six parachute-recovered containers or packs (parapacks or paratainers) slung beneath the centersection. More efficient but labor-intensive was shoving containers out of the door on the cable. Late in the war a roller conveyor system on the floor, angled out of the door, greatly simplified this task and reduced the number of passes over the drop zone required to deliver the full load. The airplane's ability to alight on unprepared surfaces was limited to grass fields or hard-packed dirt.

Douglas C-47A characteristics

Span	95.5ft (29.1m)
Length	63.8ft (19.4m)
Height	17.0ft (5.2m)
Wing area	987ft² (92m²)
Fuel, max	804 gallons (3,044 liters)
Fuel, with ferry tank	1,704 gallons (6,450 liters)
Climb rate, initial	1,042fpm (318mpm)
Service ceiling	24,000ft (7,315m)
Weight, empty	17,865lb (8,103kg)
Weight, gross	26,000lb (11,793kg)
Weight, ferry	31,000lb (14,061kg)
Speed, max (8,800ft)	230mph (370km/h)
Cruise speed (5,000ft)	160mph (258km/h)
Range (160mph)	1,600 miles (2,575km)
Range, ferry (155mph)	3,800 miles (6,116km)
Landing distance (over 50ft obstacle)	1,850ft (564m)

Proposals for more extensive alterations of the C-47 were rejected in the interest of maintaining the pace of production. More than 9,000 of the Douglas type were manufactured in Long Beach, California, and Oklahoma City, Oklahoma, deliveries reaching 573 per month in May 1944. Many hundreds were provided to allies, and more than 3,000 militarized DC-3s were built under licence in the USSR and Japan. Comprising several models, the majority were C-47As with the R-1830-92 at 1,200hp (895kW). The B model was better suited to high-elevation airfields in the CBI with two-stage superchargers – although these proved unsatisfactory and the airplanes (lacking an installed oxygen system) were unsuited to cross the Himalaya route (the famed 'Hump').

Considering the payload fraction of total take-off weight and fuel consumption per ton-mile flown, the C-47 did not match up well with other medium and heavy transports. Although there were many moves to push other aircraft to high-rate production and replace the C-47, General Arnold resisted. The Douglas airplane was at hand, a known quantity, relatively low cost, and would supply assets faster than pushing another from behind. Its performance was acceptable and airplanes built to supplement or replace the Skytrain were required to at least match those figures.

A companion airlifter, the Curtiss-Wright C-46, was derived from a 1940 commercial prototype that was to be pressurized, but only came to maturity as an unpressurized military variant. Consequently, much time was spent on development and refinement before full-rate production was warranted. It was powered by two supercharged 2,000hp

This trio of GIs are posing before the cargo doors of a Douglas C-47A with only one side (containing the troop door) open. The full entrance is wide enough to allow wheeled cargo like jeeps and a 105mm gun to be loaded, albeit ponderously with a turn. Note the rifle ports in the windows, a feel-good feature carried over to other tactical transports that all lacked gun turrets. *San Diego Air & Space Museum*

The interior of the C-47 was not an efficient volume for freight operations – one seldom had cargo that reached the ceiling and the curved sidewalls only complicated matters. This interior is fitted out for executive transport with plush seats alongside the buckets (instead of the fold-down canvas seats that came later, in common with most other tactical transports). Note the extended-range fuel tanks at the forward end of the cabin. *Author's collection*

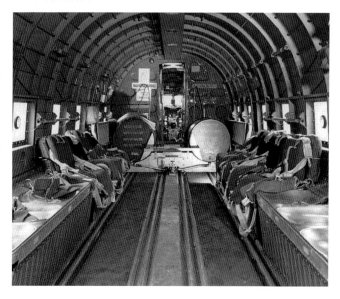

(1,491 kW) R-2800s. The three-blade Ham Standard props soon gave way to Curtiss 13.5-foot (42-meter) four blade units. With systems like hydraulic boost for flight control, an auxiliary power unit (APU), autopilot, oxygen system, and an extensive anti-ice suite, the complex airplane had a crew of four that included a flight engineer. The design used flush riveting, butted panels and low-drag cowlings that eliminated protruding scoops. Slotted Fowler flaps were featured and control surfaces remained fabric-covered. The C-46A could accommodate forty to fifty troops in fold-down sidewall seats, thirty-three litter patients, or typically around 10,000lb (4,545kg) of freight. The airplane had a loadable cargo floor length of 48 feet (14.6 meters). A freight door on the port side and an optional hydraulic winch aided cargo operations. The floor segment immediately inside the door was built level, transitioning forward to the sloping deck, to assist loading. The 'double bubble' fuselage cross-section gave a lower lobe with some stowage volume.

An order for forty-six in July 1940 was increased to hundreds through 1942, then thousands in 1943 and 1944, most as the C-46A with greater durability and power. Yet only two test examples were flying by December 1941. Curtiss had the first two production examples ready for delivery on 18 July 1942. After initially judging the Commando as contributing little to paratroop operations, the C-46D was introduced in September 1944 with changes to make it more suited for paratroop operations with a troop door added in the port side cargo doors and another on the starboard side for jumps from both sides simultaneously.* The D could also be overloaded to 51,900lb (23,541kg). These models made up most of the Curtiss production, primarily in Buffalo, New York, and Louisville, Kentucky.**

Advertised as the largest twin-engine transport aircraft in the world, the Commando could be a handful with several tricky characteristics. It entered service in mid-1942 with markedly better performance than the C-47, thus promising much, but its heavier weight limited its off-field capabilities. The C-46's tons-per-mile numbers made it most efficient for lifting cargo from one semi-prepared field (commonly on steel matting) to another, while the Skytrain concentrated on shorter-haul combat flights, paratroop drops and glider tow, with

landings on grass when necessary. Owing to its complexity and the haste with which it was pushed into production, the Commando proved a good deal of trouble. Hundreds of modifications were made to production aircraft through the latter half of 1943 to correct problems, and at one point deliveries from Louisville were halted until the production line caught up with the changes. The Marines spent nearly 1½ years trying to get the RC5s right before service introduction.

The Air Forces was still dissatisfied with the C-46 but needed the aircraft urgently in CBI, so pressed on, making changes indicated by fleet service as they went. The C-46 was vital in keeping a supply line open to China via very treacherous high-altitude flying over 'the Hump' until the Burma Road was secured. Eventually 3,180 Commandos were built during the war.

Curtiss C-46A characteristics

Span	108.1ft (32.9m)
Length	76.3ft (23.3m)
Height	21.8ft (6.6m)
Wing area	1,360ft² (126m²)
Fuel, max	1,400 gallons (5,300 liters)
Fuel, auxiliary tanks	800 gallons (3,028 liters)
Initial climb rate	575fpm (175mpm)
Service ceiling	24,500ft (7,468m)
Weight, empty	30,669lb (13,911kg)
Weight, gross	45,000lb (20,412kg)
Weight, overload	49,600lb (22,498kg)
Speed, max (15,000ft)	270mph (435km/h)
Cruise speed (8,000ft)	173mph (278km/h)
Range (173mph)	3,150 miles (1,429km)
Range (237mph)	1,000 miles (454km)
Range, long-range tanks	2,650 miles (4,265km)
Landing distance (34,000lb) (over 50ft obstacle)	1,900ft (579m)

The C-46 was a large and complex airplane, so not so well suited for tactical missions. However, its capacity was generous and it was at hand, and therefore adopted even by the Navy and Marine Corps – USMC R5D-1s are seen here at Ulithi Atoll, Caroline Islands, on 3 April 1945. The Commando remained troublesome, so it was fortuitous that when introduced in large numbers the American circumstances in the war allowed the services to operate the type satisfactorily. *National Archives*

* A criticism of the C-47 was that it permitted jumps from one side only. This dispersed the jumpers over the drop zone and thus lengthened the time before the troops could join up for effective defense.

** Curtiss also built ten machines in St Louis, while Higgins, introduced later, constructed just two in New Orleans.

Prototyping

Tactical gliders were partially developed following the German example, but also to make up for the initial woeful lack of anything approaching a tactical transport.[1] They, of course, required a large aircraft (commonly a C-47) to tow them to within glide range of the landing zone. Adding power packs to the gliders was tried, but these could serve only for repositioning or small package delivery. What was really needed was a purpose-designed high-wing aircraft with a cargo floor at truck-bed height and a loading ramp, with a wide opening aligned with the longitudinal axis of the fuselage. These would need to be built quickly and cheaply, preferably from non-strategic materials (i.e. wood). The aircraft had to support paratroop jumps, cargo parachute drops and glider tow while preferably having some off-field operational capability. Serious discussions of pursuing such a new aircraft development program to fill the tactical transport requirement began in late August 1941.

A wooden tactical transport airplane did hold merit in the view of USAAF leadership. They agreed it should be rugged, easy to operate and maintain, and with a generous payload fraction. If an aluminum shortage did occur it was vital that fighters and bombers take priority. A review in the fall of 1941 found that there was little potential for short supply of suitable woods. Congress also applied pressure to increase the availability of transports to circumvent the submarine threat,

again emphasizing wood as a good choice of material. Although wood had been common in aircraft construction a generation before, with a rich library of design literature, such aircraft still in production were generally low-performance models with a wooden frame and fabric covering. A fully semi-monocoque structure with a wood skin and carrying flight loads from the performance expected of a 1940s airplane, not to mention a rugged tactical machine, was supported by little existing design guidance. All this in a large transport, subject to high-rate production, had never been done.

Research had been under way in laminating various wood veneers with new glues. The molding of the composites under temperature and pressure for a plasticized product suggested compound shapes like airfoils and aerodynamic fairings were practical. Such was patented pre-war as the Duramold process, which produced very smooth surfaces free of joints and rivets, but this was not the only method employed. Wright Field also did some development work in building wing panels and a fuselage with various woods and glues, then subjecting them to loading trials. These data were made available to manufacturers. The US Forest Service, Forest Products Laboratory, also performed research work and produced two manuals on the design and fabrication of wooden aircraft that saved much time and eliminated some uncertainty. Consequently, there was some confidence in deciding to pursue wood as the principal material for a new transport. Some such projects were already under way in building low-performance military types to include trainers and gliders.

Left: The Americans built many thousands of the Waco CG-4A glider as their first true tactical transport – although following the German example. The raised nose permitted rapid loading and unloading of cargo with wheeled items rolled on short ramps. The glider was commonly damaged in actual combat assault landings and was seldom recovered after the battle moved on. *National Soaring Museum*

Below: A short path to a large-capacity tactical transport was via gliders. This Laister-Kauffman XCG-10A (42-61100) possessed the features sought in powered tactical airlifters in the low cargo deck with loading ramp. While providing large/heavy cargo delivery coincident with an airborne assault, the aircraft had little other utility and a high number could be expected to be destroyed in their one operational mission. *Museum of Flight*

Above: Another effort to create rugged tactical airlift capability with more flexibility than a glider was to add engines. This XPG-3 was CG-15A (44-90986), a glider converted by Waco in 1945 with twin Jacobs R-755-9 radials delivering 245hp. The low power-to-weight ratio combined with the short range gave such poor performance as to render such avenues of exploration fruitless. *National Museum of the United States Air Force*

Right: This 13 July 1943 photograph of Waco CG-4A production shows wing panels built of wood. The skin lamina, with inspection holes, has the outer sheet oriented at 45 degrees to the chord line and inner plies are likely oriented at 90 degrees opposed to this for as close to uniform properties in all axes of loading. There was much research and testing behind the move to wood as a principal material for aircraft of low or moderate performance, but shallow experience in the industry. *National Museum of the United States Air Force*

Characteristics for the twin-engine Aircraft, Low Performance, Transport, (Cargo), suitable for carrying paratroops and ordnance gear, were drafted in August 1941 and approved on 11 September. These stated a rough requirement for 1,000 airplanes and called for a modest 600-mile (966km) range at a sedate 120mph (193km/h) with a 4,500lb (2,041kg) payload or twenty fully equipped troops (225lb/102kg each). It was to operate from a 1,200-foot (1,931-meter) unimproved field surrounded by 50-foot (15-meter) obstacles. This unimproved field requirement indicated the high potential for damage upon landing, as for the gliders, to the point of calling it a 'crash landing'.[2] A ferry of 2,500 miles (4,023km) was to be possible under reduced load factors, and it was to possess a 20,000-foot (6,096-meter) ceiling. A .30-cal MG was to be installed for covering the upper hemisphere. It was also to be capable of carrying long-range-tanks for a 2,500-mile (4,023km) ferry at reduced load factors for flight to a theater of operations. A project was launched to build an airplane meeting these requirements. However, separate proposals led to three other simultaneous projects. These duplicative efforts pointed, in part, to how seriously the Air Forces took the transport airplane problem. Additionally, in the year following Pearl Harbor the country as a whole and the military in particular was willing to try anything rather than be accused of not turning over every stone in seeking military superiority. All the projects were directed to use the C-47's engines and cowlings to reduce integration issues and eliminate further burden on powerplant and propeller manufacturers. This alone dictated some aircraft weight limitations to ensure suitable performance, also compared with the Skytrain. The lower performance of the wooden airplane compared with the C-47 emphasized the expected heavier airframe weight of the wooden construction.[3]

The armed forces' need converged with an effort by the Defense Supply Corporation (DSC), Aviation Division, to develop an airplane to displace German equipment in Central and South American countries and help counter any foothold the Nazis might have in the region. The DSC formulated a requirement in the summer of 1941 for a transport to haul cargo and personnel into and out of unimproved fields, which was to be rugged and inexpensive. It recognized that there was a potential shortage of aluminum owing to War Department priorities and the fact that the highest-grade bauxite ore had to be imported. Consequently, a board of notable aviation designers proposed a steel airplane, but recognized that wood might be an acceptable substitute. They estimated that a stopgap wooden airplane could be in production within six to nine months and a follow-on metal type in twelve to eighteen months.[4] The furniture industry could be engaged as subcontractors for the wood undertaking, having thus far not contributed to the defense build-up. Since the DSC need would likely not exceed fifty airplanes, it was reasonable to seek a military partner for the endeavor.[5] At a 26 August 1941 conference the general characteristics of the airplane were formulated. In a follow-up meeting on 16 September the USAAC expressed a willingness to assist the DSC project with information, but already had their own similar projects under way, which were expected to be in production by the time the DSC machine started flight testing.

Mired (Waco C-62)

The Army's September 1941 requirement came at a time when most of the country's airframers were fully committed to defense projects. They eventually settled on the Waco Aircraft Company of Troy, Ohio.* This firm had produced very worthy cabin-class commercial airplanes between the wars, and was already designing and building the first two combat gliders types with wooden wings and tails attached to fuselages of welded steel tube with fabric covering. Instead of a competition, it appears that Waco alone was asked to undertake the wooden transport project, and responded with the patriotic zeal typical of the period. The company was given a 31 October 1941 contract for thirteen YC-62 test aircraft (42-12554/66), with production to commence in the fall of 1942.

The undemanding performance was met with a utilitarian design. Payload was to be nineteen troops or 4,400lb (1,996kg) of freight accompanying the three-man crew. The flight deck and wing box were above the cabin of the podded fuselage. The cockpit cab faired into a boom that went back to an H-tail. The cargo compartment measured 7.5 by 6.5 feet (2.3 by 2.0 meters), was 25 feet (7.6 meters) long, and was accessed through rear loading doors under the tail boom.[6] One drawing shows the fixed main landing gear with aerodynamic fairing issuing from the engine nacelles. Other drawings and the wind tunnel model show the gear post fixed to the nacelle, but with side struts to the fuselage. Oddly, the airplane was not equipped with a nose wheel. Sitting on a tail wheel, the cargo deck had about a 13-degree nose-high angle, although the rear entry sill was just 24.5 inches (62cm) above the ground. Two 1,200hp (895kW) R-1830-92 engines were intended, the same as the C-47, turning 11.5-foot (3.5-meter) three-blade Hamilton Standard propellers. The effort appeared to benefit from Skytrain equipment as Waco was provided with examples of that aircraft's engine mount and flight deck with controls. In drawings, the crew cab and nacelles look very much like those of the Douglas airplane.

Waco proposed to build the YC-62 in the same manner as the gliders, with a welded steel tube fuselage. The USAAF may have demurred, insisting on all-wood construction and fearing a looming shortage of the steel tubing.[7] The fully committed aviation industry was soon over-committed after Pearl Harbor. This included Waco, which found itself manufacturing its CG-4A glider while supporting the engineering for the type as it was being built by small firms all across the country. The company also developed the spin-off CG-15 and more advanced CG-13, as well as powered versions. Consequently the C-62 development engineering proceeded very slowly. The addition of 240 production aircraft (42-35584/823) to the contract, approved on 31 January 1942 at $114,565 unit cost, could not change the underlying difficulties in finding trained and experienced engineers or skilled workmen. By mid-1942 the design was still only a quarter complete. The first flight was set as 30 January 1943 and delivery of the thirteenth airplane on 30 June of that year.

Materiel Command attempted to help solve Waco's problems by trying to get the firm to work with the Curtiss-Wright team in St Louis, who could provide data on the C-76 effort (see later). Waco, however, was so overworked that it

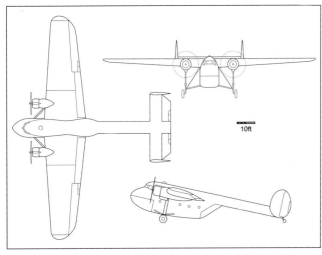

This three-view drawing of the Waco C-62 tactical transport suggests doors in the nose and the aft end of the podded fuselage, although only the rear doors are mentioned in references. No troop doors are indicated. All the lines reflect pre-war convention and Waco commercial aircraft legacy. *Author*

The wind tunnel model gives emphasis to the cumbersome form of the C-62. The tail wheel at the end of the high boom gave a notable deck angle to the cargo floor. The fixed main gear promised drag, together with the blunt shape of the fuselage. *via Fred McDougall*

Waco YC-62 characteristics (predicted)

Span	100.0ft (30.5m)
Length	73.8ft (22.5m)
Height	19.1ft (5.8m)
Wing area	1,476ft² (137m²)
Fuel, max	447 gallons (1,692 liters)
Fuel, with ferry tanks	1,574 gallons (5,958 liters)
Climb rate, initial	870fpm (265mpm)
Cruise speed	132mph (212km/h)
Weight, empty	21,660lb (9,825kg)
Weight, gross	29,500lb (13,381kg)
Weight, ferry	33,500lb (15,195kg)
Speed, max (sea level)	150mph (241km/h)
Range (132mph)	600 miles (966km)
Range, ferry (120mph)	2,500 miles (4,023km)
Service ceiling	17,000ft (5,182m)
Landing distance (over 50ft obstacle)	1,300ft (91m)

* Waco was the brand name for the originally titled Weaver Aircraft Company.

could take little advantage of this avenue.[8] The pressures to produce gliders were enormous, with keen interest from the Chief of Staff himself. Waco knew its priorities.

It was May 1943 before the building that was to house final assembly of the C-62, at a proposed rate of twenty per month, was completed. Judging by the floor space required by other manufacturers undertaking similar work, the facility was too small. The Curtiss C-76 experience with wooden structures prompted calls in spring 1943 for the similar C-62 to be cancelled.[9] By that summer Waco had just a few parts of the first aircraft completed, among them the tail boom and empennage, and was seeking subcontractors. Jigs had yet to be built for the rest of the machine. In September this discouraging progress was essentially unchanged.

In the two years since Materiel Command had deemed a need for the airplane and let a contract, the combat commands had not bought into the C-62 project. By the measures of summer 1943 the C-62's capacity was meager, the tail wheel was decidedly antiquated, and the predicted performance uninspiring. The palpable disappointment with the similar C-76 was reason to eliminate the second contract for 240 C-62s on 20 July. So it was that the lagging Waco project became orphaned. It was finally axed on 21 December, leaving just the prototype for experimental purposes, to the relief of all.[10] However, even the experimental data derived from the prototype were eventually deemed superfluous. This single example, under sporadic construction, was never finished and Waco was eventually directed to burn the parts.[11]

Low point (Curtiss C-76)

Likely taking notice of the Air Corps's specification for an all-wood transport, designer Dean C. Smith of Curtiss-Wright's Airplane Division conceived such an airplane in January 1942. This was pitched to Wright Field's Colonel Franklin O. Carroll, Chief of the Experimental Engineering Section, via a call from corporate vice president Burdette Wright on 9 February. Follow-up the same day with Brigadier General Oliver P. Echols, Chief, Materiel Division, received approval to proceed with the project provided it did not interfere with ongoing manufacturing efforts. Although a joint effort with Waco was discussed, it was set aside as potentially delaying production. However, if one design proved superior to the other, both manufacturers would be set to build the airplane.[12] In that difficult time it appeared responsible to have a second program to help ensure high-volume production and success of an undertaking with some measure of manufacturing uncertainty. It was also recommended that Curtiss manufacture some of the Waco gliders to build experience in wooden aircraft construction, but the firm demurred. It was confident that it could complete a wooden transport superior to the C-62 in just six months.[13] (Materiel Command considered nine months a more realistic goal.)

To help this accelerated program, the government agreed to give Curtiss-Wright a free hand and did not insist on approving detailed design or closely reviewing stages of progress.[14] The Curtiss team had no recent experience with wood but were highly regarded by the Air Corps given their other recent successes on defense projects. A 6 March 1942 Letter of Intent

for 200 airplanes (42-86938/7112) was followed on 8 August with a $31,174,819.80 contract. The CW-27 was then fleshed out by chief designer George A. Page Jr.

A new facility would be required to meet the production demand and suit the materials. It was also to be where plentiful manpower was available and away from coasts where enemy attacks might emerge. A search settled on Louisville, Kentucky, with Howard R. Moles as chief engineer. Priced at $11,531,398 (eventually $16,695,543), the buildings on Standiford Field had elaborate air-conditioning and humidity control equipment that, for the molded wood processes, sought to keep the facility warm and moist. However, subcontractors would perform much of the specialized wood working on subassemblies, 65 percent of the aircraft. These were the Mengel Company of Louisville, the Baldwin Piano Company in Cincinnati, Ohio, the Universal Moulded Products Company in Bristol, Virginia, and supplier Haskelite Manufacturing Corporation. These firms also required another $5,164,145 capital investment to support the program. All were learning as they went along what was required for an acceptable wooden aircraft structure.

Evolving requirements outlined a need for as many as 2,400 of the transports. Curtiss accepted a 2 December 1942 increase to 1,200 C-76s and 20 percent spares at an estimated cost of $169,171,411.97. (With later plus-ups, the total of Curtiss contracts would reach an estimated $210,962,932.79.)[15] Initial deliveries would be in August 1943, reaching eighty aircraft per month as soon as October. Another manufacturer was sought to shadow Curtiss's production and fill out the numbers. Higgins Industries of New Orleans was selected for a further 1,200 C-76s, with a 2 November 1942 contract for $167,601,600. Higgins was a shipbuilder (including wooden vessels) that the War Department hoped to turn to aircraft manufacturing with the formation of Higgins Aircraft during 1942. The contract was approved on 17 December for $162,720,000. Another $26,235,000 was allocated to build a factory in Michaud, Louisiana, on 'made' delta land 13.5 miles (21.7km) from New Orleans, where uncommitted workers were expected to be found. More investment would be needed to create an airfield nearby. Higgins promised that other subcontractors would also be used. At a rate of 160 airplanes per month from the two sites, the total fleet was expected to be delivered by the end of 1944.

The May 1942 specifications for the Curtiss transport, dubbed the Caravan, called for the hauling of 4,500lb (2,041kg) for 600 miles (966km) at 150mph (241km/h) in and out of a 1,200-foot (366-meter) field at a normal gross weight of 26,145lb (11,859kg). The wing and flight deck placement atop the fuselage gave a clear loading volume with a cargo box 6 feet (1.8 meters) high, 7.5 feet (2.3 meters) wide, and 32.5 feet (9.9 meters) long. An additional requirement was that all parts of the machine save the fuselage were to break down for transport inside a C-76. The twin had a tricycle undercarriage that gave it a level deck accessed by a swing-aside nose. The high wing gave the cargo deck a ground clearance of 3 feet (0.9 meter).

The C-76 was powered by the C-47's powerplant, to be interchangeable with the C-62.[16] This meant two 1,200hp (895 kN) R-1830-92s turning 11.6-foot (3.5-meter) three-blade Hamilton Standard 'hydromatic' constant-speed props. Plain slotted flaps got the landing speed down to 80mph (129km/h). Landing gear struts

The C-76, with its high-mounted flight deck and broad nose, was hardly easy on the eyes. However, the clean exterior, by virtue of the wooden construction, might have promised some reduction in drag. Profound design issues overshadowed any such attributes. *Author's collection*

were to be from the North American B-25A medium bomber.[17] Ferry tanks could be installed on the cargo deck to greatly extend the range for flight to theater. The airplane was to have a crew of three and could accommodate twenty troops or eighteen litters, or a predicted 11,000lb (4,990kg) of freight. Intended as a tactical transport for an airborne task force, the airplane was to be capable of towing gliders and had a troop door aft of the wing trailing edge on the port side. It was to be able to land in unprepared areas, which could well mean the gear shearing off. Although repairs were possible, the aircraft would be considered disposable to an extent. There were also accommodations for a ·30-cal MG by the radio operator's station to the rear of the flight deck cab.*

The new Louisville plant, still under construction, was not staffed to design and perform prototype assembly, so this was done in St Louis, Missouri (more precisely nearby Robertson). The first five aircraft were built there, although designated C-76s and given serials 42-86913/7 (c/n 21/5). These were to be followed by eleven Louisville-built service test YC-76s (42-86918/28, c/n 1/11).

Curtiss ran into almost immediate difficulties. In July 1942 the government identified the supply of Sitka spruce as potentially facing shortages. The Air Corps advised manufacturers to consider Douglas fir or other species, generally more dense woods (23 percent for the fir). Curtiss eventually resorted to birch, gum, hemlock, mahogany, noble fir, poplar and spruce in ply, veneer and general lumber forms.[18] Higgins also hoped to substitute sweet gum and cottonwood. The C-62 was likewise directed to greatly reduce the spruce content. Delays resulted from working with the inexperienced subcontractors, late materials, and design changes directed by the government. Estimated hand-over of the first airplane slipped to no earlier than 15 December 1942, but this was also missed. Transitioning the program to Kentucky did not proceed smoothly. Personnel from other Curtiss plants were assigned to Louisville to help establish production with some core of experienced people. Despite expectations, labor was difficult to recruit and nearly all new personnel had to be trained from zero on aircraft production and woodworking, which for Curtiss itself was a steep learning curve.

There was early concern with the use of wood as the principal construction material. A Civil Aeronautics Administration (CAA) representative was assigned to the program to assist in this regard, and the second airplane was subjected to static tests to destruction at Wright Field. The concern was warranted. The substitution of

The first five C-76s were built in Curtiss's St Louis plant while the Kentucky team was organized. Here the apparently complete first airplane (42-86913) is seen with another still under assembly, surrounded by AT-9 Jeep twin-engine trainers. These five Caravans had a nose that was raised to access the interior for loading and unloading, while the later airplanes had the nose pivoting to the starboard side. *San Diego Air & Space Museum*

* This was eventually deleted, but the side windows with small arms gun ports were adopted from the C-47.

dense woods and inexperience with the material, together with fast-paced engineering lacking completed documentation, led to an overweight structure. The specified empty weight was 18,380lb (8,337kg), but the first machine came in at 21,626lb (9,809kg). The spec also called for a 26,145lb (11,859kg) gross, but the airplane was fortunately stressed for 28,000lb (12,701kg). This would permit at least 3,109lb (1,410kg) of payload, a 6,374lb (2,891kg) useful load, or just 69 percent of the specified 4,500lb, plus any additional weight the contractor managed to recover via remedial efforts.[19] The added weight would surely hamper performance given the predetermined powerplant. Worse, the center of gravity (CG, measured as a percentage of mean aerodynamic chord, MAC) was unusually far aft.[20] Consequently, some portion of the payload would be sacrificed for ballast.* While such issues are not uncommon in prototypes, inexperience made them all the more difficult to correct.

Aircraft 42-86914 arrived at Wright Field for the required static tests on 8 February 1943. There the wooden structure was quickly found to be deficient in strength. The wing suffered multiple failures, some at as low as 55 percent of the intended operating structural load. Likewise, the fuselage, vertical stabilizer and flaps came in below par until reinforced, with some failures as low as 40 percent.[21] It appeared that one of the principal causes was that the skin of the large transport was thicker and stiffer than other wooden types, so required so much pressure to ensure contact with the underlying ribs and frames for sound cement joints that it threatened to buckle those elements. This led to insufficient pressure in some cases and lack of suitable bond. On other occasions the excessive time in the glue operation contributed to a poor bond as the cement had already set.

By the time of the first flight the aircraft weight and balance were still unacceptable. The machine could not be flown empty; requiring so much ballast just to bring the CG within limits, it was more than 1,000lb (454kg) beyond the newly accepted design gross weight of 28,000lb.[22] The maiden flight was on 5 January 1943 at St Louis's Lambert Field with Dean Smith and Russ Thaw at the controls. Reports in February sounded favorable, although Curtiss resisted having anyone but their experienced test pilots perform tests on the immature airplane.

The USAAF pilots finally flew the aircraft on 3 March and came away with quite a different assessment. For the flight, the aircraft was ballasted to 28,000lb, yet achieved a 37 percent MAC aft CG for a portion of the flight. There the aircraft was unstable, and uncontrollable with gear and flaps down. Severe elevator oscillations, or "walking", above 100mph (161km/h) were an ongoing challenge. The aircraft was difficult to trim so control forces were heavy, there were disturbing vibrations throughout the structure in a rated-power climb, it could not be landed with full flaps, and engine cooling was deficient.[23] On the positive side, performance bettered the spec marginally in a few areas, with a single engine ceiling more than 8,000 feet (2,438 meters), a high speed of 198mph (319km/h) versus the specified 189mph (304km/h), a cruise of 159mph (256km/h) versus 150mph (241km/h), and a range of 650 miles (1,046km) versus 600 miles (966 km). However, the landing distance was 160 feet (48 meters) beyond the required 1,200 feet (366 meters).[24]

The USAAF was adamant that all effort was to be expended in making the aircraft flyable empty, and suitably with a payload, with no concern for structural strength. Anything over 26,500lb (12,020kg) gross was unacceptable as this would reduce the payload to below 1,500lb (680kg). They very much wanted to carry a minimum 2,500lb (1,134kg) with 435lb (197kg) of fuel (72.5 gallons or 274 liters).[25]

The C-76 static article is shown in the test lab hangar at Wright Field lacking the full flight deck aft fairing over the wing box, which shows its wood veneer. Positioned on its side, it is probably being prepared for a vertical tail and/or fuselage side loading test series. Considerable structural deficiencies were revealed in these 'torture' tests that were never fully corrected. *National Archives*

* The C-76's forward CG limit was given as 23 percent MAC and the aft 35 percent. As first completed, the prototype had an unballasted empty CG of 37.1 percent, moving farther aft as the gear was lowered (swinging down and aft) and the flaps extended. It was not surprising that considerable forward ballast was necessary to balance the aircraft within safe limits. At the common operational loading conditions the CG was from 29.49 to 31.33 percent MAC compared with a specified nominal 30 percent. These were still close to the aft limit, versus an expected 27.09 percent, although the CG was expected to move forward as fuel was burned.

The fifth C-76 (42-86917) shows off more of the unattractive lines of the utilitarian Caravan. The aft fuselage closeout under the tail was modified during flight testing in seeking to cure the multiple ills. Note the troop door, aft of the fuselage bumper, and the fairing behind the engine that shielded the partially exposed wheel when the main gear was retracted. This airplane was sent to Kentucky to serve as a pattern for those to be built in Louisville. *San Diego Air & Space Museum*

Under tremendous pressure, measures to correct the weight, balance and strength issues were applied to the remaining airframes in St Louis in a crash program that drew on talent throughout Curtiss-Wright. The company was also compelled to consult Douglas Aircraft for advice.[26] However, the goals worked counter to each other. Strengthening included various combinations of added wood plies (doublers), metal straps, and changes to the fasteners that secured the wings to the carry-through structure. Such elements only added weight. Reducing the weight resulted in numerous changes such as drilling lightening holes that could compromise load-bearing capability. Balancing the aircraft properly sought to move the structural mass forward. Working to address the root causes got so far as to consider shifting the wing aft.* Hence a vicious cycle of changes was set up with little hope of converging on a successful design in the timescale and resource constraints of the war. A complete redesign appeared warranted, yet that was estimated to require six months.

Working to find cures saw numerous changes made to the three test airplanes such that at no time were any two alike. The outer wing panels and horizontal stabilizers were given dihedral and the stab also raised 1.5 feet (0.5 meter) with a revised tail cone, while the elevator balance weight was increased.[27] Instead of moving the entire wing, a sweep of 9.31 degrees was introduced in the outer panels.[28] The pronounced bulge of the cab was melded more smoothly into the top fuselage. Ribbed spoilers were installed across the stab and elevators. The aft CG condition also made it necessary to rework the main landing gear installation to shift the wheel centerline aft by 7 inches (17.8cm) for suitable stability on the ground (CG ahead of the axles), although this only further aggravated the inflight aft CG shift with gear extension. However, another 10 inches (25.4cm) would be necessary for the take-off attitude (nose up) and this could not be achieved without a substantial redesign.[29]

* Moving the center of lift aft by shifting the wing sought to increase the distance between this and the CG for more favorable stability, but would also move more mass aft while shortening the distance to the tail, which could undermine controllability, and so was another battle between opposing outcomes.

The fifth airplane was supposed to be production representative and was sent to Kentucky as a template. However, its empty weight proved to be 23,409lb (10,618kg), or 566lb (257kg) heavier than the first machine.[30] Curtiss had managed to get the minimum flying weight (24,074lb/10,918kg) CG with gear down to 35.98 percent, still behind the aft limit.[31] Most of the hurried changes had been abandoned, leaving the wing sweep plus dihedral (created by inserting a wedge between the outboard panels and the center box) and revised tail cone as the most evident carryovers to the final configuration.

In April it was felt that an aircraft capable of carrying 3,000lb (1,361kg) the required distance with the mandated fuel could be achieved by the fiftieth production article. An airplane meeting the original spec would not emerge before the 200th article, and only after a substantial redesign; the earlier airplanes would be subject to significant operating restrictions.[32]

The Louisville team had begun manufacturing its first YC-76s as testing revealed the need for changes. Consequently, delivery slipped from February 1943 to no earlier than May.[33] It had already been decided the nine airplanes beyond the eleven YC-76s would be YC-76As (42-86929/37, c/s 12/20), more representative of the production design.[34] All the Kentucky Caravans had the nose hinged to swing to the right side rather than upwards.* It had become clear that the first fifty airplanes would remain 'skunks' until arriving at a stable and fully satisfactory design.[35] Higgins was badly lagging in production preparation of the inconstant C-76 and there were discussions in April 1943 about the company preparing to produce a Cessna wooden transport, then in flight testing (see later), if it came together quickly. It seemed that the best the C-76 would amount to would be a 3,000lb (1,361kg) payload to 600 miles (966km) with 3,200lb (1,452kg) of ballast. The Cessna C-106A promised 2,800lb (1,270kg) to 900 miles (1,448km), and possibly with a good deal less trouble.[36]

* Discussion of this change is not found in the project file. However, disputes regarding just such a subject are found regarding gliders, with much disagreement over the best approach.

The first aircraft built in Louisville (43-86918) was in the configuration of St Louis's initial prototype (no wing sweep or dihedral). It was flown on 3 May 1943 in a very short and frightening event of just 2¼ minutes because of severe vibrations.[37] Three subsequent flights were made amounting to a total flight time of 2hr 15min.[38] For the fifth sortie on 10 May, 22 minutes into the flight the horizontal tail separated and the ship plunged to the ground.* The investigation found no cause for the fatal mishap but suspected flutter. Only later was it learned that several bolts securing the tail had not been installed.

Clearly Curtiss and its airplane were in serious trouble. Troop Carrier Command, then Air Transport Command, declared that they had no need for C-76s and would resist accepting them. Other than take-off and landing distance, the C-47 had superior performance. However, the calculations neglected the unique loading features and the ability to operate on unprepared fields. There was also a move afoot to reduce the number of types in service to lighten the supply, maintenance and training burden. A Standardization of Transports conference on 20 April 1943 concluded that the troubled C-62 and C-76 programs were no longer required or desired, as more suitable equipment would be available in 1944 when the airplanes might enter service. It appeared wise to turn the production capacity and personnel (some 8,500 people) to more beneficial ends. Elements of the Material Center had recommended cancellation as early as March, and Wright Field formally advised Material Division on 18 May to take this course.

Washington would have none of it, questioning the resolve in making every effort to aid the project. Yet on 25 May all the acquisition principals reviewed the case and mutually agreed that the facts painted a bleak picture. Still, leadership declared that it would not abandon the attempt to build a wooden transport until the then current modifications and flight tests had run their course. There would likely be political repercussions of cancellation and wasted resources, not to mention tacit confession that what appeared to be a simple task of stepping back a generation to build an airplane of wood was beyond American industry during a period of wartime urgency. The British were famously manufacturing the successful Mosquito fighter-bomber from a balsa/plywood sandwich, so why couldn't America build a plodding transport of similar stuff? General Arnold observed that even reduced performance would still leave an aircraft useful for stateside movement of materiel, freeing up more useful machines for service in-theater.[39] He also felt it was important to foster the advancement of wood in aircraft manufacturing.

At a 14 June meeting with Curtiss at Wright Field it was decided that the aircraft could not be certified for flight above 26,500lb (12,020kg) GW at 85 percent of specified load factors. Given a 165-gallon (625-liter) fuel load for the 600-mile (966km) range, and other operational necessities, this left just 1,500lb (680kg) for freight.[40] No aircraft would be accepted without short-term reinforcement permitting at least 2,500lb (1,134kg) of cargo,

with the wings passing associated static tests. The Air Forces were willing to accept a reduced fuel load (435 gallons/1,647 liters) supporting a 450-mile (724km) range to achieve the 2,500lb target for 28,000lb gross. If this proved unattainable, only ten more aircraft would be accepted to permit some service trials. This was predicated on suitable stress analysis and a new wing for static tests. Curtiss wanted to build fifty of these airplanes, and asked that different engines be considered.

A follow-up meeting was held the next day in Louisville where the path to the intermediate 2,500lb payload airplane was laid out as well as the structurally reinforced design to carry 4,500lb the 600 miles at further reduced load factors and an overload weight of 30,451lb (13,812kg). The first of the next ten substandard machines was to be delivered by 1 August (which later slipped to September) and, pending satisfactory stress analysis and static tests, would be restricted to a gross weight of 26,500lb gross and maximum fuel of 435 gallons, which, at full load factors, gave a payload of just 549lb (249kg). When approved for 28,000lb operation, the payload would increase to 2,049lb (929kg) at normal load factors. Materiel Command was clear that no more than ten of the restricted airplanes be accepted, and that they must be capable of 28,000lb operation. A redesigned wing for static testing was to be available by mid-July, when it would be given priority in the Wright Field lab. This would be introduced into the production line after the 200th article. The considerable re-engineering required to meet the original specification was estimated to require another nine months. Wright Field had little confidence that this approach would be successful.

The Army pressed ahead. Construction in Kentucky advanced but flight testing continued to struggle with the design. One airplane was cannibalized to keep the test machine flying. Curtiss finally converged on a safe and consistent configuration that passed acceptance trials. These tests included an inflight pull to 6g and pushover to -3g, bringing some confidence in the structure.[41] Full-scale wind tunnel tests with Ship 3 were envisioned to explore corrections for the elevator walk. However, the oscillation was solved in flight testing when it was determined that vertical gusts caused the port engine prop swirl to wash across the left elevator where the V-tab did its job of dampening small elevator displacement, but in this case only drove an oscillation.* The V-tab was swapped with the trim tab on the right elevator.[42]

Adding fuel to the fire, the plant inspectors concluded that Curtiss was employing inferior plywood and condoning poor fabrication techniques at subcontractor plants. Examination of the Ship 6 wreckage showed evidence of inadequate glue joints. The engineering work in Louisville, responding to design deficiencies, was judged slipshod. The inspectors questioned the structural integrity of all the airplanes. Furthermore, they concluded that the program was a complete failure and on 12 July 1943 recommended abandoning the effort.[43]

* Description of the V-tab has eluded research. It is believed to have consisted of two small surfaces fixed at angles above and below the elevator trailing edge to form a V in profile. Any disturbance causing a small displacement of the elevator would produce, possibly via separated flow, an unequal force that would tend to return the elevator to neutral force displacement.

* Fuel onboard was likely to have been light because the take-off weight was 25,243lb (11,450kg) at a CG of 29.6 percent achieved with 1,200lb (544kg) of ballast in the nose.

By mid-1943 aluminum supply appeared less likely to fall short, and resorting to wooden airplanes was no longer necessary. It had become clear that these required greater care in maintenance, were more difficult to inspect and more expensive to repair, were generally less rugged, were expected to have a shorter service life, and represented a greater fire hazard. Examples were already extant. The wooden wings of the Fairchild PT-19 trainer deteriorated rapidly in both hot/dry and hot/damp environments. When the depot found itself replacing wings after as little as two to three months service, they pleaded for a change to aluminum.[44] There was also concern that varying mass and stiffness with water absorption from humidity would complicate flutter analysis and the potential for the onset of the instabilities. With rapid runway construction perfected and steel mats to cover the ground, the need for an off-field landing capability was greatly eased. The rapid offloading capabilities were less well appreciated.

Completion of the 2,600 C-76As by Curtiss was estimated at $414,240,000, or $184,500 per airplane. The twenty-third C-76 would not be in hand before 1 January 1944. Higgins would deliver none before May 1944 and after that only 100 by the end of the year.[45] A similar number of C-47s could be produced for $166 million and in much less time. A 12 July decision was made to redirect Higgins to subcontract work on metal airplanes.[46] In a 23 July meeting in his office, Arnold agreed that the C-76 was no longer viable. Consequently, the program was formally dropped on 3 August 1943 with little fuss.

The last nineteen of the initial twenty-five machines were allowed to be finished to gain experience with a large wooden airplane. Ten were completed by August 1943 and deliveries stretched from 7 October 1943 through to 23 March 1944. All designated YC-76, they were capable of carrying 2,000lb (907kg) of cargo at normal load factors.[47] The remaining 175 C-76As on order (42-86938/7112) were cancelled.*

Aircraft 1, 3, 4 and 5 were flown to Training Command installations to be employed for ground instructional purposes. Three of the YC-76s were taken up by Wright Field (nearby Patterson) for special hauling tasks, while the sixteen others were flown by Air Services Command between air depots.[48] These operations continued over nine months but with an uninspiring outcome. One finding was excessive maintenance, with as many as 148 maintenance hours for every flight hour.[49]

One of the YC-76A aircraft (42-86931) rests on a flight line somewhere on 19 April 1944. This and a few other of the later-build airplanes were flown for several months on routine freight missions between Air Forces bases. An ugly curiosity, the maintenance demands of the type saw it quickly shuffled aside. *National Archives*

* Higgins retooled to build C-46 assemblies and eventually the entire airplane, while Louisville also turned to building the Commando.

Curtiss YC-76 Caravan characteristics

Span	108.2ft (33.0m)
Length	70.8ft (21.6m)
Height	27.3ft (8.3m)
Wing area	1,632ft² (152m²)
Fuel, allowable	435 gallons (1,647 liters)
Fuel, max+ferry	1,200 gallons (4,542 liters)
Climb rate, initial	800fpm (244mpm)
Service ceiling	22,600ft (6,889m)
Weight, empty	22,686lb (10,290kg)
Weight, gross	28,000lb (12,701kg)
Weight, ferry/overload	30,451lb (13,812kg)
Speed, max	198mph (318km/h)
Cruise speed	159mph (256km/h)
Range	650 miles (1,046km)
Range, ferry (150mph)	2,500 miles (4,023km)
Landing distance (over 50ft obstacle)	1,360ft (415m)

This table is compiled from various sources such as the weight and balance report, flight test report, and various correspondences found in the case history. Empty weight is that estimated for the seventh airplane. The summary is expected to represent the final YC-76s as close as can be created from available sources.

Flying ceased on 12 September 1944. The airplanes, with an estimated unit cost of $144,977, were disposed of soon after the war, with between 26hr 35min and 316 hours flight time. Several aircraft were written off in this period due to accidents or cannibalization.[50] The termination cost with Higgins was $2.5 million. With a total of $90 million expended, including $40 million on facilities investment and an irrecoverable $10 million for equipment and materials, $40 million was counted a loss.

Left behind (Cessna C-106)

The Cessna Aircraft C-106 was among the tactical transport candidates during the early war years, but quite a secondary project. The wooden P-260 design was a high-wing twin with a boxy fuselage and retractable undercarriage. The engines were 600hp (447 kW) R-1340s accommodating a crew of two and a 4,000lb (1,814kg) payload. Photos do not suggest any special cargo onload/offload accommodations other than port-side doors. It appeared ill-suited for any of the proposed tactical missions.

The project was launched on Cessna's own initiative at the beginning of 1943 as the company sought opportunities beyond the light twins it was building for the military. The P-260 had wooden wings and tails attached to a fuselage of welded steel tubes skinned in fabric. Control surfaces were also welded tube and fabric. All this was the same as Cessna's twin trainer design variously designated the T-50, AT-8, AT-17 and UC-78 Bobcat then in high-rate production.

The first flight of what Cessna dubbed the Loadmaster (NX24176, c/n 10001) was in January 1943, powered by R-1340-S3H1 engines, loaned from the government, with

Definitely evoking the kinship with their twin-engine trainers, Cessna adopted a high wing with more powerful engines suitable for the cargo mission of the larger aircraft. The P-260 was a company program until it gained the attention of the Air Forces, after which it became the C-106. Shown is the second prototype (C-106A, NX44600) with only the camouflage to indicate its hoped-for military customer. *Museum of Flight*

two-blade constant-speed propellers. Test pilot Reed Levy, possessing heavy aircraft experience, was brought in because he could help in the evaluation, and he and Air Forces evaluators made suggestions that led to a second airplane. This C-106A had full-feathering three-blade propellers, geared R-1340-AN-2 engines, and a refined fuselage with a large cargo door. This machine (NX44600, c/n 10002) initially flew on 9 April. These were company-owned airplanes without USAAF serial numbers.

As the Curtiss C-76 program struggled, the C-106A was considered a reasonable substitute as it was not far behind the deficient performance of the Curtiss airplane. Converting Cessna UC-78 Bobcat production to the C-106A looked as though it could be achieved readily. That and the Higgins deal could yield 100 airplanes per month with production commencing in August 1943, reaching 125 per month.[51] Although an order for 500 C-106As was placed, possibly followed by 1,200 more, this yielded to higher demand for the engines as well as wood that left the Loadmaster at the bottom.[52] More importantly, wooden aircraft construction had been discredited for military aircraft. The C-106A was eventually dropped.[53]

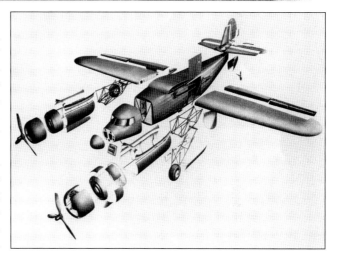

The C-106 appeared little more than a large utility aircraft rather than a tactical transport. While there were large cargo doors on the port side, the tricycle gear and general undercarriage design did not suggest a rugged, high-capacity machine, and the wooden construction of the wings was rapidly losing its luster. It was only the dismaying state of the other tactical airlift programs that prompted production consideration of the Cessna. *Museum of Flight*

Cessna C-106 Loadmaster characteristics

Span	64.7ft (19.7m)
Length	51.2ft (15.6m)
Height	11.3ft (3.5m)
Weight, empty	9,000lb (4,082kg)
Weight, max gross	14,800lb (6,713kg)
Speed, max	195mph (314km/h)
Cruise speed	170mph (274km/h)
Range	830 miles (1,336km)

Steel can (Budd RB-1 and C-93)

The original Defense Supplies Corporation requirement called for an unobstructed cargo volume cross-section of 8 by 8 feet (2.4 by 2.4 meters), and a length of 25 feet (7.6 meters). Of its specified 28,500lb (12,927kg) gross weight, fully 10,400lb (4,717kg) was to be freight. At that weight the aircraft was to be capable of departing from a 1,500-foot (457-meter) field over a 50-foot obstacle. The same powerplant as the C-47 was to be employed.

In seeking a contractor for the project, the DSC found the industry saturated with military work. The design committee eventually focused on the Edward G. Budd Manufacturing Company of Philadelphia, Pennsylvania. Budd's legacy was in shot-welded stainless steel, with streamlined railway cars and single-piece automobile bodies its noted products.* However, it had built components for the aircraft industry and had conducted much research into shot-welded steel assemblies for airplanes. In the early 1930s Budd had built an amphibious airplane of steel. Beginning in 1939, it had begun a concerted effort to research the use of steel in aircraft assemblies that had attracted some interest from within the industry, although the armed forces remained skeptical. It was expected that shot-welding instead of riveting would save construction time and reduce weight compared with that of a comparable structure built of less dense aluminum.

The DSC had no facilities for letting and administering contracts, but the US Navy took an interest in the project during 1941. Instead of competing with Army demands for existing transport types, the Navy saw an opportunity in the Budd effort to claim a unique resource for its own. After reviewing progress, the service took the project under its wing and in early 1942 Budd was asked to submit a bid. An April 1942 Letter of Intent followed for 800 RB-1s, plus a static test article. On 3 June 600 of these had been allocated to the Army Air Forces as the C-93s, the Navy's 200 identified as 39292/491**. The USAAF saw it as a 'fill-in' pending availability of the C-82 (see later) and hoped for fifty deliveries per month in 1944.[54] The Bureau of Aeronautics retained technical supervision. The formal contract followed in August 1942 in which BuAer stipulated that the aircraft was to be certified to CAA standards. This may have been because the Navy had not previously developed a transport aircraft, much less one of steel, so lacked the basis for a detailed specification and acceptance standards.

The RB-1 Conestoga was advertised as the first aircraft to be built entirely of shot-welded, corrosion-resistant stainless steel. Steel aircraft construction lacked the deep experience of aluminum with its voluminous data, dedicated machine tools, and other industrial resources. Budd's new Aircraft Division had to pave its own path, providing substantiating data every step of the way. Nearly the entire structure had to be formed from sheet steel of various gauges as there were few resources for suitable castings or milling. By the end of 1942 its laboratory testing was demonstrating that the steel parts were meeting all requirements and specifications. The War Department financed construction of a new plant for assembly of the airplanes. Budd still had to seek subcontractors for some piece/parts work.

The design was principally the work of chief engineer Dr Michael Watter, who filed a patent for the prominent features on 18 July 1942. The high wing and main landing gear issuing from the engine nacelles ensured an unobstructed cargo volume, with the floor at truck bed height. Instead of a one-piece wing or wings attaching to a box carry-through structure above the cabin, the wings were attached to stout frames that encompassed the cabin and accounted for its flaring out at the top – although this also allowed the crew to more easily walk around the periphery of a cargo load. These frames had only a shallow beam across the cabin ceiling. Wing panels outboard of the engine nacelles and flaps were detachable and interchangeable. The numerous ribs and stringers shot-welded under the skin gave a peculiar rippled surface. Some 55 percent of the wing area, aft of the spar, and all the control surfaces were fabric-covered. There was three-axis trim and the elevators and rudder featured integral gust locks. The split flaps were electrically actuated. Undercarriage actuation was also electrical and the nose wheel was castoring. A portion of the nose and main wheels were left exposed when retracted. The doors were to be of plywood, and plywood was specified as necessary for the cargo floor.

Wind tunnel tests at Langley led to changes in the vertical tail, originally meant to be broader, and dihedral was added to the horizontals. The flight deck accommodated the minimum crew of two but with a navigator station. This was set high to reduce cargo volume obstructions, making for an unusual bulbous appearance of the nose. The high placement of the cockpit, ahead of a reinforced bulkhead, also lent a measure of crash safety. The designers felt the aircraft should float for enough time if ditched to permit evacuation, so the doors were designed for a watertight seal. A pair of R-1830-92 supercharged engines and three-blade Ham Standard Hydromatic props with a diameter of 11.6 feet (3.5 meters) were mandated. The power unit, from the firewall forward, was quickly detachable and could be swapped side-to-side.

Freight loading was under the sharply upswept aft fuselage through an opening creating by manually raising two clamshell doors for overhead clearance and lowering a ramp, 10 feet (3.1 meters) long across which cargo could be passed or wheeled freight rolled. The ramp was actuated by electric screw jacks (with manual back-up) controlled from an adjacent panel or the cockpit. It could be opened in flight to jettison the cargo and could be loaded with cargo to the same surface pressure as the main cargo floor. For transferring cargo from trucks backed up to the ramp, there was a manually operated overhead hoist rated to 4,000lb (1,814kg), together with a 2,000lb (907kg) manual winch at the forward end of the compartment for pulling loads aboard. There was a troop door, 3.3 by 5 feet (1 by 1.5 meters) ahead of the ramp on both sides of the fuselage as well as a crew door in the forward port side. The aircraft was to take twenty-four troops and facilitate parachute jumps. Alternatively, it was to accommodate twenty-four stretchers together with sixteen ambulatory patients. Six parapacks could be released electrically through the opening created by raising the clearance doors. Four auxiliary fuel tanks could be installed on the cargo floor for long-range deployment.

Budd encountered plenty of engineering and manufacturing challenges even before a short supply of stainless steel further slowed the work. The program ran over-budget and more than a year behind schedule, although this was not uncommon. The company guaranteed a 29,000lb (13,154kg) gross weight and 32,000lb (14,515kg) overload, but the empty weight came in heavy so the gross was over by 1,860lb (844kg). This was also not unusual for a prototype, but brought knowing looks that this was to be expected of an airplane built of steel. Budd stuck to its guarantees by simply adding 1,860lb to all with the same

---

* Shot-welding is a unique form of spot welding. With two pieces of metal clamped together, a large electrical current is passed through them for a brief period of time. This produces a small weld joint with twice the shear strength of a rivet of similar diameter.

** This split is not explained but was likely the result of a missions and resources dispute, the Army insisting that air transport was its assigned role. The Navy agreed that NATS would service naval facilities only.

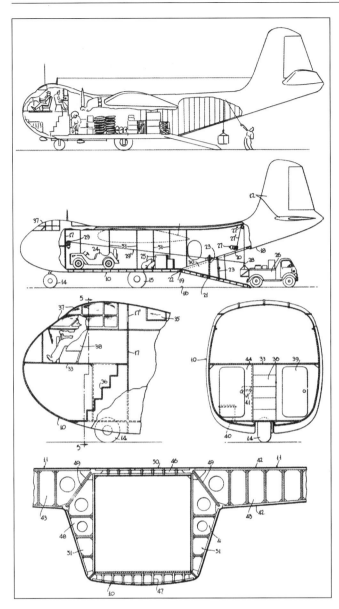

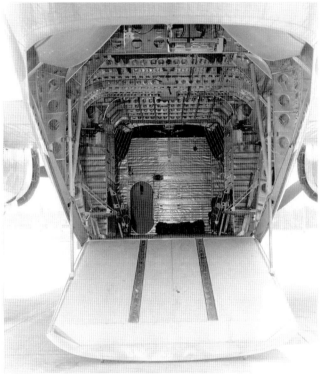

These drawings, taken from period documents, show the basic layout and original concept for the Budd RB-1, with the unusual wing attachment feature. Cargo operations with an overhead hoist and forward winch are shown. Note the navigator station on the flight deck and the original vertical tail configuration without a dorsal fillet above a horizontal initially lacking dihedral. *Author's collection*

These images of the interior of RB-1 (39294) are looking forward and aft, but lack the overhead hoist. The shiny sheet steel used in the construction shows the wavy surface that characterized the structure. Note the vertical frames to which the wings are attached outboard, the fold-down canvas seats, and the plywood cargo floor with tie-down points and fittings for litter stanchions. *National Archives, via Hayden Hamilton*

performance expectations. Hence, 33,860lb (15,359kg) became the de facto maximum GW with no normal gross.

The static article was completed on 12 August 1943 and testing began on the 19th, wrapping up on 27 October after very thorough structural trials. These supported a first flight of the number two ship, 39294, on the 31st from 'Budd Field', laid out adjacent to the plant. The Navy had instructed Budd to employ Benny Howard as the test pilot, joining company chief pilot Guy Miller. During what was supposed to be a taxi test, they took it up after just a brief roll to the end of the runway. The flight went very well, and testing in the coming weeks revealed few problems. Some complaints of heavy controls prompted Navy instructions to install an autopilot – although that had become common equipment by that point. Budd had found it necessary to add a fillet ahead of the vertical stabilizer for additional

directional stability, likely via wind tunnel testing, as it was installed from the earliest assembly. The static article appears to have been Ship 1, c/n 001, and later completed as a company flying prototype, 39292 (NX41810).

A particular issue was meeting the guaranteed 950-foot (290-meter) take-off distance at the new overload weight of 33,860lb. After trying various flap settings and rotation speeds the test team was still coming in around 1,600 feet (488 meters). They finally resorted to zero flaps but favorable nose-up trim, abrupt rotation at just the right airspeed to the point of scraping the tail bumper, followed by a quick level off while frantically rolling the trim forward and retracting the gear.[55] Budd recommended no flaps for take-off and certainly not to select anything beyond 35 degrees.*

* Full flaps was 45 degrees and there were no intermediate stops.

The RB-1 was an imposing machine on the ground with its unusual slab sides and towering bulbous nose. The unusually close ribs and stringer placement with the curious rippled skin would have attracted inevitable comments, and was just the result of the shot-welding technique employed and the use of sheet steel throughout. *National Archives*

Budd delivered its second RB-1 (39293, NX37097, c/n 002) to Patuxent River NAS on 11 March 1944, although with just a provisional airworthiness certificate and NX registration. It crashed on 12 April during a full 45-degree-flap take-off near maximum gross weight when the flaps would not retract and the aircraft could not climb at full power. It plowed into trees at the end of the runway. Of the eight men aboard, one suffered fatal injuries. The aircrew had already made several take-offs in this configuration, pulling in flaps in stages immediately after

becoming airborne and while retracting the gear, but found that this still left a meager climb rate and marginal directional control. The Navy subsequently accepted quarter-flap and no-flap take-offs. Unimpressed with Budd's artful short-field take-off procedure, this resulted in a comparatively long 2,110-foot (643-meter) take-off distance using normal rotation techniques.

An 8 May 1944 flight of 39292 ended with the airplane on its belly at Patuxent River (Pax) and the nose gear collapsed after a gear failure. However, the damage did not prevent the

This view of 39295 shows the compact lines of the RB-1 around the center cargo volume. The engines with cowlings were from the C-47, but the nacelle was a Budd design. The outboard flap segment and partially exposed wheels when retracted are evident. *Naval Aviation Archives*

Aircraft 39292 was the only one finished in the Navy's then current camouflage, all others being left unpainted. This machine was initially the static test article but was completed as a flying testbed (note the nose test data boom), used mostly at Budd's Philadelphia facility, hence the civil NX41180 registration. This angle emphasizes the notable nose-high attitude of the airplane in flight. *National Museum of Naval Aviation*

aircraft from being raised, and the gear lowered and pinned, for a flight back to Philly and repairs. Budd concluded that application of the wheel brakes during retract (a common practice) had produced excessive loads that had bent the actuation screw, and took corrective action. In the repair period the opportunity was taken to swap the R1830-92 engines for -94 models at 1,350hp (1,007kW) in the hope of boosting performance, but without remarkable results.[56] Weeks later, on 16 June, 39295 (NC45348, c/n 004) was forced to make a wheels-up crash-landing during a take-off where it failed to climb above the obstacles at the end of a 2,500-foot (762-meter) runway. Here again, the damage was minor. On 22 July the left main gear would not lock down on 39294 (NC45347, c/n 003); the subsequent emergency landing ended well enough for the airplane to be repaired. Another gear malfunction on 7 August with 39296 (c/n 005) left the crew working for 2½ hours to resolve the problem. They managing to get the nose gear down but the mains remained partially extended. The men chose a grass-field landing during which the nose gear collapsed. Budd, which had conducted very stressful landing tests to prove that the gear was not 'weak', again concluded that application of wheel brakes during retract had caused mechanical failure.

Capping the string of mishaps, both engines failed on 30 August at 800 feet (244 meters) following 39296's take-off, leaving only the Chesapeake Bay in which to put down. Air in the fuel lines was the likely cause. Aircraft 39299 (c/n 008) was ferried to Pax on 3 August but, after five accidents with two write-offs and one death in the span of five months, the Navy had finally had its fill. Cracks were also being found in the fuselage side skin, generally in line with the propellers. Overpressures from the spinning props were flexing the structure and causing fatigue cracking, which was cured with reinforcement.*

Budd completed four more airplanes in the coming months and pressed on with its testing because CAA certification had

to be attained for the company to be fully paid by the Navy. Type certification was finally granted on 27 October 1944.[57]

The final report from Pax was negative. The testers felt that stability and control was deficient, rate of climb at sea level inadequate given the intent to operate from small fields, and single-engine performance unacceptable. For this last, the Conestoga could not maintain level flight at 95 percent GW with the remaining engine at rated power.** Weight had to be reduced to 30,400lb (13,789kg) for a 100fpm (31mpm) climb rate, or 27,900lb (12,655kg) for 1,000fpm (305mpm). At maximum gross and full fuel the payload was 6,015lb (274kg). Fuel consumption also ran higher than expected.[58] These performance results are not surprising considering that Budd was compelled to use C-47 power units for an airplane thousands of pounds heavier and likely representing greater drag.

By summer 1943 the need to counter German moves in Central and South America had evaporated. Other than assault aircraft, the need to land on unprepared fields (especially for a Navy aircraft) had also been greatly reduced by the development of interlocking steel mats and other rapid airfield construction techniques.

Although the original schedule had called for thirty-six airplanes delivered in 1943 and the remaining 761 in 1944, this had proven very optimistic. Apart from the shortage of steel, the assembly plant was only completed in November 1943. A February 1944 assessment suggested that delivery of 110 Budd airplanes in the coming year was the most to be expected. Since the Air Forces planned to have many hundreds of more mature cargo airplanes available in 1945, even if lacking the C-93's unique attributes, they decided they could do without another type to sustain through training and logistics. The aircraft, by then designated C-93A, was dropped on 15 April 1944. On 13 June the Navy reduced its quantity to twenty-five RB-1s plus the static article/prototype (39292/317). This was by no means early enough to be certain of the war's outcome given existing or developmental aircraft, yet the Navy was confident that it did not want the RB-1.

* Noise levels inside the cabin during flight were tremendous and anyone lacking ear defenders was likely to suffer hearing loss after short exposure.

** Single engine performance had not been detailed in the specification.

The Navy stopped taking RB-1s in late 1944 after seventeen (39292/308, c/n 001/17). There are indications that some of the ships were used by naval units along the eastern seaboard for a brief time, but many were stored immediately after completion and their brief shakedown flights. Budd finished the remaining nine (presumably 39409/17, c/n 018/26), for a total twenty-six, with many additional subassemblies and parts also completed. Budd hoped to continue the production and offered to buy the tooling from the government. This was refused. The government assessed that $28 million had been spent on the project, with a unit cost of $378,000.

Even before the end of the war the remaining airframes were offered for sale and sold to civilian freight operators by the recently formed War Assets Administration.[59] The aircraft were let go for as little as $26,786 each. They continued to suffer more than their share of landing gear emergencies. Some were retired quite early owing to structural yielding at the wing attachment points; the wing top skin outboard of the joint buckled and the skin below cracked, while the wings assumed ever more dihedral over time.[60]

Budd C-93 and RB-1 Conestoga characteristics

Span	100.0ft (30.5m)
Length	68.0ft (20.7m)
Height	30.9ft (9.4m)
Wing area	1,400ft² (130m²)
Fuel, max	994 gallons (3,763 liters)
Fuel, with ferry tanks	1,884 gallons (7,132 liters)
Climb rate, initial	490fpm (149mpm)
Service ceiling	15,600ft (4,755m)
Weight, empty	20,778lb (9.425kg)
Weight, max gross	33,860lb (15,359kg)
Speed, max (7,400ft)	191mph (307km/h)
Cruise speed (average)	147mph (237km/h)
Range, normal	650 miles (1,046km)
Range, max (139mph)	1,540 miles (2,478km)
Range, ferry	3,060 miles (4,925km)
Landing distance (over 50ft obstacle)	1,590ft (485m)

Late winner (Fairchild C-82)

Like many aviation firms just after Pearl Harbor, Fairchild Aircraft of Hagerstown, Maryland, was eager to make a contribution to victory. Perceiving an imminent need, in November 1941 the leadership directed designer Armand J. Thieblot to begin conceptual design of a tactical transport. This would have twin booms with a podded fuselage that facilitated loading through an aft door or doors, the floor at truck bed height. A 155mm gun or three jeeps could be rolled in for rapid egress at the destination. Performance numbers suggested that 12,500lb (5,670kg) of freight could be hauled 500 miles (805km), or 8,500lb (3,856kg) to 1,500 miles (2,414km). This bettered the C-47, and the conceptual C-62 and C-76, by more than 100 percent. Fairchild Vice-President and General Manager Richard S. Boutelle presented the Model 78 to Materiel Division personnel a few weeks after Pearl Harbor and it soon came to the attention of Hap Arnold. The General directed that Fairchild was to be granted a development contract for the airplane – provided it was built of wood.

After protracted negotiations, a contract for a prototype C-82 and a static article was issued in August 1942. Fairchild had a mock-up ready for a 15 September inspection. A second prototype was added later. The contract called for the use of plywood and steel. As the prospects for the Waco and Curtiss transports faded the Fairchild remained favorable. However, although Fairchild was experienced in wooden airplane construction, it recognized the dangers and asked the USAAF to reconsider this approach.[61] Trying to ensure that the C-82 did not fall into the same wooden trap as other programs, in December 1942 the USAAF permitted greater use of steel in the design. A month later it directed that the aircraft be built of aluminum, as stainless steel was becoming scarce.[62] (The cargo floor remained plywood-covered.) These were fundamental changes that set the design engineers back months and ensured that the C-82 would not be delivered before 1945. Fairchild facilities were expanded in anticipation of assembling the large aircraft. Some similar elements of the airplane were designed to be interchangeable, reducing assembly time and support costs.

The fuselage hung from an inverted gull wing selected only to allow for shorter main landing gear struts. The nose gear was not steerable. Only the main wheel brakes were hydraulic, Fairchild preferring electric motors for all other moving parts. Inboard aileron segments drooped with flap extension to enhance low-speed lift. The slotted flaps had segments both inboard and outboard of the booms. Hot air deicing was provided to the wing and tail leading edges. The engines selected were the 2,100hp (1,566kW) supercharged R-2800s. These turned three-blade, 15.2-foot (4.6-meter) Hamilton Standard quick-feathering Hydromatic propellers, also equipped for deicing. The crew of five was made up of the two pilots, navigator, radio operator and crew chief. The aircraft was to be capable of towing gliders.

Budd RB-1 39300 was photographed at Norfolk's airbase and with the name 'Norfolk' painted on the nose, supporting speculation that the aircraft were operated by naval air units down the east coast for a short time until stored awaiting sale. This image reveals the lowered cargo ramp, overhead doors also raised. The troop doors in the aft fuselage are open, the departure path for the paratroops being clear of the horizontal tail they would face with the C-47 or C-46. *San Diego Air & Space Museum*

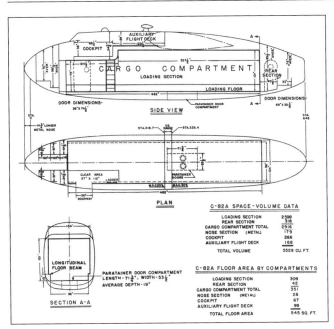

The Fairchild C-82 was another tactical transport project kicked-off in the frenzied aftermath of Pearl Harbor. Like the others, it was conceived to simplify freight operations, in this case with an aft cargo door and a ramp between the twin tail booms. This internal arrangement also reveals the parachute-recovered container drop doors in the middle of the cargo floor. *National Archives*

The Fairchild XC-82 Packet is shown during a flight test sometime after its first flight on 10 September 1944. The project had begun more than two years before, but was slowed by an initial order that it be built of wood and steel, only to have this overturned about six months into the design. Consequently, one of the airplanes were delivered by the end of the war. *Author's collection*

The principal loadable volume was roughly 8 by 8 feet (2.4 by 2.4 meters) and 28 feet (11.6 meters) long, and was essentially the same 2,598ft³ (81m³) as a railroad boxcar – hence the 'flying boxcar' moniker. This could take most of the Army's wheeled vehicles and field guns, forty-four troops or thirty-four litters. Paratroops could jump from the troop doors in each cargo door. The clamshell doors could be left on the ground to permit parachute drop of cargo from the rear – although the Air Forces still had to develop this form of airdrop. However, the C-82 was also designed to drop parapacks in a much easier manner than the C-47. These were hung from overhead rails and positioned over the opening in the cargo floor, normally covered by a hatch, to be released electrically from the shackles by the pilots or crew chief to fall from the bottom of the aircraft.

The first XC-82 (43-13202, s/n 10001) took to the air at Hagerstown Municipal Airport on 10 September 1944 during what was supposed to be a taxi tests, with Benny Howard and Dick Henson at the controls. The aircraft was powered by R-2800-34 engines and still had Duramold nose cone and cargo doors. The testing proceeded so well over the coming weeks that the second prototype was cancelled and the Air Forces directed that the 100 C-82A Packet transports (44-22959/3058, s/n 10003/102) ordered earlier that year enter production in January 1945. This was a rare dropping of the USAAF's guard for a program with which it had otherwise proceeded with uncharacteristic caution. By this point many programs had moved away from the frantic period of 1942 to assume more normal if accelerated milestones.

Series production began as planned and the initial service airplane was flown on 30 May 1945, handed over in June. The first ten mounted R-2800-22 engines. All moved from the

prototype's integral fuel tanks to rubber cells, which reduced capacity by 250 gallons (946 liters). While the airlift teams got familiar with the airplane, another 100 were placed on order in early 1945. Other production lines were established in Fort Worth, Texas, and Kansas City, Kansas, by North American Aviation with orders for 792 C-82Ns (NA-135).

Fairchild had delivered just nine C-82As by the end of 1945 – the most advanced and capable tactical airlifters manufactured during the war. Only three C-82Ns (45-25436/8) were completed, in Kansas, before the North American order was cut at the end of the war, although Fairchild continued turning out the Packet following hostilities. The aircraft were not without problems to be corrected, but they set the standard for tactical transports that followed.

Fairchild C-82A Packet characteristics

Span	106.5ft (32.5m)
Length	77.1ft (15.6m)
Height	26.3ft (3.5m)
Wing area	1,400ft² (130m²)
Fuel, max	2,834 gallons (10,728 liters)
Climb rate, initial	950fpm (290mpm)
Service ceiling	21,200ft (6,462m)
Weight, empty	29,800lb (13,517kg)
Weight, gross	42,000lb (19,051kg)
Weight, ferry	50,000lb (22,680kg)
Speed, max	240mph (386km/h)
Range (210mph)	2,390 miles (3,846km)
Range, best time (225mph)	1,075 miles (1,730km)
Range, ferry (183mph)	3,875 miles (6,236km)
Landing distance (hard, dry surface, over 50ft obstacle)	2,100ft (640m)

The C-82 cargo compartment shows what all the wartime projects sought to achieve – a clear, easily loaded volume. The lower ceiling in the forward portion provides space overhead for the flight deck and clear space for crew entry through the port door and flight deck access via an adjacent ladder. Note the cargo tie-down rings in the plywood floor panels. *National Archives*

Below: Tactical vehicles were loaded into the Packet via wheel ramps between the interchangeable tail booms and vertical surfaces; improvised wooden units are being used for this demonstration of the XC-82. The swing-aside cargo doors contain the troop doors for parachute jumps out of each side of the aircraft. Stabilizer struts have been lowered on either side of the cargo opening to reduce aircraft motion during heavy equipment loading and unloading. The main and nose gear wheels and tires were interchangeable. *National Archives*

CHAPTER SIX

Strategic Movers

Jury-rigged

T HE CONVERSION of long-range heavy bombers as transports held much appeal as it could significantly shorten the time to fielding assets. Conceivably, the existing fuselage could be modified by removing the bombing and defensive weapons hardware to install cargo flooring and doors, while the wings, engines and empennage remained unchanged. Even an entirely new fuselage would be minor by comparison to developing an entirely new aircraft. The production line was running for most of the aircraft, and personnel training as well as logistics were all in place for the majority of the systems. Anyone familiar with aircraft development understood that this was a superficial assessment, but the possibility of saving time was great motivation. The highest concern was potentially slowing the production and improvement of the bombers.

The Consolidated B-24 appeared the most suitable candidate for cargo conversion, the high wing and tricycle landing gear configuration lending itself to rapid loading and unloading across a little-obstructed floor space. The B-17 was less appealing, but both had been used to ferry aircrew and vital small cargo items when necessary. At least one B-17E (41-2593) and an F (40-6036) had been turned into XC-108 passenger transports for general officers, one with a passenger door cut into the rear starboard side. Another E (41-2595) became the XC-108A, with a cargo door on the port side. A

The earliest B-24s were not considered combat-worthy as the type was still maturing and adopting some of the required survivability features. However, its long range made it very suitable as a transatlantic transport. This YB-24 was turned to such tasks with all weapons removed and extra windows added. *National Archives*

spin-off of the B-29 was also considered at that time but dismissed as disrupting that very important program.[1]

The B-24 was well into production by November 1941 when Consolidated Aircraft of San Diego, California, proposed a troop transport variant. This only raised Air Corps ire regarding ill-focused resources, and it directed that all such studies cease. A month later matters changed with the declaration of war. The company was instructed to explore the potential without negatively impacting ongoing programs. In June 1942 the Air Staff decided to pursue the acquisition and a contract was promulgated in September. The first Liberator Express flew on 24 August 1942 in San Diego, but all the rest were built in Fort Worth. The USAAF took delivery of its first C-87 on 2 September.

Famed as the staff aircraft of General Douglas McArthur, this XC-108 (B-17E 41-2593, photographed on 29 November 1943) is a good example of an ersatz long-range transport created from a heavy bomber. All weapons save a nose gun have been removed, there is a fairing over the aft fuselage in place of the tail gunner's station, and a passenger door in the aft fuselage. Such four-engine machines were in high-rate production, and turning a few hundred to the transport role was tolerable – although the B-17 was passed over save for the few specially modified examples. *San Diego Air & Space Museum*

Consolidated built 278 of the transports alongside the bombers through 10 August 1944. Of these, five were passed to the US Navy as RY-2s and twenty-four lent to the RAF as Liberator C.VIIs. With a crew of five, the aircraft featured twenty to twenty-five seats depending on configuration, aft port side loading doors, and windows. As a freighter the aircraft carried up to 12,000lb (5,443kg), depending on fuel state. A belly structure replaced the bomb bays, the 'greenhouse' nose was replaced with a fairing hinged on the starboard side, and a fairing covered the tail turret area. Six VIP C-87As in 1943 had sixteen seats and ten berths, with the USN taking three as RY-1s.

Below and opposite bottom: These illustrations show the interior of the C-87 and how the wing box forced a very low overhead for the forward portion of the cabin. Aft of that there was ample headroom and enough height for five litters in the stanchions. The narrow width greatly limited the freight that could be accommodated. *National Archives/San Diego Air & Space Museum*

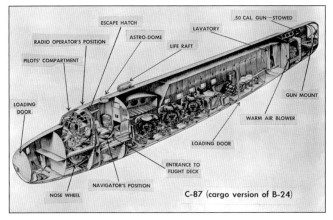

Consolidated C-87 (RY-2) characteristics

Span	110.0ft (33.5m)
Length	66.3ft (20.2m)
Height	18.0ft (5.5m)
Wing area	1,048ft² (97m²)
Fuel, max	2,814 gallons (10.652 liters)
Climb rate, average	957fpm (292mpm)
Service ceiling	31,000ft (9,449m)
Weight, empty	31,935lb (14,485kg)
Weight, gross	56,000lb (25,401kg)
Weight, ferry	62,000lb (28,123kg)
Speed, max (25,000ft)	306mph (493km/h)
Cruise speed (20,000ft)	205mph (330km/h)
Range (200mph)	2,900 miles (4,667km)
Range, ferry (163mph)	3,500 miles (5,633km)
Landing distance (over 50ft obstacle)	2,250ft (686m)

The most prominent feature of the C-87 was the lack of armament and the 'greenhouse' nose. A closer look reveals the two-segment door in the port rear side. Note how the nose fairing is hinged to swing aside.
San Diego Air & Space Museum

The C-87 was clearly an ersatz solution, as the 1,150ft³ (33m³) volume with a width of a mere 5 feet (1.5 meters), loaded through a trapezoidal door into a sloping deck segment, was cumbersome. The width was less in the early production before 15-inch (38cm) heating ducts along the floor were relocated. Personnel and packages were the only practical payload, although the ability to transport engines was demonstrated. Still, it was at hand when there were very few other options. The Navy even had a variant developed with the PB4Y-2 cruciform tail as the RY-3 (C-87C) for Lend-Lease. The intended 112 saw perhaps less than half completed, most going to the RAF as the Liberator C.IX.[2]

Recognizing these limitations, Consolidated developed a more refined transport spin-off from the B-24 as the Model 39 (later Convair Model 104) Liberator-Liner or 'Libliner', which clearly spoke of ambitions for post-war commercial sales. This used the cruciform empennage of the PB4Y-2 on an entirely new circular cross-section fuselage. With a diameter of 10.5 feet (3.2 meters), a length of 90 feet (27 meters) and a crew of four, this seated forty-eight or berthed twenty-four, or held 18,500lb (8,392kg) of freight. Grossing 64,000lb (29,030kg), it was to

A Lend-Lease variant of the C-87 was procured under the Navy designation RY-3 (the C-87C designation was not actually used). These varied by using the tall vertical tail of the PB4Y-2. Despite reports, several were used by American forces, as evident by this Marine example (90044) with firing port windows. *Gerald Balzer collection*

cruise a 202mph (325km/h) to 4,000 miles (6,437km). A large cargo door was created in the forward starboard side and another on the aft port side. This was an entirely corporate effort with the fuselage built in Fort Worth and shipped to San Diego for final assembly. However, the Navy had become interested and signed a Letter of Intent on 20 March 1944 for 253 R2Y-1s (90132/384) with delivery between August and July 1945.

The Navy deal fell apart in April when the mock-up was inspected and the proposed airplane came into sharper focus. The service objected to the fuselage volume interrupted by the wing carry-through, disappointing payload weights, and predicted long take-off distance. Yet Convair received permission to complete the first article in Navy markings while awaiting civil registration. Fitted with R-1830-94 engines, this became the XR2Y-1 (09803, later NX30039), and first flew on 15 April 1944. It was subsequently purchased by the company and a second (NX3939), with R-1830-65s, completed. Although operated for three months in the summer of 1945 with American Airlines, post-war interest was slack owing to the availability of inexpensive military surplus.

The R2Y-1 was so designated because of a Navy contract, despite the type being developed on Convair's own initiative. By the time the aircraft flew in April 1944 the Navy had withdrawn but, awaiting the civil registration, the USN permitted operations under temporary military markings. A reasonable spin-off of the B-24 with a more practical fuselage, the aircraft was still hardly easy on the eyes. *San Diego Air & Space Museum*

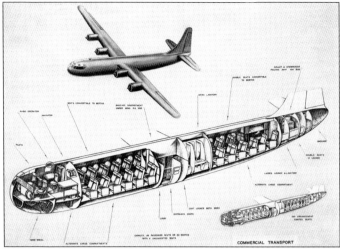

This cutaway and interior shot of the Convair R2Y-1 or Liberator-Liner shows how the cabin was interrupted by the wing box beam. This mandated two cargo doors, one at the right front and the other left rear, making for a poor freight transport. It is unlikely this would have appealed to many airlines had the market developed post-war. *San Diego Air & Space Museum*

The exigencies of the war demanded even shorter timeline conversion of bombers, some performed in the field. Liberators, Flying Fortresses and even B-29s were stripped of offensive gear and fitted with seats and bunks for priority personnel transport, or 'package delivery' of vital materiel. Jury-rigged cargo racks could be placed in the bomb bays. Late in the war a few Liberators and Flying Forts operating as transports were dubbed CB-24 and CB-17. Even fuel could be delivered within the large tanks of the bomber, and the standard long-range tanks fitted in the bomb bay, to be pumped out to storage tanks at the destination or directly into another aircraft.

The movement of aviation fuel from India to China over the Himalayas was a particularly daunting task, yet urgent in keeping pressure on the Japanese. To help improve this situation, several of B-29s were modified as dedicated 'tankers', with four bomb bay tanks and all non-essential equipment removed. All but the tail guns were jettisoned and sighting blisters faired over. These aircraft could deliver 2,410 gallons (9,122 liters) of fuel (from a capacity of 8,050 gallons [3,047 liters]), 100 gallons (379 liters) of oil, and 3,290lb (1,492kg) of other freight. They used 2.25 gallons (8.52 liters) of fuel for every gallon delivered compared with 7 gallons (26.5 liters) for a standard Superfortress. In

another example, a wing of Eighth Air Force B-24s was devoted in September 1944 to flying fuel to forward airfields on the continent for Third Army combat vehicles as they advanced ahead of their supply columns. Each bomb bay was loaded with 200 5-gallon fuel cans.[3]

The B-29s had more important tasks to perform. An example of both the B-17E (42-30190, XC-108B) and the B-24 was quickly modified in 1943 for the tanker role. Ford converted a B-24E as the XC-109, which carried an additional 2,250 gallons (8,517 liters) in seven metal tanks: one in the nose, one in each bomb bay, and three in the rear. This was roughly double the standard B-24 fuel load. An APU was provided to pump out fuel from a single point in the fuselage, but crews were wary of employing this because of fumes that could gather inside the fuselage. An inert gas replaced the fuel as it was drawn from the tanks. Ford and Martin built another 208 examples from B-24Js and Ls, but with flexible tanks, through to the end of 1944. The aircraft was marginally stable with full fuel and, following several take-off crashes, the fuselage fuel load was reduced to 1,200 gallons (4,542 liters), or at least the nose tank left empty. Two of these C-109s could carry the fuel for one B-29 long-range bombing mission over Japan.

An example of an unofficial 'CB-17' transport conversion of the Fortress was this B-17G, photographed in April 1945. Somewhere in the Pacific theater this was modified as shown with simple bench seats in the aft fuselage for what appears to be ten passengers. Comfort was clearly not a priority. *National Archives*

This 23 November 1943 image captures the sole B-17 tanker, or XC-108B. The E-model (42-30190) appears normal save for the lack of turrets and nose guns. By a judicious placement of added fuel tankage in available volume up to the overload gross weight of the aircraft, such a machine could deliver fuel to remote airfields or those inaccessible by ground transport to sustain air operations, but it remained a costly endeavor. *National Archives*

The production solution was the C-109 tanker based on the B-24J and L. These had tanks in the nose and bomb bays with a single-point fuel/defuel point (despite appearances here). The first picture shows 42-52033 from 5 December 1944, and the other 42-48979, revealing the tanks in the bomb bays. *Top National Archives/bottom San Diego Air & Space Museum*

Above and above right: The huge Coronado (PB2Y-3R shown) was bought in comparatively small numbers after it was observed that bigger was not necessarily better when it came to the patrol mission, and the flying boat was a poor bomber. Its cavernous fuselage, as suggested by the photograph looking aft, lent itself to transport conversion. It was just a matter of finding the best way to take advantage of the 6,000lb payload capacity.
Above *Left Naval Aviation Archives/right National Museum of Naval Aviation*

Diversions

As the war moved along it became clear that large flying boat patrol bombers were less effective than shore-based aircraft unless operating from the water was essential. The twin-engine Martin PBM became subject to this in 1942, with thirty-one twin PBM-3s converted to R-suffix transports and eighteen more built new in the unarmed PBM-3R configuration. This was still just 13 percent of that model's production order and 4 percent of the Mariner total. These boats normally cruised at 127mph (204km/h) and had a patrol range of 2,260 miles (3,637km) with a 1,300lb (590kg) payload. Even standard-configured boats, including the ubiquitous Consolidated PBY Catalina, could transport a few passengers in great discomfort and boxes of vital supplies.

When the four-engine Consolidated PB2Y Coronado came on force in significant numbers the Navy turned more and more to transport work. Of the 200 PB2Y-3s, ten sent to Britain were soon devoted to transport duties, as were thirty-one USN examples in 1945. Additionally there were a few PB2Y-5Rs at about the same time. These machines cruised at 141mph (227km/h) to around 2,000 miles (3,219km) carrying about 6,000lb (2,722kg). The recognized inefficiency of the large flying boats affected the enormous and costly Martin PB2M, which cruised at 141mph (227km/h) to around 2,000 miles (3,219km) on dual-row eighteen-cylinder Wright R-3350 Cyclone 18 engines. After a single Mars was flown, the remainder of the production was turned to twenty JRM-1 transports in January 1945, where the 12,000lb (5,443kg) payload was of great value. Only the reworked XPB2M-1R contributed, none of the production airplanes being completed during the span of the conflict.

The Martin PBM-1 was the most numerous Navy long-range flying boat patrol-bombers during the war. However, the Mariner and others of its ilk were soon displaced by more efficient landplane patrol aircraft. Yet the flying boat still had value as an ersatz transport to locations only accessible by sea, and many were converted like this unarmed PMB-3R. *San Diego Air & Space Museum*

A sole Martin XPB2M-1 (1520) was built in 1940-41 and tested into 1942. By then it was clear that this giant airplane was impractical for the patrol-bomber mission as it had evolved during the war. The prototype was reconfigured over six months into the XPB2M-1R transport for operations from May 1943 through the end of the war (seen here in operational camouflage), while a few others were manufactured only to fly post-war as JRM-1s. *National Museum of Naval Aviation*

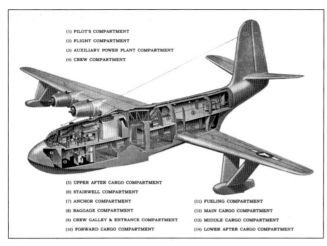

The PB2M-1 found renewed life as the JRM-1 Mars transport flying boat. This cutaway shows the considerable interior volume, albeit broken up by multiple bulkheads and two decks. None of the JRMs were completed before the end of the war. *Naval Aviation Archives*

Take-overs

The military became the customer for two developmental airliner programs, the Douglas DC-4 and Lockheed Constellation, on the verge of production. Momentum had to be maintained while unique military needs were inserted with as little disruption as possible. Such were the goals, but many factors intruded. One was an Airborne Task Force Carrier requirement. Movement by sea was time-consuming and vulnerable to the submarine menace, yet was the principal means of moving heavy equipment and high-volume freight, but air transport of a special fighting force might be possible. However, it still involved such weighty and bulky articles as 105mm howitzers and T9B1 light tanks. Innovative solutions would be essential.

Douglas C-54

The forty-two-passenger Douglas DC-4 was entering production and appeared the shortest route towards meeting minimal USAAC needs. It was powered with four 1,350hp (1,007kW), supercharged, P&W twin-row fourteen-cylinder R-2000-3s and 13-foot (4-meter) Hamilton Standard props. After Pearl Harbor the Air Corps moved quickly and negotiated for all the DC-4s then on contract for the airlines to become C-54 Skymasters.* Without time to formulate a specification for the strategic transport, the Army applied the two-engine transport spec.

The first Skymaster flew from Santa Monica on 14 February 1942, captained by John Martin, and delivery occurred on 20 March. The difficult period during 1942, with few air bases in remote locations, made it necessary to add four long-range fuel tanks for a total of 1,800 gallons (6,814 liters) in the forward cabin. This increased capacity by 78 percent but reduced passengers to thirty airline-style seats.

Nine of the aircraft already in jigs were taken as they were, while the remaining fifty-two were to be modified for the task force mission. A July 1941 meeting and subsequent mock-up

* Although to be built without pressurization for simplicity and cost, the design lent itself to the feature for later application. The military never availed itself of this potential.

conferences made clear that the C-54 could haul the bulky weapons only externally, although with the drag greatly impacting range and handling. This would be done only as a last resort.* Although 5 percent of the aircraft were built with the provision to carry the external loads, they were never employed as such.[4] Other gear was loaded through a cargo door in the port rear side, widened from 5.6 to 7.8 feet (1.7 to 2.4 meters). A door hoist was added, the floor strengthened, and freight handling features included. This became the C-54A with -7 engines. The cargo volume was 2,700ft³ (251m³) with a floor width of 8.7 feet (2.6 meters) and a length of 29.2 feet

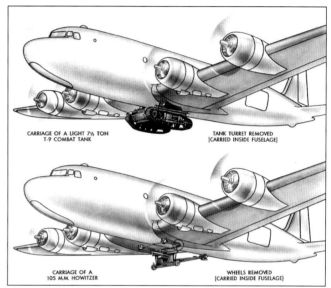

The Army had an Airborne Task Force deployment mission that required the carriage of heavy equipment like light tanks and guns. Finding no near-term solution in existing designs, the only option was external carriage of weapons that could not enter the aircraft interior, as shown in these period drawings. Some C-54As were equipped for this mission, which was considered a 'last resort' and never exercised. *Author's collection*

Douglas C-54A characteristics

Span	117.5ft (35.8m)
Length	93.8ft (28/6m)
Height	27.5ft (8.4m)
Wing area	1,460ft² (136m²)
Fuel, max	3,620 gallons (13,703 liters)
Climb rate, average	676fpm (206mpm)
Service ceiling	22,000ft (6,706m)
Weight, empty	37,000lb (16,783kg)
Weight, gross	62,000lb (28,123kg)
Weight, ferry	73,000lb (33,112kg)
Speed, max (10,000ft)	265mph (427km/h)
Cruise speed (10,000ft)	192mph (309km/h)
Range (190mph)	3,900 miles (6,276km)
Range, ferry (182mph)	4,500 miles (7,242km)
Landing distance (over 50ft obstacle)	2,000ft (610m)

* The T9B1 light tank was not produced in quantity, in any event.

(8.9 meters), expandable to 42.5 feet (13.0 meters) with the removal of the deck fuel tanks. Payload capacity was typically 22,000lb (9,979kg). In the B-model, 840 gallons (3,180 liters) of auxiliary wing fuel eliminated two of the deck tanks, permitting up to fifty-four austere seats or thirty-six litters.

It was concluded early on that converting the airplane for airborne operations would hamper rapid progress to high-rate production, given the extent of the changes necessary to permit troop and cargo airdrop. However, static cables and jump lights together with a glider tow capability were made standard installation for emergency use. Initially with an operating gross weight of 65,800lb (29,846kg), structural modifications permitted this to be increased by the end of 1944 to 73,000lb (33,112kg) and a maximum of 81,000lb (36,741kg).

The airplane had single-slotted wing flaps and a split flap under the fuselage. Control surfaces were fabric-covered with three-axis trim, the elevator having a flying tab. Nose wheel steering was commanded via a tiller beside the pilot. Apart from the main deck, there was cargo space in the belly forward and aft of the wing box. These could be accessed in flight via a trap door in the cargo floor. A hoist frame could be installed in the freight door opening to lift freight that was then manhandled into the compartment. This was used until the fall of 1943 when a swing boom hoist was adopted. The non-pressurized cabin had windows with gun ports. A crew rest area included two bunks and a john. Inflating boot deicing was standard, as was propeller fluid anti-icing. The flight engineer sat in a jump seat just aft of the center console.

A plant in Chicago was erected and began deliveries in the fall of 1943. Additional model variations were undertaken to standardize and optimize the cargo systems, further expand wing fuel to finally eliminate the cabin tanks, and mount the then current production engines possessing a modest 100hp (75kW) increase in power. These factors prevented rapid increase in the production rate. Only twenty-six of the airplanes were delivered in 1942, and seventy-four in 1943. However, this finally jumped to 355 in 1944 and 708 in the last year of the war. The total of 1,163 included 211 that were passed to the Navy and Marines as the R5D, and twenty-three lent to the RAF.

Despite the early assessment that the airplane was unsuitable for airdrop, the decision was made in mid-1944 to pursue the C-54F. This would have a troop door, self-sealing fuel tanks and flak curtains, and an ability to carry parapacks externally and to tow gliders. The inboard engines would be throttled back to produce a suitable environment for jumping. A C-54B (42-72321) was modified with two troop doors as the XC-54F for flight trials. Only after putting all this into motion was it realized that the self-sealing tanks would reduce capacity by 884 gallons (3,346 liters) and thus the range by 24 percent. The tanks would also require a substantial redesign of the wing internal structure. Observing that the C-82 was coming along, the project was dropped in March 1945.[5]

The C-54 stood out as the most effective long-range transport in the US fleet, but the level deck was well above the ground. The design was basically sound and caused few problems. It was not glamorous, but it got the job done when no others could do it as efficiently. The Air Force retained the type decades beyond the war and the DC-4 entered commercial service.

This C-54 is being refueled the hard way at a forward airfield in China, circa July 1943. The emergency exit hatch over the wing has been removed and the forward cargo door segment is open. The latter had two segments opening to the sides and was suitably wide but frustratingly far above the ground. *National Archives*

This interior arrangement in a Skymaster has several litter stanchions erected with passenger seats beyond. The view is looking towards the rear of the aircraft, the forward end typically having long-range fuel tanks on the cargo deck beyond a light bulkhead. Over the few years of production and several hundred aircraft the interior accoutrements underwent several changes, contributing to the comparatively slow production. *National Archives*

Lockheed C-69

The Lockheed Constellation was sponsored by Transcontinental and Western Airlines (TWA) and Pan American Airways. The forty-four-seat Model 049 and the heavier, transoceanic 149 (with tanks in the outer wing panels) seemed ideal for the military mission. With 2,000hp (1,491kW) engines and full-feathering props, the design goal was a cruise speed of 360mph (579km/h) over some 3,000 miles (4,828 km) at 20,000 feet (6,096 meters), mandating cabin pressurization with a circular fuselage cross-section. The triple-tail configuration was chosen so that the overall height of the airplane was compatible with existing airline hangars. In December 1941 Lockheed was told that the Air Corps would become part of the development effort, although the airlines would continue to participate. The planned eighty aircraft would be sold to the Army by the airlines, but with a tacit understanding that the companies would likely operate the machines in service.

Construction had just begun on the first Model 049s. The initial plan was for Lockheed to build the eighty airplanes on order as C-69s. The USAAC worked with the firm from January 1942 to study a variant of the 149 capable of hauling task force equipment. The results were favorable enough to issue a $138,203,767 contract on 29 September for 180 of the Model 349s (C-69B 43-94549/728), together with 15 percent spares.[6] These would be taken up after the eighty airliners were completed. However, while this was being negotiated the Air Corps declared that the Model 149 was to be dropped, while features of the 349 would be incorporated as soon as possible into the 049s, which were being limited to fifty.

With many course changes, and receiving direction from multiple airlines and military agencies, the Burbank, California, company struggled to get an airplane into production. In an effort to reduce confusion, the Army declared in May 1942 that it would procure the aircraft directly, with Material Center managing, essentially cutting out the airlines. The latter protested vehemently and an agreement was struck that the first nine 049s (43-10309/17) would be delivered to TWA by 31 July 1943, forty-one to the USAAF in the following year, and 210 349s by 31 October 1944. The first twenty C-69s would have a 65,000lb (29,483kg) GW, and be personnel transports for which a mock-up inspection was performed in May 1942. Some 21,000lb (9,525kg) of freight could alternatively be accommodated. The next thirty airplanes would be 67,000lb (30,391kg) C-69As, possessing cargo-carrying features and seats for 100, or forty litters. They were to have an upward-swinging cargo door, with an inset passenger door, in the port rear side. The floor was strengthened for freight, which was moved with a winch. Remarkably, the Army insisted on rifle firing ports in the windows. The final 210 Constellations would be long-range, 86,000lb (39,009kg) C-69Bs with full freight capabilities, including ninety-four seats. In addition to the A's cargo system, the B was to have a belly hoist and a cavity that permitted the T9 tank to be carried under the centersection. The usual selection of task force jeeps and guns could be loaded inside. It was also to have twin superchargers for efficient high-altitude operations, whereas the other models had just one 'blower'.

The model distribution was rearranged in April 1943 as ATC assessed the Constellation's value. It sought passenger versions as the first 120 machines and projected a peak rate of ten per month in 1944 to achieve seventy-nine C-69s by the end of that year. Consequently, the C-69A was cancelled and any procured beyond the 120 would be B models. Not long after this it was decided that only three pre-production C-69Bs were to be completed. Into this mix were thrown fifty of the C-69C VIP transport variant seating forty-two and with twin superchargers on each engine, the first to be converted from one of the C-69s. Lockheed had to resisted efforts to add turbosuperchargers and leading-edge heating deicing to the 'Connies'.

The Lockheed Model 049 and its derivatives would be the most advanced transports in the world. The C-69 was powered by the 2,200hp (1,641kW) R-3350-35 turning three-blade Hamilton Standard propellers with a diameter of 15.2 feet (4.6 meters). The integral fuel tanks suffered fuel seepage until a suitably flexible interior coating material was found. Lockheed went with a conventional airfoil possessing good stall and lift characteristics. Fowler flaps were incorporated. Control surfaces were hydraulically boosted, but with a manual reversion capability, augmented by servo tabs in all three axes. The boost packs were located near the associated control surfaces and an artificial feel system was necessary for the pilot controls. The hydraulic system was so extensive and complex that Lockheed was compelled to build a ground test rig for capability and endurance trials employing mass and aero force simulators of control surfaces and undercarriage. Cowl flaps were electrically controlled. Outboard engines superchargers provided cabin pressurization. The twin-wheel nose gear was steerable on the first two airplanes.[7] The basic crew was five, and the flight engineer had his own station. Bunks for a relief crew of four were provided behind the flight deck. Food service and lavatories were in the rear of the cabin. Leading-edge deicing boots were standard but not fitted initially to the first airplanes. The pilot windscreens, propellers and carburetors were anti-iced with alcohol spray.

It was understood that the Constellation would take a backseat to combat aircraft production. In September 1943 an urgent boost in P-38 fighter production forced a drastic slowdown in the Constellation except for completing the first two airplanes. The C-54 was meeting needs and the C-69 was not essential. The C-69 was also additional competition for the R-3350 engines powering the all-important B-29, with the development problems of that powerplant also pacing the Constellation's move towards flight testing. The schedule was changed to one C-69 delivered in January 1944 and seventy-eight more to follow that year, production reaching ten per month in April 1945. The three B models were to be built as purely passenger C-69s. Lockheed contributed to the distractions by proposing a heavyweight model with greater performance via a later-model R-3350 at 2,500hp (1,864kW) and possessing leading-edge thermal deicing. This was expected to haul 12,000lb (5,443kg) – to include fifty-seven passengers – to 3,700 miles (5,955km). The USAAF could not resist, and contracted in November 1943 for initial work on three 94,000lb (42,638kg) GW C-69Ds.

Given the difficulties the R-3350 had experienced through to the end of 1942, Lockheed and the USAAF agreed to consider an R-2800-powered model of the Constellation, designated XC-69E. Lockheed also explored a 'Speedpac' external cargo container 33 feet long by 7 feet wide and 3 feet deep (10 by 0.6 by 0.9 meters), or a volume of 400ft³ (11.3m³), nestled under the centersection and with some 8,140lb (3,692kg) capacity for a loss of some 10-12mph (16-19km/h). Neither of these projects yielded tangible results within the span of the war.

Despite all this program instability, Lockheed finally managed to put a Constellation into the air (NX25600, 43-10309) for the first time on 9 January 1943 from Burbank, with E. T. 'Eddie' Allen commanding. This may have been among the first test aircraft to use an onboard water ballast distribution system, via a series of tanks, pumps and lines on the cargo deck, to create different GW and CG conditions in flight. It may also have been the most heavily instrumented to that time. All the R-3350-powered aircraft were grounded between February and April 1943 owing to the crash of the XB-29 from an induction fire. After completion of an AAF test program, which included accelerated thirty-three-day service trials, 43-10309 was passed to TWA. The

A design that was well under way when the Army took it over in 1942, the Lockheed Constellation was an airliner from stem to stern. Standing well above the ground because of the very large propellers, the concept of using it for strategic cargo transport was born only out of a desperate need and the fact that it was at hand. This image of the first machine, wearing only Lockheed livery owing to airline participation in the development, emphasizes the size of the aircraft. *National Archives*

second C-69 (43-10310) flew non-stop from Burbank to Washington, D.C., on 16 April 1944 in a record 6hr 58min.

Fifteen C-69s (43-10309/17 and 42-94549/53), with 42-94550 as the sole C-69C, were accepted by the end of the war (42-94552 was subsequently static-tested to destruction). The Constellations were used primarily for training and stateside transport, with the airlines flying some of these. However, the first non-stop transatlantic flight (42-94550) occurred on 5 August 1945.

With the war winding down and C-54s meeting requirements, the contracts were reduced in late February 1945 to seventy C-69s and the three C-69Ds. Then, in August 1945, the orders were further reduced to twenty C-69s and the three Ds. The rest, already under construction, were cancelled, and Lockheed completed them as commercial airplanes.

Lockheed C-69 characteristics

Span	123.0ft (37.5m)
Length	95.2ft (20.0m)
Height	23.7ft (7.2m)
Wing area	1,650ft² (153m²)
Fuel, max	4,820 gallons (18,246 liters)
Climb rate, average	1,409fpm (429mpm)
Service ceiling	25,000ft (7,620m)
Weight, empty	48,630lb (22,058kg)
Weight, gross	72,000lb (32,659kg)
Weight, ferry	82,000lb (37,195kg)
Speed, max (10,000ft)	330mph (531km/h)
Cruise speed (10,000ft)	300mph (483km/h)
Range (300mph)	2,400 miles (3,862km)
Range, ferry (227mph)	4,500 miles (7,242km)
Landing distance (over 50ft obstacle)	2,800ft (853m)

Reaching

Under political pressures, the task force goals, and the uncertain duration of the war, the Army initiated programs to build true strategic cargo transports, and the Navy something similar. The multiple projects seeking cargo movement by air to a scale not previously addressed by the Air Forces brought a conference at Wright Field in September 1943. At this meeting standards and procedures were set to help ensure some commonality and share best practices.[8] This affected tactical and strategic airlifters alike, and must have imposed some engineering changes where possible.

All the projects suffered from low priority for resources and a general shortage of manpower. Even these reflected motivation by the manufacturers to develop airframes suitable for the post-war airliner market. By 1945, with none of the projects likely to contribute to the war, it was difficult not to conclude that the War Department was de facto subsidizing the post-war airliner industry.

Boeing C-97

After Pearl Harbor, the Boeing Aircraft Company of Seattle, Washington, stepped forward with a proposal to adopt the B-29 as a transport. Preliminary engineering was authorized in January 1942, completed by 20 June, and a formal proposal worked up. The three XC-97s (43-27470/2) were ordered on 23 January 1943 for delivery by 25 March 1944. It was strictly emphasized that the transport was not to interfere with progress on the bomber, so would follow.

The Model 367 added a twin-lobe fuselage to the B-29 wings and empennage. This was an expedient, but also permitted more floor area and simplified design for pressurization stresses. The lower lobe had the diameter of the B-29 fuselage while the upper was more capacious, a total volume of 6,140ft³ (174m³) being available. The upper deck was principally for the 36,000lb (16,329kg) useful load, with the length of 74 feet (22.6 meter) allowing alternatively 142 troops,

The first of three Boeing XC-97s is shown during an early flight test over Puget Sound. All but the fuselage was derived from the company's B-29 bomber, which held priority and, among other factors, ensures that this photo could only have been taken near the end of 1944. At this point the freighter could not be placed into high-rate production during the war. *National Archives*

eighty-five casualties with four attendants, three loaded 1½-ton trucks, or two light tanks. Vehicles were loaded via a ramp lowered through clamshell doors in the aft fuselage. The ramp was two joined segments folding in half and raised above the level of the doors for flight. Other items could be hoisted up and moved forward using an overhead traveling hoist running the length of the cabin. The hoist could also winch articles up the ramps. The lower hold was split into two volumes by the wing

The interior of the C-97 shows a clean volume thanks to the low wing. However, it also meant that the cargo floor was well above the ground and an electric hoist traveling on the overhead rails was required to bring cargo aboard that did not move under its own power. Here a Boeing technician is using a hand controller to operate the hoist as it brings up a slab of ballast through the aft fuselage opening. *National Archives*

box and loaded via a pair of doors. Ladders permitted inflight movement between the two decks. A crew of five was common. The aircraft mounted R-3350-23 turbosupercharged engines with 16.5-foot (5-meter) Hamilton Standard props. The B-29 laminar flow airfoil wings came with the standard Fowler flaps. Complex and heavy hydraulics were avoided by the use of flying tabs and many electric motors.

The C-97 took a big step forward in strategic airlift with the aft clamshell doors and loading ramps, across which wheeled articles could be driven or pulled with the hoist. It was, however, an imperfect solution owing to the grade of the ramp and the time required for the loading and unloading operations, as shown by these GIs straining to guide a 75mm gun up the ramp as it is hoisted aboard. Note the aft fuselage skid, stabilizing struts, and the ramp supports with a hinge joint halfway down the length. *National Archives*

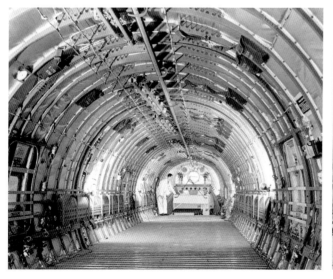

Paced by its supremely important bomber sibling, XC-97 construction in Renton was slow. The aircraft did not fly until 9 November 1944. The first set a speed record for transports with a 3,323-mile (5,348km) flight from Seattle to Washington, D.C., in 6hr 3min with a 20,000lb (9,072kg) cargo. The second XC-97 was delivered in June 1945, but the third did not appear until July 1946 owing to slowing of work post-war.

Being pleased with the C-97, but seeing that the war was reaching a conclusion, the USAAF took the peacetime approach of ordering service test airplanes. However, it also saw likely massive scaling-back of defense expenditure, so stacked the contract with three models of quite different characteristics. On 6 July 1945 six YC-97s, three YC-97As, and a passenger-only YC-97B (45-59587/95) were placed on contract. The only major differences in the YC-97s were the adoption of the 'Andy Gump' chinless cowling planned for the B-29A, additional fuel, and an electrical system of greater capacity. The A model, originally proposed on 2 June 1943, was to carry over the features from the B-29D, which included R-4360 engines, an extended vertical stabilizer but with fold-aside capability, thermal deicing replacing the boots, hydraulic rudder boost, and nose wheel steering (the basic model had none). The B had A model features save for deleting freighter accoutrements. Radar came later still. These aircraft flew well after the war concluded, and the type went on to an illustrious post-war military and commercial career.

Boeing XC-97 characteristics

Span	141.3ft (43.1m)
Length	101.3ft (30.7m)
Height	33.3ft (10.1m)
Wing area	1,739ft² (162m²)
Fuel, max	5,785 gallons (21,899 liters)
Climb rate, average	500fpm (152mpm)
Service ceiling	28,700ft (8,748m)
Weight, empty	71,150lb (32,273kg)
Weight, gross	120,000lb (54,431kg)
Weight, ferry	140,000lb (63,503kg)
Speed, max (25,000ft)	332mph (534km/h)
Cruise speed, average (25,000ft)	253mph (407km/h)
Range (228mph)	2,850 miles (4,589km)
Range, ferry (217mph)	4,100 miles (6,598km)
Landing distance (over 50ft obstacle)	3,350ft (1,021m)

Douglas C-74

Purveyor of many successful airliners, Douglas moved quickly after the US declared war to propose a heavy, long-range transport for the Army. Its January 1942 Model 415 proposal was met with desire but also sticker shock. One airplane without the engines and other government-furnished equipment (GFE)

was projected to cost $5 million, or 150 at $1 million each. Douglas came back a month later with the reduced-weight 415A at $900,000 each for fifty, or $500,000 for 300. The first was to be delivered in eighteen months, with production reaching three per month by November 1943, because it was well within the state of the art and Douglas's experience. With a nod from General Arnold, a Letter of Intent was issued in March. The 25 June $50 million contract reflected confidence with fifty airplanes (42-65401/51) designated C-74, without X- or Y-prefix examples, plus a static article.

Any innovations had to be developed within the tight schedule or left out. The cabin remained unpressurized although the circular cross-section certainly lent itself to the option. A laminar flow wing, adapted to production on a large scale, brought concerns with required manufacturing tolerances. Apart from wind tunnel tests, flight test data was collected with laminar wing 'gloves' representing the proposed C-74 airfoil flown on a Douglas A-17 test aircraft, with various skin joints and finish smoothness.

The C-74 was the largest landplane transport in production at the end of the war. As originally conceived this was to gross 125,000lb (56,699kg) carrying 26,000lb (11,793kg) to 2,700 miles (4,345km) at 200mph (322km/h). With a light payload its range was enough to reach any point on the globe from the US. A 48,150lb (21,840kg) payload could include two angle dozers, two T-9E1 light tanks, or two 105mm guns with a ¼ton truck plus an ammunition carrier and crews.

The cabin length was 75 feet (23 meters) with a volume of 6,800ft³ (193m³), enough for 125 troops or up to 115 litters with attendants. With a tricycle gear arrangement and the C-54's steering nose wheel, the level cargo deck stood 13.3 feet (4.1 meters) off the ground. The need for loading ramps was reduced by incorporating two overhead traveling hoists of 8,000lb (3,629kg) capacity. These could be positioned to support a rear lift that dropped down through fuselage pedal doors. Wheeled cargo or other articles placed on the platform, measuring 6.7 by 12.5 feet (2.1 by 3.8-meters), were lifted into the aircraft. A hoist could be swung out of a forward cargo door opening. Such electrically powered equipment was supplied by an auxiliary power plant (APP) during ground operations. Loading remained difficult but feasible, as demonstrated with a full-scale mock-up.

The largest landplane in production at the end of the war, the prototype Douglas C-74 is shown with the forward cargo door raised and a hoist in the opening. Although a 'clean sheet' design meeting the Army's task force deployment goals, it still appears to be a converted airliner, reflecting Douglas's ambitions for post-war commercial sales. This was a thoroughly advanced design reflecting safety and operational features expected of peacetime airliners. Although not pressurized, the fuselage design definitely lent itself to this feature. *National Archives*

The interior of the Globemaster shows exemplary workmanship and good use of the volume despite the curved sidewalls. The overhead electric hoists are positioned over the aft floor opening, the rails for longitudinal displacement evident. Despite this being a strategic airlifter, the Air Forces insisted on including gun ports in the cabin windows. *National Archives*

Loading heavy cargo and vehicles into the C-74, with its cargo deck 13.3 feet off the ground, was done with a lift platform in the aft fuselage. A portion of the floor was lowered, using the overhead hoists, through the opening created by opening two fuselage-bottom doors. Wheeled items were rolled onto the platform via wheel toes and, once inside, rolled about manually or positioned with the rerigged overhead hoists. *National Archives*

Full-span Fowler flaps, with double-slotted inboard segments and triple-slotted outboard, were augmented with a split flap segment under the fuselage. The outboard segments were ailerons that operated as 'flaperons' in the high-lift configuration. The large, fabric-covered control surfaces were operated via flying tabs.[9] However, the flaperons were hydraulically boosted, and operating in manual reversion mode, although accompanied by very high control forces, risked overloading the outer wing. The unusual double-bubble ('bug eye') canopy improved all-round visibility.[10] The five-man flight crew could be augmented with a relief crew given the long duration missions planned.

Thirteen combustion heaters, using engine fuel, warmed the cabin as well as the leading edges for anti-icing. Propeller anti-icing was via an alcohol pumping system for fluid migration along the blades. Douglas chose R-3350 engines that, as mentioned, ran into trouble and led to the B-29 demanding the lion's share of production. Performance figures with the powerplant were coming in with a disappointing rate of climb at cruise altitude to get over weather fronts. In March 1943 the engine was changed to the more powerful R-4360-27, which was also late in reaching production. This was coupled with four-blade reversible Curtiss Electric propellers that were automatically synchronized. The ability to back up and the APP gave the aircraft a self-sustaining capability at a forward airfield that appealed to the USAAF. Engine changes were facilitated by a hoist that could be attached to the nacelle.

The 4360s represented a substantial increase in weight, so the gross was raised to 145,000lb (65,771kg) and the cargo capacity to 49,000lb (22,226kg). The time lost in redesign meant that the first delivery was moved out to 25 December 1943. It was clear from the outset that Douglas was aiming at the C-74 being easily adapted as a commercial airliner post-war. A close eye was kept on the program and it soon because evident that the C-74 engineering was affecting progress on

the very important A-26 medium bomber, which was seriously behind schedule. In January 1943 the priority for the C-74 was reduced and personnel reassigned. Only materials acquisition for the first airplane was given priority. Hence the first jigs were not completed until August 1944.

The prototype of what Douglas called the Globemaster (s/n 13912) finally rolled out in July 1945 and flew on 5 September. Save for lack of pressurization and tank inerting, this was a thoroughly advanced aircraft. However, production was terminated in January at just fourteen, one to serve as the static article. Ultimately, it became the basis for the post-war C-124, with nose doors and loading ramp, which was built in the hundreds. As planned, it also served as the basis for an airliner proposal, but this was too much airplane at the time and found no market.

Douglas C-74 characteristics (estimated)

Span	173.3ft (52.8m)
Length	124.3ft (37.9m)
Height	43.9ft (13.4m)
Wing area	2,510ft² (233m²)
Fuel, max	11,000 gallons (41,640 liters)
Climb rate, initial	2,605fpm (794mpm)
Service ceiling	22,000ft (671m)
Weight, empty	83,000lb (37,648kg)
Weight, gross	145,000lb (65,771kg)
Weight, ferry	172,000lb (78,018kg)
Speed, max (16,400ft)	300mph (483km/h)
Cruise speed (10,000ft)	214mph (344km/h)
Range (214mph)	2,700 miles (4,345km)
Range, ferry (198mph)	7,000 miles (11,265km)
Landing distance (over 50ft obstacle)	2,900ft (884m)

Lockheed R6O

In 1942 NATS's initial transoceanic flights employing Pan American aircrews were difficult given the available aircraft. Before the war, Pan Am had worked with industry in developing the next generation of world-spanning airliners, but this was interrupted. The company then influenced the Navy in pursuing better solutions. The airline was empowered to again engage industry, and Lockheed offered its Model 89 Constitution that had been conceived during the preceding year with Pan Am collaboration. The firm's draft specification on 20 November 1942 claimed a range of 5,000 miles (8,047km) at better than 250mph (402km/h) above 25,000 feet (7,620 meters), with a useful load of 17,500lb (7,938kg). It took another year of preliminary design back-and-forth, with Pan Am engineers acting as USN consultants, before the Navy contract for the R6O was finally issued on 1 November 1943. This was for fifty aircraft at $111,250,000. It was clear that both Pan Am and Lockheed were aiming at the post-war airliner market, but this also served USN interests.

The pressurized fuselage was split into two decks in a 'figure of eight' configuration connected at the front and rear by spiral staircases. Each deck had 6.7-foot (2-meter) ceilings. The upper cabin was principally for 168 passengers in normal seating, or 204 in more utilitarian accommodations though initially configured for just 92. The lower cargo deck was separated into two compartments by the wing box beam, and had a volume of 7,375ft³ (209m³). They were accessed via hydraulically actuated starboard side doors, one ahead of and another behind the wing. The sill of these doors was 7-8 feet (2.1-2.4 meters) off the ground, so an electrical cargo hoist at each could be swung out to bring cargo into the opening. The low overhead limited this to vehicles like jeeps or shallow bulky cargo like engines. The crew was to be twelve: the captain of the ship (having his own curtained-off 'berth'), two pilots, primary and assistant flight engineer, navigator, radio operator, two flight orderlies, and three relief crew members. With galleys, lavatories and drinking fountains as on a train, the aircraft was clearly more inclined to comfortable passenger travel than military transport.

A crawlway in the wing leading edge permitted inflight access to the engines. Although mounting R-4360-18s, the engine mounts were designed to take projected future powerplants such as turboprops. The 19.5-foot (5.9-meter) Curtiss Electric propellers included reversible inboard pairs. Lockheed had originally planned to use steam-driven superchargers, with water tanks and boiler, but his was eventually set aside for exhaust-driven turbosuperchargers. A complete engine and nacelle assembly was tested in propulsion wind tunnels, especially to optimize cooling. The total fuel capacity was 9,600 gallons (36,340 liters).

Each main landing gear was two tandem two-wheel struts interconnected by links such that they acted together. Integral electric motors spun-up the wheels to about 80mph (129km/h) prior to landing to reduce drag loads. A laminar flow airfoil with Fowler flaps was adopted. The vertical tail went through some evolution to seek the best stability and control. Leading edges were heated via engine exhaust gases for anti-icing. A weather and navigation radar was placed in the nose, like that to be found in subsequent post-war airliners. Full-time control system hydraulic boost was necessary given the size of the aircraft, with minimal manual control in a failure state. This and driving other articles like flaps, brakes, nose wheel steering, landing gear actuation, retractable tail bumper, and even windshield wipers, compelled Lockheed to build a full-size hydraulic laboratory rig for development optimization. Tabs were electrically operated, and an electrical system test rig was also built.[11]

The final design was a very large airplane for the period, with a 3,610ft² (335m²) wing area. Empty weight was to be 114,575lb (51,970kg) and maximum take-off GW 184,000lb (83,461kg). Performance estimates were a range of 6,300 miles (10,139km) at 238mph (383km/h) cruise, an initial rate of climb of 1,000fpm (305mpm) to a service ceiling of 27,600 feet (8,413 meters), and a 2,300-foot (701-meter) landing over a 50-foot obstacle.

Lockheed had many higher-priority projects and the R6O required construction of a new six-storey hangar in Burbank. The first airframe also served as the static test article. Consequently, the first Constitution was incomplete when the war finished, at which time the USN reduced the order to two XR6O-1s (85163/4) at $23 million. The first example flew in November 1946. Performance fell short of expectations and there was no follow-on military or commercial production.

Lockheed conceived a beautiful double-deck aircraft with the R6O-1 Constitution; planned for Navy long-range transport, it only flew after the war. Every bit an airliner, it stretched credulity as a utilitarian military cargo airlifter. Freight was loaded via hoists through the two starboard side cargo doors, while passengers occupied the upper deck. *Author's collection*

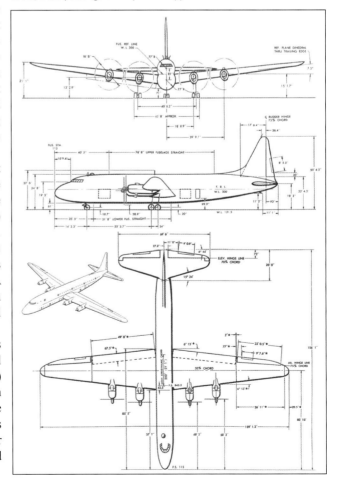

Far out

Two additional projects were aimed at super giant airplanes, and were longshots at yielding anything during the war. Yet considerable progress was made, with important technological advancement worthy of review.

Consolidated XC-99

On 1 August 1942 Consolidated proposed a transport variant of its intercontinental XB-36, having performed studies since May. This Model 37 (initially 36), using all but the fuselage of the bomber, was intended to increase interest by vendors and subcontractors in support of the slow-moving XB-36. Initiated in November 1941, the program lacked a production contract and needed a boost to perhaps move it along faster. It was also a move to position the company for the post-war airline market.

Agreement was reached with the Air Staff on 8 August 1942, and the contract was approved on the last day of the year for a single XC-99 prototype (43-52436) at $4,680,000. The machine was to be delivered on 31 September 1944, twenty-one months later. However, the contract stipulated that the transport must follow the bomber by no less than three months. The priority of the XB-36 fluctuated throughout the war and the transport was rated below nearly all other efforts within the company. The enormous bomber had six 3,000hp (2,237kW), turbosupercharged R-4360 engines in a pusher arrangement with reversible pitch propellers. Flight control surfaces were servo-tab driven and leading edges were heated.

The transport was to have a crew of five, and similar relief. The 16,000ft³ (371m³) loadable volume in a double-deck fuselage would be able to accommodate an astounding 400 troop seats, or 305 litter patients with thirty-five attendants, or 5 tons of freight, including vehicles. The two decks were to be connected via staircases at the forward and aft ends. The lower deck was divided by the wing center box beam into two loading zones, 40 feet (12 meters) long, each with a hatch in the floor to the exterior. Two sliding cargo doors were to be located along the centerline of the airplane, one forward of the wing box and

This period three-view drawing and concept art shows the basic profile of the XC-99 transport derived from the XB-36 bomber program. It has the single-wheel main landing gear, retracting into the wing, which was standard for the bomber and installed for initial flight testing of both types before being replaced by the more practical four-wheel truck. Note the two-deck fuselage of enormous dimensions. *National Archives*

the other at the aft end of the fuselage. Both were to slide forward and outside the skin. Two pair of clamshell cargo doors were to be installed immediately aft of the rear sliding cargo door to provide clearance for rolling vehicles aboard. A pair of cargo hatches in the upper deck floor were positioned over the lower deck cargo doors. Cargo was to be loaded, unloaded or shifted within the compartments by means of four electrical hoists, two on each deck, which ran on overhead rails. The two hoists in the lower compartment were designed to permit inflight drops through the opening made by the sliding doors. Even with these impressive notional attributes, the aircraft did not fit any Army mission requirement. Its enormous size and footprint, with a single-tire main gear, would limit the airfields from which it could operate to a very small number around the world, from where the cargo would have to be redistributed for further transport.[12]

The giant airplane, 135,914lb (61,650kg) empty, was to gross 265,000lb (120,201kg), or overload to 295,000lb (133,809kg). Operating without cabin pressurization, it was restricted to 10,000 feet (3,048 meters) – although any production model was planned to be pressurized. The optimal range at this impractical altitude and with 10,000lb (4,536kg) of freight was 8,100 miles (13,036km) at a ghastly 180mph (290km/h) average, or something like 45 hours flight time. This would likely use nearly all of the 21,116-gallon (79,933-liter) fuel capacity in inerted tanks. Alternatively, with a 100,000lb (45,359kg) payload and at 200mph (322km/h), the range was reduced to 1,720 miles (2,768km), or an 8.6-hour flight. The spec called for a 9,400-mile (15,128km) ferry at 173mph (278km/h). Like the XB-36, the

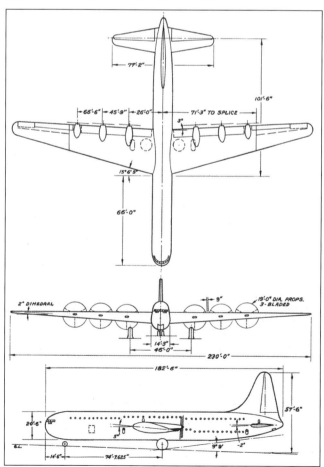

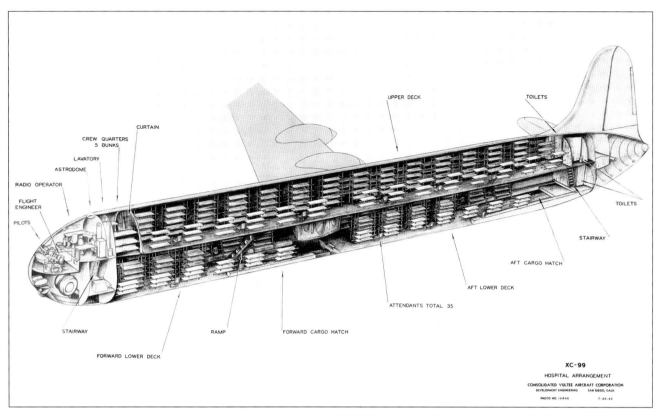

These period cutaways reveal the cargo handling features and internal arrangements of the Convair XC-99, the 'hospital ship' layout accommodating 305 litters and thirty-five attendants. While notionally impressive, the loading and unloading of all these patients via the steep stairs in the fuselage would have been time-consuming and exhausting. Note the flight deck arrangements, lower deck hatches and separation of this volume by the wing box.
Above San Diego Air & Space Museum/right Author's collection

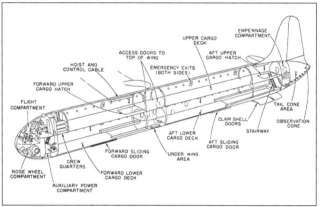

super-heavy airplane needed a runway at least 10,000 feet (3,048 meters) long for safe acceleration-stopping distances, and an unobstructed departure path of 5 miles (89km) because of the very low climb gradient.

A mock-up was inspected in Fort Worth on 24 February 1943 and a section of the fuselage was assembled for loading trials. The XC-99 suffered the same schedule slips as the XB-36, with propulsion and general engineering development delays. By the end of the war construction of the XC-99 had just begun, with the wing and empennage assembled at Fort Worth and shipped to San Diego, where the fuselage was designed and built. Aluminum was substituted for much of the magnesium present on the B-36 in the interest of construction simplicity and because magnesium was unsuitable for pressurized assemblies.

Consolidated Vultee (Convair, merged on 17 March 1943) did not fly the bomber until a year after the war, and the transport more than two years, with more than $6 million overrun. At the time it was still the largest operational airplane in existence, setting a payload record. It performed to expectations, which is to say graphically illustrating the utterly impractical nature of the airplane. Just as the Air Forces had largely lost interest in an unequalled intercontinental bomber, so did they see no future use for a transport counterpart. While it could carry the load of several then-extant Air Forces cargo airplanes, those aircraft could be loaded and unloaded more easily, access more fields, and get there faster.

Despite the myriad transports in development and production by August 1944, the Army still suffered from a lack. A committee meeting that month found that no existing or prospective design met the needs for a troop transport to sustain and exploit captured areas, and they recommended a new acquisition program. Men and equipment requirements broke down into two widely separated loadings, and thus drove consideration of two different aircraft: the troop carrier aircraft (heavy cargo) with a payload of up to 40,000lb (18,144kg), and troop carrier aircraft (special) with 70,000lb (31,751kg) freight. Wright Field believed that rewriting the Special Requirement slightly would permit the C-99, with a redesigned fuselage, to meet the need, and this was done. In May and June 1945 letters inviting preliminary design data were sent to prospective manufacturers. However, by September it was clear that funds would not be made available for such a program in the post-war era, and the solicitation was withdrawn.[13]

Hughes-Kaiser HK-1

During the clamor in early 1942 over the dearth of strategic transports, industrialist Henry J. Kaiser declared that he was ready to convert his shipyards to aircraft production. He observed that the steel for one ship could be used to build 200 airplanes. Looking at the sole Martin Mars patrol bomber, Kaiser was confident that he could be manufacturing these within ten months. He made extraordinary public statements about building 200- and 500-ton airplanes, proposing to produce 5,000 giant flying boats to span the ocean with materiel to defeat the Axis. He believed that in six months he could be laying the keel for such boats in his shipyards, then floating them to facilities where the wings, tails and engines could be installed. Although aircraft manufacturers, knowledgeable regarding complexities of aircraft development and production, were leery, if not dismissive, of such pronouncements, they could not ignore the public and Congressional agitation over the submarine scourge. The irrepressible Kaiser had worked industrial 'miracles' before, so why not give him a chance?

Kaiser's first plan to build 500 PB2M flying boats met with resistance from Martin and the Navy. Kaiser then moved to design an aircraft of his own using his engineers who hastily studied aeronautical design. Initially favoring a twin-hull flying boat, they conceived an all-wing airplane with four engines and cargo distributed across the span within the centersection. This 290-foot (88-meter) wing was to have an area of 7,920ft² (736m²) area and the aircraft would gross approximately 175,000lb (79,379kg). This was apparently intended as a landplane, but where such a goliath would take off and land was unclear. With the US Navy as sponsor, a model was tested in the Langley tunnel in 1943 and underwent considerable changes to seek a stable configuration. While it certainly showed uninhibited conceptual design, the path to a safe and practical production article appeared long. The Kaiser Cargo Wing was ultimately abandoned.[14]

Working with the established aviation industry, it was not surprising that only Howard Hughes was willing to partner Kaiser in this sensational effort. They formed the Kaiser-Hughes Corporation, in which Hughes would design the airplane and Kaiser would produce the Kaiser Flying Cargo Ship in what was proclaimed the "most ambitious aviation program the world has ever known". The knowledgeable and experienced aviation advisor to the War Production Board (WPB), Grover Loening, felt that this was enough to give Hughes a chance to design this fantastic airplane while Kaiser detailed his equally fantastical production plans. Hughes also gained the voice of fellow Texan and family acquaintance Jesse H. Jones, Secretary of Commerce and the Federal Loan Administrator. Washington decided that there was little to lose in letting them try.

The notional giant, dubbed the HK-1, was to employ the Duramold process for largely wood construction so as not to further burden the aluminum supply. A Letter of Intent was issued on 17 September 1942 followed by the $18 million contract approved on 16 November 1942. This called for three airplanes, one a static test article, delivered in twenty-four months. Hughes-Kaiser was not to 'poach' talent from the aviation industry and was to make no profit from the effort. The Defense Plant Corporation supervised the contract with financing through the Reconstruction Finance Corporation, ensuring that no military bias or preconception would hinder

The three-view drawing of the HK-1 reveals the enormous dimensions of the aircraft. The layout was entirely conventional and the lines were very clean given the laminated wood construction. Not shown are the clamshell doors planned for the nose, opening to the sides to permit a loading ramp to access the cargo floor, as this feature was not built into the prototype. *Author*

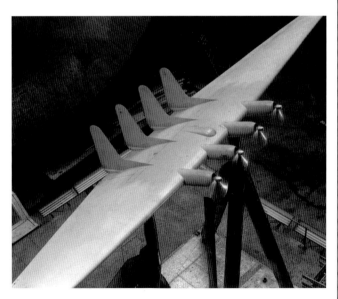

The 1.7-percent scale model of the Kaiser Cargo Wing is shown at NACA Langley during wind tunnel testing in 1943. Initially just a wing, the NACA researchers quickly concluded that directional stability was inadequate and the four vertical tails were added and ultimately twin booms to two vertical tails and a horizontal stabilizer with elevator. Note the canopy bulge in the centerline near the leading edge. *NASA*

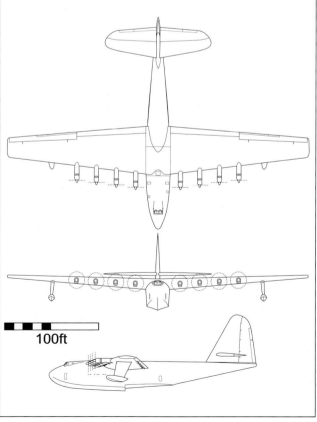

the development. Since the WPB was not an aeronautical development agency, it relied upon its few aviation experts, NACA and the CAA for assessment of progress in addition to managing the contract. Hughes Aircraft could proceed without detailed military specifications or close scrutiny.

Design began in the fall of 1942. To construct the major assemblies, an enormous 8-acre assembly building was erected at the Culver City facility, at the time the largest free-standing wooden structure in the world. In preliminary planning it became obvious that Kaiser's shipbuilding and other heavy industry assets and experience would be of little value in the undertaking.

Any idea of building the Martin Mars of wood was impractical. The team therefore went even bigger, seeking a machine to carry significant quantities of men and materials previously only transportable by sea. The goal became direct flight over ocean distances (3,500 miles/5,633km) with up to 120,000lb (54,431kg) of freight. From an expectation of building a 145,000lb (657,708kg) gross airplane, the team settled on 400,000lb (181,436kg). This was simply the result of deciding on eight engines as a practical limit and using the most powerful powerplant then available. The result was an airplane that stood eight storeys high and spanned more than a football field. This could carry a battalion of troops (750 men) or 350 litter patients and attendants, or such bulky and dense articles as two M-4 Sherman tanks at 31½ tons each.

The Hughes team worked with NACA Langley on the hull layout before doing the final design and providing a model for water basin tests. Howard Hughes was greatly concerned with hull step placement with respect to CG and deck angle, and performed extensive flight trails with his Sikorsky S-43 to explore options. In usual fashion he did not adhere to a rigorous flight test progression, so none of the data were useful. When building a sub-scale example for testing some of the more uncertain features was considered, Loening suggested instead that a PB2Y be used for the purpose. One of the big flying boats was eventually acquired from the Navy, but Howard Hughes could never divide his attention enough to do anything with it. Langley also contributed to the wing section design. In all, the NACA engineers considered the Hughes flying boat of superior aerodynamic and hydrodynamic design.

Applying Duramold, using mostly birch, to such enormous structures required additional research, new materials, and new tools. At the wing root the laminated wood front spar was 13 feet (4 meters) high and 3 feet (1 meter) across. There was great concern whether laminated wood was suitable for such a large aircraft structure and its attendant weight. Yet, when offered the chance to switch to aluminum in early 1943, at least for the wing, Hughes declined. The company was too invested in the process and was too far behind schedule.

The two wings were one-piece panels that joined on the centerline for an area of 11,430ft² (324m²). All control surfaces save the single-slotted flaps were fabric-covered. The fuselage was unpressurized, so flight would be limited to comparatively low altitude. The cargo doors (not built into the prototype) were planned to be two clamshell units in the bow opening to the sides, with an extending loading ramp. The bilge space consisted of eighteen watertight compartments, twelve of which could flood and the aircraft would remain afloat. The keel skin was an inch thick. Beach balls were placed in the hull voids for added buoyancy if flooded, later to be replaced with form-cut styrofoam. All fuel was stored in the bilge spaces, within fourteen 900-gallon (3,407-liter) tanks. Only eight tanks were built into the prototype. A 300-gallon (1,136-liter) supply tank was located in each wing.

The decision to employ eight supercharged R-4360-4As with synchronized, four-blade, 17.2-foot (5.2-meter) Ham Standard propellers meant relying on the production of a new engine as a pacing item for a schedule-critical program. The four inboard engine props were planned to be reversible for deceleration and surface maneuvering, but this was dropped after the XF-11 mishap. The pilot had just four 'master' throttles, one for adjacent pairs of engines, while the flight engineer had eight throttles. There was also a throttle 'inching' system for fine control using toggle switches. The leading edge was accessible, permitting crewmen to reach equipment therein. Engine cooling via cowl flaps and oil cooling via a radiator beneath the cowling was entirely conventional. There was no direct control of the engines, given the great distances between the throttles and engines – a pneumatic system with 'pneudynes' was employed through the first flight, but this was never suitably accurate and was replaced by electrical servos after the first flight.[15] An unusual 120-volt DC system was chosen to reduce the weight of the conductors.

Flight controls were hydraulically boosted with electrical flying tabs as back-up. The term 'boosted' was misleading as hydraulics alone moved the surfaces for what may have been the first full-time hydraulic actuation of primary flight controls with no manual reversion, given the impracticality over the great distances involved. Artificial feel had to be provided for the pilot controls to ensure proper senses such as stick force per g. All this was such new technology, with myriad challenges, that what may have been the first 'iron bird' simulator was constructed to test the system in the laboratory before installation on the aircraft.[16] Originally the pilot controls directly moved the hydraulic servo valves that altered the pressure within the lines to the actuator at the control surfaces. However, this design was found to be too sensitive, with violent oscillations given the smallest input. The change was to move the valves out to actuators, and the feedback cables became the command lines between the controls and the servo valves. Full redundancy was provided for this vital system.

After a number of plant visits and inspections by Loening and consideration by other senior aeronautical personalities, the War Production Board concluded that the HK-1 was taking too long and was unlikely to produce an airplane of value to the war effort.[17] Although of high-quality engineering and workmanship, there was considerable concern that the HK-1 would come in excessively heavy and that wood was operationally unsuitable. The services concurred that Hughes's resources could be put to better uses. Kaiser and Hughes were therefore called to a meeting in October to respond to these observations. They extracted a verbal agreement to await the results of static tests on major components over the coming thirty days. Unfortunately, the tests were largely negative, with repeated failures of glue joints (typically between stringer and skin) followed by reinforcement.

The enormous wings of the HK-1, 11.5 feet thick at the root, near completion in the cavernous assembly hall at Hughes, Culver City, then the largest free-standing wooden structure in the world. The wings joined on the centerline of the flying boat, so this appears to be a fit check. Note the three-storey-high wing float in the foreground, the laminated wood material readily apparent. *Museum of Flight*

More study and reporting followed, assessing that the HK-1 had passed the point of size efficiency in a trade-off between structural weight and payload. The tipping point probably lay somewhere between the PB2M and the HK-1.[18] There was also disagreement between the government and Hughes regarding the predicted performance, especially as an overweight condition was expected.[19] However, the HK-1 was reasonably expected to cruise around 185mph (298km/h) to 2,000-2,975 miles (3,219-4,788km).

Major construction of the first aircraft finally began on 6 March 1944, with $12.4 million already expended. On the 24th the government moved to cancel the program, sending stop-work orders. Kaiser withdrew but Hughes chose to fight for the airplane. He again sought the intercession of Jesse Jones, and President Roosevelt soon intervened to allow a new contract on the 27th under similar terms, but with the one prototype and no additional funds, to gain some research value from the money already spent.

Redesignated the H-4 Hercules, or HFB-1 (Hughes Flying Boat), the program was dragged out in no small measure due to the inherent engineering challenges but also the perfectionism and close association of the mercurial Howard Hughes and his unorthodox business practices. He was soon spending his own

money with as much as another $7 million and his personal reputation on the line as charges of wartime profiteering arose.[20] Resources had to be diverted to the XF-11, and the flying boat was given reduced status by the government.

It was June 1946 before the large assemblies were moved by road 28 miles (45km) to Long Beach Harbor. There the airplane was assembled in a purpose-built drydock for launching. It would still be more than a year before it flew, and just once in a brief hop above the water by Howard Hughes in a just-to-show-'em gesture. The flight was terminated when a crewman reported the fuselage skin below the tail was splitting, with daylight showing through.[21] This suggests inadequate design or poor workmanship and deficient structural ground testing. Although repaired and upgraded, the aircraft was then hangared until after Hughes's death in 1976. It remains the largest aircraft in the world by some measures.

CHAPTER SEVEN

Autogyro Apogee

Legacy

A T THE START of the war the USAAC had a small contingent with autogyros it had operated for a few years. This had begun in 1935 with acquisition of the best offerings of the Kellett Autogiro Corporation and Pitcairn Autogiro Company for evaluation.[1] A variant of Kellett's successful civil KD-1A direct-control autogyro, with rotor spin-up, became the YG-1 (35-278) with a Jacobs seven-cylinder YR-755-1 engine of 225hp (168kW).[2] This machine had a 'longitudinal bungee control' that set a fixed incidence of the rotor for trim, in the manner of an airplane elevator trim, for a greater CG envelope. A much larger Pitcairn direct-control PA-33 with a 400hp (298 kW) engine, designated YG-2, was also purchased but lost in 1936.

During 1936 the YG-1 underwent trails at various Army sites. With the blades folded along the fuselage, the ship could be towed on roads with difficulty. It was twice almost destroyed in ground resonance mishaps. Both times it was rebuilt at Kellett and, the second time, returned at about the same time as the company also delivered a YG-1A (36-352) with an HF radio. This machine was initially tested at Wright Field before moving on to field trials, where it was badly damaged in a landing accident. Soon after the A-model mishap, the YG-1 was also lost when a blade came loose and

In the mid-1930s the USAAC procured a small number of direct-control autogyros for evaluation in the observation mission. A school was set up in Dayton, Ohio, and the YG-1Bs traveled far and wide to participate in exercises and show their capabilities. While possessing some unique capabilities, they offered to the mission too little that was new and were no substitute for the long-sought helicopter. *National Museum of the United States Air Force*

the unbalanced rotor instantly separated from the machine. At this time, seven YG-1Bs (37-377/82 and 37-635) with 225hp (168kW) R-755-3s were ready for delivery, but were held up by the accident investigation.

After repairs, the YG-1A was sent to Langley and tested in the full-scale wind tunnel. There it again suffered a rotor imbalance, which tore up the ship and damaged the tunnel test section. Consequently, YG-1B 37-377 was accepted and test equipment installed for flight testing at Wright Field. A weak forging was identified and redesigned components installed before the remaining YG-1Bs were taken up. One of these last (37-378) was modified as the YG-1C and redelivered in December 1938. It had a 'constant speed' rotor with a diameter of 41.6 feet (12.7 meters) that also raised the GW by 195lb (89kg). This was a limited 0-4-degree collective blade pitch control for accelerated take-off.[3]

The USAAC came away from its first eighteen months of flying its two autogyros with the impression these were 'tricky' aircraft requiring carefully trained and skilled pilots. In general, they had some benefits in the observation mission, but were found too limited in endurance and payload, together with CG travel, the observer being unable to employ tactical cameras, flares, radios, etc. Their suitability as a military aircraft was therefore marginal. It was also observed that the burgeoning light airplane market was producing inexpensive machines that could serve as liaison and observation platforms nearly as well and with greater safety, as well as much less support cost. If fitted with slotted flaps for effective slow flight, these airplanes could match that aspect of the autogyros' performance.

No additional autogyros were to be procured. However, despite the desultory evaluation results, there was also confidence that the helicopter was coming, so the autogyro was a means for building rotorcraft experience. Thus the service established the Autogyro School at Patterson Field in April 1938 using the YG-1Bs. It graduated its first class in May 1938, but the aircraft also continued to fly in trials. The NACA's work led it to attain rotorcraft expertise and conduct fundamental research with published reports, which helped those working towards helicopters. The Air Corps soon established a project office for rotary-wing aircraft development.

The number of these autogyros remaining at the dawn of the war is unclear. However, when the country joined the conflict the machines were shuffled off to Texas in 1941 to serve border patrol duties.

The US Navy had also briefly explored the potential of the autogyro by acquiring a trio of winged Pitcairn PCA-2s in 1931 as XOP-1s (eXperimetal Observation Pitcairn, 8850, 8976/7). These had four-blade rotors, dual controls and radio installations. In September of that year an XOP-1 was evaluated during take-off and landing trials aboard the carrier USS *Langley*, marking the first rotorcraft operation from a

Kellett YG-1B characteristics

Rotor diameter – therefore	40.0ft (12.2m)
No. of rotor blades	3
Length	28.8ft (8.8m)
Height	10.2ft (3.1m)
Fuel	30 gallons (1,149 liters)
Best climb rate	1,250fpm (381mpm)
Weight, empty	1,580lb (717kg)
Weight, max	2,254lb (1,022kg)
Speed, max	125mph (201km/h)
Speed, slow flight	17mph (27km/h)
Range (103mph)	205 miles (330km)
Service ceiling	14,000ft (4,267m)

ship. The next year the Marines evaluated 8976 for the observation mission in Nicaragua, where they were combating an insurgency. The payload was judged inadequate and the range too modest to be useful as a military machine.

In 1936 the USN ordered 8850 to be rebuilt as a direct-control XOP-2 (PA-34), shorn of its wings and with a three-blade rotor. Redelivered in 1937, this was much like the Army PA-33/YG-2. It was again evaluated by the USN and USMC, with no enthusiasm generated. In the mid-1930s the Pennsylvania Aircraft Syndicate built an autogyro for the Navy based on a rigid rotor design by Edward Burke Wilford. This XOZ-1 used a Fleet N2Y-1 (8602) biplane that had been placed on floats as the XN2Y-2, the rotor replacing the upper wing.

It is doubtful if any of the Navy rotorcraft remained operational when war dawned. The experience had led the service to conclude that rotorcraft held no value for naval operations.

While some of the Kellett YG-1Bs were turned to research projects, those that remained were shipped off to Texas for border patrol duties when America entered the war. There they all met unfortunate ends. These machines are shown during the late 1930s at Patterson Field, Dayton, Ohio (near Wright Field). *National Archives*

Colonel Frank Gregory (left), USAAF rotary-wing aircraft project officer, shows off the new XR-5 to Brigadier General F. O. Carroll, Chief of Materiel Command Engineering Division (seated), with Colonel H. Z. Bogart observing. Gregory was among the first Air Corps pilots to be introduced to the YG-1 autogyros and was selected as a Lieutenant to manage the new helicopter development programs. He remained in the role throughout the war, managing acquisition of all helicopter types and participating in the flight testing of each. *National Museum of the United States Air Force*

Carry-over (Kellett XG-1B, YG-1C, XR-2 and XR-3)

As the war began overseas and America prepared for possible conflict, the USAAC looked again at rotorcraft. Another attempt to develop a practical helicopter was begun as part of a national endeavor, but it would clearly be some time before it yielded fieldable results. In the meantime, the latest autogyro technology could be evaluated to remain abreast of maturing rotorcraft technology. By this time, Materiel Division had assigned Captain H. Frank Gregory as its rotary-wing project officer. With progressive promotions, Gregory would continue in this capacity until the end of the war. He had been a pilot assigned to adopting the YG-1Bs into the service.

In 1939 Kellett was contracted to further modify the YG-1C (37-378) as the XR-2, with a jump capability and a 300hp (224kW) Jacobs seven-cylinder R-915-1 turning a constant-speed Hamilton Standard prop, and fitted with improved rotor starter transmission. Collective pitch was increased to 9 degrees for jump, and the maximum speed went up to 120mph (193km/h). Tapered rotor blades were adopted with a 'constant center of pressure' and attached with a tension-torsion rod method. A rubber rotor mount reduced the vibration transmitted to the stick and the source

of pilot fatigue. The outrigger landing gear was also replaced with a clean cantilever 'high travel' arrangement. It appears that some of the modifications for this XR-2 were added through a series of contract changes to bring the total to approximately $80,000.[4]

Flying began in January 1940 with the flexible engine mount, rotor-starter, and accelerated take-off gear. It came to an end on 21 February when a crack-up followed a bad take-off. During repairs the R-915-1 with a constant-speed prop was installed. Testing in this configuration had only just begun when another take-off accident ensued owing to a failure of the rotor clutch to release. Repaired yet again with all planned features added, the XR-2 was then destroyed on 11 November 1941 during a rotor 'rev-up' test owing to ground resonance.

One can learn even from a failure, and so it was in this case, with resources expended for work at Kellett and NACA to understand and prevent the ground resonance phenomenon that seemed to be exacerbated by higher rotor speeds. The results would benefit rotorcraft projects that followed, but were immediately applied to another YG-1B in the form of a stiffer rotor pylon and inter-blade dampers. Known as the XG-1B, the results remained mixed.[5]

During 1940 the USAAC set out to perform tests of current autogyro features using existing YG-1B airframes. The XR-2 'jump giro' represented the most current rotary-wing technology at the time to include the simplified cantilevered landing gear strut and power shaft running directly to the rotor head. Here it is seen before and after being wrecked prior to delivery owing to a violent ground resonance event. *Left National Museum of the United States Air Force/below left National Archives*

Under a 29 June 1940 contract that ran to $52,548, yet another YG-1B (37-380) was bailed back to Kellett for modification as a 'jump gyro', and with cyclic pitch control in place of direct control. The blades were tapered and a 225hp (168kW) R-755-3 fitted, possessing an improved rotor starter. The 'flexible' rotor hub (probably meaning that it was rubber-mounted) was also designed to further ease the stick vibration issue.[6]

The aircraft was delivered to Kellett in October 1940 and the modifications were apparently protracted. This XR-3 then became a testbed for resolution of the ground resonance and vibration problems that were seen as the greatest impediment to safety and operational utility. This occupied it throughout most of 1942 while the new rotor hub was completed in August and bench-tested. Refinement continued until the new rotor was installed on the aircraft in June 1943. The initial flight in this configuration was on 23 November, after which the USAAF accepted the machine. Remarkable progress had been made, with the stick free of vibrations and control very smooth. However, response was sluggish in some regimes and the autogyro appeared to be neutrally stable in others.

While generally advancing the rotary wing aircraft state-of-the-art, these projects also lent confidence that there might be promise in further evaluation of production-representative militarized autogyros.

Another early war experimental rotorcraft was the XR-3 (again derived from a YG-1B), possessing jump capability, and cyclic rotor articulation replacing the tilting head. It was put through its paces for data collection. The enclosure above the rotor is a camera for filming blade behaviour in support of a helicopter development program.
National Archives

Foreign dalliance (Pitcairn PA-39)

Facing the ruinous U-boat scourge, Great Britain needed a shipborne submarine-spotting aircraft when convoys were beyond range of shore-based patrol airplanes. The direct-lift jump autogyro was a natural choice for this mission, as it could be made available with little delay and flown off small platforms affixed to freighters' decks. Additionally, the RAF might need replacements for the autogyros devoted to the coastal early warning radar calibration mission. The local Cierva Autogiro Company was already saturated with other war production, so the UK turned to America.

The British Purchasing Commission included RAF Wing Commander Reginald 'Reggie' Brie, who was an accomplished autogyro pilot and a personal friend of Harold Pitcairn. Brie approached Pitcairn in late 1940 with the notion of a naval autogyro employing technology demonstrated in the one-off PA-36 'jump gyro'. The Royal Navy (RN) expressed a desire for fifty PA-34s, but this was met with discouragement from the US Navy.[7] The RAF persevered with a cautionary seven unique PA-39 jump autogyros with direct control (BW828/34), ordered on 5 November 1940. Because the United States was already moving to a wartime economy, original manufacture presented manifold problems for a quick reaction on a commercial contract. Instead, these were PA-18 machines purchased from private owners and reworked with PA-36 features. The inactive Pitcairn Autogiro Company was reorganized as the Pitcairn-Larsen Autogiro Company with long-time associate Agnew Larsen partnering.

The modifications to the PA-18s saw the wings discarded, the empennage replaced, a direct-control rotor installed with its collective pitch, and the engine swapped for a 175hp (131kW) Warner 165-D Super Scarab fitted with a constant-speed propeller. The collective control hydraulically set the step-tapered blades to 3.5 degrees on command after spin-up to 285rpm. Like the PA-36, the 'upside-down' stick for direct control was replaced by a wheel at the end of a control column that moved fore and aft for longitudinal pitching of the rotor, and turned for lateral tilting. The resulting PA-39 could jump to 25 feet (8 meters).

First flown in February 1941, all the Royal Air Force PA-39s were completed before the close of the year. Five were delivered in the second half of 1941 to Norfolk, Virginia, for shipment to Canada and then on to England. Another (possibly BW832) was retained in Willow Grove for additional testing as follow-on orders were anticipated. The seventh machine was also held in the US under RN supervision for pilot instruction and testing. Three aircraft were damaged in Canada during January 1942 before loading (BW228/30), owing to suspected sabotage.[8] The two (BW833/4) that did arrive were evaluated but set aside after a weak component was identified in the rotor drive system.[9] The machines did not go into service and no further purchases were made.

The example PA-39 remaining in the US was employed by Brie in further testing to include trials in May 1942, with take-off and landings from ships like that intended for sea operations. This included operations from a 40 by 90-foot (12 by 27-meter) deck on the stern of the British SS *Empire*

Pitcairn-Larsen Autogiro PA-39 characteristics

Rotor diameter	42.3ft (12.9m)
– therefore	
No. of rotor blades	3
Length	20.4ft (6.2m)
Height	10.0ft (30.4m)
Fuel	20.4 gallons (77.2 liters)
Climb rate, best	933fpm (284mpm)
Service ceiling	14,500ft (4,420m)
Weight, empty	1,340lb (608kg)
Weight, max	1,946lb (883kg)
Speed, max	117mph (188km/h)
Speed, slow flight	22mph (35km/h)
Range (83mph)	205 miles (330km)

The UK was one of the few nations to employ autogyros in military service at the dawn of the Second World War. The U-boat menace in the Atlantic brought forth the idea of flying them off platforms on merchantmen to scout for submarines. To this end, Pitcairn assembled seven PA-39s for the British, but only two made it to the island (this example lost to suspected sabotage before it reached the UK), and there was no follow-up given the advent of the helicopter. *National Museum of the United States Air Force*

Mersey, as well as aboard the escort carrier HMS *Avenger* in Long Island Sound and the Chesapeake Bay.

Another go (Kellett XO-60 and YO-60, and AGA XO-61 and YO-61)

By the time of America's entry into the Second World War it appeared the two-seat liaison airplanes' limited ability to take off and land on roads and other areas in short distances might soon be trumped by the helicopter's vertical operation feature. The jump take-off demonstrated by some autogyros, especially the PA-36, with which the Army was now acquainted, offered a potentially shorter path to the direct-lift capabilities it sought with familiar if maligned hardware. While possessing a very constrained vertical capability, the 'jump gyro' might present some advantages over liaison/observation machines and the Army Ground Forces were pushing for the technology to be explored further. The nation's former autogyro companies were producing none of their wares in support of the war effort. Consequently, characteristics were drafted in mid-1941

This pair of photographs shows one of only two G & A YO-61 'jump gyros' completed. The pusher configuration offered superior vision for the observer in the forward seat and also forced the then rare tricycle gear arrangement, but produced engine cooling problems. The aircraft never advanced to the service trials stage before the contract was cancelled. *National Archives*

and the USAAF solicited proposals from Kellett and Pitcairn-Larsen for a jump-capable autogyro that would meet observation mission requirements. It already had designs in hand following a 1940 competition that led to a helicopter program (see later). Both were placed on contract for prototypes as Project MX-156 and 157.

The PA-36 and PA-39 efforts had been money-losers for Pitcairn, which had twice essentially abandoned the field.[10] The small company changed its name to the A.G.A. Aviation Corporation (standing for Autogyros, Gliders and Airplanes) on 11 October 1941 to appeal to a wider potential customer base. While hundreds of CG-4A gliders were built there, their clean-sheet-designed gliders were too ambitious and failed, with nothing flown. On 25 August 1942 the name was changed again to G & A Aircraft Incorporated because of a similarity to another business, and 'Autogyros' was dropped, being out of favor.* Yet the new autogyro contract was dated 22 November 1941.

The proposed aircraft had already acquired a PA-44 designation as the last Pitcairn design. The renamed firm was to construct a static test article and six XO-61s with 225hp (168kW) R-755-1 engines. The order was soon changed to one XO-61 (42-13611) and five YO-61s (42-13612/6) taking 300hp (224kW) R-915-3 engines turning a Hamilton Standard constant-speed propeller with a diameter of 102 inches (25.9cm).

The autogyro had an unusual tricycle gear and pusher configuration (though not the first), with the tail plane on booms on either side of the propeller. The engines on autogyros are typically tilted down such that the trust line passes through the vertical CG – unusually high for an aircraft due to the rotor.

* The company was acquired in 1943 as a division of the Firestone Tire & Rubber Company.

The short distance between the engine and rotor mast of the YO-61 meant that the engine was more steeply tilted than usual. Wind tunnel testing was required to determine the optimal fin design for suitable directional stability. The XO-61 mock-up inspection was conducted on 15 October 1941.

Perhaps only one or two were competed, the first in spring 1943 and likely with a 325hp (242kW) R-915-A4. Only a single YO-61 has been observed in photographs. It first flew on 7 April 1943 but encountered an unstable speed range during a tethered ground 'rev-up' that caused the pylon braces to fail and damaged the rotor. The company had also run into other mechanical difficulties and deficient directional stability. While the pusher layout permitted an unobstructed plex enclosure for the pilot and observer, the engine suffered cooling challenges and never delivered the power sought. Resolution of these problems proved protracted and contract overruns were also racked up for a total expenditure of $912,984.32.[11] By the end of 1943 the Army lost interest in the project. Although 75 hours' flight time had been logged, none of the aircraft were delivered or subjected to service trials. The contract was cancelled in late January 1944.

G & A YO-61 characteristics

Rotor diameter – therefore	48.0ft (14.6m)
No. of rotor blades	3
Length, overall	39.0ft (11.9m)
Height	12.0ft (3.7m)
Fuel	33 gallons (125 liters)
Take-off over 50ft	250ft (76m)
Landing over 50ft	250ft (76m)
Climb rate, best	625fpm (191mpm)
Service ceiling	11,000ft (3,353m)
Weight, empty	2,340lb (1,061kg)
Weight, max	3,038lb (1,378kg)
Speed, max	103mph (166km/h)
Speed, slow flight	29mph (47km/h)
Endurance	2hr

The forward end of the YO-60's front cockpit is busy with levers that had to be operated in the correct sequence to avoid disaster. The parking brake had to be set and the cyclic stick locked forward before starting and during initial rotor spin-up. The clutch was then disengaged and the cyclic released and pulled aft and to starboard for the jump take-off. *National Museum of the United States Air Force*

Kellett built the XO-60 as another version of the KD-1A that had been the basis for the YG-1B. The principal external difference was the enclosed canopy and windows in the floor. The 330hp (246kW) R-915-3 engine turned a Hamilton Standard constant-speed propeller with a diameter of 8.5 feet (2.6 meters). Internally, the pilot was moved to the front seat and provided rotor collective control. The observer's seat could pivot so he could face aft over a small table. Each blade was tapered and had a fixed trailing-edge tab near the tip for trim. The welcome feature of rotor blade folding, common to all Kellett autogyros, was retained. Features easing disassembly simplified potential overseas shipment.

The design was reworked with Kellett's spin-up jump system of the YG-1C, although with many improvements introduced based on the XR-2 and XG-1B experience. When the spin-up clutch was release, counterweights were also released that automatically moved the blades from feather to an 8-degree pitch. When the rpm dropped back to that for normal forward flight, the blades naturally returned to the typical 3 degrees. The take-off process was complex and if not performed precisely could lead to unfortunate consequences. During rotor spin-up, the cyclic stick was locked forward near the instrument panel to prevent it whipping about at less than 200rpm. The clutch was then disengaged and the collective handle released. The stick was held aft in preparation for maximum translation lift and to starboard to counter any residual torque.

Before the Kellett XO-60 had flown it was selected for a service evaluation run of one XO-60 and six YO-60s (42-13610 and 42-13604/9 respectively), plus a static article. This was codified in a 19 November 1941 contract that eventually reached an outlay of $483,026.10. The first machine was completed in February 1943 and the last delivered by the end of the year (accepted by April 1944). The manufacturer changed its name to the Kellett Aircraft Corporation in June and eventually established a new residence in North Wales, Pennsylvania. The XO-60, delivered last, had a cantilever main landing gear like the XR-2, while the YO-60s had the common braced gear. YO-60 42-13605 was severely damage on 27 June 1943 before delivery when the jump setting was accidentally tripped while the cyclic was still locked at the forward stop. It was not repaired.

In a secret program, the aircraft were put through their paces in Orlando, Florida, at the Air Forces School of Applied Tactics by the 445th Test Squadron.[12] They were then thoroughly evaluated in combat exercises. Lessons included the care required to keep the rotor balanced, preventing heavy vibrations, by adjusting the trim tabs before flight. The YO-60 was judged too complex and fragile to fly as a field liaison, as well as being costly, for a marginal advantage over light airplanes.

Kellett YO-60 characteristics

Rotor diameter (XO-60)	42.0ft (12.8m)
Rotor diameter (YO-60)	43.2ft (13.2m)
– therefore	
No. of rotor blades	3
Length, blades folded	25.9ft (7.9m)
Height	10.3ft (3.1m)
Fuel	34 gallons (129 liters)
Take-off over 50ft	250ft (76m)
Landing over 50ft	50ft (15m)
Climb rate, best	1,150fpm (350mpm)
Service ceiling	19,000ft (3,353m)
Weight, empty	1,960lb (889kg)
Weight, max	2,640lb (1,198kg)
Speed, max	127mph (204km/h)
Speed, slow flight	30mph (48km/h)
Range (103mph)	217 miles (349km)
Endurance	2hr

The Army's long association with the Kellett autogyros ended with the YO-60 'jump gyro', yet another evolution of the KD-1. A single XO-60 and six YO-60s were evaluated for potential work in place of liaison light airplanes, but were found to have few advantages to outweigh the disadvantages. The maturing helicopter rendered them anachronistic. *National Museum of the United States Air Force*

For vertical flight performance, controllability and safety, the maturing helicopter rendered the autogyros anachronistic. General Arnold had already decided in June 1942 not to pursue autogyro production for these reasons (based on early XR-4 testing and Colonel Gregory's judgment), even before the Kellett and G & A machines had flown.[13] This suggests that the entire effort had been a means of placating the Ground Forces for a period while the helicopter advanced to the point of pilot production. Additionally, it was assessed that Sikorsky (see later) had greater capacity to rapidly enter large-scale rotorcraft production than either of the autogyro firms. The contracts were cancelled, spelling the end of the line for the autogyro in military service. The YO-60s were subsequently sent to Texas to fly border patrols, and all but one expired in crack-ups.

This YO-60 was probably photographed during border patrol work in Texas, likely in 1944. This was the last operational US military use of autogyros. The pinnacle of autogyro technology, the type remained a challenge to fly and had a poor safety record. *National Museum of the United States Air Force*

CHAPTER EIGHT

Helicopters Leap Ahead

Army initial strides

IN THE LATE 1930S concern was raised in the US over the progress made in Germany with helicopters. The Focke-Achgelis Fw 61, with twin lateral-tandem rotors, broke records in a flurry of performances during 1937 and 1938. Hovering and translating in all directions with precision, it showed that the problems of the helicopter could be solved. It was known that a helicopter with twin intermeshed rotors, the Flettner Fl 265, had also flown. After start of the war, word of helicopter progress in Germany ceased or was unreliable.

The sensation of the German success with helicopters, and the general discomfort with its rearmament and bellicose Nazi rhetoric, created urgency in fostering American aviation advancement. Congress passed the Dorsey Bill on 30 June 1938 (the Dorsey-Logan Act when signed by President Roosevelt on 1 August), which authorized $2 million to boost development of rotorcraft. However, the wording of the bill said "and other aircraft development" to permit some freedom if and when the funds were actually appropriated. Nearly a year later the appropriations bill had just $300,000. Although many branches of government and the War Department were consulted in this undertaking, the House Appropriations Committee had specified

that the Army would be the lead agency. At a 31 May 1939 meeting at the office of the Chief of the Air Corps, which included senior Navy and Coast Guard service members and representatives of other government departments, it was decided that the USAAC would spend the money on developing an experimental helicopter. No mission goals were set, but some general requirements and evaluation methods were selected. It was recognized by those involved in this development that the helicopter was as immature as the airplane was in its first decade, and that expectations had to be held to realistic objectives.

The Army issued its draft specification on 10 June 1939, approved on 25 August. A Circular Proposal was released soon after, seeking solicitations to build and fly a single experimental helicopter. This lacked detailed specifications apart from general performance requirements for a two-seat machine with the ability to take off vertically and clear a 50-foot (15.2-meter) obstacle.[1] The competition brought forth many unsolicited

The first American helicopter development program of the war (before US entry) was under Army sponsorship and employed the lateral tandem rotor layout that the Germans had demonstrated successfully. The new firm of Platt-LePage struggled with the project, flying the prototype XR-1 late and with numerous problems. This angle on the machine, early in its existence, reveals the ground-adjustable empennage surfaces. *National Archives*

proposals from design teams and hobbyists. When the formal proposals were opened on 15 April 1940, one was dismissed outright and four substantial submittals evaluated in detail. The contenders were Kellett and Pitcairn with autogyros, and Platt-LePage and Vought-Sikorsky with helicopters. Estimates ranged from more than $400,000 to just under $200,000. The evaluation board met on 27-28 May and reported on the 28th, with the Pratt-LePage design judged superior.

A single $199,075 contract was subsequently issued on 19 June 1940 to Platt-LePage for a single XR-1 prototype (MX-167) and a static test article for delivery on 1 January 1941. The fact that this design had a lateral tandem twin-rotor layout like that of the successful Fw 61 was a significant consideration.

While these moves were being made, another avenue of progress appeared via a Russian immigrant in Connecticut. Igor I. Sikorsky had left his mark in large, multi-engine airplanes, most recently with the United Aircraft Corporation. With recent advances in rotorcraft technology, he saw an opportunity to bring his helicopter aspirations to life and convinced the corporation to fund development of an experimental helicopter to explore potential control solutions. This began with a rotor ground test rig wherein methodical tests could be made with rapid flight control design changes. Likewise, the single-seat, single-main-rotor VS-300 helicopter was a flying test rig with a 75hp (56kW) engine, in which design changes could be made quickly and fresh data collected. Although initially employing both collective and cyclic rotor pitch, the latter proved unsatisfactory and was temporarily abandoned for attitude control with collective control of various auxiliary rotors at the aft end of the craft.

The VS-300 first flew tethered in 14 September 1939, then made a free flight on 13 May 1940. It would ultimately have four major reconfigurations, eighteen functional changes, and numerous small alterations as the team converged on the most promising solutions through careful testing and a few accidents. Captain Gregory and members of the Materiel

Division rotary-wing staff followed this progress with keen interest, examining Sikorsky's work at various stages, and were also permitted to fly the helicopter. The machine operated so effortlessly and under such precise control, repeatedly breaking records, that no one could deny the helicopter had come of age – well ahead of the XR-1 and without Army financing. The defense build-up offered the opportunity to exploit this progress.

Gregory consulted the inter-agency board and there was agreement to seek the remaining Dorsey Bill appropriations to fund an Army prototype spin-off of the Sikorsky work. At a 17 December 1940 meeting in Washington, D.C., senior members of the responsible government agencies approved a proposal drafted by Vought-Sikorsky for a parallel prototype observation-trainer. They endorsed helicopter development by another team, with a different design approach, as a hedge against failure of the XR-1. No specifications were levied, but performance goals were set such as a weight not to exceed 2,000lb (907kg), a useful load of more than 549lb (249kg), hovering under good control, vertical take-off and landing over a 50-foot obstacle, and all controls for longitudinal and lateral motion to be incorporated into the rotor hub. Only $50,000 was available (another $12,946.51 was added later), but Vought-Sikorsky agreed to fund a considerable portion of the effort. The company had already expended some $100,000 on the VS-300 and could expect to front another $150,000 for the Army prototype under MX-245.[2]

First steps (Platt-LePage XR-1 & XR-1A)

From the mid-1930s, Dr Wynn Laurence LePage and Havilland H. 'Hal' Platt had worked intently on detailed helicopter rotor designs and filed several patents. LePage was an Englishman long working in the US, having served as an engineer at both Pitcairn and Kellett. Platt was a gifted engineer with helicopter ambitions who had developed the first automatic transmission for cars. In early 1938 LePage observed the Fw 61 in flight during a visit to Germany. He acquired a film of the flight

By the mid-1930s Germany was rearming rapidly and devoting prodigious resources to aeronautical development. Its success in the field of helicopters was evident to the world with public displays of the Focke-Achgelis Fw 61. This revelation prompted a concerted effort at catch up in the United States. *National Archives*

demonstrations and the American manufacturing rights for the helicopter.[3] He promptly reported his observations to NACA and the Army, so was at the front of the pack when the service sought prospective contractors. Suitably encouraged, the Platt-LePage Aircraft Company was incorporated in Eddystone, Pennsylvania, in November 1938.

The partners immediately set to work designing and assembling the PL-1, which possessed the laterally displaced twin rotors and empennage of the Fw 61 but was otherwise an independent development. Their analysis showed the performance benefits of the layout. However, unlike the Focke-Achgelis helicopter, they planned to enclose the outrigger structures to the rotor hubs in an airfoil as wings (cantilevered 'pylons') to provide lift during forward flight and partially offload the rotors. This became the basis for their PL-3 design submitted in the USAAF competiton.[4] After the contract award, the PL-3 was developed as the XR-1 (41-1). Given the scope of the work and remarkably short schedule, the program ran months behind.

Unlike the Fw 61, Platt-LePage mounted the XR-1's 440hp (328kW) R-985-21 engine amidships. The rotors, 3 feet (0.9 meter) apart on the centerline, featured cyclic and collective pitch. An innovation was the incorporation in the power transmission of differential to automatically apply slightly more collective power to one rotor during a turn. Designed for observation duties, the tandem-seated crew had liberal glazing in the sliding canopy and lower quarters. Although fitted with dual control, the principal pilot station was the forward seat. What appeared to be a conventional airplane empennage consisted of ground-adjustable but not pilot-controllable

elevators and rudder. The construction was typical of aircraft of the period, including fabric covering over a welded tube frame and fixed undercarriage. The undercarriage wheels were castored so that they would not resist sideload in a sideways landing and contribute to an overturn event. While the contract very aptly funded the development, the USAAF insisted on standard accoutrements in the prototype aircraft such as radio, intercom, exterior lights, relief tube, etc. This and the detail reporting requirements of a government contract greatly burdened the infant company undertaking its first project.

Mock-up inspection took place on 26-27 September 1940. The first flight of the XR-1 was tethered, on 12 May 1941, under the control of Lou Leavitt, and unrestrained on 23 June. Many of the most serious design challenges were successfully meet, such as long drive shafts free of detrimental vibrations, a successful transmission, and engine cooling. Despite being a bit heavier than anticipated, there was generous excess power. However, longitudinal and lateral control deficiencies together with resonant vibrations greatly slowed progress as multiple alterations were introduced. The differential tended to produce uncommanded roll that promoted control reversal and pilot-induced oscillations. Excessive control sensitivity as the machine began to move forward at 5-10mph (8-16km/h) was a matter of great concern, making Leavitt extremely cautious and contributing to the desperately slowing progress. The breakout moment came when Colonel Gregory took the ship up on 9 June 1943, accelerated smartly through the sensitive speed range to 75mph (121km/h), and executed a closed course. Leavitt was so abashed by this performance, feeling that he had lost the confidence of his employer, that he promptly left the company.

Vought-Sikorsky built and tested the VS-300 from 1939 until 1941 as a testbed exploring helicopter control techniques. Once the firm had a contract for an Army helicopter prototype, the VS-300A became a means of converging on the best layout for that design. Among the final steps along that path was this late-1941 configuration, with Les Morris at the controls, which still had a horizontal tail rotor for pitch control until full cyclic was reintroduced to the main rotor. *National Archives*

Later in the career of the XR-1 the tail gear shows changes, but many alterations of the control system had been affected. The helicopter appears to have always flown without panels on the lower half of the forward fuselage. Although development continued after a crash, the focus shifted to a greatly revised version. *National Archives*

Despite two years of work, the controllability issues lingered. The static article had also suffered a failure during testing of the tail, requiring modifications. The firm's inexperience was evident, evincing more of a trial-and-error approach to development, and it was unable to hire the necessary skilled and knowledgeable personnel given wartime demand. Funding was also difficult despite increases to the contract amount, so the company took on subcontracting work.

On 4 July 1943 a preliminary installation of fairings about the blade roots at the hubs was mistakenly flown prematurely. One came loose and caused the separation of one blade. Although pilot Jim Ray managed to get the ship down, albeit badly damaged, he suffered a back injury from the severe vibrations and hard landing.

Although repaired and returned to flight on 1 August 1944, the XR-1 appeared a lost cause without profound design changes. These came by way of a 26 April 1941 proposal. The Army decided on 28 July to pursue this after the XR-1 had flown. The XR-1A was born with a $144,662 contract on 29 October for another prototype (42-6581). This was hastened by using the static test airframe as a starting point.[5] Substantial changes to the rotor system were introduced and the CG was further aft. The most evident changes were the formed plexiglass nose enclosure, displacement of the pilot to the aft seat, and fairings around the rotor hubs. Engine power was increased to 450hp (336 kW) with the R-985-AN-1. A mock-up was inspected at the beginning of November.

Completion of the XR-1A was held in abeyance while the cause of the XR-1 accident was investigated and corrective measures taken. It flew tethered on 27 October 1943 and freely in December, soon reaching an altitude of 300 feet (91 meters). Instead of shipping the helicopter, it was flown to Dayton after Gregory was convinced of the practicality by coming to Eddystone and flying it above 500 feet (152 meters) and at more than 135mph (217km/h). The delivery occurred in June 1944 (arriving on the 20th) with pilot Buck Miller and a mechanic on board. Accepting the aircraft on 15 August, the Rotary Branch of the Air Technical Service Command then undertook testing at Wright Field.

The XR-1's altered control system had, in the meantime, shown promise. Although the two machines were found to possess improved flight characteristics, control was still poor. Longitudinal control during transition to forward flight was particularly deficient, with notable lag in cyclic response. Although smoother to control, the XR-1A's response was sluggish, it retained issues in the lateral axis, the collective pitch control was inadequate, and it had uncomfortable vibrations. Rotor downwash on the wings sacrificed hover performance. Yet a letter contract was issued in January 1944 for seven YR-1A aircraft, the same as the XR-1A save for change from a 12-volt to a 24-volt electrical system. The formalized $1,096,455.36 contract followed in October, with the first helicopter due in January 1945. This action may have been partially to placate members of Congress who saw favoritism in the generous helicopter contracts going principally to Sikorsky, who was dominating Army purchases. However, the struggling Platt-LePage simply lacked the means to fulfill the contract.

The XR-1A was gravely damaged on 26 October 1944 at Wright Field, owing to a hub mechanical failure and the starboard rotor striking the ground. It was returned to the manufacturer but repairs were interrupted by the end of the war. The XR-1 was evaluated again on 21-22 March 1945 and, while finding some improvement, azimuth control was still considered unsuitable and there was considerable vibration, particularly in turns. The future of the helicopter had been

An improved Platt-LePage machine was funded in the hope of resolving many of the more serious deficiencies. However, the XR-1A, most easily identified by the revised forward enclosure, was still beset by controllability issues after four years of development, and was therefore dropped. Note the addition of a second strut under the horizontal stabilizers and fairings around the rotor hubs.
National Archives

Platt-LePage XR-1 and XR-1A characteristics

Rotor diameter	30.5ft (9.3m)
– therefore	
No. of rotor blades	3 each
Span	64.0ft (19.5m)
Length, overall	35.0ft (10.7m)
Height (XR-1)	8.8ft (2.7m)
Fuel (XR-1)	100 gallons (379 liters)
Weight, empty (XR-1)	4,030lb (1,828kg)
Weight, loaded (XR-1)	5,200lb (2,359kg)
Weight, loaded (XR-1A)	5,300lb (2,404kg)
Climb rate, best (XR-1)	1,000fpm (305mpm)
Service ceiling (XR-1)	16,000ft (4,877m)
Speed, max (XR-1)	110mph (177km/h)
Speed, max (XR-1A)	100mph (161km/h)
Range	400 miles (644km)

The XR-1A continued to suffer controllability issues through years of development. It paled in comparison to the Sikorsky models and a modest production order was eventually set aside. While the laterally displaced twin rotors appeared the approach of least technological risk when the program was initiated, this image shows the considerable width of the helicopter, requiring a much greater operating area than the single-rotor Sikorskys.
National Archives

sealed by the marked success of the Sikorsky models and there was dissatisfaction with Platt-LePage's performance. On 7 April 1945 efforts began to close out the long-running contracts that amounted to $560,518.60 for the XR-1, and $327,580.92 for the XR-1A. The XR-1A was bailed to the firm for further development as a commercial product, but that proved stillborn. Flight testing ceased in 1946 and Platt-LePage did not continue long beyond that point.

Winner takes all (Sikorsky R-4, R-5, R-6, R-7)

The second Army prototype helicopter was to be a two-place Vought-Sikorsky aircraft more suitable for military missions than the VS-300 but directly derived from that machine. Fortunately, the company was well acquainted with War Department contracts and its team highly experienced. The letter contract for the XR-4 (41-18874) was signed on 17 December 1940 and the formal contract let on 10 January 1941.

The original design of the XR-4 reflected one of the early successful configurations of the VS-300 with a main rotor possessing collective control only and three tail rotors. The latter consisted of a horizontal rotor on each side of the centerline for pitch and roll, and one vertical for countering main rotor torque, all with collective pitch. In forward flight the main rotor downwash on the tail units disrupted fine control. Although not intentionally working to avoid duplicating the Harold Pitcairn patented cyclic pitch control approach, Sikorsky's configuration changes had moved away from features like main rotor cyclic, which had been the initial design. However, the Army urged him to return to that solution, referencing Pitcairn's work and negotiating a licence.[6] Consequently, the VS-300 went through a further series of modifications, initially with partial main rotor cyclic for lateral control, a horizontal tail rotor on the centerline for pitch, and a vertical anti-torque rotor. It also got a 90hp (67kW) Franklin engine turning the 30-foot (9.1-meter) rotor, and the helicopter, with a gross weight of 1,150lb (522kg), was reregistered as the VS-300A (NX28996). The next step was returning to full cyclic in summer 1941 and elimination of the tail pitch rotor. Translated to the XR-4, all this greatly reduced the weight and complexity of the machine while improving stability and control, making it a more suitable military asset. This testing greatly facilitated Sikorsky's progress with rotor control while the XR-4 was in detail design and construction. About halfway through the XR-4 fabrication the new control layout was adopted, and several weeks were taken for reworking.

The XR-4 (Model VS-316) had full dual controls with line-abreast seating, putting the crew mass closer to the CG. It retained the most successful configuration of the VS-300 with a single three-blade main rotor with a diameter of 36 feet (11.0 meters) and an anti-torque tail rotor. Geared to the rpm of the main rotor via a long power shaft, the tail rotor automatically countered the torque but typically consumed 10 percent of the available power. Moving the pedals changed the pitch on the tail rotor blades to cause a change in thrust to one side or the other and swing the tail for directional control or to counter main rotor torque during power adjustments and resisting a heading change. Usually any change in main rotor lift/power required a compensating pedal input. The tapered main rotor blades were a riveted steel tube section spar with wood ribs and fabric covering. The three tail rotor blades were all wood. The fuselage was a welded steel tube truss with fabric covering. Initial plans to use a Franklin 125hp (93kW) engine was set aside for a seven-cylinder Warner R-500-3 Super Scarab of 165hp (123 kW) buried amidships.[7] It was cooled by a ventilator that drew air in through an opening ahead of the tail rotor. There were "basic provisions for carrying external litter or bomb racks".[8]

The US military's first successful helicopter, the Sikorsky XR-4, flew in January 1942 (shown here during an early test flight), little more than thirteen months after award of the contract. It quickly showed the promise of the type but underwent steady improvement as the Army sought a combat capability to go with the hovering and slow-flight maneuvering antics. This would take to the end of the war, with only a few machines performing a handful of non-violent combat missions during the conflict. *National Museum of the United States Air Force*

The XR-4 emerged in late December 1941 and Charles L. 'Les' Morris took it up for the first time on 14 January 1942. The craft had covering only around the crew stations and the tail wheel was also below the tail rotor until later moved forward. The usual corrections and refinements quickly converged on a practical if limited helicopter. Tests progressed apace to include full engine-off autorotation to a landing on 3 April. Tests were also performed in February with a rudder installed, but this proved unsatisfactory.[9] With only 9½ hours logged, the machine was demonstrated to government officials on 20 April. This included lifting straight up to 500 feet (152 meters), flight to 5,000 feet (1,524 meters), precision control exercises, gently lifting and delivering minor loads, telephone communications, and a man boarding and exiting the hovering helicopter by rope ladder.

This was clearly the most promising of the helicopters under development, and the Army moved immediately to exploit the advance. Although a rudimentary and very limited helicopter by today's standards, the XR-4 stood head and shoulders above anything seen to that time in terms of controllability, performance and practicality. It demonstrated this by flying a delivery flight on 13-17 May from Stratford to Dayton, with sixteen stops over 761 miles (1,225km) and a flight time of 16hr 10min. Subsequent delivery flights went over the mountains and took just over a day with 9hr 30min. The XR-4 was demonstrated to General Arnold on 7 July and passed the 100-flight-hours mark on the 24th.

The top speed of the 2,450lb (1,111kg) – design gross – helicopter was 80mph (129km/h) and flight to 12,000 feet (3,658 meters) was demonstrated. Yet at maximum gross on a hot day at the 800-foot (244-meter) Wright Field, the aircraft struggled to get airborne. Doors and radios would be removed, only partial fuel loaded, and careful choice of pilots by weight was occasionally necessary. Even under the best of circumstances the helicopter could seldom hover out of ground effect. Control was not crisp, the pilot needing to make constant small corrections, and vibrations, especially in the cyclic stick, were uncomfortably persistent. The industry had much to learn yet about building fine helicopters, to include uniform rotor blade construction and dynamic balance.[10] Once military observers got past the wonder of an aircraft hovering and translating precisely, their thoughts naturally turned to how it could contribute to their missions.

Wright Field flight testing began almost immediately. Among these was checking the aircraft's potential as a 'bomber'. This began with the observer lobbing a 25lb (11.3kg) bomb from his lap out of the door while the pilot hovered a few hundred feet over the outline of a submarine chalked on the ground. The best results were actually achieved while passing over at 40mph (64km/h), employing a simple bombsight, with a rack of five of the small bombs affixed under the fuselage. The ability to carry and accurately deliver a depth charge was judged confirmed. In late August or early September pneumatic rubber float pontoons were fitted. Some ground resonance was encountered, but was avoided by making a quick and positive take-off and landing. Water operations were then performed. The XR-4 completed its tests on 5 January 1943, by which time the country was at war and everything moved more quickly.

The type was ready for service trials, for which fifteen YR-4As (Model VS-316A) were ordered on 21 December 1942 for an eventual $3,528,726.98. This was soon altered to three YR-4As (42-107234/6) and twenty-seven YR-4Bs (42-107237/48, 43-28223/35, 43-28247, and 43-47953 for static testing). All had the R-500-1 at 180hp (134kW) and a 38-foot (11.6-meter) rotor. Instead of the engine exhausting from the bottom of the fuselage, where it might start a grass fire, the new ships had side exhausts with the pipes extending up the fuselage. The fuselage was revised to include an extended top fairing closer to the rotor hub. The opening near the end of the tail boom was eliminated in favor of air drawn in at the front of the top fairing by a fan that directed it down onto the engine and out of the bottom of the fuselage. The tail wheel and support structure was moved farther aft to help ensure against a tail rotor strike in a severe tail-down attitude during autorotation landing. Fuel capacity was increased by 5 gallons (19 liters) and radio gear added. The YR-4Bs are credited with provisions for external litter or bomb racks, and float pontoons could replace the wheeled undercarriage.[11] The changes brought the weight up to 2,535lb (1,150kg) and performance fell off to a maximum 75mph (121km/h). The features were initially tested on the original experimental machine after modification in 1943 as the XR-4C.

The first YR-4A took flight at Stratford on 3 May 1943 and was delivered on 3 July; the final YR-4B was handed over on 14 April 1944. Three YR-4Bs went on to the US Navy and seven to the Royal Navy as Hoverfly Is. The helicopter was displayed publicly for the first time on 16 May 1943 during an event at the nation's capital.

Tests included shipboard work on 6-7 May 1943, initially with the XR-4C operating from a wooden landing deck measuring 60 by 78 feet (18.3 by 23.8 meters) fitted to the tanker SS *Bunker Hill*. The tests were conducted in Long Island Sound, just offshore of the Sikorsky facility at Stratford. The helicopter wore the pontoon undercarriage, but Morris had added wooden cross-members to help reduce bouncing on landing.[12] The *Bunker Hill* was not the ideal vessel for the tests as the platform was built near the fantail between the pilot house and a mast, together with stays, leaving a margin of just 14 feet (4.3 meters) fore and aft, with the helicopter in the center of the deck. This forced the helicopters to approach from the gunwales and translate over the deck, and the reverse on departing. Colonel Gregory flew twenty take-offs and landings from the ship, both at anchor and sailing at 15 knots, and with various wind azimuths, but all with moderate seas. The air burbles off the superstructure added to the difficulty, but all was accomplished safely. Unlike the PA-39 demonstration a year before, from which Gregory had come away judging that only a highly experience autogyro pilot could accomplish the feat and only into the wind with a proper ship's heading, the helicopter offered much less difficulty and fewer restrictions.

Many of the officials observing the demonstration that day aboard the *Bunker Hill* came away with visions of helicopters aboard ships helping convoys detect and evade or attack submarines without the aid of the few and costly aircraft carriers. In particular, fast troop ships that did not travel in convoys were expected to benefit from the airborne eyes in areas of the Atlantic crossing beyond the range of land-based airplanes. This potential was further explored in tests aboard

The reworked XR-4C is shown operating from the SS *Bunker Hill* while fitted with pneumatic floats. The considerable change to the landing gear struts to accommodate the floats is clear. Although appearing ungainly, the positive handling of the helicopter was not impeded during the very successful demonstration on the ship's added aircraft deck. *San Diego Air & Space Museum*

the troop ship SS *James Parker*, which had a trapezoidal deck measuring roughly 40-50 by 62 feet (12.2-15.2 by 18.9 meters) installed on the fantail, large enough to accommodate two R-4s simultaneously. The XR-4C on floats and a YR-4 on its wheels participated in the tests on 7-8 July 1943. They operated in weather that would have grounded airplanes, with rough seas and 40mph (64km/h) winds.

The Sikorsky aircraft appeared practical and the first series production of a helicopter in the United States was initiated with approval of the Authorization for Purchase on 26 May 1943, followed by a 6 February 1944 contract for 100 R-4Bs (43-46500/99) at $4,595,806.46. Great Britain contemplated an order of 150 to 240 R-4Bs.[13] A factory in Bridgeport, a few miles from Stratford, was converted for helicopter production so as not to interfere with higher-priority Vought F4U fighter production. Unlike other wartime aviation endeavors, United Aircraft again invested its own money in preparing for production in anticipation of orders.

The first R-4B was handed over on 22 June 1944 and the last on 7 September. They mounted the 200hp (149kW) uprated Warner R-550-3s and with further changes to the aft fuselage (likely by alterations in the tail rotor drive shaft mounting) that included eliminating a step ahead of the angle change to the tail rotor structure, increasing the clearance with the main rotor. Apparently there had been a tendency for the helicopter to nose-over, so skids were placed under the corners of the nose on many of the aircraft. Some of the helicopters had the tail wheel structure relocated to the end of the boom, just ahead of the tail rotor. As with the other models, a single collective lever was placed between the seats that otherwise had dual controls. This introduced standardization and training issues (and so safety) as the pilot had to change hands and remember the direction to twist the throttle when moving between the seats. The standard was soon a left-side collective for each pilot. The R-4B possessed greater range and could accommodate a rack of three 100lb (45kg) bombs or a litter.[14]

The Navy was given nineteen R-4Bs that went on to the Coast Guard, and Great Britain got forty-five Hoverflys via Lend-Lease, nine of which went to the RAF and the remainder to the RN, with one passed along to Canada. The RN intended to operate the helicopters on escort ships for ASW work and fit

the bomb carriage equipment. The RAF employed them for coastal radar calibration (replacing the last of its autogyros), liaison work, and VIP transport. The UK order plans were eventually greatly truncated, given the late date of anticipated delivery and a realization of the limited performance of the type.

The YR-4s were being rapidly consumed through mishaps and wear, but did serve their purpose. The Army aircraft were put through field trials, to include winter conditions in Alaska at the end of 1943. A YR-4B was transported aboard a C-46 in a disassembled state to Ladd Field, Fairbanks.[15] The helicopter flew with a framework supporting a litter on the port side covered by a collapsible canvas cover.

Tests were also performed in tropical conditions, for which Burma was selected. Four YR-4Bs were shipped east in March and April 1944 to the 1st Air Commando Group at Lalaghet, India, a special unit supporting insurgency teams against the Japanese in the forests of Burma. The unconventional unit operated an odd mix of aircraft including gliders and light planes able to get in and out of small landing strips. The leadership actively sought the helicopters but was granted only the four YR-4Bs as part of the operational trials.[16] Together with the aircraft came four pilots and four mechanics, recent graduates from Sikorsky training, and a Sikorsky service representative. One of the helicopters was destroyed in transit when the C-46 carrying it crashed. Another was destroyed soon after assembly when it hit a power line, one pilot being killed and the other seriously injured. A third pilot was wounded in an unrelated incident. The remaining helicopters and pilot were soon at work performing rescue operations that greatly challenged the limited performance, but won some acclaim. In total, twenty-three combat sorties were flown and some eighteen men lifted to safety before the machines were withdrawn, the engines showing the wear.

In an unrelated activity, the crash of a B-25 prompted the emergency shipment of another YR-4B and two pilots to Burma. From the 'go' on 18 January 1945, the helicopter was loaded into a C-54 and flown with its crew to Burma, arriving on the 22nd, only to learn that the bomber crew had already been rescued. Instead, the team flew a rescue to the top of a 4,700-foot (1,433-meter) mountain. While successful, the hot and high conditions again challenged the performance of the helicopter.[17]

A few YR-4Bs were also assigned to USAAF Aircraft Repair Units (Floating) operating in the Pacific theater. These ARU 'floaters' were depots on Liberty ships sent to areas of concentrated activities. Several of the vessels were fitted with platforms from which the helicopters served as ship-to-shore transports. Support of operations in Iwo Jima and Okinawa, together with B-29 bases in the Marianas, are most noted.

While the performance limited potential operational roles, the R-4 was a fitting introductory and training model. With the technology advancing quickly, the Army kept production to just a modest 131 machines.

Service test and production R-4s were deployed to combat zones for trials and operation. Among the most noteworthy was employment as ship-to-shore transports in the last struggles of the Pacific war, as well as rescue platforms in Burma. One of the four shipped to India for the Burmese campaign is shown under heavy maintenance in theater, supported by a Sikorsky 'tech rep'. *National Museum of the United States Air Force*

Sikorsky R-4B characteristics

Rotor diameter	38.0ft (11.6m)
– therefore	
No. of rotor blades	3
Length, overall	48.2ft (14.7m)
Height	12.4ft (3.8m)
Fuel	30 gallons (114 liters)
Weight, empty	2,020lb (916kg)
Weight, gross	2,535lb (1,150kg)
Climb rate, best	187fpm (57mpm)
Service ceiling	8,000ft (2,438m)
Speed, max	75mph (121km/h)
Range (65mph)	130 miles (209km)
Endurance, typical	1hr 25min

The production R-4B had numerous refinements that made the helicopter more practical, but it was still a marginal performer suitable for little more than training or non-combat search and rescue. The engine cooling air intake ahead of the rotor mast and the exhaust pipes below are clearly indicative of these late-model machines. Size is also evident by relation to the men in the shot. *San Diego Air & Space Museum*

While the R-4 moved to production, Sikorsky's development team was kept busy working on a type more suitable to the observation mission. This demanded a greater speed, endurance, service ceiling and payload. Although an Army program (MX-256), the XR-5 was aimed at providing capability more suitable to the Navy. The Army was hesitant to move forward because it feared it would slow the march to production of the R-4 and R-6 (see later). Nonetheless, procurement of two prototypes was sought on 8 May 1942 for an estimated $650,000. However, funding was lacking and only after transferring money from another program could a letter contract be sent on 13 June. The final contract also included two machines for British evaluation (XR-5As to include radio gear), funded via Lend-Lease, bringing the total value to just under $1 million. A mock-up was inspected on 14 August. A fifth XR-5 prototype was added on 21 December (43-28236/9, 43-47954), bringing the project value to $2,159,359.30.

The specifications called for a useful load of 1,100lb (499kg) with a gross of less than 4,000lb (1,814kg), a top speed of 120mph (193km/h), 3 hours endurance, a 5,000-foot (1,524-meter) service ceiling, and vertical take-off and landing surrounded by 50-foot (15.2-meter) obstacles. Although a spin-off of the successful R-4 configuration, the XR-5 (VS-327) was entirely new in detail design. A more aerodynamically rounded airframe was sought after it was realized that rotor downwash on the slab-topped R-4 fuselage compromised hover performance. It mounted the 450hp (336kW) R-985-AN-5 mounted horizontally and turning a 48-foot (14.6-meter) main rotor. The two crewmen sat in tandem with dual controls (save for the one collective), the pilot at the back within a streamlined nose. This had generous plexiglass, like the YO-61, and was narrower at the base to enhance downward vision. Floats could be substituted for the wheel gear. Initially intended as an all-wood aircraft, this was set aside because of

United Aircraft's lack of familiarity with the construction techniques and the growing availability of the more common aircraft materials.[18] However, design and construction of the prototypes was slowed by material shortages caused by the war. Substitute materials included a plastic-impregnated plywood monocoque tail structure, and the same material replacing some panels. The fuselage centersection with the engine and rotor mast was a welded tube truss while the cabin was the more common lightweight aircraft structure partly skinned in aluminum. The main rotor blades (which could be folded) were wooden spars and ribs with fabric covering. The tail rotor blades were all wood. There were to be provisions for bombs under the fuselage (two 325lb depth charges or six 100lb demolition bombs) or litter capsules mounted two per side. A baggage compartment had a capacity of 75lb (34kg).

The first XR-5 took to the air on 18 August 1943 at Bridgeport with Morris again doing the honors. Heavy vibration was just one of the teething issues to be resolved, but the team made rapid progress. A 13 September flight had two persons in the cabin and four sitting on each main gear strut arm to demonstrate useful load. A tail rotor disintegrated during a flight on 12 October at about 70 feet (21 meters) altitude. The pilot, Jim Viner, brought the ship down despite the torque rotation, but the helicopter was heavily damaged. While the aircraft was rebuilt, the team was without a test machine for more than a month but made steady progress thereafter. The formal government inspection was conducted on 22 February 1944.

Conceived as a more practical observation platform, the Sikorsky R-5 established a layout that became common in post-war utility helicopters before performance advances permitted proper cabins. The XR-5 shows the excellent view provided for the front-seat observer. The helicopter spent the latter half of 1943 in development tests and refinement. *San Diego Air & Space Museum*

The experimental helicopters, all delivered by 29 March 1945, were quickly followed by service test machines, with twenty-six YR-5As (43-46600/25) incorporating a few changes including hardware to actually carry the weapons load. Two were passed to the Navy. Then 250 R-5As were ordered on 26 February 1944, soon increased to 450 (including fifty for the USN and 100 for the UK). Among the first machines were those equipped to mount litter carriers on each side of the fuselage, and these were operated by the Air Rescue Service. With the technology moving ahead so quickly, the less-than-desirable handling qualities of the helicopter, and the looming end of the war, only thirty-four of the helicopters were completed (43-46626/59, with -46660/725 being cancelled, the other 350 apparently never being assigned serials). This made a total of sixty-five of the type manufactured.

When the RN ordered the two XR-5 prototypes, it had expressed a desire for 250 production machines. This enthusiasm cooled during the year of development, and production would be a longer wait still. However, the RN requested twelve YR-5As and forty-eight R-5As, while the RAF sought two YR-5As and eight R-5As. During the wait the Battle of the Atlantic had turned in the Allies' favor and the need for convoy ASW was greatly diminished. The UK order was cancelled on 25 March 1944, the USAAF taking up the two XR-5As before the special electronics gear was installed, and any British testing of the type is unclear. With the cancellation of the XR-5A, the Army was free to designate the production model R-5A instead of the original R-5B.

Sikorsky R-5A characteristics

Rotor diameter	48.0ft (14.6m)
– therefore	
No. of rotor blades	3
Length, overall	57.1ft (17.4m)
Height	13.1ft (4.0m)
Fuel	100 gallons (379 liters)
Weight, empty	3,780lb (1,715kg)
Weight, gross	4,900lb (2,222kg)
Climb rate, best	1,570fpm (479mpm)
Service ceiling	14,400ft (4,389m)
Speed, max	120mph (193km/h)
Range (85mph)	300 miles (483km)

A planned YR-5C was to be a modification to the second YR-5A with more power and an enlarged cabin to accommodate three litters, an attendant, and the pilot. Alternatively, it was to enclose the pilot, copilot or attendant, and three passengers, or pilot and 600-800lb (272-363kg) of cargo. It was to have a main rotor enlarged to 52 feet (15.9 meters) turned by an R-1340-AN-1 of 550hp (410kW) with an R-985 rear section. The twin tail rotors had a diameter of 8.3 feet (2.5 meters), one mounted horizontally but both driven off the same gearbox. The horizontal unit was thought necessary to trim pitching moment resulting from the potentially large CG travel. A hoist was to be mounted off the forward portion of the fuselage, which was to have a tricycle undercarriage. This project was begun via a 4 December 1944 contract change, and a mock-up inspection was conducted on 13-14 March 1945. However, emphasis was placed on moving expeditiously with R-5A production, so the R-5C effort was suspended, then finally cancelled.[19]

Modifications of YR-5A 43-46606 to a YR-5D configuration was approved on 14 May 1945 at $40,000. This was to have a nose wheel, a widened cabin for two seats in the rear, and the pilot was moved to the single forward seat. A sliding side door was installed on the port side and a Vickers hydraulic rescue hoist added above it. The gross was increased to 5,100lb (2,313kg). This aircraft was redelivered after the war, in December 1945. Others followed and the type was revised further with greater cabin capacity and saw continued production post-war.

Apart from external stores and litters, other experiments were performed with the new helicopters to explore their military potential, benefiting from their unique flight characteristics. Among these was employing an external hoist to winch personnel and materiel aboard. This was taken further by fixing a hook to the end of the line, itself attached to a trailing arm under the helicopter. This allowed articles to be snatched off the ground (presumably when hover performance was lacking) by flying over a line passed between two poles, which carried the article to be retrieved. The hooks engaged the line and 'snatched' it and the article away to be hauled into the helicopter; tests were performed with an R-5. A means to extend the range of the helicopter involved towing it behind a transport. The helicopter's engine was left shut down and the rotor disengaged from the transmission to permit autorotation during take-off and initial flight. Before release, the helicopter's engine would be started and prepared to engage the rotor. The line was released by the pilot at the helicopter end for autorotative flight, after which the transmission was clutched to the rotor for powered operation. The limitation of the system was that the transport could only fly as fast as the maximum airspeed of the helicopter, which was typically quite inefficient for the airplane. Such tests with an R-5 and R-6 were performed, at least in part, by Lieutenant Carter Harmon, the pilot who had flown the

All the US Army helicopters of the Second World War had the ability to carry some external stores as the military explored the potential of the new aircraft. This XR-5 displays under-belly bombs and a depth charge (probably balanced with another on the opposite side). While helicopters could serve as a light bombing platform when fitted with a rudimentary bombsight, their slow speed and low altitude made them vulnerable and this was not the best use of the machines. *San Diego Air & Space Museum*

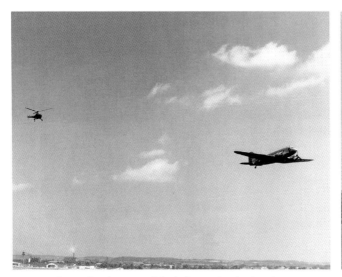

A means of extending the range of the helicopter involved towing one behind a transport airplane (a Douglas C-47 is seen here with an R-5 in high tow). The helicopter's engine was shut down and the rotor disengaged for autorotation until ready to be released for powered flight. The method was inefficient for the tug at the slow maximum speed of the rotorcraft, and also proved hazardous as demonstrated by a fatal accident. *National Archives*

Among the numerous experiments performed with the new helicopters, seeking to exploit their unique flight profile, was the snatching of articles and pouches from the ground. This R-5D, equipped with nose gear, also has a rescue hoist that provided a hooked line attached to the trailing arm. The hook engaged a line between the poles to 'snatch' the article aloft as the helicopter passed overhead; the article was then pulled into the cabin. *National Soaring Museum*

Burma YR-4B rescues in 1944. He was killed when the line was inadvertently released from the tug and whipped back to become entangled in the helicopter's main rotor.[20]

It was seen early in the design of the XR-4 that it had little growth potential, although providing invaluable insight to guide later developments. The Navy would also eventually reject it for anything beyond training. Only a substantial redesign, markedly reducing empty weight, would approach desired performance for a more practical military aircraft. Initially the YR-4A was to be given a vertically mounted 220hp (164kW) horizontally opposed engine, but this entailed so many changes that a new model appeared more reasonable. The 16 September 1942 recommendation for an improved spin-off was forwarded up the chain. It met with some opposition until the Navy threw its weight behind the concept with 43 percent of the funding. Nonetheless, the helicopter was designed to an Army specification.[21] The Brits opposed the program as it might slow R-4 production and R-5 progress. Hence, in parallel with the R-5 was a less ambitious R-6 (VS-316B), begun in October-November 1942; this folded a lighter and more streamlined fuselage around the transmission and rotor system of the R-4, but substituting the Lycoming O-435-7 at 225hp (168 kW) and more than double the fuel capacity.[22] Additionally, the tail rotor was mounted to the port side of the boom, as opposed to the starboard side on the R-4. The contract for a single XR-6 (43-47955, MX-333) was estimated at $800,000.[23]

Sikorsky quickly set the standard for light helicopters, including the cockpit layout. This XR-6A (rigged for remote control vibration endurance tests) shows the center console between the two pilot seats, each with a cyclic stick (a remote control pushrod attached for the 22 December 1944 test) and generous transparencies, including between the legs. However, it had a single collective level (another non-standard link attached) between the seats, which quickly proved to be a false economy for aircrew standardization and flight safety. *National Museum of the United States Air Force*

A mock-up of the new helicopter was inspected on 7 December 1942. The line-abreast seats were enclosed in a simple plex cab with autoclave-molded fiberglass framing and doors over the semi-monocoque aluminum floor structure that extended as a keel beam under the centersection. The dual controls did not extend to the collective, which remained a single lever between the seats. The curvaceous airframe included considerable clear panels in the cockpit, including the bottom quarter. The semi-monocoque tail boom was almost exclusively magnesium, while magnesium castings for fittings and bulkheads were found elsewhere in the airframe, some secured with new heli-arc welding. Other non-traditional materials were found to reduce the content of aluminum needed for high-priority combat aircraft. The engine was mounted in the usual welded steel tube truss but enclosed by paper and resin cowl panels cured in the autoclave. A nose wheel supplemented the tail wheel to protect the cabin in the event of a nose-over and to simplify taxiing, which was

encouraged with this model. Floats could be installed and a radio was fitted as standard equipment. The rotor hub was improved and made more compact. The rotor blades and transmission were interchangeable with the R-4, but the blades included a folding feature. There were also provisions for two litters or two bomb racks accommodating two depth charges or four 100lb bombs. However, the weapons capability was deleted on 16 November 1944.[24]

The Lycoming engine ran into development troubles and was dropped. The powerplant was changed to the six-cylinder Franklin O-405-9 at 240hp (179kW), which was apparently installed in the reworked XR-6 before it flew and was redesignated the XR-6A (initially XR-7). This delayed the detail design and the military took advantage of this to add additional prototypes. A contract change for five more XR-6As (43-28240/44) was signed on 30 April 1943, bringing the project to $1,977,846.19.[25] Three were allocated to the Navy because of their fiscal contribution to the program.

Morris took the initial XR-6A prototype (43-47955) aloft for the first time on 15 October, but the flight was very brief owing to exceptionally heavy controls and vibration. Subsequent changes included adding mechanical boost to the collective lever. It took into 1944 to work out all the bugs, but changes were still being made as production moved to high rate, mandating post-delivery modifications. An automotive muffler to reduce engine noise was also added, quieting cabin levels to that of a bus, according to Colonel Gregory, making unaided conversation possible. There was also criticism that compactness of the design made for difficult maintenance access. On 1 March Gregory and Ralph Alex flew the helicopter to Washington National Airport where they demonstrated overload flight with a pilot, observer, and two litter 'patients', although this required a running take-off into the wind. The next day the two men set out for Wright Field.

In early 1943 the Army sought twenty-six YR-6A variants incorporating minor changes, but Sikorsky demurred. Bridgeport could not handle the size of manufacturing envisioned for the R-6 and manpower was lacking in Connecticut, given ongoing higher priority defense work.

Consequently, a licence agreement for the R-6 work was concluded with the Kelvinator Division of Nash-Kelvinator, an automobile manufacturer that turned to wartime aircraft production in Detroit, Michigan. The decision was then made in March 1943 to order 900 R-6As (including 100 for the Navy) at $39,455,769.60, the YR-6As apparently falling under this contract. The deal was concluded in September 1943 but with the quantity reduced to 731.

Nash-Kelvinator began with the twenty-six YR-6As (43-45316/41). The initial YR-6A flew and was delivered in October 1944, and the last in January 1945. The company then took on the R-6As, shifting into high gear for mass production on a moving assembly line. They delivered 193 R-6As (43-45342/534) beginning in February 1944, running at twice the requested production rate, before the contract was cancelled at the end of the war. The first was handed over in February 1944 and the last in October 1945, for a recognized total of 225 R-6s. The production line was moving so efficiently that Nash-Kelvinator completed an additional 200 machines in August 1945 alone and five more beyond, in addition to voluminous spares, before the effort was halted. This makes for a total of 430 R-6s – and the company was prepared to manufacture 500 more over the next ninety days. The 205 helicopters sat for months before being accepted and shipped off to storage, only to deteriorate to scrap over the next few years of neglect.[26]

Some thirty-six R-6s were passed to the USN. Although 150 were ordered by Britain as the Hoverfly II, the war was in its closing phase as they were delivered and the UK cut its order to thirty-six. Of these, only twenty-seven were actually shipped and distributed between the RAF and RN, with one passed to Canada and two returned.[27]

Five R-6 helicopters were shipped to China in April 1945, arriving in June, for service testing and emergency search and rescue (SAR) duties. One rescue mission at 8,500 feet (2,591 meters) is mentioned, although others occurred.[28]

The numerous and efficient R-6 was also the subject of experimental testing. One project was optimizing the helicopter for Coast Guard rescue operations. The YR-6C was

The R-6 moved steadily between prototype and service test examples, then production, with only minor changes. The 2½ years between concept and production deliveries was rapid by peacetime measure but a bit slow in wartime, reflecting the application of full albeit accelerated development milestones. This XR-6A is fitted with two litter capsules. *National Archives*

Sikorsky R-6A characteristics

Rotor diameter	38.0ft (11.6m)
– therefore	
No. of rotor blades	3
Length, overall	48.0ft (14.6m)
Height	11.0ft (3.4m)
Fuel	75 gallons (284 liters)
Weight, empty	2,070lb (939kg)
Weight, gross	3,108lb (1,410kg)
Climb rate, best	1,000fpm (305mpm)
Service ceiling	13,400ft (4,084m)
Speed, max	115mph (185km/h)
Range (70mph)	350 miles (563km)
Endurance	5 hours

Above: Conceived as a better-performing variant of the R-4, the Sikorsky R-6 was to wrap a lighter and more streamlined airframe around the heart of that machine. This state-of-the-art model saw the largest production run of any Second World War American helicopter, exceeding that of all other models combined. Essentially a helicopter version of a liaison aircraft, with two seats and a modest but useful load, it was deployed to China for search and rescue duties, as seen here with a YR-6A on 4 June 1945. *San Diego Air & Space Museum*

Right: This YR-6A (43-45327) has been substantially modified as the YR-6C to test a configuration more suited to Coast Guard rescue operations. A hydraulic hoist has been installed over a door opening, facilitated by the door redesigned to slide aft. The fuel tank was removed to permit additional internal volume for two more persons, replaced by the external cells. *San Diego Air & Space Museum*

a modified YR-6A carrying two additional passengers to permit a survivor to be brought aboard via an added external hoist. To make room for the individual and an attendant/hoist operator, the internal fuel tank was removed and replaced by two external cells. To give the pilot (port seat) better downward vision for positioning the aircraft over the survivor, flooring at his feet was removed and the outer skin opposite replaced with transparency.[29] The side door was redesigned to be mostly transparent and opened by sliding aft rather than swinging forward, and a step added beneath. A Vickers external hoist and other radios were to be added. Although the $29,210 project was completed, the added weight gravelly impacted performance to an unacceptable extent.[30]

The USAAF set up a helicopter flight training and mechanics school at Freeman Field, Rantoul, Indiana, on 29 January 1944 with YR-4Bs. This was moved in December to Chanute Field, Illinois, then Sheppard Field, Wichita Falls, Texas, in May 1945. The YR-4Bs were soon replaced by R-4Bs. During the move to Texas, fourteen R-4s and three R-6s flew in a mass formation to the new location. By the end of the war the

school had graduated 200 helicopter pilots, transitioning from a fixed-wing background.[31]

Eggbeater (Kellett XR-8 & XR-8A)

Its very competitive autogyro work placed Kellett in a good position to step into helicopters. While the company worked on the YO-60 contract it was also doing preliminary design on a helicopter it called the 'Synchrocopter'. This would have two three-blade rotor hubs so closely spaced laterally above the fuselage (4 feet [1.2 meters]) that they were geared to be intermeshed, i.e. the blades of one passed through the disc of the other but were synchronized to ensure against blade-on-blade strikes. Rotating in opposite directions, the design eliminated the need for an anti-torque device that sacrificed power. The Kellett aircraft would be much more compact and thus be able to operate in more confined spaces.

Kellett's presentations were initially met with skepticism at Wright Field, but a closer examination was informed by comparative model testing. This appeared to substantiate Kellett's analysis that the layout would offer significant reductions in operating vibrations as well as eliminating the weight and downwash penalties of laterally separated rotors. Kellett was invited to offer a formal proposal, which it submitted on 11 November 1942. The Army received authorization on 7 January 1943 to proceed with the project and ordered a single XR-8 (43-44714, MX-348) in May. A mock-up was inspected in July. The formal contract of nearly $1 million followed on 11 September, calling for two prototypes and development of a two-blade rotor system.

The XR-8 had a cockpit with side doors for the pilot and observer who were seated line abreast. Behind, the six-cylinder Franklin O-405-9 engine of 245hp (183 kW) was buried in the fuselage with spiral-bevel gear transmission and shafts to the rotors arranged overhead in a 25-degree V with hubs 4 feet (1.2 meters) apart. The rotors employed collective (the same side-to-side or differentially) and cyclic pitch control with pilot input by the then common stick and rudder pedals (cyclic), and a single collective lever between the seats with a throttle twist grip. Collective change was automatically accompanied by throttle change (throttle advanced with added pitch and vice versa), making manual throttle adjustment rare. There appears to have been a 10-degree fore-aft tilt feature

for trim.[32] The rotor blades were a step-tapered steel tube spar with wood airfoil and trim tab. The airframe structure was welded steel tubing with aluminum ribs and stringers, and aluminum panels forward and fabric covering aft of the engine bay. The aerodynamic fuselage tapered gracefully to a close-out with a twin-tail empennage of wood and fabric. A steel spar in the horizontal member was attached to bearings that permitted adjustment to optimize its contribution to torque opposition. There were provisions for two 235lb (107kg) or six 100lb (45kg) bombs.[33]

It was 7 August 1944 before the XR-8 flew, with Dave Driscoll doing the honors. As soon became the convention, flight testing began with rigidly restrained runs, then tethered hovers, progressing to low-altitude translations and hover-taxi before moving to up-and-away forward flight. It was quickly learned that directional control was inadequate owing to rotor downwash interacting adversely with the empennage.[34] It appears that the aft fuselage was extended rearward a bit and a shallow strake added at the top as a partial measure. Wind tunnel testing at New York University provided data for a 28 percent increase in fin area. The rudders at the aft end of the fuselage may have been added at this time, as early drawings and photos suggest that they may not have been intended originally. The span of the rudders may also have been subsequently extended. However, flight testing then revealed excessive directional stability such that maneuverability was

Pursued as an alternative to the Sikorsky helicopters and exploring the intermeshed rotor design that the Germans had demonstrated as feasible, Kellett was contracted to develop its 'Synchrocopter.' The XR-8 was expected to have greater performance than the R-4 series and present a compact profile for operating in confined areas. The first prototype (XR-8) is shown here in its near-original form with the initial vertical stabilizers but the addition of the aft fuselage strake and an extension of the boat-tail close-out evident in a new fabric-covered structure of slight altered contour. *National Archives*

hampered. Additional changes included differential pitch of the rotors fore and aft for greater yaw control power.

The blades on the test aircraft were instrumented to detect blade-on-blade contact, indicated by lights on the instrument panel.[35] The flickering of these lights was a reason for growing disquiet. On 7 September 1944 blade-on-blade contact caused a sudden jerk of the cyclic during maneuvering flight when the blades were subject to the greatest dynamic flapping motion. Myriad placards resulted, including prohibiting abrupt maneuvers and translations in excess of 5mph (8km/h), and autorotation within 500 feet (152 meters) of the surface. While common in early flight tests, the restrictions could not be safely lifted. Although 400lb (181kg) heavier than the XR-4, the Kellett machine possessed superior performance, but this could not be exploited until the control issues were resolved. Solutions remained elusive.[36]

In an effort to understand the blade dynamics, an XR-8's rotor hub and blades was installed on the XR-3 autogyro. An $11,199 change order to the XR-3 contract funded this work, which also saw a camera mounted above the shaft in such a way as to photograph a single blade through its revolutions.[37] A rigid rotor without flapping hinges was believed to hold the answer, so the decision, based on a 10 May 1945 Kellett proposal, was made to have the company develop such a system for $55,120. It was also decided that the firm would install the twin-blade rotor it had been designing on the second helicopter (44-21908). In the meantime, progress was being made with the initial rotor design, continuing development that permitted the airspeed to be expanded to 100mph (161km/h), at which the helicopter flew quite smoothly, but still with little maneuvering permitted.

Further testing in the fall of 1944 produced additional blade strike events. Another $170,000 was authorized for substitution of the two-blade rotors on ship No 2, becoming the XR-8A. This was to be delivered in June 1944, but development ran long. When flights commenced in March 1945 the rotors generated severe vibration and an additional protracted period of development was indicated. Further design work yielded altered 'umbrella' controls for the three-blade rotors that were installed on the second prototype. Consequently, the rigid rotor work, which entailed considerably more engineering, was set aside together with the two-blade rotor. The aircraft performed some feats beyond mere flight testing to include a landing atop the roof of the central Philadelphia Post Office and a 340-mile (547km) round trip from Upper Darby, Pennsylvania, to Schenectady, New York.

By March 1945, with the end of the war in sight and aircraft programs starting to be cut back, further USAAF funding of the XR-8 did not appear warranted. The blade contact problem was not entirely resolved and Kellett was looking to an alternative control system. The Air Forces, however, balked at the extended cost, as the program had already run well over budget to the tune of $186,830 by September 1944. So, while much had been learned from the 'eggbeater', production had become very doubtful given the additional development time anticipated. However, continuing development served to aid the twin-engine Kellett XR-10 work (see later).

The machines were not accepted for service trials until January 1946, but with no sterling assessment forthcoming. Both were bailed back to the contractor where work continued until the program was terminated that December with more

Kellett XR-8 characteristics

Rotor diameter – therefore	36.0ft (11.0m)
No. of rotor blades	3 on each rotor
Span	40.0ft (12.2m)
Length, overall	36.0ft (11.0m)
Height, overall	14.8ft (4.5m)
Rotor area, each	1,018ft^2 (95m^2)
Fuel	34 gallons (129 liters)
Weight, empty	2,320lb (1,052kg)
Weight, max	2,976lb (1,350kg)
Climb rate, best	714fpm (218mpm)
Service ceiling	6,700ft (2,042m)
Speed, max (design)	104mph (167km/h)
Range (85mph)	170 miles (274km)

This image shows the original XR-8 after the vertical stabilizers had been expanded and rudders added to the aft fuselage close-out. Contracted well after the XR-4 and suffering a long development of the intermeshed rotor system, this 'Synchrocopter' was not competitive for an Army production contract, but was carried on for its technological insight.
National Museum of the United States Air Force

than $1,154,032.78 of government largess and $1 million of Kellett's money exhausted.

Too little, too late (G & A XR-9 and Rotorcraft XR-11)

Although focused on the major helicopter programs and the very successful Sikorsky types, the Army also sponsored smaller experimental work. There were surprisingly many privately funded helicopter programs under way in the late war years, some from what would later become familiar post-war helicopter brands such as Bell and Hiller (see later).[38] Among these was the extensive development work by Bell Aircraft in Buffalo, New York, employing a unique rotor design by Arthur M. Young. This was a two-blade semi-rigid linked to a cross-beam gyro-stabilizer bar with tip weights perpendicular to the blades, all on universal joints as a self-stabilized teetering

Bell Aircraft experimented with an entirely new helicopter rotor stability concept designed by Arthur Young. The company built a series of testbeds during the war, including this Bell Model 30 Ship 1A, flown by Floyd Carlson in spring 1944. Bell was but one of a number of teams flying experimental rotorcraft during the Second World War, outside the purview of the War Department. *National Archives*

arrangement. As the bar tilted it caused blade angle changes to right the unit. Wright Field evaluated the rotor in ground tests during spring 1943. First flying as a single-seat testbed in 1943, Bell's work resulted in a two-seat helicopter in 1944 that formed the basis for light helicopter production post-war, which would have a profound influence on military and civil aviation for decades to come.

Among the other work, Aeronautical Products built several versions of a three-blade helicopter with a conventional layout (a single main rotor and anti-torque tail rotor), having the engine in the nose. Bendix had the Model K contra-rotating coaxial machine with a single occupant. Gazda Engineering built the Helicospeeder with a two-blade rotor and a jet-exhaust anti-torque mechanism. The Helicopter Corporation of America flew a coaxial rotor machine in 1940 with the engine and fuel tank above the fuselage and between the two three-blade rotors. Higgins Industries flew its EB-1 two-seat helicopter with a four-blade main rotor (actually two twin-blade units, one immediately above the other) and tail rotor. Landgraf Helicopter Company flew the lateral-tandem twin rotor H-2 with synchronised and intermeshed non-hinged blades fitted with aileron-like surfaces at the tips that rotated the blades' airfoil shells about their fixed spars as commanded via the cyclic stick. Others were at work on designs that did not fly, or only went aloft post-war; these included the Brantley B-1 co-

axial helicopter. The Georgia School of Technology experimented with a single blade/single rotor driven by a tip compressed air jet. Nemeth Helicopter Corporation developed a two-blade rotor machine of conventional configuration but with the engine in the nose. Roteron had a coaxial machine, with the engine between the two rotors. And the Twin Coach Company branched away from its buses to develop a coaxial rotor helicopter. Army attention to a few of these efforts came about as means of fostering useful technological developments in the new helicopter field and keep alive inventive design teams. Political pressures may well also have had a role in some of the contracting decisions – Congressmen seeking largess for businesses in their constituencies.

One experimental type funded by the War Department included the G & A Aircraft Model 45B. Following the failure of the YO-61 autogyro, Firestone had encouraged its division to move into helicopters based on that work. It made what appears to have been an unsolicited proposal to the Air Forces and won a contract. The procurement was approved on 26 October 1943, with a letter contract issued on 25 November for two helicopters. The design work began in 1943, employing the company's advanced rotor design but with an anti-torque tail rotor on a long tail boom. It used elements of the XO-61, most obviously the plex-enclosed pilot and observer station at the front. However, the first incarnation was a single-seat machine, notably small, light and simple compared with the XR-4. The initial government contract (MX-463) was apparently in 1944 and possibly only for development. The Army lent technical assistance to the effort and gained derived data. The program did seem to proceed much like a typical acquisition program, including a mock-up inspection in about July 1944.

The XR-9 had a welded tube structure covered with aluminum panels, together with a balsa core tail boom skinned

This elegant-looking helicopter is the two-place Higgins EB-1 with two twin-blade rotors, one atop the other. It is a fine example of a raft of commercial projects that were undertaken in the United States during the war as the era of the helicopter blossomed. Such rotorcraft creativity, with considerable technological innovation, far exceeded anything similar across the globe. *National Archives*

in light-gauge aluminum. A second individual could be squeezed into the cockpit, between the pilot and the aft bulkhead, during an emergency. Only 126hp (94kW) from a Lycoming XO-290-5 was needed for the light helicopter, with just 291lb (132kg) of useful load. Installation of an XO-290-C was also developed. An electro-hydraulic governor maintained a constant rotor speed via automatic blade pitch control regardless of power setting. This permitted the pilot to make the helicopter climb and descend using throttle alone. Additionally, the rotor hub was gimbal-mounted to reduce the magnitude of blade flapping in an effort to reduce vibration.

The helicopter (490991, s/n 1) flew initially on 4 December 1944 under the control of long-time Pitcairn test pilot Fredrick A. 'Slim' Soule.[39] It operated extraordinarily well, with little vibration and even capable of being trimmed for minutes of hands-off flight. It was damaged on 3 February 1945 when a wind gust during landing rolled it onto its side. It had returned to the air by 19 March and was flown by Colonel Gregory. Unfortunately, on 21 June the single prototype was gravely damaged again, this time by a service test pilot who flew the aircraft aggressively despite emphatic instructions. The assessment was that "in certain flight conditions the change in control phasing was such as to require stick movement not normally encountered". Soule, who observed the pilot make a full-forward cyclic input from a low hover, would claim later that the accident was an intentional act planned by the Army.[40] However, the USAAF chose to continue development but insisted that there had to be two seats with dual controls to enable suitable training to be given in how differently the helicopter handled.

The initial contract was closed out with $595,742 having been expended. This had included development of a two-blade rotor

intended for the second helicopter, to be the XR-9A (GA-45C), and that would have greatly simplified hangaring. However, the second single-seat machine was never completed and the new rotor, the design nearly completed, was not built.

A 14 July 1945 letter contract funded two XR-9B (GA-45C revised) helicopters with dual controls but, with the pilots seated in tandem, with only a single forward instrument console. It was also to provide a means of locking-out the floating hub feature and incorporated offset flapping hinges. As many as possible of the parts from the XR-9s were employed. This was a slightly lighter aircraft at 1,380lb (626kg) gross and 1mph faster. It had an O-290-7 of 134hp (100 kW) and, although reported to be 9 inches (23cm) longer, this may have referred to the cabin only, as the official numbers indicate an 8.8-foot (2.7-meter) reduction in overall length.[41] It went back to a three-blade rotor 28 feet (8.5 meters) in diameter. The XR-9B's maiden flight was in October 1945.[42]

The second contract called for aircraft delivery with a serial number applied (46-001, perhaps suggesting a post-war contract change). Consequently, the formal military machine was delivered for evaluation in March 1946.

In 1945 the USAAF also funded a longitudinally displaced tandem-rotor, two-place machine with line-abreast seating and a tricycle undercarriage. This was from a new firm, Rotor-Craft Corporation of Los Angeles, California, founded by designer and president Gilbert W. Magill. Called the X-2 Dragon Fly by the development team, it employed the rigid blade concept pioneered and licensed by Landgraf. The wooden rotor blades were rigidly attached to the hub without

A variant of the XR-9 was sought with alterations in the rotor hub but principally possessing dual control (the aft pilot seat not visible here) but both pilots referring to the same instrument panel. As this photo of the XR-9B illustrates, the helicopter had a longer cabin, an engine change, and the tail boom bumper with an aerodynamic fairing wrapped around it. The nicely executed prototype flew within two months of the war's end. *National Archives*

G & A XR-9 characteristics

Rotor diameter – therefore	28.0ft (8.5m)
No. of rotor blades	3 on each rotor
Span	28.0ft (8.5m)
Length, overall	35.0ft (10.7m)
Height	8.0ft (2.4m)
Fuel	25 gallons (95 liters)
Weight, empty	1,153lb (523kg)
Weight, max	1,464lb (664kg)
Weight, overload	1,676lb (760kg)
Climb rate, best	1,000fpm (305mpm)
Service ceiling	12,400ft (3,780m)
Speed, max	94mph (151km/h)
Range (74mph)	262 miles (422km)
Endurance	3 hours

The Army partially funded the lightweight G & A Model 45 project as the XR-9 during the war years. Shown is the initial incarnation with a single occupant and three-blade rotor, with a second person squeezed in to sit on the canted bulkhead behind the pilot's seat. The very lightweight machine possessed very smooth flying characteristics. *Author's collection*

hinges, although collective and cyclic control was retained via a 'feathering hinge'. The helicopter was predicted to be inherently stable. Apart from the mechanical simplicity of a rigid system, it was also advertised as safer since blade droop would be less, reducing the hazard to personnel around the machine. It was also important to avoid disc-to-disc interference as the rotors overlapped with a clearance of just 6 inches (15cm). The $55,000 contract was based on a 27 March 1945 Authorization for Purchase.[43]

The XR-11 was to be powered by a single Continental A-100 flat four-cylinder engine of 110hp (82kW) with power shafts extending fore and aft under the floor to the vertical rotor shafts. The three-blade rotor diameters were first 18.4 feet (5.6 meters) for the rear and 17.9 feet (5.5 meters) for the front, then 19.5 feet (5.9 meters) for both with 12.3 feet (3.8 meters) overlapped. The swash plates for blade control were mounted at the base of the drive shafts rather than beneath the rotor hubs, with pushrods to the blades within the hollow drive shaft. This had the front shaft rising just ahead of the instrument panel in front of the pilots. It had a welded steel tube frame and employed numerous inexpensive automobile components. Overall length was to be 26 feet (7.9 meters) and height 7.5 feet (2.3 meters). Maximum airspeed was predicted at 110mph (177km/h) with a service ceiling of 12,000 feet (3,658 meters) and an initial climb rate 667fpm (203mpm). Range, however, was estimated at just 77 miles (124km) with a 6-gallon (23-liter) fuel capacity. Gross weight was planned at 1,100lb (499kg).

The experimental XR-11 is shown in 1945 concept form and 'undressed' for post-war testing. The four-cylinder flat engine and underfloor transmission is visible buried in the welded tube frame, with power shafts running to each vertical rotor shaft. The small machine was an unusual experimental effort funded late in the war by the Air Forces. Right Author's collection/below National Archives

The single aircraft (45-9478) flew post-war with a 100hp (75kW) O-118 engine, possibly with rotors reduced to 18 feet (5.5 meters) in diameter, and a 70lb (32kg) increase in weight. The helicopter had significant technical issues with the rotor hub.

Army twin (Kellett XR-10)

With a few years of experience and reasonably practical flying helicopters, the Army kept up the pressure for technological advance in the field. It naturally wanted to move beyond two-seat machines to something with greater utility. An AAF Technical Instruction on 31 August 1944 sought "a large helicopter capable of carrying wounded personnel, passengers, and cargo within the fuselage". The Air Surgeon requested a minimum capacity of four litters. This suggested a rotor lifting disc area requiring two rotors and likely two engines.

Kellett's frustrating work on the XR-8 had led the company to design an enlarged version of the 'Synchrocopter' as the twin-engine KH-2X-C. This preliminary design was pitched for the Army's twin-engine helicopter competition, which included

Bell, Platt-LePage and Sikorsky. The Kellett offering received a preliminary go-ahead followed by a 16 October 1944 letter contract for two XR-10 helicopters (45-22793, 43-22795), a static test article capable of flight, a mock-up, and float landing gear. The contract was valued at $1,281,545.47, but would nearly double. The static article was cancelled via a 25 May 1945 change order and spares substituted. This MX-558 was the largest helicopter the USAAF had under development during the war years.

The mock-up was inspected on 11 December 1944. The XR-10 was to have two 525hp (392kW) Wright R-975-15 Whirlwind 9 nine-cylinder engines (Continental production) in side nacelles so as not to intrude on cabin volume. These were to be cooled by the engine exhaust directed into steel venturi-shaped ducts and drawing outside air through the nacelles. The engines turned three-blade rotors with a diameter of 65 feet (19.8 meters) and inclined 12.5 degrees from the vertical for a total width of 71 feet (21.6 meters). The fuselage construction was entirely metal, employing common aircraft practices. The center of the three vertical stabilizers had a rudder. The helicopter was to carry ten passengers along the sidewalls or six litter patients, and a crew of two seated line abreast.[44] Just behind the cabin was a hoist over an opening in the deck to raise and lower cargo or personnel. The aircraft weighed 7,555lb (3,427kg) empty and 13,500lb (6,124kg) gross, and was expected to have a 2,200lb (998kg) useful load and fly to 99mph (159km/h) with a typical range of 270 miles (435km). It was to operate up to 4,600 feet (1,402 meters) on a single engine via a connecting

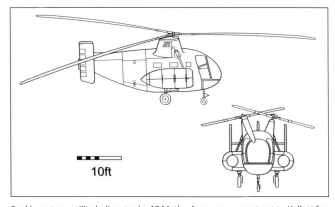

10ft

Seeking a true utility helicopter by 1944, the Army gave a contract to Kellett for a twin-engine 'Synchrocopter' (with intermeshed rotors), which flew post-war. The XR-10 was an enlargement of the XR-8 concept with a cabin and all-metal construction, making it the largest Army helicopter under development during the war. The rotary engines housed in side sponsons, with generous cooling openings fore and aft, gave the appearance of jet engines. *Author*

cross-shaft between the upper gear boxes.

Scheduled to fly in December 1945, this did not occur until more than a year later, after the second prototype had been cancelled. The XR-10 suffered weight growth but also performance gains. A preliminary production order was cancelled.

Navy seeks its own (Sikorsky HNS-1, HOS-1, HO2S-1)

The Navy had not been idle while the Army forged ahead in rotorcraft development, although largely benefitting from its sister service's efforts and moving ponderously. Rear Admiral John H. Towers, BuAer's chief, directed on 24 July 1942 the procurement and evaluation of four R-4s. However, while awaiting the helicopters there was little interest within the Bureau for the program. The USCG was much more enthusiastic about the potential of the machines, especially for SAR, and was a persistent voice behind the effort in the face of general disinterest within the Navy. The Coast Guard emphasized the ASW role rather than SAR in order to curry favor with Navy leadership.[45] Replacing USN airships for ASW patrols also appeared worthy of exploration, these not being able to accompany convoys across the ocean. Helicopters operating off small decks on merchantmen might be an answer where aircraft carriers were not available. The Royal Navy was also eager for helicopters as ASW assets, seeking YR-4As as early as April 1942. The potential benefits of a helicopter for ship-to-ship and ship-to-shore transport, replenishment and scouting/observation were notable compared with the difficulty of achieving the same with seaplanes or small boats. Aboard an aircraft carrier the helicopter could serve as 'plane guard', ready to react quickly if a crew member ended up in the drink.

Movement occurred only after more than a year of near inactivity and nay-saying following demonstrations of the XR-4 and continued Army helicopter development. No naval officers took the opportunity to fly the existing helicopters during any of the demonstrations.[46] Helicopter adoption also had to be paced by the number of vessels that could accommodate the craft, and its integration into carrier operations. Here again limitations were emphasized, but few solutions explored. Even the normally progressive aviation community was dismissive, the highest levels at BuAer deriding rotorcraft, so the pace of work remained lethargic. By 1943 there was mounting public and Congressional pressure on the Navy to make serious efforts at adopting helicopters in the face of their evident distain of rotorcraft yet the increasing losses of shipping and men to submarines.

After observing further flights of the VS-300 and XR-4 in early 1943, Vice Admiral Russell R. Waesche, Commandant of the Coast Guard, bypassed the non-responsive BuAer and went directly to Admiral Ernest J. King, Chief of Naval Operations (CNO), asking to acquire more of the Army helicopters at the earliest opportunity for training, ASW and SAR. The RAF's Wg Cdr Brie was at the forefront of urging acceptance of the Sikorsky helicopters within his country. With the promised helicopters finally due to be delivered, King directed on 15 February 1943 a program for test and evaluation of helicopters for use with sea-going supply convoys. In May 1943 the RN, USCG and USN formed the Combined Board for the Evaluation of the Ship-based Helicopter in Antisubmarine Warfare, the NACA and War Shipping Board added later that year. The Coast Guard was directed to take the lead in development of the naval applications, as it had wished. On 18 December 1943 the CNO further directed that helicopter testing and training be separated, with the latter to be conducted by the USCG at Floyd Bennett Field, Brooklyn, New York. Although BuAer was ostensibly responsible for the testing, it was almost exclusively executed by USCG personnel in Brooklyn.

First up was a YR-4B that was designated HNS-1 (42-107239 as BuNo 46445), assigned in 1942, followed by two more in March 1943 (42-107241/2 as 46699/700).[47] The service accepted the first machine on 16 October 1943 and the other two in November. On 29 June 1943 the Coast Guard began conducting sea trials of HNS-1s aboard the cutter SS *Governor Cobb*, which had been fitted with a helicopter deck. Beginning on 28 November of that year the USCG and USN, in cooperation with the RN, performed comprehensive sea training aboard the *Cobb* and the British merchant vessel *Daghestan* in Long Island Sound. Hundreds of transitions were flown by pilots from the three services. The *Daghestan* had a deck installed that measured 40 by 80 feet (12.2 by 24.4 meters), accommodating two helicopters. In January 1944 the vessel sailed with a fifty-ship convoy to Liverpool carrying two Hoverflys and four pilots (one USCG, one RN and two RAF) to provide anti-submarine patrol duties. The weather was predictably so bad during the crossing, and the vessel so loaded, that it rolled excessively and only two 30-minute patrols could be flown. One helicopter suffered rotor damage while U-boats sank three vessels.[48] It was evident that the R-4 could not operate from a deck on a vessel the size of a cargo ship subject to the motion from high sea states, unlike an aircraft carrier (on which the Navy would not contemplate trials). Although the circumstances of the voyage were about as adverse as conceivable, the Combined Board concluded that, given the present development of the helicopter, such operations should be confined to coastal waters. So pronouncing, the Board was dissolved.

Within the USCG, Lieutenant Commander Frank S. Erickson was the principal motive force behind the integration and experimentation with helicopters. The service, in cooperation with the UK, established Coast Guard Air Station Floyd Bennett Field in November 1943 with the three HNS-1s and four RN Hoverfly Is, Erickson commanding and Brie again a major player. There, many naval aviators as well as the initial batch of British pilots and mechanics were also trained. To assist the training, the Otis Elevator Company of Philadelphia designed and built a helicopter simulator. A gimbaled platform, 40 by 60 feet (12.2 by 18.3 meters), was also assembled on which helicopters could take off and land while it rocked to simulate the motion of a ship at sea. Shipboard training was with the *Governor Cobb*.

The team in Brooklyn also experimented with rescue

The Royal Navy and Royal Air Force adopted many R-4s and R-6s for evaluation and operation, the initial motivation being to operate from decks on cargo vessels crossing the Atlantic and assist in spotting enemy submarines. This is one YR-4B Hoverfly on the deck of the *Daghestan* after a trial crossing in January 1944 as the ship arrives off Ireland and is greeted by a Fairey Swordfish torpedo plane. Unfortunately, the experience was not a good one and it was clear that the R-4 was inadequate for the task. *National Museum of Naval Aviation*

Naval helicopter flight training at Floyd Bennett Field included an introduction to landing aboard decks attached to cargo vessels. Although a ship was employed in this training, an initial step was this 'galloping flight deck' simulator that reproduced the pitching and rolling of a ship at sea. The aircraft is an HOS-1 (75612), which should be an R-6A but appears to have the supposedly unique modifications applied to YR-6A 43-45327. *National Museum of the United States Air Force*

devices such as, in December 1943, a litter mount initially suspended below the floats whereby a person in the water could crawl into it while the helicopter hovered above. It was later mounted off the side of the helicopter. The first improvised rescue hoists were demonstrated in August and September 1944, initially with an electric unit, then hydraulic. This work then led to a rescue harness being attached to the winch cable hook. At least one HNS-1 was fitted with skids in place of the wheeled undercarriage, probably to reduce weight and assist rescue work.[49] The USCG began immediate training for SAR tasks with its helicopters and was soon performing actual emergency operations.

The Navy then took up three more YR-4Bs (43-28227, -29229 and -28231 as 39033/5) and nineteen R-4Bs (39036/52 and 75727/8), three of which (39042/3, 39045) went on the USCG for pilot training. The last was brought aboard in December 1944. The first twenty were clearly Army-contracted aircraft whereas the final two (75727/8) are uncertain, especially in light of a further twenty-six (39053/55, 46701/23) that were cancelled with no associated Army serials.[50] The USN took on three of the XR-6As as XHOS-1s

This Coast Guard HNS-1 39040, an R-4B flown by Lieutenant Commander Frank Erickson, performs a sea rescue test on 26 September 1944 with an unlucky sailor. The rudimentary rescue hoist and harness are evident, the cabin doors removed both for weight saving and to allow the survivor to scramble aboard. The USCG was perhaps the most enthusiast operator of the Sikorsky helicopter and quickly developed rescue equipment that would become common for generations after. *National Museum of the United States Air Force*

The 'workhorse' R-5 was developed to perform naval missions in addition to Army roles, given its greater payload and obvious growth potential. However, the Navy paid it little heed, letting the Coast Guard perform the evaluation of the two HO2S-1s acquired. All the Army production helicopters had the ability to operate on floats, as demonstrated by this XR-5. *National Museum of the United States Air Force*

(43-28241/3 as 46446/8). Contracted for on 20 March 1943, the first was accepted in September 1944 and passed along to the USCG at Floyd Bennett Field. Two R-5s (HO2S-1, 43-46613 as 75689 and 43-46618 as 75690) were ordered on 22 June 1943, but only formally accepted in December 1945 and subsequently moved to the Coast Guard.

The CNO moved to procure twenty-three R-4Bs for training, fifty R-5As, and 100 R-6As.[51] Follow-through was less than these numbers after the Combined Board's conclusion regarding non-suitability for the ASW mission. The Navy acquired thirty-six production R-6As as XHOS-1s (75589/624). Another sixty-four may have been planned as BuNos 75625/88 were blocked out for the type, but no order placed.[52] An order for thirty-four production HO2S-1s was also dropped – the very helicopter of the period that may have done some real work for the Navy. The UK dropped its plans to procure hundreds of Sikorsky helicopters.

Beginning in February 1945, operating from the *Cobb*, XHOS-1 46448, with excess power for the job, performed tests fitted with a dipping sonar, lowered into the sea from the hovering helicopter to detect a participating submarine.[53] It was important that the helicopter remain motionless above the surface, not dragging the device through any translation motion and generating self-induced noise. This was difficult to judge and the use of float lights and dye markers was ineffective because the rotor downwash blew them away. The answer was the Sunday comics page thrown out into the sea, where it clung to the water as a fixed and colorful reference point. Another rescue mission in April-May 1945 gained further acclaim, but no high-level reaction. Learning of a military aircraft crashed in the frozen, remote wilderness of Labrador, one of the Coast

Guard HNS helicopters was disassembled and flown to Goose Bay in a C-54. Assembled there, it was used to rescue eleven crewmen. However, the Navy's apathy had already caught up with Erickson and his team. The Brooklyn school was closed on 6 February 1945 after training 102 pilots. Many of the helicopters were placed in storage.[54]

The performance of these early model Army helicopters was also cause for hesitation. Yet a not-invented-here attitude played no small role in the Navy's antipathy; the sea service always held to the preordained conclusion that no Army aircraft would ever be suitable for a naval mission. In a decision seen as partially to dismiss the existing models of helicopters and a reluctance to even try the then current machines despite demonstrated capabilities, requirements for a naval helicopter were stated as a 4-hour endurance, a payload capacity permitting radar and depth charges or no less than 1,000lb (454kg), suitable radios and life rafts, and equipped for blind flying.[55] This far exceeded anything then in work, and the Department was skeptical that anyone could meet the requirements, yet BuAer did little to encourage development to meet the goal. Conventional thinking at the time was that empty weight as a percentage of gross increased directly proportional to rotor size, and an impractically large rotor was necessary for a large/heavy helicopter of useful performance. So it is not surprising that the Department chose not to adapt a helicopter but to develop one on its own initiative. It would seek a machine meeting its very ambitious useful load figure, provided that was even possible. Additionally, BuAer authorized the Floyd Bennett Field team on 17 May 1944 to work with the Sperry Gyroscope Company on an autopilot for the HNS-1. Flight tests had occurred by August, but were unsatisfactory.[56]

This XHOS-1 (46448) wears floats, the engine access panels have been removed for added cooling, and it has extra gear installed in the nose for the dipping sonar submerged beneath. The test shown was conducted on 13 April 1944 from Floyd Bennett Field, although it was also flown from the SS *Governor Cobb*. This advanced equipment pointed to future capabilities when the Navy adopted the helicopter with more enthusiasm than they mustered during the war.
National Museum of the United States Air Force

Milestones (Piasecki XHRP-1)

The maturing nature of helicopters and the wartime aeronautical workload favored new and emerging firms seeking War Department contracts, provided talented engineering and shop personnel could be recruited. As such endeavors came after the initial build-up to combat aircraft output wherein all the established aviation firms were fully committed, start-ups with fresh ideas had an advantage. There were no lack of these, with more than 300 firms pursuing helicopters emerging and failing during and immediately following the war. Among these aspirants was Frank N. Piasecki, a young (23 in the fall of 1943) yet experienced engineer (having worked at Platt-LePage) with vision and drive to succeed in developing helicopters and win military attention. Teaming with fellow engineering graduates including Harold Venzie, and attracting Elliot Daland, Platt-LePage's chief designer, they formed P-V Engineering Forum, incorporated in 1943 in Pennsylvania.

Initially performing aviation subcontractor defense work, the P-V team of youthful and enthusiastic individuals built the PV-2 single-place helicopter with a three-blade rotor and anti-torque tail unit. With an engine of just 90hp (67kW), the 1,000lb (454kg) PV-2 hovered and translated in addition to possessing a top speed of 100mph (161km/h). First flying on 11 April 1943, it was only the fourth helicopter type in the country to fly and the second as a private venture shown to the public. The PV-2 was demonstrated in the nation's capital on 20 October. The Navy took notice and, assessing the small PV-2 and its equally small team with confidence, gave them a task to develop the largest helicopter in the country.[57] The group had already conducted a conceptual design of a naval helicopter.

The work began with a study contract that included evaluation of the PV-2 rotor in a Langley tunnel. The goal for the helicopter, as proposed by P-V rather than BuAer, was an extraordinary 1,800lb (817kg) useful load and a crew of two for the Coast Guard SAR mission, especially rescuing sailors from sinking ships after being torpedoed. With a fuselage 47.2 feet (14.4 meters) long, this would provide a sizable cabin like that of a transport airplane. Piasecki performed careful concept design studies and settled on the longitudinal tandem rotor layout. Longitudinally displaced twin rotors reduced frontal area and thus drag while also permitting a generous CG travel. Distributing the lift across two rotors reduced disc loading and downwash velocity. It would require a long interconnecting shaft between the rotors for uniform free-spinning rate in autorotation, although this was omitted from the first demonstrator ship until very late in its testing. Aerodynamic influences were partially verified through model testing in a University of Pennsylvania wind tunnel. A formal proposal was drafted and, although it met with deep skepticism at BuAer, development go-ahead was given on New Year's Day 1944. On 1 February 1944 the Navy formally ordered two XHRP-1 prototypes (37968/9, eXperimental Helicopter tRansport Piasecki).

Power for the XHRP-1 (PV-3) was supplied by an R-975 at 450hp (336 kW) connected via power transmission shafts to a reduction gearbox beneath each rotor. The fuselage curved up at the rear to place the aft rotor above the front to avoid blade contact. The layout would soon earn this and like designs the moniker 'Flying Banana'. The construction was principally welded steel tubing with wood ribs and stringers covered with fabric. The interior volume was 400ft³ (11.3m³). Moving to a new site at Sharon Hill, still near Philadelphia, the small P-V team worked quickly.

In the event, only 37968 was completed during the war and referred to as the XHRP-X while it remained an experimental demonstrator. It was soon being called the 'dogship' because of its hard workout as an experimental aircraft, initially flown without external covering. The helicopter's maiden flight on 7 March 1945 had Piasecki and George Townson at the controls, these men having received helicopter training on R-4s at Floyd

Frank Piasecki and his P-V Engineering Forum had developed and flown only one single-place helicopter when the Navy contracted with them for America's largest helicopter undertaken during the war. The 1,800lb (817kg) load was far beyond anything attempted to that time, but the Navy insisted that this was what was required to meet its requirements. Yet the prototype XHRP-1 flew fourteen months after go-ahead, initially without the fabric and metal covering as seen here during initial shipboard trials with floatation bags. *National Archives*

Bennett Field. The machine was first demonstrated to Navy officials a month or two later. Much work remained to improve controllability. The company moved quickly under Piasecki's forceful leadership, sometimes cutting corners and safety, and suffering some close calls, to keep a step ahead of the competition. Fear by some of front rotor downwash disrupting the performance of the aft rotor during forward flight proved unfounded. Likewise, transmission weight and shaft vibration were all dealt with successfully. Testing uncovered mechanical deficiencies, especially with automotive parts incorporated into the prototype, but refinement showed the promise of the machine. It soon demonstrated the requisite payload with an external sling load of a log (another American first) only to encounter load pendulum motion, the ship being saved only when Piasecki jettisoned the log. The furthest it likely flew was to the Navy Yard in Philadelphia for a demonstration, yet it did eventually perform an autorotation to landing.

The second airframe, with an R-1340 of 600hp (447kW), was completed post-war by the then Piasecki Helicopter Corporation as the Static-Dynamic Test Article for more extensive testing to include sea trials. A production contract was let well after the war, and these machines would begin a long history of Piasecki 'Flying Bananas' with the US military.

Piasecki XHRP-1 characteristics

Rotor diameter	41.0ft (12.5m)
– therefore	
No. of rotor blades	3 on each rotor
Span	41.0ft (8.5m)
Length (fuselage)	48.0ft (14.6m)
Height	13.9ft (4.2m)
Weight, empty	5,041lb (2,287kg)
Weight, loaded	6,900lb (3,130kg)
Speed, max	110mph (177km/h)
Speed, uncovered	95mph (153km/h)
Range (100mph)	300 miles (483km)

Experimentation (Hiller UH-1X)

The Navy was finally focusing some engineering attention on rotorcraft and began to collect data and establish personnel with specific expertise. It took an interest in several helicopter design efforts. Among these was the work of Stanley Hiller Jr, who formed Hiller Aircraft in 1942 at 17 years of age, and in little more than a year had built the first successful American co-axial contra-rotating rotor helicopter. The layout, well known in helicopter circles, eliminated the weight and power loss associated with a tail rotor as well as the drag associated with tandem rotors. The single-place XH-44 Hiller-Copter of 1,244lb (564kg) empty weight was powered by a four-cylinder Franklin of 90hp (67kW, derated to 65hp [49 kW]).[58] The rigid rotor, 25 feet (7.6 meters) in diameter, was made especially stiff with all-metal blades. Essential in preventing flapping and flexure that could produce blade contact between the closely spaced rotors, the stiffness also reduced complexity and the other hazards associated with flexible wooden blades on hinges. Construction and balancing was also simplified.

The XH-44 flew in the San Francisco bay area during summer 1944 with remarkable stability and crisp response to controls. The small machine attracted the attention of Henry Kaiser, who had already attempted to develop a helicopter with Polish designer Bernard Sznycer working for Fleetwings (although reportedly designed by The Franklin Institute) and with the approval of the US government. The Kaiser-Fleetwings XH-10 Twirly Bird (NX41804) had a three-blade main rotor and a tail rotor. Mounted on floats, it was to accompany shipping convoys to scout for submarines. Although flight-tested in either 1944 or 1945, the results were apparently disappointing and the program did not advance from the prototype stage. The XH-44 appeared much more promising. Kaiser and Hiller formed the Hiller-Copter Division of Kaiser Cargo and began development of the X-2-235, a two-place, all-metal helicopter with a 235hp (175kW) Lycoming based on the XH-44.

Some Navy funding came for the X-2-235 during design and construction in the fall of 1944. In 1945 the company became United Helicopter and the aircraft the UH-1X. The third of the three flight test machines was delivered for Navy testing in a

Piasecki adopted the tandem rotor design for the XHRP-1 and it flew remarkably well. It met all performance goals and a production contract for the first naval helicopter was let in the final days of the war. With a capacity of ten passengers and a top speed of 110mph (177km/h), the Navy's cautious approach appeared well-rewarded. *National Archives*

Another youthful design team that flew a private-venture helicopter gaining military attention was that under the guidance of Stanley Hiller Jr. Their XH-44 Hiller-Copter, seen here, had a co-axial rigid rotor with metal blades. It flew in summer 1944 so effortlessly that the Navy funded development work on the X-2-235 spin-off. *Museum of Flight*

NACA Langley tunnel. This was not a full-up aircraft and may have been the rotor system alone; hence it received no military designation or BuNo. The Langley team hesitated to test the article to its limits in the tunnel for fear of vibration-induced failures. However, useful data were collected. While Hiller began ground testing the UH-1X in summer 1945, it appears that the Navy never went beyond the tunnel work, as the end of the war forced a marked constriction of expenditures.[59]

Pushing on (McDonnell XHJD-1)

The disappointing XR-1 work bore fruit in another form via a Navy contract with McDonnell Aircraft. The young St Louis, Missouri, firm under James McDonnell was eager to find niches in which it could make money and leave a mark. Hence McDonnell had a small team study rotor design and construction. An early financial backer of Platt-LePage, engineers were sent to Pennsylvania to assist and learn during development of the XR-1. Via this contact, McDonnell learned of the PL-9 twin-engine helicopter design that extended the XR-1 configuration but failed in the Army twin competition. The two companies agreed in June 1944 to permit McDonnell to develop the twin in return for further investment in Platt-LePage.[60]

McDonnell approached the Navy with a proposal to build the Model 65 as a testbed and possible ASW craft. In the former guise, it could be employed in researching rotor design variables. BuAer looked with favor upon this proposal as it had already concluded that the laterally displaced twin rotor configuration was the most favorable for such a mission. While slowly coming around to the idea of a naval helicopter, the Navy still saw that all existing rotorcraft companies, save for P-V Engineering, were fully engaged by the Army. McDonnell therefore represented a new avenue and a hedge against potential failure of the less-experienced P-V. Consequently, a Letter of Intent was issued on 15 May 1944 for a single XHJD-1 (44318), a contract following on 23 March 1945. The design at that time was well advanced but the helicopter was not finished until after the war.

The XHJD-1 'Whirlaway' was intended to accommodate up to ten occupants. The initial rotor diameter was 50 feet (15.2 meters) for a full span of 87 feet (26.5 meters). The height was predicted at 12.2 feet (3.7 meters) and the fuselage length 32.2 feet (9.8 meters). The empty weight was to be 8,000lb (3,629kg) and the loaded weight 11,000lb (4,990kg). Nacelles outboard of the fuselage each contained a 450hp (336kW) R-985-AN-14B engine. The pylons to the rotors constituted wings that generated about 10 percent of the lift during cruise flight and up to 30 percent during engine-out autorotation. Cross-shafting allowed any single engine to power both rotors with enough lift to sustain level flight at maximum gross weight. These features emphasized the inherent safety of the design. Downwash on the wings from the rotors would compromise somewhat the hover performance. The cruise speed was to be 90mph (145km/h), maximum 120mph (193km/h) at 5,000 feet (1,524 meters), with a range of 300 miles (483km). The anticipated rate of climb was 1,300fpm (6.6 meters per second) with an absolute ceiling of 12,900 feet (3,932 meters).

The XHJD-1 was flown post-war as the first twin-engine helicopter in America. Development was slowed by struggles with shaft and pylon resonances. The 'Whirlaway' served well as a testbed but was not manufactured as a service type.

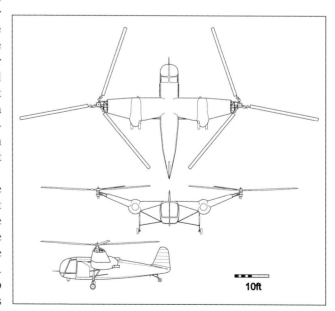

This drawing depicts the McDonnell XHJD-1 as it was first built, although initial testing had the outer wing skin paneling removed. Later testing would see a horizontal stabilizer added to the tail with lower struts. Some tests also had a winch arm protruding from the port wing leading edge just outboard of the sliding left-side door. *Author*

CHAPTER NINE

Targets Aloft

Foundation

THE NAVY INITIALLY took the lead in the US on target airplane development, for ship heavy anti-aircraft gunnery, and assigned Lieutenant Commander Delmar S. Fahrney at BuAer to head up the effort. Radio control of an existing airplane was the objective and the NAF handled the hardware and served as the base of test operations, while the Naval Research Laboratory (NRL) in Washington, D.C., worked the radio electronics. Almost the entire electronics and actuation system for the first such targets were fabricated in NAF and NRL shops. The BuAer's Radio Control Unit team adopted the name 'drone' for such aircraft. Within fifteen months, no-pilot solo ('nolo') flights were being made, and by early 1939 the targets were being flown over ships during exercises.

A dozen radio channels were selectable, each associated with axes of motion or specific functions like opening and closing of cowl flaps. Lights on the control box indicated that a channel was clear and ready for a command, followed by a tone.* The channels were created via a circuit that vibrated a reed for an audible tone transmitted over a high frequency (HF) carrier signal to a circuit tuned to the same oscillatory frequency. Radio direction from a control airplane was via a box with a short toggle that, when displaced, sent such commands over the selected channel with magnitude increasing proportional to the time the toggle was displaced. This came to be termed 'beeping' and the operators were

The initial team working on radio-controlled drones within the US Navy is shown with its leader, Lieutenant Commander Delmar S. Fahrney in the middle. They are standing before a Stearman-Hammond JH-1 target drone at the Naval Aircraft Factory in Philadelphia on 14 December 1936. Fahrney would go on to guide the drone work into various weapons during the Second World War and interface with his Army counterpart. *National Museum of Naval Aviation*

occasionally referred to as 'beeper pilots' employing 'beeper boxes'. The reeds were soon replaced with crystals (vacuum tubes) chosen to oscillate at harmonics of the carrier frequency such that crystals needed to be changed to alter the carrier. Even with the crystals, the tones were audible (one reason why the operators wore headphones) and any disturbance of the carrier heard could be indicative of radio interference.

Common were hydraulic servo motors with valves controlled by a solenoid operated via a radio control channel. Tricycle landing gear was chosen as the only practical arrangement for remote take-off and landing given its inherent stability during ground operations compared with a conventional ('tail dragger') undercarriage. For operations with a safety pilot aboard, the man could disable the drone system instantly and take over control.

* Radios during that era required careful monitoring and adjustment to ensure that a channel remained on frequency, as the electronics 'drifted'. This made them only marginally suitable for the remote-control tasks demanded of them in drone work.

The US Navy's target drone program of the late 1930s provided the foundation for turning the aircraft into strike weapons. The means for remote radio control of the unmanned aircraft were well established and projects were in work to improve these when the Americans were drawn into the war. Here a Navy operator prepares for either the take-off or landing of a drone, showing off the control unit to a cameraman while cables run to the generator and radio gear inside the van behind. *National Soaring Museum*

The drone was typically launched and landed by a ground operator at a field control station consisting of the control box connected to the transmitter typically installed in a van beside the runway running a power generator. At an altitude of about 200 feet (61 meters) following take-off, control was handed off to an inflight operator aboard a nearby aircraft, coordinated via voice transceiver. The control aircraft had to remain within sight of the drone, or no more than 2-3 miles (3.2-4.8km), or handed off to another control plane. For landing, the hand-off occurred at about 50 feet (15 meters). A lesson learned was to employ redundant controller systems at both ends. All these features of drone systems and operation became common for the wartime projects that followed.

Adaptation of manned airplanes to drones initially used just remote control and a simple wing leveler. Automatic stabilization evolved to include an autopilot. This operated with battery power and hydraulic servo motors. The rudder and ailerons were at first interconnected to simplify the control to only aileron actuation, this after initially having the rudder fixed. Modifications included a triple parachute emergency dive recovery system, the chutes being cut away after recovery. Likewise, emergency floatation bags were included to permit recovery in the event of alighting on water. Direct reading of aircraft course, airspeed or altitude was felt unnecessary as the judgment of the remote pilot was sufficient. A system was developed for automatic reaction to loss of radio signal (carrier): the drone would enter a shallow turn that would persist for 10 minutes before the throttle was cut automatically and a glide set up for ground impact.

Complementing the drone work, the Navy also advanced its remote control, auto-stabilization and radio telemetry hardware through use on aircraft undergoing very hazardous flight trials where a test pilot could not be risked. This was primarily high-speed dives of fighter-type aircraft. Along these lines, a compact system was developed that could be adapted to most aircraft. This single unit encompassed all mechanical, hydraulic and electronic elements.

By the time of the war, the Navy had a very adequate drone system with the Curtiss N2C-2 airplane, fitted with a fixed tricycle landing gear and capable of about 100mph (161km/h), and a Great Lakes TG-2 control plane.[1] An O2U-3 was also converted, retaining the conventional undercarriage, but this proved unsuccessful, with ground loops experienced until a plough on the tail wheel, improved brake control and greater rudder command available on the ground was introduced. In time, control of conventional-gear aircraft improved so that such measures were unnecessary. However, the tricycle undercarriage was still preferred.

By 1939, the drone program within the NAF was known as Project Fox. Operational units formed that year were Utility Squadron VJ-3 at Otay Mesa, San Diego, and VJ-5 at NAS

Cape May, New Jersey, to support fleet exercises as the system passed beyond the test stage. About this time the radios were change to those operating in the VHF band, permitting the use of a whip antenna.

Purpose-built drones

Feeling that they had a sound system, in early 1939 the Navy had contracted with the W. L. Maxson Corporation to produce a monoplane with a span of 30 feet (9.1 meters) and a 100hp (75kW) Menasco engine. The aircraft could be flown with conventional or tricycle gear. When tested, the equipment failed to meet requirements and the contract was cancelled on 27 May 1941. In the meantime, dozens of obsolete fleet aircraft were identified for conversion as drones. These included the Vought O2U, O3U-3 and -6, the Boeing F4B-3 and -4, the Curtiss SBC and the Vought SBU. By March 1941 a Beech JRB was also converted as a control plane. Six higher-performance, permanent-control aircraft (Northrop BT and Grumman JRF Goose) were also sought.

The use of converted outmoded types as anti-aircraft artillery (AAA) target drones continued after the US entered the war, and perhaps a dozen airplanes per month were being modified by 1941. This increased rapidly as airplanes were lost to hits or mishaps. An arrested landing (presumably employing a shore-based system) was demonstrated in August 1939 with a Vought O2U-3 drone (almost certainly on the conventional gear), then a catapult shot in May 1940 of an O2U-3 drone at the NAF (safety pilot aboard). Drone night flying began in the fall of 1944.

Guided by the same training motivation, the Army resumed remote-controlled drone development for training of ground forces (commonly much lighter weapons than naval vessels). Captain George V. Holloman was central to these efforts, having been working in the field of automatic flight systems and pilotless aircraft at Wright Field since 1935. He continued to lead the wartime guided missile work in the AAF, rising to Colonel before the end of the Second World War. Captain Leon D. 'Sparky' Hoffman supervised the Army's target drone and control aircraft development.

The USAAC had been working with Reginald Denny Industries of Hollywood, California, on a radio control (RC) airplane of small size and seeking a unit cost of a few hundred dollars. The firm was founded by Reginald L. Denny, an actor and Englishman possessing an aviation background, with Paul Whittier, modeler and National Guard flyer. They engaged electronics engineer Walter W. Case to develop the remote control systems and Walter Righter to build a small gasoline engine for their aircraft. The initial design had two side-by-side counter-rotating propellers to eliminate torque.

Denny demonstrated iterations of his system (RP-1 to RP-3) to the Army several times, beginning in 1935. None of the aircraft actually flew in a controlled manner and all ended in heaps. The service worked together with Denny to reach a reliable and practical system until a successful demonstration of the RP-4 won an order for three, delivered in May 1939, then fifty (despite another crash after a wild flight) of what became the OQ-1.[2] The firm became the Radioplane Company in November or December 1939 with a factory at the San Fernando Valley Airport, Van Nuys. Engines continued to come from Righter Manufacturing while the control equipment came from Bendix Aviation and Doolittle Radio. Further refinement into 1941 yielded the RP-5, suitable for high-rate production. It had the two propellers on concentric shafts for contra-rotation and thus yaw reduction. Originally designated A-2 and later OQ-2, deliveries of these began in June 1941 as the A-2A then the OQ-2A (Model RP-5A).[3]

The OQ-2A had a span of 12.2 feet (3.7 meters), was 8.7 feet (2.6 meters) long, weighed 108lb (50kg), and had a welded steel tube triangular fuselage with a wood structure wing, all covered in fabric. It was powered by a two-cylinder Righter engine that the Army would eventually designate the O-15 of 5-10hp (3.7-7.5kW) turning 26-inch (0.7-meter) wooden props. It had only elevator and rudder control surfaces. The tiny airplane could reach approximately 60mph (97km/h). With 1.8 gallons (6.8 liters) of fuel, endurance was about 70 minutes. Selling for $600 each, the little airplane was rapidly assembled, with many parts interchangeable and easily repaired.

The production system, with a single propeller, generally used a catapult for launch rather than the wheeled landing gear, although the gear was sometimes retained to help prevent damage on landing under parachute. The remote control module had five channels for up-down and left-right (beeper stick), and parachute deploy – interrupting a magnetic solenoid for spring release of the cover and chute from atop the fuselage. Recovery was via this 24-foot (7.3-meter) parachute, which would also deploy automatically if the aircraft was hit or the control signal interrupted. Controlled from the ground (line-of-sight transmission and a requirement for the controller to see the small airplane), it had a range of less than 1,000 feet (305 meters). There was a time delay of a split second that could promote over-control with new pilots. Additionally, the single propeller produced yawing torque that required controller compensation.

Small improvements then yielded the OQ-2B. In early 1944 the OQ-3 (MX-378) entered service, lighter in weight at 97lb (44kg) and with an uprated engine for 102mph (165km/h). The OQ-6 and OQ-7 were passed over for the OQ-14 (RP-8), which first flew in July 1944. This was also very similar, but the Righter/Kiekhaefer O-45 four-cylinder engine of 22hp (16kW) gave a top speed of 140mph (225km/h). It had a unit price of around $700. These three models were being built at such a quick rate and in such numbers that the Frankfort Sailplane Company of Joliet, Illinois, had to be brought in to supplement Radioplane's output. The Navy also took an interest in this development, and by 1943 it was purchasing the TDD (Target Drone Denny) in the -1, -2 and -3 models, catapulted from ships for small-caliber AAA practice (up to 40mm), and shore-based for Marine Corps training. Radioplane and its subcontractors delivered 14,891 of these small RC airplane drones during the war.

The US Army sought targets sized like model airplanes for small-caliber anti-aircraft guns supporting troop movements. The Radioplane Company supplied thousands of the OQ-2, OQ-3 and OQ-14 targets, at prices in the order of $700, to be gleefully shot out of the sky by American soldiers. This image shows a Navy TDD (OQ-2A) being prepared for launch from a ship's catapult, after which it would be controlled by the pilot shown.
Left National Archives/right National Museum of Naval Aviation

In the quest for a suitable and cost-effective aerial target for AA gunners, the Air Corps contracted in mid-1939 with three companies for prototypes. Fleetwings ended up as the only firm to deliver the aircraft, the A-1, spanning 20 feet and weighing 628lb. Testing in 1940 proved the type disappointing and the effort was closed without production. Note the lack of rudder. *National Museum of the United States Air Force*

The USAAC was interested in a drone between the size of the RC airplanes and a converted full-size machine, and by summer 1939 had types with spans of approximately 20 feet (6.1 meters) under development. A contract was given for two aircraft, designated A-1, from each of three companies. Fleetwings Incorporated, of Bristol, Pennsylvania, got its contract in May, for prototypes to be delivered on 17 February and 17 April 1940. The radio-controlled Fleetwings A-1 was on tricycle gear and spanned 20 feet (6.1 meters), mounting an 80hp (60kW) engine. Weighing 628lb (285kg), it was to reach 180mph (290km/h) and a climb rate of 1,000 fpm (305mpm) to a 10,000-foot (3,048-meter) ceiling. Tested at Aberdeen, Maryland, on 10 August 1940, the first example crashed due to an inadvertent stall and over-control following take-off. Flights of the second prototype were very difficult and the Army chose not to proceed further with this type. The other contenders, the DeSoto Airplane Company and Vega Airplane Company, appear to have been dropped before their fall 1939 delivery dates.

The conversion of full-size USAAC machines to power-driven targets had proceeded, and by December 1940 forty-nine A-4 targets had been created at Materiel Division from North American BT-2 basic trainers, modified with tricycle landing gear and capable of 130mph (209km/h). Another ten became control ships. The use of other converted USAAC airplanes was examined through experiments that included the Boeing P-12 (drone A-5), Douglas O-38 (A-6) and Bell P-39 (A-7). How far this program proceeded is unclear as the A-7 is known to have gone no further than the planning stage.[4] While the others were clearly outmoded types, the P-39 had value and by 1941 none could be discarded as targets. Seeing the need for hundreds if not thousands of such airplanes, a more permanent solution was sought in new-built drones from light plane designs, all single-engine, monoplane machines with tricycle gear. These PQ types could be flown manned, for ferry and system check-out, or remotely with a safety pilot or unmanned. In August 1940 the USAAC introduce the concept at a Wright Field meeting with about twenty light plane manufacturers invited, urging them to bid.

The Army quest led to conversion of the Culver Airplane Company's Model LFA Cadet two-place sport plane with retractable landing gear and semi-monocoque aluminum construction. Originally in Columbus, Ohio, Culver moved to Wichita, Kansas, in 1941. Delivered in December 1940, the

Army evaluated the aircraft as the XPQ-8 (initially A-8, project MX-79) prototype in 1940 and found it suitable. However, it insisted on a fixed undercarriage for simplicity, and wood, plastic and fabric construction. To help ensure against a spin that the RC operator could not hope to recover, the wing was altered to greatly delay stall and enhance stability. This included adding a leading-edge slot ahead of each aileron. The rudder was used for taxi but locked up and away so that turns were not coordinated. The engine was also changed from a Franklin to the Continental YO-200-1 of the same 90hp (67kW).

An order for seventy-five PQ-8s (Model LAR-90) was placed, at $2,875 apiece. It was soon evident that Culver had underestimated the airframe cost and the Army raised the price to $3,275 each. The remote control gear, jokingly referred to as 'Yehudi' after a contemporary magician, was $1,100. This was installed behind the cockpit where it could interface with the control cables. The gear in the control plane was another $1,000 or so.[5] An operator typically required about 50 hours of practice with a safety pilot aboard to become fully proficient. The wing had a span of 26.9 feet (8.2 meters) and the maximum gross weight was 1,305lb (592kg). It topped out at 118mph (190km/h) and could go 450 miles (724km).

A further order followed to total 200 PQ-8s and a like number of PQ-8As (A-8A), all delivered in 1942. With a 125hp (93kW) Lycoming 0-290-1 engine and an enlarged balanced rudder, the A model could make 128mph (206km/h) for 300 miles (483km) or 2.1 hours, on 18.8 gallons (71 liters) of fuel. By spring 1941 the quantity of obsolete naval types available for drone conversion was being rapidly drawn down, so the USN looked to the Army's PQ examples for the role. It requested a PQ-8 on 14 February 1942 for testing. This proved a satisfactory substitute for the Maxson drone, and the first contract with Culver soon followed for 200 TDC-2 (Target Drone Culver, PQ-8A) aircraft. These assets were even deployed to the war zones for ongoing training.

The maximum airspeed of the PQ-8A/TDC-2 was woefully non-representative of enemy combat aircraft. Hence the Culver PQ-14 (Model NR-D, MX-264) was developed as an enlarged

and improved version of the PQ-9, the drone conversion of the commercial NRB that was passed over for production because of its unfortunate flat spin characteristics. All wood with the wing spanning 30 feet (9.1 meters), the PQ-14 was powered by a Franklin 155hp (116kW) O-300-11. It featured retractable landing gear and a sliding canopy. Control surfaces were increased in area for enhanced maneuverability. Grossing 1,820lb (826kg), it had a maximum airspeed without pilot of 188mph (303km/h). The Navy also acquired production PQ-14As as TD2C-1s. On 16 October 1942 the fleet requested BuAer to deliver twenty per month for firing exercises. The production PQ-14A saw nearly 2,000 built in various models, most going to the Navy. The marginally heavier B model had different models of the O-300, 594 of which were produced.

There were a number of other such light planes evaluated by both the Army and Navy for potential production as drones. Among these, the Fletcher Aviation Corporation of Pasadena, California, built ten wooden PQ-11s (42-46892/901) powered by a 450hp (336kW) R-985-AN-1 and with electrically actuated flaps, before the order was dropped. The PQ-11s were a redesign of the CQ-1 drone control aircraft (see later). Fletcher had completed a single YCQ-1A (41-38984) in 1942, but a follow-on preproduction order was cancelled.

Fleetwings was contracted in 1941 for a fixed-gear XPQ-12 (Model 36). This was altered before completion to an XPQ-12A and eight YPQ-12As for bomb drone trials (see Chapter 10). These airplanes, delivered in 1942, were powered by a 225hp (168kW) Lycoming XO-435-5 turning a constant-speed propeller. Unique for targets, the airplanes also had self-sealing tanks and some small quantity of armor plate for the remote control equipment.[6] An additional forty-two PQ-12As were cancelled.

Drone control aircraft were also created by adopting existing designs. These were the one-off Fletcher CQ-1, the Stinson CQ-2 derived from the L-1A, and the CQ-3 derived from the Beech UC-45F twin (1944 conversion). The CQ-1 was itself a redesign of the unsuccessful Fletcher FBT-2 wooden trainer with fixed conventional gear and an R-985-A-1 engine.

The Culver PQ-8 drone (seen here as a Navy TDC-2) was a diminutive alternatively manned drone with a 125hp engine and a radio aerial stretching from wingtip to wingtip across the post above the cockpit. The Culver was the first of a series of targets based on light plane designs that offered better performance than the tiny Radioplane models. The picture at right shows the interior with the basic pilot station and remote control gear.
Left National Archives/right National Museum of the United States Air Force

The Culver PQ-9 was a drone conversion of the commercial NRB, which did not go into production. For unmanned target operations, it had the cockpit faired over for reduced drag. This approach would be employed in some of the bomb drone types. *National Archives*

The Culver PQ-14 was a significant improvement on the PQ-8, derived from a private light plane with a larger airframe and engine but only a single seat under a sliding canopy. A top speed of 185mph (278km/h) made it a more representative target for gunners. The picture at right shows the cockpit with the quadrant on the left for the throttle and a switch from manual to servo control. *National Museum of the United States Air Force*

A Navy drone operator lands a TD2C-1 (PQ-14B), displaying the makeshift controller station mounted off the front bumper of the truck that contains a generator and transmitter. The smaller picture is an image of the controller box with joystick and several single-channel selector switches. Such technology fed directly into the assault drone program. *Left: Naval Aviation Archive/ Right: Air Force Test Center*

Another competitor for the USAAF light airplane target drone role was this Fleetwings design, designated PQ-12. After a prototype, eight YPQ-12A aircraft were delivered in 1942. Seen here in a manned configuration preparing for take-off, the diminutive size of the craft is evident. *National Museum of the United States Air Force*

For unmanned flights, the windscreen and roll-over bar of the YPQ-12A were removed and a fairing installed over the cockpit. This view of the aircraft shows the fixed-pitch wooden prop, the cowling for the flat Lycoming engine, and the fixed landing gear. Although the Fleetwings type did not go into high-rate production, the airframes would serve a vital test role in weaponizing target drones. *National Archives*

AMERICAN AIRCRAFT DEVELOPMENT OF WWII

Fletcher developed a wooden light trainer before the war, but it did not interest the military services. However, it was explored as the PQ-11 drone target, the CQ-1A drone control ship (shown here), and as a powered missile armed with a bomb, but was found unsuitable for each. The PQ-11 retained the windscreen and a roll-over bar, but eliminated the canopy and faired over the rear seat. *National Museum of the United States Air Force*

By mid-1944 the performance of the Culver drones was considered inadequate by the USN. Stating a need for a true airspeed of up to 400mph (644km/h) at 10,000 feet (3,048 meters), only combat types were expected to be suitable. The conversion of a Grumman F6F-3 Hellcat was begun in June 1945, with 100 examples the initial goal. Such aircraft required more modifications to be suitably operated remotely given their greater complexity, including multiple fuel tanks and powerplant controls. Ten channels of control were required.

Sitting duck

Some of the moderate-performance Army aircraft turned to drones, like the P-39 becoming the A-7, could have served as targets for aerial gunnery. For decades such shooting was taught using fabric banners or, much more commonly, sleeves towed by another aircraft. The fired rounds were painted with a dye that left a mark on the sleeve, permitting hits to be counted after flight and the scoring gunner or pilot identified via the associated color. The USAAF also employed Bristol C-1 towed glider

A Navy operator executes a landing of an unmanned Grumman F6F-1 Hellcat fighter using a control unit positioned beside the runway. The parallel to drones flown in this manner today is striking. The Army-derived targets were not satisfying mission needs by mid-1944, so ageing machines like the Hellcat, backed by a prodigious industry output of new fighters, permitted high-performance machines to be substituted. *National Soaring Museum*

Above: This Martin JM-2 (91983, TB-26G) was photographed in 1945 towing a target sleeve. This was the common means of practicing aerial gunnery for many years, at least for deflection fighter firing. However, it left much to be desired, including lack of maneuvering. *National Archives*

Left: In the early war years the Air Forces used this C-1 towed glider as an airborne target. The simple device spanned 35.0 feet, was 33.0 feet long and 6.3 feet high, and was towed at the nose from takeoff to landing. Bristol Aeronautical of New Haven, Connecticut, assembled 21 of the targets in 1942 and 1943. *National Museum of the United States Air Force*

targets. This allowed only moderate maneuvering, if any. For fighters, only deflection shooting with intercepts from the side were permitted. The tow planes were usually second-rate machines performing a job that challenged them little before retirement. Combat results showed that the training left much to be desired, especially for gunners.[7]

More effective aerial gunnery targets were sought during the war. The Navy experimented with a towed glider that may have had some measure of maneuverability. The Army wanted high performance with considerable maneuverability, and rounds that would not damage the aircraft or pilot. Flying in relatively close proximity to manned aircraft (bomber with gunnery students) demanded a manned target. Such a system was conceived and fostered by USAAF Major Cameron D. Fairchild, beginning in spring 1942, eventually with the assistance of the National Defense Research Committee (NDRC). The complexity of the task emerged over time, contributing to nearly three years elapsing before the concept was put into practice.

The gunners would be firing only frangible rounds, which disintegrated on impacting the armor added to the exterior of the target aircraft. The bullets were made of a lead and phenolic mix developed at Duke University by Professor Paul Gross, with the assistance of Princeton University, as well as the Bakelite Corporation, which manufactured the rounds. Only ·30-caliber guns would be used, requiring changes to the mounts that commonly accommodated ·50-cal guns. The guns and sights also required modifications, combined with slower engagement speeds, because of the different muzzle velocities and ballistics.

To explore this concept, the wing from a Douglas A-20 Havoc medium bomber was armored and subjected to fire from handmade frangible bullets in early 1944. Later that year an A-20C (41-29205) was modified at Wright Field as a target for further testing. It was armored to take hits over some 75 percent of its outer surface in the forward and center fuselage, inboard wing panels, and nacelles. Louvered panels covered the forward face of the cowlings. The entire top decking and cockpit enclosure was removed and faired over,

Seeking a more effective aerial gunnery target, the Navy developed a towed glider, shown here behind a JM-1 (TB-26). The bifurcated tow lines, attached above the nose of the glider, enhanced stability on tow. There are clearly two lines to each post, suggesting cables around pulleys for some manner of maneuvering control, although the glider clearly has no moving control surfaces – possibly just pulling the nose over to yaw and causing a skid to the side. *National Archives*

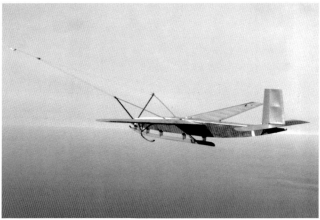

The solitary A-20C modified as an airborne target was photographed on 1 April 1944. Evident is the added outer layer of thick-gauge metal (painted green) on the fuselage and on the wings as far as the outer panels, but not on the tail. Note the louvered covers on the forward face of the cowlings, the open top entry hatch of armored glass, and the plexiglass nose, which was frequently damaged in the testing. *National Museum of the United States Air Force*

with the exception of an armored glass cupola added over the pilot's station, the top panel hinged for pilot entry. All armament was removed.

The A-20C testing began with the frangible rounds fired at the aircraft on the ground in Dayton from about 25 yards (23 meters), with men in the cockpit to win the confidence of the skeptical pilots assigned to the project. The first frangible bullet flight testing was conducted at Buckingham AAF, Fort Myers, Florida, with the A-20 flying against a YB-40.[8] All seemed to work well until an engine of the A-20 quit and it could not hold altitude in its heavyweight condition. Fortunately, the pilot was able to bring it down to an emergency landing at an auxiliary field (an unrelated engine issue was to blame). The trials proved the practicality of the maneuvering manned target and frangible round concept, but the A-20 was clearly not the best target airplane. What was sought was an aircraft more like a Messerschmitt Bf 109, and the Bell P-63 was selected.

The frangible bullet program became one of the few American roles for the P-63 Kingcobra, which was almost exclusively exported and not employed by main-line US combat units. The intent was relative invulnerability within 30 degrees of broadside, the 'pursuit curve', with orders that gunners cease firing once the attacker angled off in order to preclude hitting unarmored elements of the aircraft. All weapons and normal armor for the cockpit and vital components were removed to permit an outer skin of some 2,000lb (907kg) of thicker-gauge aluminum to be added throughout. Most was attached over the

original skin. The aluminum plating varied from 0.050 to 0.375 inches (1-10mm) thick. Full gear well doors were added to cover the main gear tires. The canopy framing was reinforced to take armored glass, and the cockpit rear transparency was eliminated. The internal fuel capacity was increased to compensate for an inability to carry external tanks. The carburetor intake scoop on the spine was a source of several solutions, including removal and a smaller, then retractable, scoop installed. A single cover or individual shrouds were installed above the exhaust stubs. The wing leading-edge intakes for the engine coolant radiators had baffling installed in an attempt to deflect the bullets. Hits were detected by 109 vibration sensors under the aircraft skin, which electrically tripped a counter as well as setting off a large red light on the spinner. This light proved ineffective (being seldom observed), so several lights were later installed elsewhere, including at the wingtips.

Two P-63As were modified in July and August 1944 to become RP-63As, the first flying on 1 September.[9] Trials with the first RP-63 and the A-20C were flown at Laredo AAF, Texas. After three more RP-63As, production began in late summer 1944. Another ninety-five were created from P-63As, followed by 200 RP-63Cs and finally thirty-two RP-63Gs. This last had more lights and 100hp (75kW) additional power as well as, more importantly, heavier and better-oriented armor to permit other forms of attack than the outdated pursuit curve.

The lighting up of the aircraft when hit by rounds inevitably gave the frangible bullet program the nickname 'Pinball'. All assets were in hand by late 1944, but training did not begin in

An RP-63G armored target aircraft, with white stripes over the orange finish, awaits attention in a hangar. The image reveals the baffling in the wing root intakes to the coolant radiators intended to deflect the frangible rounds, as well as the reduced-height spine carburetor air scoop. These modified machines were developed to be intentionally fired at by aerial gunners aboard bombers during mock attacks, shooting frangible bullets. *Jay Miller Collection*

earnest until April 1945. Although some 11,000 student training missions were flown and 12 million rounds expended, this late date ensured that benefits did not affect the outcome of the war. It still had developmental issues but was considered the most effective aerial gunnery training system to that time.

While the 'Pinball' effort was successful, it was not carried off without some harm to the target airplane, which increased risk. Some gunners kept firing after the attacker turned away in the break, and therefore hit the radiator exhaust. Bullet fragments occasionally damaged the cooling system and loss

of coolant or engine oil was the cause of several forced landings. This was finally the reason for grounding the fleet in early August 1945 when five RP-63s had been 'shot down' in the span of a week, a pilot dying in one of the forced landings. An order for 450 RG-63G targets was cancelled after the first thirty-two were delivered in September. The RP-63Z was being designed with a heavy structure to which the armor could be directly attached, but this, too, was dropped.

One of the two prototype RP-63G 'Pinball' target aircraft, painted bright orange, is shown with a large bull's-eye marking on the flank. Evident is the metal replacing the rear transparency, shrouds on the exhaust stubs, full main gear doors, and the flush carburetor intake on the spine. The frangible bullet training proved practical and valuable, but hits on the coolant system and the end of the war saw demise of the program and the RP-63s. *Jay Miller Collection*

CHAPTER TEN

Drones Proliferate

Gizmo

THE PATH to an operational target drone and on to bomb-carrying types depended on reliable stability, control, guidance, and targeting hardware. All this was developed before the war in the period of economic hardship, then under wartime pressures as a combat system.

For the Army, just contemplating loss of an expensive gyro in a terminal test caused anxiety. In time, the Hammond Organ Company developed an electric gyro sold at just $15 each. By 1943 a single-package autopilot servo unit had been developed to fly the PQ airplanes. This included three-axis stabilization and control together with radio channels for throttle, nose wheel steering, and brakes.

Drone targeting would require a more precise means of flying the aircraft to a specific point than watching it from another aircraft miles away. The solution appeared to be television (TV) images of the view ahead transmitted from the drone in daylight, and possibly the instrument panel or other collection of instruments by day or night. Television was then still in its infancy, but the Radio Corporation of America (RCA) of Camden, New Jersey, had before the war developed a lightweight yet relatively rugged unit and operated it from an aircraft, but only by compromising image quality. When

This Piper LBP-1 towed glider bomb is an example of a parallel class of weapons employing much the same technology as the assault drones. They also employed radio remote control and television guidance, although autonomous steering was also explored. Unlike the Army, the Navy pursued the glider bombs quite a long way before abandoning that route. *National Archives*

RCA's proposal to adapt its unit to a radio-controlled glide bomb was met with indifference from the service, the company worked with the NDRC.[1] Fortunately, this work was then mined by the services in support of drones and other projects.

The Naval Aircraft Factory was authorized to purchase its first TV equipment from RCA on 14 October 1939, and it performed preliminary ground tests of the gear under a 24 February 1940 contract. The 70lb (32kg) of equipment was taken to flight evaluations aboard a tricycle gear Lockheed XJO-3 in January and February 1941. Continuing into June, the trials showed that an individual 20-30-miles (32-48km) away could direct (from ashore) a pilot of the aircraft mounting the camera to fly directly over a target. RCA had continued development and built a camera and transmitter unit called the Jeepette weighing 35lb (15.9kg) and measuring 8 by 13 by 15 inches (20 by 33 by 38cm). Resolution of the 7-inch (18cm) cathode ray tube display was 350 scanning lines at a rate of forty frames per second. (The power supply weighed another 26lb [12kg].) It operated at around 100 megacycles (megahertz, MHz) with the option of four individual channels. The receiver weighed 20lb (9kg), with a 37lb (17kg) battery. Pictures could be received at a range of 50-60 miles (81-97km), and a target such as a vessel at sea identified 8 miles (13km) from the camera plane.

Trials on 7 August 1941 with the camera mounted in a pod under the port wing of a TG-1 drone resulted in the first ever successful guidance via TV under radio control. Some fifty simulated torpedo drops were made with the airplane beyond sight of the controller, at up to 6 miles (10km) distant, with clear picture reception. The Army bought the same RCA sets with few changes and conducted its first flight tests in April 1941 aboard a Douglas B-18 bomber. The system was ordered into production in 1942 as the Block I, which got the camera weight to 33lb (15kg) and the transmitter to 26lb (12kg), measuring 9 by 10 by 20 inches (23 by 25 by 51cm). It also operated at around 100 MHz with the option of four individual channels. The follow-on Block III used a 264-312 MHz band with five individually selectable channels, and was believed less susceptible to jamming. It separated the camera and transmitter, but the total weight of the gear rose to 90lb (41kg). The cost of such systems was approximately $2,000 per unit.

Radar (an established technology) offered a means of directing the drone in periods of darkness or in weather where sight and television were ineffective. Radar guidance was explored via a project begun on 31 March 1941 with the NAF, NRL and NDRC participating. The NRL developed a 3cm wavelength (microwave) system that could employ a scanning concave antenna under a radome instead of the aerials used theretofore. An airborne example was tested in a blister under the fuselage of a Beech JRB-2, permitting an all-around sweep to track sea targets and drones. Instead of 'skin paint' reflection tracking, the NAF sought an Identification Friend or Foe (IFF) radar beacon in the 3cm wavelength for installation aboard the drone to permit directing it via radar and as a means of targeting and terminal guidance (automatically steering to radar reflections from the target).[2] The NRL was at work on this beginning on 1 August 1941 in cooperation with the Radiation Laboratory at the Massachusetts Institute of Technology (MIT).

The radar work converged to a decision on 28 August 1942 to use the 10cm ASV radar for tracking and IFF, this system already being well progressed at MIT, while NRL developed the drone's 3cm targeting and terminal guidance radar. The JRB-2 was assigned to support this work. The NAF also tested the 60cm ASB radar characterized by external 'comb' antennae under each wing, which had to be manually rotated. This was hardly suitable for a drone, but the tests explored the 'repeat-back' function (scan results sent via radio link). During March 1943 the flight test team managed three simulated engagements out of thirteen attempts against a lighthouse. Further refinement and training on 3-4 June yielded sixteen 'hits' out of twenty-one engagements of the lighthouse and ships under way.

The weapons applications came to focus on glide bombs and missiles riding the radar energy generated by the 'mother ship' as an adjunct to manual TV guidance. This appeared the shortest path to a practical system. The more complex problem of homing on reflected radar energy had to compete against the other urgent programs. Hence the Navy defined its requirements for the drone as radar homing to generate correction signals to the drone control system as it rode the beam from the control aircraft. All this envisioned a control plane illuminating a target with radar energy and initially guiding one or more drones indicated by IFF signals. The radar Plan Position Indicator (PPI)

display would show targets within the scan and range of the Aircraft Search Unit radar, permitting the controller to direct one or more drones towards the target with radio signals, with the final run-in via TV. All had to operate on 12-volt power. Both 3cm and 10cm systems were to be pursued. Desired ultimately was a self-contained homing system, transmitter and receiver, aboard the drone for autonomous terminal guidance. An AT-11 aircraft (possibly referring to the Navy's JRB variant of the Beech 18) was to serve as the development platform, while the surrogate drone would be a TG-2.

In early 1940 progress was already being made on precision radio altimeter control for exact flight above the sea supporting drone torpedo runs. Work was conducted by Western Electric in cooperation with the NAF. The initial 95lb (43kg) set derived from a 1939 development and, demonstrated in flight on 29 January 1941, was too bulky to fly in a drone. However, the NAF began working with RCA in early May 1941 for a more practical airborne kit, which was to be installed in two Vought observation planes in preparation for the torpedo tests. It represented the first successful such system in the world. Manufacture of 36lb (16kg) units followed for both services.

The RCA radio altimeter work was also turned, literally, to a horizontal scan for target ranging. In the frequency-modulated (FM) radar spectrum, it resulted in a lighter unit demanding less power, and one that was easier to tune than other radar then in use. In a switching mode, looking to the sides in a repeated scan, it could also serve for target homing. Tests showed an effective range of 2 miles (3.2km). This RL 101 'sniffer' provided the means for automatic weapon release at a preset range from the target. Tested in April and May 1943 with an SNB (Beech 18) drone, good automatic bomb releases between 98 and 207mph (157 and 333km/h) were achieved. The RL 102 'supersniffer' sought the automatic homing feature employing an arc search. A specification was issued in February 1943 for the RL 102 with an initial range of 2 miles (3.2km), then 6 miles (9.7km). Trials with the 'supersniffer' in May 1943 were the first successful radar homing experiences in the world, with a drone seeking and locking onto a moving tanker vessel target at a range of 2 miles. They soon yielded ranges of 4.5-5 miles (7.2-8.1km) when flying at 50 feet (15 meters), and 6-8 miles (9.7-12.9km) at 200-300 feet (61-91 meters).

Tests of the 'supersniffer' for autonomous weapon release were promising. Development was also conducted on infrared (heat) detection for autonomous guidance, with good outcome. All these advanced systems were ordered into production with the intention that they be introduced at the earliest opportunity into new drones then being produced.

The NRL also worked to ensure against enemy jamming of the direction signals by employing pulse signals. This does not appear to have progressed far during the war, and such jamming remained a true concern if widespread combat employment of such systems followed.

These resources had applications beyond the drones, which represented the first obvious guided missiles. Applications of the control, guidance, targeting and homing technology to missiles were a natural follow-on to the assault drone effort. The services had numerous air-launched and surface-launched missile programs, but these were a step behind the drones in maturation, so appeared even less likely to contribute to the war. However, as the duration of the war remained uncertain and the missiles were clearly going to be important in post-war developments, the drones endured as clearly short-term weapons of circumstance.

The work also extended to Army and Navy gliders (modified as well as uniquely designed aircraft), stabilized automatically on tow and, following release, guided remotely from the tow plane via television cameras or steered autonomously via the various sensing methods. Onboard electrical power was usually derived from a wind-driven generator charging a battery that might also power a hydraulic pump. The Navy efforts advanced to actual guided impacts in target areas, but the Army dropped its program earlier. None of these systems were deployed. The limitations of the immature technology were just too great.[3]

Parallel missiles

Before Pearl Harbor, the American armed services had developed auto-stabilization via gyroscope to an operational level while the various guidance methods were emerging in the laboratory. Apart from target drones, this prompted an interest in steered gravity bombs, stand-off glide bombs, then powered missiles. While a remotely piloted airplane appeared the shortest path to a guided missile, these other approaches were pursued in parallel. In January 1944 the USAAF ranked guided missiles

second only behind fighter range-extension tanks as the number one Air Forces materiel acquisition project, but they were clearly a long-term effort.[4] The Navy projects were under the Special Weapons Ordnance Devices (SWOD) program, but the service also participated in some of the Army projects. Few of these weapons reached production and even fewer combat, but some of the technology development benefited the drones.

The initial impetus was a glide weapon that provided a stand-off from heavily defended targets and a flat trajectory for impacting tall targets. These included standard bombs and torpedoes with lifting and control surfaces attached, together with auto-stabilization systems to keep them upright during flight. Dropped from external mounts on a bomber, their direction of travel and range were dependent on launch conditions and preset control surfaces. Range was typically a few miles and accuracy roughly half a mile. The Army's initial effort, beginning in May 1941, adopted a 2,000lb (907kg) bomb as the GB-1, which were pressed into production in the thousands. The path to combat proved frustratingly long, and it was three years before they were employed. Poor workmanship and low system reliability were evident in the disappointing results. The bombing outfits disliked the performance impact on the parent bomber and were confident that they could do better with conventional techniques. The Navy equivalent was the Dragon, with a more aerodynamic airframe encompassing a 1,000lb bomb. The glide torpedo (GT-1) had a similar experience and more refined variants were abandoned.

A quick path to a winged bomb was just that: aero surfaces added to a general-purpose bomb to permit stand-off from heavily defended targets and a flat trajectory impact of vertical targets. It required gyro-stabilization and external carriage on the bomber (this B-17 carrying two GB-1s) with a performance decrement, but reliability was poor. They were produced in large numbers and provided a basis for follow-on guided glide bombs. *National Archives*

For precision targeting, the Army had started a Controlled Vertical Bomb Program in November 1941 in cooperation with the NDRC. This sought to provide the bombardier with a means for correcting the fall of the bomb to hit a point target. Initial guidance was by the bombardier visually directing the bomb to the target via radio control, usually aided by a flare at the top end of the weapon. The first had a pair of rudders in the tail unit that also incorporated a gyro stabilization unit to counter roll, and a radio receiver, all added to a 1,000lb bomb. The package provided only azimuth (yaw) control, hence the name VB-1 Azon (AZimuth ONly). This proved more effective than conventional bombing in hitting long narrow targets, such as bridges and roadways, from a distance of 1-2 miles (1.6-3.2km) radius. It still required three radio channels (left, right and flare ignition), but multiple bombs (typically six) could be so controlled simultaneously, although it was vulnerable to jamming. Thousands were built and widely used throughout 1944 and 1945, though with little acclaim. A 2,000lb (907kg) version (VB-2) was manufactured in small numbers.

Arresting roll to permit the azimuth control meant that fall dispersal increased owing to bomb exterior irregularities. Addressing this by permitting some spin during the initial portion of the fall – as the Spazon – was successful, but came too late. The addition of range control to the controlled bomb yielded the 1,000lb VB-3 and 2,000lb VB-4 Razon (Range and AZimuth ONly) weapons, which then encountered parallax issues that made it difficult for the bombardier to judge the potential impact point. An infrared seeker was incorporated in the VB-6 Felix version. Applying the Razon technology to the 12,000lb (5,443kg) 'Tallboy' bomb yielded the VB-13 Tarzon. These weapons did not reach an operational stage during the war.

The natural next step was for control of a glide bomb via radio and guidance by sight. The resulting GB-8 was given priority and finally ordered into production in the thousands on 10 November 1943. It possessed control similar to target drones, requiring bombardier control in three axes mechanized as three separate radio channels. Excellent results were only achieved

Providing some remote control and targeting guidance to free-fall bombs was another path pursued with very modest results. The VB-1 Azon (AZimuth ONly) shown here was manufactured in thousands and used with some success. The photo shows the 1,000lb bomb with its tail kit containing rudders, the box containing the stabilization and remote control gear, and brackets for mounting the tracking flare. *Air Force Test Center*

under test conditions, requiring a high degree of operator skill to be employed accurately. Carried externally, they slowed the parent aircraft and were themselves slow and thus vulnerable to AAA. Combat introduction in Europe during summer 1944 yielded disappointing results. The GB-9 variant included a radio or barometric altimeter to level off for low-angle impact.

Control by radio and guidance via TV (GB-4, VB-7 and VB-8, and Navy Robin variant of the Dragon) with a radar beacon was manifest principally in the GB-4, a spin-off of the GB-1 (although more streamlined), quickly devised and tested in early December 1941. A Block III TV camera and transmitter were placed in a faired container beneath the bomb, with an antenna on the tail. This mandated another radio channel for the TV signal, and it was thus much more complex and subject to jamming, while remote flight control was challenging. Delayed by Block III development issues and emphasis on the GB-1, the GB-4 was not tested operationally until late summer 1944 with very poor results owing to low television reliability and clarity limitations, in addition to the need for near perfect weather. Lacking a propulsion system, the speed of such single-pass weapons could not be controlled and was too fast (especially the VB) to effect last-second flight path changes once the target (if any) was resolved.

Some work was done on a light-contrast seeker for the free-fall bombs (VB-5 variant of VB-3 and VB-9/VB-10) and glide bombs employing a photo-electric cell. This was expected to be successful against a vessel at sea (GB-12), homing on a flare (GB-13) dropped on a target by an aircraft, or homing on enemy searchlights. For the anti-shipping application, the device proved too sensitive to the position of the sun and general lighting conditions, and the time required to stabilize the weapon after launch could cause the target to be lost. The flare-seeker weapon took too long to develop. Infrared seekers were explored (GB-6 and VB-6/VB-11), but again sun angle and reflections, in addition to humidity and haze, offered difficulties. The VB-9 and VB-10 Roc had cruciform wings and tail for a less steep descent. A variant of the Roc (both 1,000 and 2,000lb variants) possessed a gimbaled ring wing (lift vectoring) for range and azimuth control, while the ring tail had vanes for roll control and a decelerating shroud to slow the weapon for more practical manual guidance via TV. The ring arrangement permitted internal carriage in a B-29. Although showing promise, none of these projects advanced to production during the war.

Radar targeting began with semi-active homing (GB-7 and VB-9) in which the weapon steered autonomously to radar energy reflected off a target illuminated by an aircraft. The Navy equivalents were the Pelican (500lb/228kg bomb or 325lb/147kg depth charge, and enlarged for 1,000lb/454kg and 1,500lb/680kg bombs) and the Moth (650lb/229kg bomb) in a new glider body. The NDRC independently developed the radar-homing Pelican weapon, which eventually gained the interest of the USN. Active homing had the radar aboard the GB-14 gliding weapon and a Navy Bat (the same airframe as the Pelican with a 1,000lb warhead). With an effective range of 12-13 miles (19-21km), the Bat's radar was locked onto a target selected by a radar operator aboard the bomber. Three thousand were built, but only thirty-three were deployed in spring 1945 against Japanese shipping, with decidedly mixed results.

The only American radar-guided weapon to see service during the Second World War was the Navy Bat. Active homing, with onboard radar, required the radar operator to lock the weapon on a target before release. It was deployed from Consolidated PB4Y-2 Privateers, as shown, against Japanese vessels with quite mixed results. *National Archives*

Adding a propulsion system to the glide weapons offered the opportunity to increase the range and speed. Among these was the Navy Gargoyle radio-controlled and TV-guided airframe enclosing a 1,000lb bomb. A solid rocket motor was installed to boost speed for greater-impact kinetic energy and armor-piercing potential. The USN also pursued a series of Gorgon winged missiles with either a liquid-fuel rocket motor or turbojet engine and various guidance and targeting means. Little progress was made on these weapons during the war. The Army initiated a series of Jet Bomb (JB, implying rocket or turbojet propulsion) weapons that proved too ambitious for the technology of the period and few moved beyond the design stage. The JB-1 was a tailless airframe with two rudimentary turbojets in a center body and a 2,000lb bomb in each wing root. The one rail launch test ended in failure.

A short path to a JB weapon was the only known example of a reverse-engineered weapon in the US arsenal, advancing the program well ahead of others in development. The JB-2 was a copied German V-1 'buzz bomb'. Air Forces labs used components collected from missiles wrecked in the UK to recreate the pulsejet engine, guidance system and airframe of the missile in just sixty days. The first flight was in October 1944 using a ground rail launch system like the Germans, although some were air-launched from B-17s for flight trials. A radio-command targeting system (allowed by air superiority) was more efficient than the German preset targeting, yet still had a large impact error. It transitioned to production, with plans to rapidly manufacture and deploy tens of thousands, but was curtailed by the end of the war. The pulsejet engine was used on several other experimental weapons including the JB-4 as a powered GB-4 and the JB-10 spin-off of the JB-1.

An agreement in the fall of 1944 saw review and elimination of redundant Army programs. Among those surviving this culling was drones created from bombers (see Chapter 11, dedicated drone airplanes having been largely abandoned by this point), several freefall and guided glide bombs, and the JB-2. It left untouched duplication between the Army and Navy, especially galling as both sought resources from the same national agencies. An ad hoc subcommittee under the Joint Chiefs of Staff (JCS) had been formed in June 1942 to study needs and potential for such weapons and to offer suggestions. It recommended a division of the NDRC to supervise development activities, and this Division of New Munitions (Division 5) was instrumental in undertaking basic scientific research beyond the weapons procurement activities of the services. The JCS body became more formalized in January 1945 as a committee that (belatedly) was to reduce duplication, which also included NACA.[5]

Robot sea attackers

Simulated dive-bombing runs by target drones during fleet firing exercises in the fall of 1938, guided by the control plane 2-3 miles (3.2-4.8km) away, readily brought forth the realization that an armed drone could be dived into an enemy vessel as a guided missile without risking an aircrew aboard a bomber. Sacrificing an unmanned airplane to sink a capital ship was readily acceptable. Recommendations to undertake such development dated from that period, but budgets and other priorities precluded action. Finally granted authorization on 29 November 1939, what was referred to as the assault drone program was formally kicked off in a 22 March 1940 BuAer directive to the NAF. This followed an order from the CNO, Admiral Harold R. Stark, in February to facilitate tests of bomb fusing and bounce from low-altitude release for which drones were expected to be used for safety reasons. This allowed the NAF to pursue gear that would be directly applicable to assault drones.

The Factory began working towards essential elements for flying a drone in an attack profile like a torpedo plane or delivering 1,000lb (454kg) bombs. The first tests along these lines were conducted in July 1940 by diving a drone against a smoke trail. The aircraft passed within 100 feet (31 meters) of the smoke while directed visually by the controller in his airplane 3,000 yards (2,743 meters) behind. Dives were also made against an automobile moving along a beach. It was postulated that if the control pilot guided the drone via a TV image of the view from the drone's nose, the control plane could be as far away as the range of the radio gear. Progress remained slow though 1940 owing to short budgets and staff, but was re-energized on 17 January 1941 by direction of the Chief of BuAer, Rear Admiral Towers.

The immediate goal was to develop a TV-directed torpedo bomber drone which was considered the most valuable application of the drone for offensive operations. This made urgent the completion of a radio altimeter. Conversion of a TG-2 director plane as a demonstration platform was made possible by the arrival of the first purpose-built drone director aircraft, the Beech JRB-1, in October 1940. Eleven of these Beech C-18S twins (2543/7, 4709/10 and 4726/9) were acquired late that year, modified at Beech with a raised fairing above the flight deck and forward cabin as a windowed 'cupola' for greater controller all-around vision and photography. They could easily accommodate two control sets and were employed in Philadelphia and by VJ-3 and -5. However, a BG-1 torpedo plane was also being converted to a drone.

The growing scope and complexity of the drone flight tests mandated a single site with more freedom of operation. This was one motivation for establishing the Naval Air Test Center at Patuxent River. First sought out in August 1941, 'Pax River' began operations on 29 June 1943.

During 1941 on the east coast, VJ-5 conducted tests by dropping torpedoes and depth charges from drones as low as 50 feet (15 meters), checking for the hazards of bounce and splash – trials too risky for a manned aircraft, yet showing the drone's offensive potential. During these operations one bomb, only partially released upon command, shorted the entire system, prompting the aircraft to impact the water.

On 9 July 1941 Lieutenant Robert F. Jones, commanding VJ-5, suggested a radio control fighter, rigged with explosives, as an 'aerial ram' or 'flying ram', which could be flown into the middle of a bomber formation and detonated. This was approved on 8 October as Project Dog, among the first determined efforts to test and operate drones as offensive weapons and train personnel in their use. Unfortunately, although Jones had suggested a four-month development period, the operational unit lacked the time and means for the task and was duplicating work at the NAF. Additionally, effort converting Brewster F2A-3 Buffalo fighters rigged as drones had led to two crashes, one killing an experienced control pilot. Consequently the project passed to Project Fox at the NAF in June 1942, where the ram application faded away.

By October 1941 the NAF, then commanded by Commander Leslie C. Stevens, had concluded that the assault drone experimental stage had yielded satisfactory results, with all elements of a practical and all-weather system in place. It recommended that the Navy undertake a full-on development program en route to production. The CNO, Stark, concurred

One of eleven Beech JRB-1 drone control aircraft, 2543 models the 'cupola' added above the flight deck for the control operator and photographer. A hatch in the crew door in the aft fuselage also facilitated photography. The size of the aircraft permitted redundant controller equipment and more than one controller crew to support training. *San Diego Air & Space Museum*

towards the end of the month, but emphasized that the already heavily tasked aviation industry should not be additionally burdened by the new program. BuAer went on to request obsolete torpedo bombers for conversion in the form of 100 TBD Devastators, expecting them to be supplanted later by other current types as they were replaced by newer aircraft. However, it was also considering a remotely piloted torpedo plane to be built quickly and cheaply of wood.[6]

The attack on Pearl Harbor gave impetus to the new-design approach since no torpedo planes could be spared for drone conversion. In March 1942 a board of representatives from each USN bureau and the office of the CNO was formed under Captain Oscar Smith to monitor Project Fox progress and ensure nothing stood in its way. The undertaking was given the highest priority and the normal terms of acquisition regulations were set aside.

Flight tests on 4 March 1942 with the TV-equipped TG-2 included mock torpedo and low-altitude bombing runs against targets in the Delaware River, as well as simulated collisions. Fully 80 percent of the terminal runs met the success criteria, while only 32 percent of the torpedo runs and 12 percent of the bombings were successful.[7] These results, combined with the abrupt thrust of America into the war, prompted a shift from a drone delivering a bomb or torpedo to the aircraft being directed into a terminal flight path while carrying explosives to impact. Earlier, the actual crashing of the drone into the target was not expected to be necessary. It was recognized that the limit dive speed of an aircraft (not very dense) before structural break-up would provide inadequate kinetic energy to penetrate even the weather deck of a vessel, let alone an armored deck or reinforced concrete bunker. Success appeared to demand release of a bomb, with a suitable fuse, from a steep dive. The drone target experience, with few drones actually shot down, suggested that a high ratio of assault aircraft would return from an attack. What changed the calculus to expecting good results from a relatively low-velocity impact is unclear. Other than a self-guiding torpedo, delivery of a bomb was problematic because no manner of remote-reading bombsight was possible at that time. Lacking this, any visually judged release was certain to have such a large error as to make the exercise fruitless.

A visually directed crash of a nolo BG-1 into a towed target raft was attempted on 1 April 1942 by VJ-5, but a system failure saw it impact halfway between the tug and raft. Another attempt on 3 April saw impact just short of the target, making a glancing blow, with the control pilot a little over 1 mile (1.6km) distant. Neither of the drones was fitted with the radio altimeter. An attempt by VJ-5 to hit a wreck in Chesapeake Bay by visual guidance (and without radio altimeter), the drone fitted with an armed bomb, was also unsuccessful. The airplane passed 10 feet (3.1 meters) over the target and impacted beyond, but did not explode. It appeared that the controller had to be much closer to the drone to affect a precise impact by visual means alone (especially judging altitude), placing the control plane at greater risk of engagement by the enemy.

A torpedo drop from a drone by the NAF was moved forward with alacrity. The drop, with an inert warhead, was performed on 9 April 1942 with a TG-2, equipped with radio altimeter control, against a destroyer that steamed parallel to the oncoming bomber as in an actual combat scenario. The bomber was launched from Quonset Point and flown nolo to the attack. The target was acquired at a range of 8 miles (12.9km) on the TV image and the distance closed. Lieutenant (Junior Grade) Molt B. Taylor commanded the torpedo release at 300 yards (274 meters) astern of the vessel, the control plane then at a range of 6 miles (9.7km). Running at a depth of 38 feet (11.6 meters), the weapon passed directly under the keel along its full length.[8] The TG-2 was then flown back for a successful recovery.

On 19 April the NAF team set out to crash a BG-1 nolo drone into a raft towed at 8 knots (9mph, 15km/h) on Chesapeake Bay using TV guidance and radio altimeter control. The target was acquired at a range of 5 miles (8km), but the drone failed to respond to the final turn command and gave a near miss. This may have been due to Taylor in the JRB control plane being 16 miles (26km) distant, so the signal was weak. Fortunately the drone was recovered and brought around for another attempt. This time the drone struck the raft with the control plane 11 miles (18km) away. This was the first time a maneuvering 'missile' had been directed to a precise attack from beyond the visual range of the guiding operator – and on a moving target as well.

Fahrney and Smith put together a presentation with films of the drone demonstrations for senior staff, which received considerable attention. Word of the drone success brought requests from combat commanders for immediate employment against high-value targets like submarine pens in Europe (flying into the low opening) and heavily defended Japanese bases. Many leaders lacking experience in weapon system development assumed that the successful assault drone tests meant that a deployable weapon was near at hand. Nothing could be further from the truth.

BuAer had directed on 23 March 1942 the production of 200 expendable assault drones for $1 million with the highest priority. This was clarified on the 30th as NAF production of 100 of its wooden aircraft design, designated TDN-1, by 1 November 1942, and to seek a commercial source for another 100 of possibly unique design. The Interstate Aircraft & Engineering Corporation of El Segundo, California, was selected for this contract, formally ordered by the CNO on 3 April. These were expected to meet only low-performance goals given the limited resources available at that stage of the war. The NAF team expected them to serve strictly for service tests in advance of a high-performance model.

In a 22 May 1942 follow-up to a meeting with the Commander in Chief (CinC) US Navy, Admiral King, the total number of drones to be produced was expanded to 1,000 aircraft, delivered at up to 300 per month, with 500 per month desired. Eighteen squadrons were each to employ 162 control planes and 500 drones, with another 500 drones in reserve. Delivery of the first 500 drones was set for mid-summer 1943 to support plans for combat operations to begin on 15 December of that year. The next 500 were likely expected by the end of 1943 as operations ramped up and replenishment became necessary. This ensured that combat introduction of the weapon would be overwhelming and exploited to the fullest before the enemy could develop countermeasures.

The program was approved by the CinC in its full scope at an early May 1942 meeting. Remaining requirements for a war-ready system were listed as:

- Manufacture, test and training with a purpose-built, combat-ready assault drone
- All-weather operations using radar, although now sought from take-off to landing and requiring a 'repeat-back' of the received radar information at the drone to the controller
- Selectable altitude hold feature
- Jettisonable or retractable landing gear to improve performance
- Automatic weapon release at a preset condition
- Ability to detonate an onboard explosive above a target vessel to destroy deck installations and eliminate personnel, and an equipment destruct command in the event of the bomb failing to detonate
- Autonomous guidance systems, especially with radar
- 'Tie-in' of any such autonomous guidance with the electronic control system that, in turn, interfaced with the mechanical aircraft controls
- Drone control from a surface vessel and submarine, possibly assuming control of the drone launched from much further away from another ship or carrier

These neglected, of course, the formation and training of units that could then deploy to the war zone with a full logistics 'tail' and prepare to engage the enemy, followed by reaction to operational lessons. To those familiar with such endeavors, a year or two appeared a reasonable estimate. The strictest secrecy was enforced.

This decisive move by King to rapidly develop drones was a means of backing up US naval aviation, which was essentially still new and untested. Aircraft carrier operations were little more than a decade old and had not been tested in a major war. The first generation of aviators was only just reaching senior command postings. Initial combat results against the Japanese had been disquieting, at best, and against German submarines especially dismal. The number of carriers had been reduced to desperate levels. Until naval aviation proved itself with significant victories and reached decisive mass, it appeared prudent to ensure that there was a fallback means of asserting airpower. Many other new weapons were being pushed rapidly through development to deployment, so King's move was not unusual.

Admiral Towers and the NAF leadership cautioned against plunging headlong into such a vast and fast-paced production and deployment program. They pointed out that such an effort would tie up 10,000 people, including 1,300 aviators, and the program could cost an estimated $235 million. The ability of Interstate to deliver at any sizable rate could not then be reasonably estimated. With the fleet hard-pressed to replace losses and train new pilots, such a diversion of resources could set back conventional naval aviation efforts. The development leadership (Towers also considered a voice for the operational aviation forces since BuAer then also included operational elements) recommended in June a 500-aircraft program as Project Option, which included Project Dog, and this was

approved by the CNO (also King after 18 March) on 12 August 1942. These were to consist of the 100 TDNs and 200 Interstate TDRs of low performance, together with 100 TD2Rs and 100 TD3Rs of high performance, which were to be controlled from medium bombers. A review of guided missile programs within the country during this period concluded that only the USN drones were likely to yield a deployed guided and powered missile within the duration of the war.[9]

The revised goal, as of May 1942, had been to deliver all 100 TDN-1s, plus 10 percent spares, and 444 control units by 1 November at a cost of $2.75 million and $1.32 million, respectively. Subcontractors would provide some of the large plywood assemblies, but final assembly and testing of the secret airplane would be in Philadelphia under project engineer John S. Kean. The first six production examples were to be available in August and eventually reach ten aircraft per week. The best that was achieved was delivery of the first dozen TDN-1s in December 1942 (against a 1 January 1943 deadline) after a tremendous effort by the NAF. Deliveries did not resume until mid-March 1943, and the last of the 100 was finally completed by 1 November 1943, a year late.

The initial test results with the first dozen TDN-1s generated another wave of exuberance, and on 23 March 1943 the Vice CNO, Admiral Frederick J. Horne, ordered BuAer to ramp up drone production, increasing the total to 3,000 aircraft with an objective of 250 per month by June 1944. Rear Admiral John S. McCain, then commanding BuAer, protested about the enormous pressure this would place on industry and manpower, in addition to a probable $227 million bill and the diversion of 291 aviators. Once again, the quantity was halved, with 1,500 drones to be acquired beyond the 500 already on order for delivery by the end of September 1943 from Interstate. Carefully calculated estimates were submitted on 1 May, showing that the 500 drones with support equipment were going to cost $40,875,874 while the additional 1,500 would be $101,583,350. Expecting that some $50 million would be recoverable if the program was prematurely halted on the basis of poor results, the CNO endorsed going forward and BuAer responding accordingly. Interstate's production obligation increased to 1,100 units, consisting of 100 TDR-1s, 400 TDR-2s, 100 TD2R-1s and 500 TD3R-1s.

The TDN testing through the fall of 1943 excluded a combat evaluation because of conflicting views about the necessity of this before commencing large-scale production while maintaining operational security to preclude the enemy developing defenses before the new weapon could be brought to bear in a decisive manner. Yet the accumulating TDN assets provided a means for early and urgent deployment against high-value targets. Again, the CNO remained firm in resisting early introduction as isolated, one-off attacks on high-value targets. However, while waiting for the higher-performance models was tempting, the CNO was firm that the initial models must be pressed into combat as soon as quantity represented a decisive mass of combat resources.

A vital mass of combat drones proved elusive. Progress at Interstate was slow to the point of calamity. By 1 November 1943 none of the TDRs had been delivered and King had requested weekly progress reports. BuAer dropped work on the advanced model to help Interstate focus on pushing out forty-eight airplanes by 15 March 1944.[10]

Even at this late date the system was being refined to correct issues such as radio altimeter control reliability and its tendency to 'hunt' for the correct height, together with abrupt climbs and descents when the system was engaged or disengaged. The weapon was formally called the Airborne Remote Controlled Bomb (ARC Bomb), but 'assault drone' stuck.

In forming up to meet the ambitious CinC goals, Project Dog was broken away from BuAer on 18 May 1942 to become the responsibility of VJ-6. Testing was shifted from Cape May to Traverse City, Michigan, on Lake Michigan, in January 1943, where work could be undertaken from the training carrier USS *Sable*. Training facilities were established at Clinton, Oklahoma, with auxiliary fields on the Gulf of Mexico and the Great Lakes. The teams initial employed Beech twins as control planes and converted Vultees as drones. Moving to preparation for combat, VJ-6 and all Project Option personnel and equipment became part of Training Task Force Command in Clinton on 23 March 1943, together with the formation of combat units, all under then Commodore Oscar Smith. Although not an aviator, Smith felt strongly about the potential for offensive drones, and his assignment showed King's confidence in him. The goal became nine Aircraft Radio Controlled Bomb Units, under three wings, combat-ready by 15 March 1944. VJ-6 retained an instructional and advisory role at Cape May, employing most of the TDN-1s. On 12 August 1943 the combat units were renamed Fleet Special Air Task Forces (SATFOR) with three Special Task Air Groups (STAGs) composed of eight VK squadrons (STAGRONS) and three headquarters squadrons. The baseline was nine control planes and fifty-four drones for each of the nine squadrons. A deployment plan drawn up on 16 March 1943 called for 441 officers and 3,210 men in three combat units operating ninety-nine control planes, and 891 drones supported by a training team of 259 officers and 2,238 men with twelve control aircraft and forty-five drones.

Operational training was at Traverse City. Carrier training was performed in the winter of 1943 from escort carriers operating in the Chesapeake Bay. This included catapult launches of drones carrying their full complement of 2,000lb (907kg) of ordnance.[11] Towards the end of November 1943 STAG-1, intended for carrier-based operations, moved to Monterey Naval Auxiliary Air Station, California, for additional operational training, and conducted flight operations at Half Moon Bay in preparation for deployment to the Pacific theater. STAG-2, intended for land-based European deployment, was deployed to Eagle Mountain Lake, Texas, and STAG 3 remained in Clinton.

Seeking an opportunity for operational testing and commencement of planning for full deployment of the STAGs, a 10 November 1943 conference was held in Hawaii with Admiral Chester Nimitz, CinC US Pacific Fleet, and his Commander of Aircraft, Rear Admiral John Towers (formerly of BuAer).* The outcome was a rude awakening. Nimitz, while supporting development of advanced weapons, doubted the value of the drones compared with more conventional weapons. He was very hesitant to employ the TDN/TDR types because their low speed and maneuverability greatly reduced

potential usefulness. He recommended holding out for the high-performance drones or converting SBD dive bombers instead (then a second-line type). In the meantime, he had not the deck or airfield space, nor other resources, to host the new drone outfits. Yet Nimitz insisted that they be fully proven before being introduced. Towers was more blunt, opposing drones in principal (although not missiles) and especially the scope of the program.[12] He also felt that the best time for combat introduction had passed, the Pacific campaign having moved from a static to a mobile phase.

Consequent to the Hawaii meeting, Commodore Smith directed that TD2R/TD3R production be accelerated and an SBD-5 be converted immediately. However, McCain at BuAer opposed the conversion of SBDs, feeling that the prototype stage had passed and diverting combat aircraft prior to a demonstration of combat effectiveness was unwise. Towers judged the SBD near-outmoded, therefore lending little additional value as a drone.

King ordered Commodore Smith back to Hawaii to work out combat trials. Arriving near the end of January 1944, he found a willing partner in Admiral Raymond A. Spruance, Commander 5th Fleet, who was then planning the assault on the Marshall Islands. After investing the islands, a STAG could move into one of the airfields in the Gilbert chain and respond as targets were selected to test assault drone effectiveness. Nimitz and King approved this plan. However, the speed of the Marshall Island campaign, decided by the end of February 1944, was such that STAG-1 was not ready to deploy in time to participate. King then directed Nimitz on 23 February to seek some other scenario of drone introduction such that combat experience could be gained as soon as possible.

Bad news piled up in March 1944 when Captain H. B. Temple, heading guided missile activities for the CNO, expressed his conclusion that the drones offered too little at that time and circumstances of the war to be useful. The carrier was dominant and the drone did not augment its striking power, the low-performance drones being considered unsuitable for integration into carrier flight operations. He recommended that the program be greatly reduced in scope to a combat test program. McCain likewise felt that augmenting carrier-based aviation with guided missiles was the best course of action. With no such Navy weapons likely to be available in the near term, he recommended the Army Razon and Felix types be adapted to naval aircraft while ongoing missile programs such as Bat be continue at a deliberate pace. Even the Pelican was to be scrapped after it failed a final test series, and the concept of operations no longer fitted the Pacific campaign conditions. Additionally, higher leadership levels in the form of the well-regarded Doctor Vannevar Bush, heading the Officer of Scientific Research and Development (OSRD) under the President, opposed the drone on the grounds that the instances where sacrificing an entire airplane to hit a single target with perhaps 50 percent reliability were too few for the resources expended.

King's attitude towards the drones had likewise shifted. Naval aviation had come to dominate the Pacific theater,

* John Towers was considered by many to be the premier naval aviator and his judgment was held in high regard.

steadily eroding Japanese air power. True air-launched missiles were in the wings, the 'Bat' showing promised by the last quarter of 1944 and the Germans having demonstrated the potential of such weapons. Although only the drones among the guided missile programs had reached a point of potentially contributing anything during the war, the drone production effort had essentially failed and the character of the war had changed in a manner that made them of too little value.[13]

The CNO reacted in March 1944 by cutting the aircraft buy to 100 TDN-1s (already in hand), 188 TDR-1s, and fifty each of the TD2R-1 and TD3R-1. The combat teams were reduced to just STAG-1 with STAGRONS 13 and 14 in addition to its two existing squadrons. However, production of electronic gear for drone conversions and control continued apace as there were prospects for other applications.

Maritime fowls (TDN, TDR, TD2R, TD3R)

The BuAer assault drone design in the fall of 1941 was a high-wing type with a jettisonable tricycle undercarriage. It stood high off the ground for ease of weapons loading in the belly. The TV camera peered out of a window in the apex of the nose. Expected to be expendable, it was to be built inexpensively, simply and quickly from non-vital materials (read plasticized wood laminate over a welded steel tube frame) like a light plane, yet be suitably reliable. It had to be easily disassembled for crating and shipment overseas. The low-performance model was to be capable of catapult launch and have a maximum airspeed of about 200mph (322km/h) and a 2½-hour endurance at full throttle.[14] Two 150hp (112kW) 'flat' engines were assessed as delivering suitable power while not placing additional demand on the production of radial engines for manned combat aircraft. The airplane was to be configurable to accommodate either TV or radar guidance. A torpedo was to be accommodated in addition to a 100lb (45kg) internal explosive for detonation when the airplane impacted the target.

Conceptual design and general specifications were completed on 29 November 1941 and forwarded to the NAF, which responded on 15 January 1942 with a preliminary design supporting construction of prototypes. The Factory proposed to complete a full design, build a static article, and construct four prototypes for $354,000. The first flight was expected in July 1942. The Bureau directed the NAF on 14 February to initiate development of the XTDN-1 for TV guidance.*

Seeking a firm to take on the development and manufacturing of a similar type, yet not already engaged in large-scale war production, proved challenging. After examining the field, Lieutenant Taylor informally broached the subject with Interstate on 18 March 1942. This firm dated from April 1937 as a producer of hydraulic components and other precision aircraft gear. Its S-1B Cadet two-place light airplane became the L-6 liaison machine for the Army, with 250 built. The company was hungry to take on meatier challenges and visited Philadelphia on the 25th with conceptual drawings of its proposed drone. A Letter of Intent was issued to the firm on

* The Naval Aircraft Factory became the Naval Air Material Center (NAMC) on 20 July 1943. In August 1943 Lieutenant Grayson Merrill took over the Navy project from Fahrney as head of the BuAer Special Design Branch.

4 April to build the XTDR-1 prototype. Again showing its enthusiasm, Interstate had a mock-up ready in just weeks, inspected on 23-24 April. The contract then called for two prototypes XTDR-1s, and a Letter of Intent for 100 TDR-1 aircraft followed on 1 June.

The Franklin O-300 was the original engine choice for the TDNs and TDRs, but the Lycoming 220hp (164 kW) XO-435-2 six-cylinder engine, with a fixed-pitch Sensenich wooden propeller, was ultimately selected by BuAer as more readily available. This proved somewhat misleading as Lycoming had difficulty meeting the schedule and XO-300s had to be used on the first XTDN-1. These low-performance models were then expected to reach 150mph (241km/h) and 600 miles (966km), carry 2,000lb (907kg) of weapons, and be radio-controlled as well as television-directed. The TDN could be fitted with a belly drop tank for ferry.

A wind tunnel model of the TDN was available in March 1942. The aircraft had a span of 48 feet (14.6 meters) with a length of 37 feet (11.3 meters), and grossed 7,000lb (3,175kg). Maximum airspeed was around 180mph (290km/h). Although adding costs, counter-rotating propellers had to be adopted for adequate directional control.[15] The mock-up was inspected on 1 June and numerous minor alterations requested. Work fell behind the very optimistic schedule, and it was directed that it was not to impede the PBN-1 flying boat effort also at the Factory. The first XTDN-1 (27853) made its initial three flights at the NAF's Mustin Field on 15 November 1942. After shakedown, it was passed to BuAer in December for trials at Mustin and the Philadelphia Municipal Airport. The preliminary test results of the XTDN-1s were reported on 19 January 1943, although testing ran into March 1943, with very favorable conclusions. A final test was to detonate the 100lb charge in the cockpit over Patuxent River. This machine was devoid of TV and had an incomplete radio control system. The remaining three prototypes (27854/6) featured the full kit and took up the testing. The first twelve of the 100 TDN-1s (17292/391) were completed by the end of the year and deliveries did not resume until mid-March 1943.

Tests into 1943 extended to January twin bomb releases against a floating target in the Delaware Bay on at least two occasions. Despite flying over the target at very low altitude and with the control plane less than a quarter of a mile to one side, the bombs fell short each time. In another test a TDN, apparently armed with a bomb (and with undercarriage still attached), was flown at a billboard-size target erected on Bloodsworth Island in the Chesapeake Bay. It overshot and impacted several hundred feet beyond. During August, flying included catapulting nolo TDN-1s off the *Sable* in Lake Michigan. The first launch from the ship was on the 10th, but this or another launch on the same day did not do well, with the aircraft veering to the left edge of the deck during the rolling take-off until corrected right by rotation. The aircraft may then have been lifted off too abruptly to avoid further on-gear dynamics as it was climbed very steeply and apparently suffered a wing stall. The airplane rolled off on the left wing and impacted a short distance off the port side.[16] The team demonstrated control from an onboard station to a distance of 15 miles (24km), suitable for ship-to-ship combat. The

Above: Details of the TDN-1 are evident, in addition to the simplicity of the design, in this 19 May 1943 image of 17309. The high stance eased weapon loading. The hinge line for the port bomb bay door can be seen.
National Museum of Naval Aviation

Right: The Naval Aircraft Factory TDN-1 was occasionally flown with the bomb bay doors removed for unclear reasons. Inclusion of the bay seems to run counter to the goal of simplicity, and was not reflected in the sister Interstate TDR-1. This machine, photographed on 2 March 1944, has cowling holes covered in addition to temporary changes to the exit flaps, perhaps as an effort to better control engine temperatures. *National Archives*

jettisonable undercarriage was conceptually the simplest aspect of the aircraft, but there was uncertainty about it separating cleanly. In June 1943 the NAF had to undertake development of a hydraulic release system for retrofit. Tests also included uncrating, assembling, then flying a TDN to judge the number of flight hours with safety pilot before the system was considered suitably shaken-down to attempt a nolo flight. A figure of 3 hours was determined.

The use of subcontractors for the TDN-1 woodwork helped accelerate the effort, which was well behind schedule. The Brunswick-Balke-Collender Company of Muskegon, Michigan, and the Singer Manufacturing Company in South Bend, Indiana, were engaged. Deliveries reached four or five machines per day. Despite initial plans to retain secrecy, Singer assembled the last thirty machines, the first taken up by the NAF in August 1943. Here the effort was halted owing to the slow rate and high cost, the alternative TDR appearing a better avenue. The NAF hoped to reduce the aircraft unit cost to $21,000, but missed that mark by a wide margin.

The TDR-1 showed much in common with the TDN-1, but with significant changes. The bomb bay was eliminated, allowing a low wing with the option of wing-mounted bombs. The engine cowling was considerably reduced in volume. Apart from the torpedo or 2,000lb of bombs, the TDR-1 could carry two 650lb (295kg) or four 325lb (147kg) depth charges. The

The bay doors were both fully enclosed and also cut-out types, providing clearance for stores while eliminating some drag. Shown at Clinton, the aircraft is carrying two depth charges. The main gear attachments support inflight release, while separation of the nose gear is less obvious. *National Archives*

Above: Lacking wheel brakes, ground movement of the TDN and TDR required towing it to the runway using 'wing-walkers' for any low-speed taxi. In most cases the aircraft was restrained until take-off power was attained and engine instruments checked, then it was abruptly released. In the case of this TDN-1 flying nolo (no pilot solo) from Clinton on 14 November 1943, a rope between the tie-down point at the end of the fuselage ventral strake and a truck bumper has been cut. *National Archives*

Left: On 10 August 1943 two TDN-1s were tested aboard the USS *Sable* training carrier in Lake Michigan. This example is clearly unmanned, with TV and remote control antenna installed, as it rolls for take-off. While the aircraft lacked wing flaps, it evidently had a low enough stall speed that a rolling take-off with wind-over-deck was acceptable. *National Museum of Naval Aviation*

fully enclosed canopy and headrest were removed and the opened covered by a fairing for nolo operations. These were facilitated by setting a hydraulic control lever on the port side of the cockpit and an AC-DC switch in an electrical control panel. For simplicity and weight saving, engine instruments were mounted in the engine cowlings, visible from the cockpit, instead of in the cockpit panel. The aircraft also lacked wheel brakes or nose wheel steering; making 'wing-walkers' with chocks at the ready an essential element of ground operations. For take-off, a line ran from the drone to the bumper of a truck, this being released after full power was achieved to initiate the take-off run. For catapulting, the bridle on the shuttle was attached to points on the aircraft wing box, under the fuselage, and the holdback shackle to a point just aft on the centreline. Unlike the Army bomb drones (see later), the TDR lacked any armor protection or fuel system protection. The landing gear could be jettisoned, adding about 11.5mph (18.5km/h) to the top airspeed. If it was planned to expend the aircraft, the gear was usually retained until just before the final run-in. The TDRs were designed to be easily broken down and crated for shipment overseas (electronics separately), then quickly reassembled.[17]

By the time of the 1,100-aircraft order, it was estimated that Interstate could build thirty TDRs per month in El Segundo. A

comparatively tiny organization, the daunting Project Option schedule demanded a herculean effort from Interstate, which would need to grow enormously and rapidly to meet its obligation. Although it was already expanding, the full production rate number and date was still impossible to predict. Experienced in manufacturing wooden musical instruments, R. Wurlitzer would contribute from a facility in DeKalb, Illinois. Interstate also located other firms to manufacture the airframe from its drawings and under its guidance. These other prime contractors were the American Aviation Corporation of Jamestown, New York, with 100 TDR-1s and 300 TDR-2s (unknown planned changes), and Brunswick-Balke-Collender with 400 TD2R-1s. Several subcontractors apart from R. Wurlitzer made significant contributions with airframe parts, including the General American Aerocoach Corporation of Chicago, Illinois, the Schwinn Bicycle Company for the welded steel tube frame, and Singer. Some difficulty was encountered with these well-established firms taking direction from the less experienced Interstate, with complaints about drawings and their late delivery.

Interstate delivered two XTDR-1s (37635/6, but delivered as 27857/8) for testing by the NAF. A structural defect was uncovered following a fatal crash during the formal Navy trials board testing, correction of which may have slowed production progress. The TDR-1s were delivered from 1943 to 1944, though totaling just 189 machines (27859/958, 33515/31, 64497/568). The remaining 828 airframes (64569/5396) were cancelled.

Interstate TDR-1 characteristics (configured without pilot unless otherwise noted)

Span	48.0ft (14.6m)
Length	35.7ft (10.9m)
Height	13.9ft (4.2m)
Wing area	371ft² (34.5m²)
Fuel, max (both)	100 gallons (379 liters)
Climb rate, best	476fpm (145mpm)
Service ceiling	10,000ft (3,048m)
Weight, empty	3,320lb (1,506kg)
Weight, gross	6,314lb (2,864kg)
Weight, ferry	4,763lb (2,161kg) piloted
Speed, max	162mph (261km/h)
Cruise speed	152mph (245km/h) piloted
Range (172mph)	425 miles (684km)
Range, ferry (152mph)	375 miles (604km) piloted

An often-published photo, this is still a fine study of the Interstate TDR-1 flying over the Philadelphia Navy Yard with Lieutenant Molt Taylor in the cockpit. The antennae for remote control installed on the spine are noteworthy, the pilot trying to show that he is not flying the airplane. The simplistic nature of the aircraft construction is evident. *Air Force Test Center*

All the drones were radio-controlled (the equipment codenamed 'Cast') with gyro stabilization and hydraulic servo control. The F.M. Link Company of New York, New York, manufactured the FM control elements. These also featured a radio altimeter (code-named 'Ace') with an altitude hold feature selectable from 50 to 1,500 feet (15 to 457 meters) in roughly 300-foot (91-meter) increments, and a radar beacon (code-name 'Roger'). The television camera and transmitter gear (Block) began with the RCA Block I kit, the follow-on Block III not being available at the time of combat trials. The radio altimeter also came from RCA, which was additionally responsible for the 'sniffer' automatic bomb release.

The Grumman TBF-1C Avenger (more specifically the General Motors TBM-1C version) was selected as the control plane. The television, radar and radio control antennae were within a retractable radome housing (called 'Roger') extending from the belly, and the radio compartment was aft of the weapons bay. The radar had a scanning parabolic dish antenna. Aside from the control box with beeper stick, the channel selection and command means was via a telephone dial unit mounted on the port side of the rear cockpit. A command had to first be dialed, then executed with a button, or cancelled. The Control Plane Pilot (CCP) in the front seat would fly the drone into the target area visually (although he also had a TV screen and radar repeater) before hand-off to the Drone Control Pilot (DCP) in the rear seat. The DCP would first acquire the target on his 6-inch (15cm) TV screen, observed under a black hood over his area for better viewing of the displays. Seated shoulder-to-shoulder beside him was a radar operator with a roughly 12-inch scope possessing a

The canopy and windscreen of the TDR-1 (XTDR-1 27858 shown) were designed to be quickly removed and a flush fairing put in their place. Only the rudder and elevator had trim tabs, the ailerons normally with a fixed tab. Note the clean exterior derived from the wooden construction. *National Archives*

This series of photographs show the TDR-1 in various store configurations. The torpedo (a production TDR-1, 33515) and large bomb, both 2,000lb, are surrounded by a drag-reducing fairing that was not actually used in combat. The loading of four 325lb (XTDR-1 27858) depth charges, on the centerline and outboard stations, or two larger 650lb depth charges on the centerline, could be substituted by bombs. *National Archives*

Unusual features of the TDR-1 are shown here. The cockpit itself is fairly standard if spartan, save for the servo instruments and master switch, but the toe brakes are unusual given that the aircraft had no wheel brakes. The engine instruments were found in the inboard side of the nacelles where the pilot could observe them from the cockpit during shakedown and ferry flights. *Left National Archives /right National Museum of the United States Air Force*

PPI display. The radio altimeter control feature could be used to ease the control task until the final approach to the target. Once the DCP announced that the target had been acquired on the TV, the CCP would turn away to open out the stand-off range from the TBM's target. The rest of the crew comprised a radioman and gunner.

The ground control station was named 'Command', with the gear in a 'command car' panel truck. Hand-off to the TBM was via the voice radio command "take control". Although naval aviators were initially selected to fly the drones, they tended to be more interested in flying the Grummans. In time, enthusiastic enlisted technicians took over much of these responsibilities. During training, converted Beech SNB-1s (Army AT-11s) were employed as drones (presumably with safety pilot) and command ships. An R4D-5 (C-47A) was also modified with the 'Roger' gear, the radome raised and lowered out of the bottom of the aircraft, for use at Clinton.[18]

The higher-performance drones were conceived as a twin-engine airframe with two engine options and carrying 2,000lb

A number of TBM-1C torpedo bombers were modified to serve as control planes for the Navy's combat drones, as in this image of a VJ-6 bird from 12 October 1943 over Traverse City. Accommodating the radome saw the elimination of the bottom aft tunnel MG station, a fairing in its place, and ventral flow-straightener strakes aft of the radome. The 'Roger' radome protruded roughly 1 foot (0.3 meter) when retracted, but note also the curtains that could be drawn over the aft cockpit for improved TV image viewing. *National Archives*

Some of the gear from within the TBM-1C is shown in these photographs. The first shows the drone control pilot's station in the aft cockpit with a gun camera mounted to record the TV screen, while on the left is the control stick and on the right the radar display and radar operator. The second picture shows the control stick and function selector (telephone rotary dial), channel indicator, and amplifier box. *National Archives*

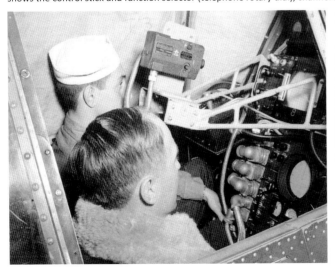
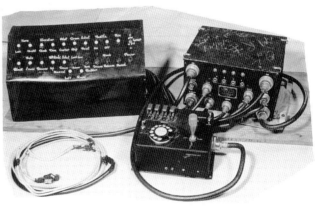

Above: The TBM-1C and TDR-1 combat team is visible in this shot, taken on 18 March 1944, probably off Half Moon Bay, California. The TDR-1 is in the drone configuration with a fairing covering the cockpit after the canopy was removed, and a 2,000lb bomb on the centerline, while the Avenger does not have the 'Roger' radome deployed, suggesting drone control from another aircraft. In actual service the control plane typically trailed the drone by several miles and the drone undercarriage was dropped once an attack was imminent. *National Archives*

of explosives. The TD2R would mount a twelve-cylinder Franklin O-805-2 of 450hp (336 kW), and had more internal fuel, for a maximum 230mph (370km/h) and a range of 1,700 miles (2,736km). Two XTD2R-1s (33921/2) were ordered but were finished as TD3Rs after it was discovered that the experimental Franklin suffered cooling issues. The otherwise identical TD3R mounted two 450hp (336 kW) R-975-13s with constant-speed propellers. These were also planned to be manufactured by the NAF. All these aircraft were very similar to the TDR-1, including engine instruments in the nacelle, and with considerable wood content in their construction. Departures were the addition of wheel brakes and flaps. Completed were three XTD3R-1s (33921, 33923/4) and an XTD3R-2 (33922, variant differences unknown).[19] No production examples were finished, the forty on contract (33881/920) being cancelled.[20] There are also no indications that the aircraft was flown unmanned or with the full-up drone systems installed.

As a drone system trainer, several Beech SNB-1s (Army AT-11 Kansan bombardier and navigator trainers) like this one were modified, the turret replaced with an antenna but no indication that radar was added. The pictures at left show one of two nose antenna configurations and the TV receiver with control box at the copilot station, which was also duplicated in the cabin. *National Archives*

Interstate TD2R-1
(TD3R-1 believed to be similar) estimated characteristics (configured without pilot unless otherwise noted)

Span	48.0ft (14.6m)
Length	35.7ft (10.9m)
Height	13.9ft (4.2m)
Wing area	371ft² (34.5m²)
Fuel, max (drone)	350 gallons (1,325 liters)
Fuel, max (piloted)	480 gallons (1,817 liters)
Service ceiling	13,500ft (4,115m)
Climb rate, best	714fpm (218mpm)
Weight, empty	5,653lb (2,564kg)
Weight, gross	10,268lb (4,658kg)
Weight, ferry	9,797lb (4,444kg) piloted
Speed, max (drone)	227mph (365km/h)
Speed, max (piloted)	185mph (298km/h)
Cruise speed	185mph (298km/h) piloted
Range (227mph)	1,070 miles (1,722km)
Range, ferry (185mph)	1,180 miles (1,899km) piloted
Take-off distance (over 50ft obstacle)	1,165ft (355m)

The Interstate XTD3R-1 appears to have been fundamentally the same airframe as the TDR-1 save for substitution of the more powerful radial engines. If the prototype possessed the greater range and airspeed claimed of the type, many hidden changes must have been incorporated to strengthen the structure and add fuel cells. This photo is proof that, despite many printed statements over the decades, the Interstate aircraft did fly. *Naval Aviation Archives*

The cockpit of the TD3R-1 shows significant changes from the TDR-1. Apart from more trim wheels and toe brakes, a notable departure is the lack of prominent drone controls such as a switch for remote control. This is further indication that the type never reached the stage of drone system installation. *National Archives*

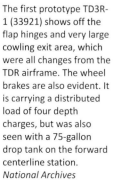

To carry the standard torpedo, the XTD3R-1 added a fairing under the fuselage to reduce interference drag (similarly used for the 2,000lb bomb). Note the constant-speed metal propellers, easily removed canopy, and nose port for the TV camera. No photos have emerged revealing the aircraft fitted with drone antennae or with the canopy replaced by a fairing. *National Archives*

At least one TD3R-1 made it to Clinton for evaluation. After the program was terminated, an example was used as an aerial target, destroyed by an experimental Gorgon missile on 20 March 1945.

The first prototype TD3R-1 (33921) shows off the flap hinges and very large cowling exit area, which were all changes from the TDR airframe. The wheel brakes are also evident. It is carrying a distributed load of four depth charges, but was also seen with a 75-gallon drop tank on the forward centerline station. *National Archives*

Interstate XBDR-1

At the far end of the Second World War drone spectrum was work on a jet-powered, TV-guided aircraft. The advent of turbojet engines brought forth this idea, which had the potential to avoid at least a tail chase intercept by enemy fighters. The project was formulated in the latter half of 1943 and Interstate offered a design mounting two 1,600lbf (7,117N) Westinghouse 19B axial-flow turbojets. This XBDR-1 was based on a Northrop Aircraft 'all-wing' or 'tailless' concept and promised a maximum airspeed of 486mph (782km/h). The engines would be buried in the wing on either side of a centersection containing control gear and the explosives.

The aircraft was to have a span of 51.6 feet (15.8 meters) with a 362ft² (33.6m²) area, and a gross weight of 10,800lb (4,899kg). The earliest drawings showed tip vertical surfaces while later drawings and wind tunnel models had a single vertical tail, extending above and below the centerline, containing a large rudder that could split open to the sides and serve as an airbrake. Wingtip split drag rudders served for directional control while inboard elevator/ailerons (elevons) provided roll control and lift improvement. The undercarriage may have been intended as droppable, but a manned version was drawn with retractable gear. There was the option of a cockpit with an enclosed canopy. The TV camera would have been in the apex of the nose, which also contained a release clamp for towing. The mockup was reportedly towed as a glider.

Two prototype XBDR-1s (337635/6) were ordered from Interstate and a board reviewed a mock-up on 15 September 1943. Gust wind tunnel tests of a 1/17th scale model were conducted at Langley during October, with and without landing gear, and later tests there employed a larger model.

Development of the engine was slow and early production went to priority fighter projects. Support for the drone program faded in 1944 and the XBDR-1 never moved forward. Interstate was so overwhelmed making progress on the TDR and TD3R projects that diverting its attention was unwise and its chances of success on such an advanced aircraft appeared remote.

This wind tunnel model of the jet-powered XBDR-1 was tested at NACA Langley, Virginia. The aircraft was to be a high-speed drone, optionally manned and with either a retractable or droppable undercarriage. The 'flying wing' layout, with wingtip split drag rudders and vertical tail drag brake, came from the fertile design shop at Northrop Aircraft, which pursued several such aircraft and missiles during the war. While likely practical, the XBDR-1 was never built as the appetite for drones receded and the intended engines were not available for such applications during the war. *National Aeronautics and Space Administration*

The XBDR-1 mock-up shows a swing-aside canopy. The openings in the vertical tail ahead of the drag brake, also evident in the concept art, are unexplained. The project was a step too far given the scarcity of the engines and the capabilities of Interstate. *National Archives*

The concept art for the XBDR-1 was quite exciting, showing a compact little jet-powered airplane with swept wings and leading-edge slot intakes. The manned version (note the tow hook opening under the TV window) may have been intended for flight test as the retractable undercarriage appears too complex for a drone of the period and would have consumed volume required for the explosive load. Presumably removal of the cockpit on the deployed version would have accommodated the bomb. *National Archives*

Proof-of-concept for the Glimpy was flown on 3 March 1944 with Piper NE-1 26197 mounted on blimp XM-1 for purely captive-carriage trials. The landing gear has been removed but the airplane is otherwise not mission-representative. It lacks the remote control gear and side generator, there is a line running from the tail wheel to the cabin window for added stability, and another line runs from the cab to the vertical tail, then forward. *National Archives*

Glimpy

Another drone mission that was explored was release from an airship to attack a surfaced submarine. The airships moved slowly, so once a sub was spotted it had to maneuver overhead before attacks with depth charges, and the sub could escape during that time. A radio-controlled airplane would, if launched rapidly, reach the target much more quickly and be guided into a collision or close enough impact such that the depth charge had a greater chance of damaging or sinking the boat. An aircraft for the role had to be very light so as not to exceed the capacity of the airship, and be mounted in a practical manner. Releasing aircraft from airships had been done before, but releasing one to serve as a missile was new.

Chosen for the drone was a Piper Cub or Navy NE-1 trainer with a 65hp (49kW) engine and fixed-pitch propeller. The low stall speed of the Cub made it ideal for the mission of release from the very slow-flying blimp – the M-class airship's maximum airspeed was just 68mph (109km/h). The NE-1 was mounted beneath the control car of the M-class blimp, suspended from its wing centersection structure on a trapeze arrangement. It hung just ahead of the forward windows of the car from which the control operator watched. A notch had to be created above the propeller where it passed through the control car's outer moldline. The rear cockpit of the NE-1 (seat removed) was fitted with the radio and control gear while the front seat was replaced by a mount for the depth charge. For manned flights of the concept, the pilot had to sit in front – contrary to normal practice. The aircraft had a wind-driven generator attached on each side of the fuselage.[21]

Tests of the concept, which was dubbed 'Glimpy', were performed with Airship Squadron 32 at NAS Lakehurst, New Jersey, in March and April 1944 using the Goodyear M-class airship XM-1.[22] On 3 March 1944 NE-1 26197, sans undercarriage, was flown unmanned and mounted on the blimp

as 'captive-carriage' proof-of-concept. This was followed on the 5th by NE-1 26328 fully configured for remote control but manned and with landing gear installed. The engine may have been run on this flight and remote-control functions checked. On 13 March NE-1 was released at about 1,000 feet (305 meters) and flown back to landing by the pilot. Other drop tests were performed on 17 and 27 April from greater altitude and possibly involving remote control. A local farmer wanted his barn demolished and the project personnel were considering using the building as a target for the final test. The Glimpy was not taken that far, and whether a free flight without the undercarriage was undertaken (supposedly ending in a wreck) is unclear.

The Piper Cub test subject for the Glimpy tests is shown in the first picture with the radio control gear replacing the rear seat, a depth charge in place of the front seat, and one of two wind-driven generators aft of the door. This NE-1 appears to be the same one that performed the piloted flights with the blimp, in the second picture. The depth charge does not appear to be mounted in a manner permitting a drop from the aircraft.
Top Air Force Test Center/right National Archives

There are many unknowns about the Glimpy program and this has brought forth much speculation. There have been suggestions that the aircraft could redock with the airship in flight, the trapeze being extendable. This is not reasonable because the trapeze seen in photographs does not appear to be extendable, the position of the airplane ahead of the windows portion of the control car would make line-up impossible, and the fine remote control of the drone would be so challenging as to make the task a hazard to the airship. Additionally, the drone program had by that stage adopted collision of the aircraft with the target as the operational concept. There are also discussions of a pilots climbing into the NE-1 to start the engine, then evacuate before release. Photo evidence does not show such paths of ingress, and starting the engine remotely should have been a relatively simple mechanical design. Also, the attack is mentioned as both depositing the depth charge from the airplane and diving the airplane into the sub. Photographs show the charge secured in the cabin such that discharge appears doubtful because, if rolled out of the door, it would have struck the wing strut. However, if the aircraft was to hit the sub and detonate an onboard explosive, a depth charge seems a poor choice. An explosion on the surface with an impact fuse would disable a submarine only through luck. There is no mention of TV guidance, so targeting would be by 'Mk I Eyeball' from the airship perhaps a few miles away, this having been shown to involve considerable error for either attack option.

Army not-so-dumb bombs

By 1939 the Air Corps was seeking an aerial torpedo or "power-driven bomb" with a range in excess of an artillery round, where weather or enemy defenses made manned air operations impractical. Only an area target could be hit, so a vehicle of low cost was indicated. The service acquired a Navy target drone system consisting of an N2C-2 and TG-2 together with a field control set.[23] Fifteen USAAC members were trained by Navy personnel in Philadelphia in the use of the drone equipment. The assets were assigned to the USAAC on 24 May and taken to Wright Field for study and to build experience.[24] This facilitated the Air Corps's own drone program of converting outmoded planes at air depots for AAA exercises.

The first inflight release of NE-1 26328 from XM-1 on 13 March 1944 is said to have been at an altitude of 1,000 feet, but this is clearly higher so likely a later drop in May. The shot from the cabin shows the complexity of the mounting mechanism but also reveals the added aerials running out to the wingtips as well as a light bulb that may have provided positive indication of a remote control link being established. The aircraft appears to have remote control gear in place and a generator wind turbine mounted off the port side. *National Archives*

For the aerial torpedo, a review of options in August 1938 resulted in a design competition being approved on the 29th. Specifications of 29 September called for the carriage of a standard 300lb (136kg) bomb or 200lb (91kg) of explosive within a range of 20-50 miles (32-81km) to strike an area target of 2 square miles (5.2km²). Beyond line-of-sight of the ground controller (an airborne controller not then considered), the aircraft would have to proceed on a preset flight profile. A unit price of $300-800 was sought. A request for data issued in April 1939 brought only a bid from Vega, which was judged unsuitable. Finally, General Motors Corporation (GM) made a convincing offer. Over an extended development program its A-1 showed promising results (see later), but ultimately could not meet evolving requirements.

By January 1942 the notion of saturating a target area with scores of directed (not guided) airplanes with modest warheads was no longer considered reasonable – the rapidly growing fleet of American bombers could perform such missions. It had been considered essential that a target worthy of expending an entire powered airplane on would require a 1,000lb or 2,000lb (454kg or 907kg) warhead, the objective 900-1,200 miles (1,448-1,931km) distant, and the aircraft possessing speed to remain with a B-17 bomber control plane (roughly 220mph [354km/h] and 15,000 feet [4,572 meters]). Given such requirements, the USAAF had concluded that the shortest route to a controllable bomb was a ground-launched airplane that was optionally manned for testing, check-out and repositioning (in daylight and via dead reckoning, although oxygen would provide for flight above weather if necessary), but otherwise fitted with a standard bomb casing (sans the fins). Beginning from a pre-existing design would also be advantageous, and project MX-53 was kicked off in March 1942 (later augmented as MX-183). By the fall of 1942 radio control with television for guidance had been judged the most effective means of precision targeting, mandating a 'mother plane'.

Although conversion of training and combat aircraft to bomb drones (BQ) was considered at the time, they were rapidly becoming scarce resources as US air combat forces increased in size, so this option was dismissed. If light plane technology and associated engines were to be employed in avoiding further burdening the principal warplane manufacturers, a twin-engine design was indicated in meeting the performance goals. In the meantime, the USAAC was already working with Culver and Fleetwings on the PQ target drones, and these single-engine types were examined with the concept of adding TV for targeting. A weapon load of at least 1,000lb (454kg) was sought, so this eliminated the very light PQ-9. Radar target-seeking gear for the PQ-8 was requested on 8 April 1942 from the NDRC, although already under way with the Radiation Laboratory.

The PQ-11A and B (differences unclear) were PQ-11 targets modified to carry the 1,000lb warhead and fitted with a self-sealing auxiliary fuel tank for extended range. The weapon would likely have had the TV camera in a fairing abutting the port landing gear strut. Appearance with the bomb has not been revealed. The PQ designation for an armed drone suggests that the project may have been intended as a testbed for the BQ types put into development during 1942. Flight

Fletcher PQ-11 characteristics
(configured with 1,000lb bomb unless otherwise noted)

Span	30.0ft (9.1m)
Length	23.9ft (7.3m)
Height	10.4ft (3.2m)
Wing area	125ft² (12m²)
Fuel, max (target)	75 gallons (284 liters)
Service ceiling	17,000ft (5,182m)
Weight, empty	2,402lb (1,090kg)
Weight, gross	3,124lb (1,417kg)
Weight, ferry	3,324lb (1,508kg) piloted
Speed, max	200mph (322km/h)
Range	750 miles (1,207km)

This photo shows an example of the Fletcher XBG-1 during flight testing in a manned configuration in April 1942. As a PQ-11 drone, the engine would have been in place of the aerodynamic nose plug. The canopy would also be replaced with a fairing over the cockpit.
National Museum of the United States Air Force

trials of the revised but manned aircraft at a representative gross weight revealed unsatisfactory flight characteristics and it was never flown unmanned. The ten aircraft subsequently had their engines removed to become XBG-1 bomb gliders, but were also set aside before completion.

Of the fifty Fleetwings PQ-12As on order beyond the XPQ-12A (41-39098), eight were finished as YPQ-12As (41-39049/56), optionally manned or carrying a 500lb (227kg) bomb. These aircraft cost perhaps $12,000 each and the full TV/remote control suite was $3,500. The camera/transmitter was in a fairing ahead of the starboard wing gear strut fairing to be outside the optically interference of the propeller. These were employed in experimental trials of the bomb drone concept. Performance made the YPQ-12A unsuitable for most envisioned operational missions, yet tests and demonstrations were intended to collect data for the purpose of determining the future of the BQ-type weapon.

Testing associated with the MX-53 program included trials with a PQ-8 modified with the Doolittle Radio multi-channel

Above and left: The USAAF's cancelled Fleetwings PQ-12 drone program yielded nine airplanes that could serve to test the assault drone concept. The line of Fleetwings YPQ-12A drones at Muroc Army Air Field, with a B-17F beyond, shows the red paint applied to all unmanned airplanes and the deep fairing under the starboard wing containing the TV camera. The post behind the cockpit served as roll-over protection for the pilot, but was also used for mounting the television antenna, in addition to the other antennae for remote control that are visible. *Top Air Force Test Center/left Jay Miller collection*

Below: A YPQ-12A target drone is followed by a CQ-3 control aircraft, a 1944 derivative of a Beech UC-45F, above the dry lakebed at Muroc. The poor image shows the drone with the original shallow fairing over the cockpit, suggesting that it was not a weapons test. With flaps up on the twin Beech suggesting take-off, it would be unusual for the control plane to direct the drone at this stage of flight. *National Museum of the United States Air Force*

remote control system intended for the power-driven bombs. The FM gear with eight channels was also tested on a YPQ-12A and AT-7 aircraft. A 7 October 1942 test at Muroc AAF, California, saw a small bomb dropped from the PQ-8 as commanded from a CQ-2 control plane. Another Muroc test in May 1943 involved flying a PQ-8 using TV guidance. The camera was in the cockpit and aimed through a hole cut in the windscreen, and a small bomb was mounted under the belly. Flown in November aboard a YPQ-12A, the system permitted the aircraft to be maneuvered solely by reference to the TV image to include a dive to low altitude and recovery from an inadvertent spin.[25]

This Beech C-45 is clearly modified for electronic testing and very likely supported the drone development program. The top antenna appears to be a television receiver, and the aerial strung from near each wingtip back to the tail is like the HF receivers on drones. The added fairings probably covered other antennae or mounts for television cameras. *Jay Miller Collection*

These images (the right from motion picture film) show the stages of preparing an armed YPQ-12A for a test mission. Note the larger fairing covering the 500lb bomb casing. Placement of the television camera is not visible. *National Museum of the United States Air Force/Air Force Test Center*

An unmanned Culver PQ-8 drone is flown remotely by a Vultee CQ-2 control plane (converted L-1 40-3113) in a close formation for the camera. A remote drop of a small bomb is performed on 7 October 1942 in support of bomb drone development. The picture below shows the aircraft being prepared for the demonstration at Muroc AAF.
National Museum of the United States Air Force

As an indicator of further progress towards the BQ system, a large-scale demonstration was arranged at Muroc for 10 October 1943.[26] The first exercise was to show how a drone could be flown into a bomber formation and detonated. A controller aboard a UC-78 Bobcat flew a PQ-8 at 2,000 feet (610 meters) above the observers. A YPQ-12A drone was prepared with a 500lb (227kg) bomb and Block I TV system. Controlled from an AT-7 fitted with the TV receiver and controller system, the drone was directed to close on the Culver from behind, both control planes about 1 mile (1.6km) distant. Within 75 feet (34 meters) the bomb was remotely detonated. The YPQ-12A was obliterated and the badly

Fleetwings YPQ-12A characteristics (configured with 500lb bomb unless otherwise noted)

Span	30.0ft (9.1m)
Length	19.9ft (3.0m)
Height	7.0ft (2.1m)
Wing area	100ft² (9.2m²)
Fuel, max (drone)	33 gallons (125 liters)
Fuel, max (piloted)	40 gallons (151 liters)
Climb rate, best	1,042fpm (318mpm)
Service ceiling	18,000ft (5,486m)
Weight, empty	1,740lb (789kg)
Weight, gross	2,916lb (1,323kg)
Weight, ferry	2,088lb (947kg) piloted
Speed, max (piloted)	161mph (259km/h)
Speed, max	171mph (275km/h)
Cruise speed	175mph (282km/h) piloted
Range	375 miles (604km)
Range, ferry	510 miles (821km) piloted
Take-off distance over 50ft obstacle	1,570ft (479m)

This PQ-8 has a Block I television camera installed in the cockpit, aiming through a hole cut into the windscreen, and transmission antenna on the spine. This permitted evaluation of the TV combined with the drone as a stepping stone towards the TV guided bomb drones. The smaller photograph shows the camera unit. *Top National Museum of the United States Air Force/left Bart Everett*

damaged PQ-8 flew on briefly before spiraling into the ground. Another TV-guided YPQ-12A was directed into a white target square measuring 30 by 30 feet (9.1 by 9.1 meters) on a 45-degree sloping hillside. With the control plane 3-5 miles (5-8km) distant, the drone impacted 30 feet (9 meters) from the center, probably owing to directional mistrim misleading the controller as to the line of flight.

The twin-engine BQ drones represented some technological risk in that remote control of a twin-engine airplane had not been definitively demonstrated and represented directional control uncertainty (identical engine settings). Tests by February 1943 with a remote-controlled AT-11 had shown the risk to be tolerable. However, an engine-out situation might be irrecoverable.

As a means to likely reduce the take-off roll for the BQ types, a Project MX-642 was approved to seek a method of launching pilotless aircraft using powder rockets.[27] The JB systems were a natural adjunct to the drones but would clearly have a prolonged development. Any immediate hope of a powered and guided missile lay with drones. A separation of missile activities between the Ground and Air Forces was arranged to ensure against duplication. The USAAF focused on air-launch and wing-borne missiles.

After take-off, drones were controlled from a 'mother ship' fitted with an operator station and suitable transceivers, and possibly radar. This B-23 bomber was so configured for 7 October 1942 drone testing at Muroc Army Air Field. Note the TV receiver antenna atop the tail. *National Museum of the United States Air Force*

For purely visually control the operator in the B-23's copilot seat performed as shown with the box of toggles and switches. When the drone was equipped with a television camera, he looked at the received image while controlling the drone. This was only for terminal guidance – the visual method employed to that point. *National Museum of the United States Air Force*

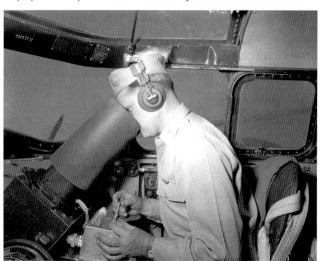

The guided munitions program in the USAAF did not benefit from the flag-rank sponsorship the Navy enjoyed. This did somewhat undermine the ability to move forward rapidly and acquire necessary resources. There were many influential voices that opposed all the many missile development activities, seeing them as contributing little or nothing to the present war. Yet General Arnold continued to press them, and on 16 February 1943 directed continued development of power-driven bombs, including various methods of remote control and targeting. It occasionally took specific direction from the General to induce a commander to permit a field test of the guided weapon in his area. Arnold again urged renewed effort in November 1943 when the Germans began to employ their guided bombs against such pin-point targets as naval vessels. He instructed Materiel Command to re-energize similar Army projects and move to deployment with all haste. At that point the systems under development were far from combat-ready, so even this push could not generate any immediate outcome. Subsequently, a Special Weapons Branch was formed within the Equipment Laboratory at Wright Field with Colonel Holloman directing. Construction of suitable testing facilities at Muroc, Tonopah, Nevada and the Proving Ground at Eglin Field, Florida, was authorized on 3 June 1944. Yet the effort continued to move at a lackluster pace, struggling for priority in acquiring the men and materials required. Additional high-level impetus was applied in August 1944 when the Germans showed on a large scale that these were not just 'Buck Rogers' concepts and the Navy was making decisive strides. A Special Weapons Unit at Muroc was formed and $445,000 approved for new construction. Efforts to streamline the development process saw a Pilotless Aircraft Branch established within the Engineering Division in February 1945.

All the BQ projects were under way by 5 February 1943 as high-priority efforts, progress followed with interest at levels as high as Chief of Air Forces. Arnold was known as an air leader not likely to become enamored with new or conceptual aircraft or weapons. Especially under the pressures of the war, he was loath to expend resources on projects unlikely to yield operational systems within a year or two. Hence, after the initial flurry of activity following the US entry into the war and as the likely course of US involvement became clearer, he had second thoughts about the drones. On 16 June 1943 the General directed that "no further quantity procurement of this type of bomb will be made for other than experimental and development purposes. This is primarily based upon the fact that until definite determination of the capabilities of this type equipment can be made and a definite plan of action formed, Operations, Commitments and Requirements cannot establish future requirements." In a 5 July 1943 letter to the Engineering Division, he directed that no procurement beyond developmental quantities was to be undertaken until they had demonstrated system capabilities, and operational requirements for same were clarified. This equated to a request for the BQ-4 and BQ-5 (see later) be cancelled, and that 200 BQ-types determined to be the best were to be obtained with the least delay.[28]

While the Muroc demonstration of October 1943 showed the progress being made, only the PQ-12A experimental drone could be shown in action. The purpose-built aircraft were still in development and would take too long to produce and reach operational units. An assessment in spring 1944 stated that, "Actual production in any quantity would probably take at least a year... Doubtful whether any quantity will be ordered. Too long to procure, too hard to use and too expensive in comparison with glide bombs."[29] The BQ types were too slow for the tactical environment at that point in the war and were comparatively costly as a one-shot weapon. Another document said that such aircraft "... requires clear weather, suitable fighter protection and a control airplane with highly trained crews."[30] And another, "The BQ program was dropped because it was slow and expensive, requiring almost as much time and money as the development of combat airplanes, without sufficient tactical utility to justify the expenditure of that much time and money. The power-driven XBQs also required clear visibility for use, extensive fighter protection, and highly trained crews."[31] Accuracy remained an open question surrounded with considerable doubt. The simple calculus of tactical utility in comparison with more flexible manned aircraft found the drones wanting.

All these points were reiterated in a 15 April 1944 summary. The XBQ-4 and XBQ-5 had already been dropped. By September, only the XBQ-3 project was still running. It would ultimately be judged no more efficient than other weapons then in service, and was cancelled. Progress on glide weapons and missiles clearly pointed to the future, and these were pursued while drones as a weapon were left behind.

Return of the Bug (General Motors A-1)

General Motors replied to the USAAC's 1939 aerial torpedo solicitation on 7 September proposing an inexpensive two-cycle, 150hp (112kW) engine and other components for a predicted drone all-up weight of 1,200-1,500lb (544-680kg) to include a 300lb bomb within the fuselage.[32] General Arnold was personally involved in the discussions with GM and expressed the opinion that, in suitable quantities (GM suggested 10,000), costs could be reduced to as low as $700 per unit. The General Manager of the corporation's Research Laboratories, Charles F. Kettering, had developed the pioneering Kettering Bug drone for the US Army during and after the First World War (with a younger Arnold participating).

Revised requirements were released on 26 February 1940, which included an accuracy to hit within a half-mile (0.8km)-diameter circle at a range of 20 miles (32km) and an overall range of 100 miles (161km) and to be impervious to enemy interference. A proposal was offered by GM by September, the heart of which was its X-250-D 200hp (149 kW) engine (military designation XR-250-1) turning a 7.3-foot (2.2-meter) propeller in a Cessna Aircraft Airmaster.[33] A $250,000 contract of 14 February 1941 called for ten Type A-1 Power Driven Bomb aircraft (USAAC Aerial Torpedo, renamed Controllable Bomb, Power Driven, on 21 May 1941) together with launch equipment and control gear.[34] Automatic control with barometric altimeter was the baseline. However, the installation of radio control equipment was approved on 30 April for flight test purposes and provided by Wright Field.[35]

The A-1 aircraft as built had a span of 21.1 feet (6.4 meters), was 16.3 feet (5 meters) in length, and grossed 1,550lb (703kg) in its final configuration with payload and 50lb (23kg) of fuel.[36] A maximum speed of 198mph (319km/h) and a range of 400 miles (644km) was expected (although 200 miles [322km] proved more practical). Tests in the Langley full-scale tunnel during July-August 1941 found the rudder and elevator surfaces to be of inadequate area (no ailerons). It otherwise appeared to have suitable stability and control.

The first A-1, dubbed the GM Bug, was initially flown at Muroc on 15 November 1941 with Kettering supervising. It was launched from a four-wheel carriage moving on a track, pulled by a tow vehicle, until 175lb (79kg) of lift caused a restraining spring to release. On the first launch attempt the release occurred at 91mph (147km/h), which proved too slow, the airplane crashing owing to wing stall. The team determined that at least 1,500 feet (457 meters) of travel was required to reach flying speed.[37] The next attempt on 5 December saw lift-off at 100mph (161km/h). Stability appeared poor and control sluggish, both on radio and

automatic control, with the aircraft crashing 2½ minutes into the flight. Another try on 7 December, with elevator and rudder travel reduced by more than half, revealed a tendency to over-control both manually and on automatic flight. Following 10 minutes of flight, the radio transmitter was inadvertently disconnected. The drone continued down range for another 5 minutes before crashing. The next day, elevator and rudder travel were limited even further and the displacement rate also reduced. The flight was more successful, lasting 1hr 35min, but still struggling with over-control on both radio and auto control. A landing attempt, lacking wheels or skids, ended in a wreck.

A program review was conducted at Wright Field on 7 January 1942. It was decided to employ a motorized launch car, install gyros, and add spoilers for roll control (wing design making the addition of ailerons impractical). The gyros permitted stabilization in pitch, acting through the elevators, and roll through the spoilers. This would reduce operator workload and hopefully the over-control tendency. The calculus by that time that the power-driven bomb required a 1,000lb or 2,000lb bomb and a range of 900-1,200 miles (1,448-1,931km) effectively eliminated the A-1 from any useful role, and the unit price appeared well beyond the original intent. Consideration of a practical launching technique brought thoughts of a short track with rocket assist via catapult from landing gear. However, the A-1 might still provide useful information and experience in meeting such goals.

The General Motors A-1 Bug was an early attempt by the USAAC to develop a power-driven bomb, designed to carry a 300lb bomb 20 miles. Here the aircraft is being positioned on a rail for launch from the dry lakebed at Muroc, while the smaller picture shows an example in flight. Although teaching much, the program ran for 2½ years, expending a dozen airplanes, without yielding a fieldable weapon. *National Museum of the United States*

In February the A-1 baseline was changed to radio guidance with TV aiming. An airframe was shipped to Wright Field that month for installation of a TV camera and transmitter. On 30 April 1942 the service ordered a further five articles with TV transmitter, three-axis stabilization, and tricycle undercarriage so they could be recovered and flown again. A monorail catapult driven by a rocket motor was also to be procured, the drone to have droppable tricycle gear for that application.

Flight testing resumed on 10 March at Eglin using an A-1 equipped with two-axis gyros. It was released at 100mph (161km/h) from atop a 'souped-up' Cadillac. A strong side wind and erroneous control installation resulted in a prompt crash. The 19 March attempt was more successful. During the 1hr 55min flight, several passes on a target were made both with and without gyro stabilization. The gyro system provided smoother flight in rough air, but control was lost briefly in this mode. The drone was finally dived to impact. The next machine had the roll gyro control acting through either the spoilers or rudder and further adjustment to the elevator control. It was flown on 2 April for 1hr 40min but still with poor response directionally. Failure of the power generator caused receiver failure and loss of the drone after another 10 minutes of flight.

As a precursor to follow-on aircraft, another original A-1 prototype was fitted with the three-axis gyro package and a TV camera for a test flight on 17 July at Eglin. Launched from the car, it failed to respond to radio commands and crashed after just 2 minutes' flight time. Moisture in the electronics from humidity was suspected, so testing returned to Muroc.

After the rail launch method proved fraught and cumbersome, another launch method for the A-1 was release from a speeding automobile, in this case at Eglin and probably during March 1942, with the engine starter device positioned ahead. This still required a high-speed run on a good surface, but did not rely upon the power of the drone. The crane on the back of the lorry was used to place the aircraft atop the vehicle. *National Museum of the United States Air Force*

An A-1 had its wings badly damaged on 7 September in a taxi test mishap on the tricycle gear with steerable nose wheel. Fitted with new wings, taxi in a straight line to 75mph (121km/h) was demonstrated on the 22nd. A flight attempt on the 25th also ended in a heap, possibly prompted by a seized brake, dumped directional gyro with full rudder and nose wheel deflection at 50mph (81km/h). Brake pressures were subsequently reduced. Another machine was lost in the next take-off attempt on 30 September with the new undercarriage owing to inability to maintain control.

The support truck for the GM Bug chased the aircraft on its take-off run, whether on track, vehicle or its own landing gear. The cab view shows the initial arrangement with the operator inside the cab (the tests in the California desert prompting casual attire) to control directional steering when on the gear, command the take-off and climb-out, then hand-off control to an airborne operator or direct the airplane visually from the ground. The later arrangement in the bottom right view has the operator atop the vehicle and more regulation wear. *National Museum of the United States Air Force/Air Force Test Center*

An October 1942 review reaffirmed the conclusion that a weapon like the A-1 would need a much heavier explosive charge and hundreds of miles range for the targets envisioned. The radio control would need to become standard, mandating a 'mother plane' with remote pilot to guide the bomb to the target. Both would be vulnerable to enemy fighters and AAA. Air-launch might permit a marginally heavier payload and extended range, and GM had made a proposal on 16 June 1942 for a 'pick-a-back' arrangement of the missile launched from atop a North American B-25 Mitchell bomber. Under such conditions, the radio-controlled and TV-equipped airplane with a 500lb bomb might fly at 185mph (298km/h) for 15 minutes. In any event, the tricycle landing gear was eliminated as it appeared improbable that a safe and consistent take-off and landing technique would be found. Arnold still held out hope for the system, which appeared to require a considerable redesign and a big step backwards in development. In December 1942 he approved the proposed changes, seeking a range of 1,000 miles (1,609km) with a 2,000lb (907kg) warhead and 100 aircraft.[38] However, a twin-engine drone appeared more suitable. Nonetheless, the A-1 was proving instructive, so it was decided that additional automobile launches would be performed to perfect stability and control before attempting an air launch.

The testing was taken up again on 24 May 1943 at Muroc. An A-1 prototype was flown on that day under radio control and TV guidance. Although the flight was unsteady, likely due to improper setting of the directional gyro, it went on for 1hr 35min before being steered to impact within 75 feet (23 meters) of a ground target. The aircraft still responded slowly to commands and was unstable in turns. Having worked these problems with another drone, a test on the 27th found no control (selecting gyros off) or command combination that gave satisfactorily stable flight characteristic, turns especially being tenuous. After 1hr 20min the machine crashed after rolling over in a turn.[39]

Although wind tunnel tests were performed at Wright Field in 1943 with a 1/22.2-scale A-1 attached above a B-25 model, full-scale flight tests were not to be. The discouraging A-1 experience was cause for reflection. Clearly, development of such an aircraft, without an onboard safety pilot to compensate when the automatic or remote control proved inadequate, and to record data since telemetry was unavailable, would be prolonged and costly in wrecked hardware. Performing such hazardous unmanned tests with launch from the back of a bomber appeared unsafe.

A 24 August 1943 report from Materiel Command estimated that the now-inadequate A-1 would require another eighteen months, 100 tests with destroyed test articles, and $700,000 to yield a product already determined not to meet current needs. The radical redesign to perhaps twin engines and accommodating a safety pilot would take two years and $200,000. A GM study of such an aircraft employing the same engine had suggested a range of 900-1,200 miles at 150mph, and a 20,000-foot ceiling with a 2,000lb bomb. The engine, which had failed some Air Forces bench tests, had flown more than 600 hours by January 1941 on a Cessna aircraft.

Based on the report's findings, program termination was recommended on 6 September 1943. Demonstration of the YPQ-12A at Muroc in October and progress on the optionally manned BQ drones were the final nails in the coffin. The GM project was formally cancelled on 18 November and the stop-work order sent on 23 December after the expenditure of $350,000. The remaining airframes were broken up.

The A-1 is seen on experimental tricycle landing gear in September 1942 at Muroc dry lake, with the engine starting rig positioned before the propeller, and in flight as inert. The fairing beneath the fuselage houses the television camera system, with the transmit antenna on the spine, all added late to the design like the landing gear. The similarly equipped example in flight, launched from an automobile, was filmed over Muroc on 27 May 1943, the last A-1 to fly. *National Museum of the United States/Air Force Air Force Test Center*

The BQ mixed bag

Fleetwings was engaged in March 1942 to undertake development of two airplanes suitable as drones, one to carry a 2,000lb (907kg) bomb and the other a 4,000lb (1,814kg) weapon. On 10 July 1942 the firm was awarded a contract to build two types of drones to carry the 2,000lb bomb for delivery completed in February 1944. The airframes were almost identical, so only a single static test article was called for. They were built largely of wood and designed such that the top of the fuselage, with the cockpit complete, could be removed and replaced with a streamlined enclosure.[40] It is presumed that the bomb was loaded into the belly of the aircraft. The unit production cost (less GFE) was estimated at $26,000.

The first airplane, the XBQ-1 (42-79561), featured a jettisonable undercarriage and two supercharged Franklin XO-405-7 flat engines of 250hp (1,866kW). Experimental Wickwire-Spencer two-blade, constant-speed propellers were employed. Armor protected the remote control gear from the front and bottom aspects, and the self-sealing fuel and oil tanks and their lines. Even with the assistance of the PQ-12 test effort, the XBQ-1 project ran well behind schedule. The single prototype (42-79561) was supposed to be delivered in July 1943 but was delayed until on or about 15 May 1944. It crashed on its first flight in July due to unclear causes and the contract was cancelled.

Fleetwings XBQ-1 characteristics
(configured without pilot unless otherwise noted)

Span	48.6ft (14.8m)
Length	28.0ft (8.5m)
Height	11.0ft (3.4m)
Wing area	203ft² (19m²)
Climb rate, best	736fpm (224mpm)
Service ceiling	29,500ft (8,992m)
Weight, gross	7,815lb (3,545kg)
Weight, ferry	6,225lb (2,824kg) piloted
Speed, max	222mph (288km/h)
Cruise speed	194mph (312km/h) piloted
Range (188mph)	1,700 miles (2,736km)
Range, ferry (160mph)	3,021 miles (4,862km) piloted
Take-off distance (over 50ft obstacle)	3,480ft (1,061m)

The work continued with the second prototype, the XBQ-2 (43-79562), to be delivered in May 1943. This was identical except for substituting 220hp (164kW) Lycoming O-435-3s. It was itself set aside for the XBQ-2A (42-79562) with 295hp (220kW) Lycoming nine-cylinder R-680-13 radials. Although delivered to Dayton late and flown, the project was becoming costly. The effort was closed out on 15 December 1943, and the airframe broken up. The total cost was $1,343,000.

Fleetwings XBQ-2A characteristics
(configured without pilot unless otherwise noted)

Span	48.6ft (14.8m)
Length	28.0ft (8.5m)
Height	11.0ft (3.4m)
Wing area	236ft² (21.9m²)
Fuel, max	226 gallons (856 liters)
Fuel, max (piloted)	418 gallons (1,582 liters)
Climb rate, best	775fpm (236mpm)
Service ceiling	16,300ft (4,968m)
Weight, empty	4,130lb (1,873kg)
Weight, gross	7,606lb (3,450kg)
Weight, ferry	8,062lb (3,657kg) piloted
Speed, max	179mph (288km/h)
Range (188mph)	1,650 miles (2,655km)
Range, ferry (127mph)	2,950 miles (4,748km) piloted
Take-off distance (over 50ft obstacle)	2,850ft (869m)

Above: These photos illustrate the Fleetwings XBQ-2 during a standard photo shoot at Wright Field. This aircraft is almost identical to the earlier XBQ-1 save for the radial engines. Note the television transmission antenna on the tip of the vertical tail. *Top Museum of Flight/bottom National Archives*

Left: The Fleetwings XBQ-1 had a very brief history, crashing on its first flight and subsequently cancelled. It shared an airframe with the only marginally more successful XBQ-2, the primary difference between the machines being the 'flat' engines on this XBQ-1, shown on its one and only flight (retouched image). The flying bomb airplane has a jettisonable undercarriage for drag reduction. *Jay Miller collection*

More desirable was a recoverable aircraft with bomb shackles. Along this line, Fairchild Aircraft, at its Farmingdale, Long Island plant, was engaged in May 1942 for conversion of its XAT-14 wooden twin with retractable gear. Built as a bomber crew trainer, this cabin-class airplane had gun turrets and a 4,000lb bomb load capacity or two bombs/torpedoes in its weapons bay.[41] Fairchild had set up production in Hagerstown, Maryland, and Burlington, North Carolina, with Bellanca Aircraft and McDonnell Aircraft also manufactured the baseline airplane. The drone contract was let on 1 October 1942 for two prototypes (43-25252/53) with delivery in February and April 1944.[42]

For the XBQ-3 drone (Model 79, MX-53A), a new fuselage was designed for reduced weight, although retaining a cockpit for a pilot and navigator, and a weapons bay for mounting a single 4,000lb (non-droppable), or two 2,000lb bombs (droppable), or two torpedoes (droppable). Like the Fleetwings airplanes, the minimum airspeed with the bomb load or ferry fuel was too high to permit a safe landing in either the drone or piloted configurations. This meant that with the 4,000lb non-droppable load the mission was one-way. The two Ranger V-770-15 engines of 520hp (388 kW) with constant-speed props were retained. Suitable but readily removable navigation equipment was to be included to facilitate ferry. Armor protected the forward aspect of the TV equipment. The TV camera presumably viewed from the tip of the nose.

Delivered on approximately 20 April 1944, the first flight of an XBQ-3 was in July after a substantial development period for a variant. The airplanes were tested at Wright Field, including remote control trials, during which the first was damaged in a forced landing on 19 July, and repairs ran through to November. The second was delivered after July and was destroyed by fire following another forced landing. By August 1945 the project had been downgraded to routine priority/future operations. It was closed out with the end of the war at a total cost of $1.4 million and all terms still incomplete.

The AAF officers working the controllable bomb program maintained a close communication on progress with their Navy counterparts and wanted a look at the USN assault drones. On 25 September 1942 the service requested two each of the XTDR-1 and XTR2R-1 for testing under MX-264, and BuAer

agreed on 9 October. The intent was to assess suitability for the USAAF mission and practicality of substituting Army remote control gear. The TDRs were expected in November 1943 and January 1944, the TD2Rs in December 1943 and February 1944.

Ultimately only one XTDR-1 was provided in April 1943, to become the XBQ-4, the other being cancelled on 21 March 1944. The one aircraft was studied but seldom flown, ultimately suffering cracked spars and being returned in December 1943.[43]

The XBQ-5 was to be the TD2R-1 with Franklin O-805-2 engines, but none were ever completed for the Navy or Army. Substituted were the YBQ-6, which was the XTD3R-1 powered by O-805-2s, and the XBQ-6A, with the R-975. The Army had drafted a requirement on 16 February 1943 for 100 XBQ-5s, three YBQ-6s and ninety-seven BQ-6As for service trials, but received none.[44] In March 1943 the Army provided a list of

Fairchild XBQ-3 characteristics (configured without pilot unless otherwise noted)

Span	52.8ft (16.1m)
Length	36.2ft (11.0m)
Height	13.3ft (4.1m)
Wing area	376ft² (34.9m²)
Fuel, max (drone)	500 gallons (1,893 liters)
Fuel, max (piloted)	800 gallons (3,028 liters)
Service ceiling	14,000ft (4,267m)
Weight, empty	7,685lb (3.486kg)
Weight, gross	15,340lb (6,958kg)
Weight, ferry	14,203lb (6,442kg) piloted
Speed, max	220mph (354km/h)
Cruise speed	197mph (317km/h) piloted
Range (203mph)	1,500 miles (2,414km)
Range, ferry (197mph)	2,900 miles (4,667km) piloted
Take-off distance (over 50ft obstacle)	4,200ft (1,280m)

Twin-engine power permitted a range and payload that made an assault drone worth the expense of a sacrificial airplane. Conversion of two Fairchild AT-21 bomber crew trainers (as seen at left) to the XBQ-3 offered this in a more mature airframe than the Fleetwings machines. Note the extensive modifications for the drone application. The first prototype is seen below after a forced landing in an oat field near Wright Field in the summer of 1944. *Below National Museum of the United States Air Force/left San Diego Air & Space Museum*

The XBQ-3 was perhaps the most promising of the Army bomb drones, with twin engines giving it a payload more worthy of expending an entire airplane hitting a target somewhat precisely. Development ran long and the concept had lost its appeal by the time flight testing had begun. The wood construction was probably more suitable to these expendable airplanes than some of the other applications attempted by the US military during the war. *Museum of Flight*

required and significant changes to the aircraft to permit incorporation of USAAF remote control gear. This was surely unwelcome given the stressed state of the Navy program. Yet Interstate expected to make delivery in September. With test and production, none of the aircraft were expected to be delivered until November or December 1945. The unit production cost (less GFE) was estimated to be approximately twice that of the BQ-1 or BQ-2A.[45] The program remained moribund and was abandoned by the Navy in 1944. Any USAAF production plans had been dropped in July 1943.

The USAAF and USN unmanned aircraft and missile developers remained in close contact immediately before and during the Second World War. They sought to benefit from each other's progress, but the Navy was generally out in front of the Army. In exploring its sister service's efforts, the Air Forces acquired an XTDR-1 for evaluation as the BQ-4, shown here at Wright Field during 1943. *National Archives*

CHAPTER ELEVEN

Drones into Combat

On the line

ONLY THE NAVY assault drones saw combat. The tireless Commodore Smith was dispatched to the Pacific on 1 March 1944 to work out the details of STAG-1's deployment and combat trials. He requested that a detachment of two TBM control planes and four TDN-1 drones be placed aboard an escort carrier (CVE) for deployment within range of a suitable target. The CinCPac was not forthcoming, instead passing Smith along to Admiral Bill F. Halsey Jr, commanding the 3rd Fleet in the South Pacific where Smith was, in turn, directed to the air arm commander. The decision was taken on 18 March to dispatch STAG-1 to the Russell Islands, where opportunities for tests would be sought. However, higher-priority operations meant that it was May before the unit (squadrons VK-11 and -12, joined by VK-13 and -14 from Eagle Mountain Lake) set sail from Alameda, California, arriving in the Russell chain the following month. The TBMs and a number of fully assembled TDRs were transported lashed to the deck of the USS *Marcus Island* (CVE-77). Other TDRs were transported crated for a total of about eighty drones.[1]

With some 1,000 men, STAG-1 set up on Banika Island beside the just-completed Sunlight Field airstrip, which measured 4,400 by 150 feet (1,341 by 46 meters), while revetments and other secure areas were being completed. The rough conditions, characterized by high humidity promoting corrosion, coral dust, and crude shelters were most challenging. From arrival on 5 June, a manned engineering test flight with the initial TDR-1 (now referred to as 'dogs') occurred on the 20th, with the first nolo flight on the 26th. The TBMs were also conducting training flights, which saw several

The STAG-1 team had trained well for its combat deployment, using a variety of training aids as well as the actual systems. Here the team conducts flight operations at Half Moon Bay in March 1944 prior to shipping out. A launch of three TDR-1s (production aircraft 27860 and 27860 visible) is being undertaken, with one still tied to the truck before release of the rope restraint; each aircraft is manned, but with the TV and remote-control antennae installed. *National Archives*

lost to accidents or simply going missing. There were also mishaps with the drones, one being written off in a take-off accident during which one engine did not power up properly and the aircraft departed the runway.

The crew were also modifying the command links to FM to avoid potential jamming, for which a Philco Corporation, of Philadelphia, technical representative (tech rep) was present to assist.[2] The training flights included laying down smoke screens using one to three Mk 10 smoke generator tanks mounted under the belly. Other flights had two and four dummy 500lb (227kg) bombs mounted under the wings. The four weeks of training included ninety-six drone flights with a safety pilot, of which only 45.3 percent were judged successful. The radio control system had a 23.7 percent failure rate, the television 36.1 percent, and the radio altimeter control 22.7 percent. In nine of the take-offs the safety pilot had to take control to prevent a mishap.[3]

During the Half Moon Bay operations the Block camera is shown being adjusted after being replaced. The image gives a look at the panel truck equipped as the ground control station 'command car' and serving as an impromptu work platform. The paneled nature of the TDR-1 skin is also evident. *National Archives*

Another shot of the Block camera being adjusted prior to a mission gives a close-up look at some of the TDR-1 features and the moderate workmanship evident in the construction. The Sensenich Brothers propeller with spinner and detail of the nose gear are provided, the forward vertical post of the nose gear apparently designed to slip out of the tube when released. Aircraft maintenance in a war zone during the Second World War was often performed out of doors with makeshift support equipment. *National Archives*

The first operational test involved strikes on the beached cargo vessel *Yamazuki Maru* off Cape Esperance, Guadalcanal, about 34 miles (55km) distant. By this point, 15 July, the operational concept was to crash the plane, armed with a 2,000lb (907kg) bomb, into the target. Many practice runs were made. For the staged and filmed event, two out of four TDRs hit the target and detonated, the TBMs never closer than 7 miles (11km). One pilot had difficulty disengaging the radio altimeter control, so did not properly correct for drift. The drone struck a glancing blow on the bow and went into the drink without the bomb detonating. A fourth passed over the ship at about 10 feet (3.1 meters) and exploded ashore. A fifth machine, replaced by a spare, never left the ground when a pin retaining the nose gear sheared and it separated at power-up, falling onto its nose and cowlings.

This 25 August 1944 image shows a TDR-1 fitted with three Mk 10 smoke generator tanks. How the aircraft was selected for this mission is unclear, but it showed how the STAG-1 team was able to adapt to requirements. Production aircraft 27870 is shown at Sunlight Field on Banika Island in the Russell Island chain. *National Archives*

On 15 July 1944 four TDR-1 drones, each armed with a 2,000lb bomb and retaining the landing gear, were directed at a grounded Japanese freighter near Guadalcanal as a demonstration of the assault drone concept. The first is shown moments before impact, one of the following three also hitting the static target. The film of this event failed to stir a surge of enthusiasm, but limited combat operations did ensue. *National Archives*

Commodore Oscar Smith, in wheel cap, is shown with Commander Robert F. Jones, middle, beside a Beech GB executive transport on 15 July 1944 at Banika Island. Smith, although not an aviator, worked tirelessly to get combat drones to a combat-ready state. Jones had been involved with target drones since before the war and commanded the only unit to actually engage the enemy with the Navy attack drones. *National Archives*

The film of the strikes show several interesting aspects. In one take-off the pilot rotated the nose too early, so the run was long and the aircraft was clearly on the edge of stall (66mph [106km/h]) as it staggered into the air. The update (refresh) rate on the TV screen, with crosshairs, was slow, as was response of the airplane to final flight path adjustments, making a precise hit somewhat tricky. The contrast of the image changed dramatically with altering lighting conditions (such as passing from bright daylight to cloudy conditions), and this also complicated precise guidance.

Certain that the successful demonstration would engender more favorable consideration by Nimitz, Smith flew to Hawaii while his deputy, Commander Robert F. Jones, began converting tired SBD-3s and 5s for operation off a carrier against other targets. Thirty of these machines were drawn from storage in Espirito Santo and flown by STAG-1 pilots the 1,800 miles (28,968km) to Banika.[4] A television camera and transmitter appear to have been placed in a modified parachute drop container mounted on the starboard wing hardpoint for the drone, while others were modified as command ships.[5]

Smith found no change in the attitude that an experimental unit did not belong in a war zone. The intent was to return STAG-1 to the States for immediate disbandment. This news only spurred Bobbie Jones into action to make a true combat showing before the axe fell. Seeking guidance from local headquarters, he was granted a thirty-day reprieve. Only secondary targets of bypassed Japanese garrisons and facilities far removed from the front line of engagement were possible to avoid scrutiny from those opposed to the drones.

Between 27 September and 26 October, forty-six TDR-1s (approximately half those available) were expended against targets in the Rabaul and Bougainville areas (northern Solomons). Strikes were VK-11 from Ocean Field on Green Island, north of Bougainville, and the field on Stirling Island, off the south end of Bougainville. This forward deployment required manned staging flights from Sunlight of 450 miles (724km) with an intermediate fuelling stop. The drone operations were mixed with other flight activities at these fields, and in one strike were in cooperation with other units. With four Block I channels available for the transmitters, typically four-ship or three-ship elements (one control plane and one drone to avoid interference) were flown on the same mission against the same target. Strikes from Green were against Rabaul and so out to about 160 miles (258km) – near the range limit. Those from Stirling went out to about 60 miles (97km). Control planes normally remained 6-8 miles (10-13km) from the target, but as far as 15-20 miles (24-32km).

Of forty-six aircraft launched (number of aborts not recorded), twenty-one hit their targets with six misses and one probable. Destruction of the targets was rarely recorded,

As a short path to acquiring a high-speed attack drone, outmoded Douglas SBD dive bombers were drawn from storage and conversions begun in-theater. This included creating command ships as well as the drone – this SBD-3 (6537, photographed on 15 August 1944) has been given a hastily modified parachute drop container under the starboard wing hardpoint with a window added for the television camera. The aircraft would presumably have been armed with a centerline bomb. *National Archives*

An often-published photo, it shows the preparation of a TDR-1 in the Pacific for a combat mission with a 2,000lb bomb. The nose camera gear is exposed and the standard fixed-pitch wooden propeller evident. The wooden structure was covered with many panels held by Dzus fasteners. *Naval Aviation Archives*

Another image from the Pacific deployment of STAG-1, dated 23 September 1944, reveals TDR-1 27878 probably recently arrived at a forward base for launch against the enemy. The canopy has yet to be removed but remote-control antennae have been added. The primitive operating conditions are noteworthy; not conducive to operating such complex equipment. *Naval Aviation Archives*

This shot of a TDR-1 in the combat zone provides details of the 2,000lb bomb mounting. An alternate hold-back means has been devised with a cable running from a fitting on the back of the nose gear strut to a truck bumper out of frame to the right, and a sandbag wheel chock is in place to resist rearward motion. A wire also runs out of frame, either to release the hold-back via a tug or electrical signal. *National Archives*

suggesting little or no post-strike reconnaissance. That this 46 percent success rate was considered remarkable, especially with no loss of Allied personnel, is testament to the modest accuracy of bombing during the war. The Japanese under these attacks did not feel much threatened as they saw many failures and wondered what the intended targets were.[6] Of the TDRs launched, twenty-two were lost en route and ten crashed (seven as a result of 'material failures', suggesting some airframe issue or engine failure), and three to five were shot down by AAA. Four TDRs suffered last-minute TV failures making final flight path corrections impossible, two were lost owing to radio interference from naval vessels until the frequency was secured, seven others suffered unspecified system failures, and three bombs failed to detonate. Of the twenty-nine actual target engagements, some were difficult to discern on the TV screen due to limited contrast, such as AAA batteries, caves, specific buildings, and low bridges. Of four TDRs aimed at cave entrances in the Rabaul area, only one hit (but did not go in) and one missed without the bomb exploding, two others being lost en route. Likewise, it took five aircraft aimed at a lighthouse before one hit and destroyed the target. Eight drones were flown against a bridge but none reached the target due to system failures and shoot-downs. Several strikes were made against beached ships serving as AAA platforms.

Towards the end of the campaign, the drones dropped their bombs and were then dived into softer targets. These met with the same mixed results. In one case a drone carried two 500lb weapons on the belly and four 100lb bombs under each wing (1,800lb/817kg total). An attempt to return one to base failed when it crashed, likely due to a hit during the attack. The crashes without explosions meant wreckage that the Japanese were able to scavenge for classified materials.[7] An attempt was made to locate a few of these and destroy them in air strikes; two were spotted but appeared to have been completely demolished.[8]

Regardless of the measure of success, the fate of STAG-1 had already been sealed. Rather than transport the top-secret

gear back to the States, two TDR-1s were expended as AAA targets and the thirty SBDs were dumped into the ocean. Back home, remaining drones took up the role of targets again, some for new air-to-air weapons.

At an effective operational radius of 160 miles (258km), the TDR/TBM combination was deficient for the theater at that island-hopping stage of the Pacific campaign. The TDR's low speed made it vulnerable to AAA and fighters (though none of the latter were encountered, with the Japanese capabilities diminishing rapidly). Even as a carrier-based system, such performance did not compare well with naval attackers, which would typically be measured in hundreds of miles. Manned naval attack aircraft were then also making closer to 300mph (483km/h), so even the 'high-performance' drones that never emerged would have been comparatively slow. The drone lacked folding wings and other features, making it unsuitable for integration into a carrier air wing. The airplanes also had to be lifted onto the ship from the dockside, so the carrier

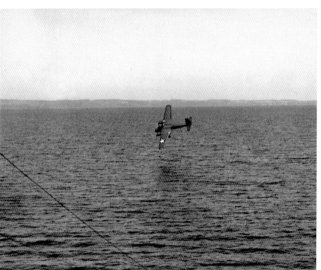

Although the TDN-1 was reported to have had a catapult launch capability, most or all test flights from a carrier were simply flown off, such as this 10 August 1944 unmanned flight from the USS *Sable* (which appears to lack a catapult). The launch clearly went badly, with over-rotation, stall, falling off on the left wing despite full opposite controls, and imminent water impact. This graphically illustrates one of the limitations of the drone system with the potential for under-speed take-off or over-rotation. *National Archives*

Other drone tests with the TDN-1 involved attempts to hit a target with inert bombs released from the weapons bay (lacking doors). For this January 1943 test in Delaware Bay by VJ-6, flying over the target an unrealistically slow speed and altitude were not enough to hit the floating target. The drone lacked a bombsight or targeting system other than sighting via the low-resolution television and pilot judgment when to command bomb release. *National Archives*

Having decided that terminal impact of the armed drone into a target was the most effective attack method, tests were performed. These included this TDN-1 dive at a billboard target on Bloodsworth Island in January 1943 by VJ-6. The dusk event again illustrated the limitations of the drone system with a miss despite an evident last-second attempt to correct the flight path. The impact does not appear to have been within lethal range, as the wooden billboard remains standing. *National Archives*

would need to withdraw to port to replenish the attack force, even if it was assembled onboard. Crosswind take-off limits appeared to be less than 10 knots (12mph [19 km/h]) due to lack of landing gear steering.[9] Conversion of operational fighters and bombers would likely have been more suitable. And, given what became a vast supply of these aircraft, the decision not to follow that route and instead start from a 'clean sheet' with an untried and ill-equipped contractor was likely fatal to the program. Yet limitations of the technology, such as too few Cast channels, made any avenue risky.

The 2,000lb explosive load of the TDR-1 was judged by some too small for one-off decisive attacks against high-value targets. Impact would be at such low kinetic energy, compared with a free-fall 2,000lb demolition bomb, that penetration of armor plating was doubtful. The *Yamazuki Maru* demonstration showed that a good deal of the blast was directed outward and to the side, not into the vessel, although gratifying holes were created in the thin skin.

The radio and control gear was admittedly fragile and cheap, contributing to breakdowns that compromised readiness and mission effectiveness. The unintentional self-jamming experienced was indicative of the vulnerability of the system to this countermeasure. Japanese forces recovered the radio gear from several wrecked TDR-1s and attempted to ship it back to Japan for analysis.[10] Although the airplane carrying the equipment went missing, any sustained use of the drones would have eventually seen the enemy determine the operating frequencies and quickly develop jammers. At the time of the combat deployment the system was still amplitude modulated (AM), which was more easily jammed than the FM gear that was just being introduced.

Bombers into bombs

The application of drone technology to war-weary heavy bombers was attractive because of their range and the mass of explosives they could carry, in addition to the short amount of time required for development at that point in the drone work. There were a number of vexing targets that could be serviced by such a weapon. Submarine pens had almost impenetrable roofs and narrow vertical openings at sea level. Surrounded by very dense anti-aircraft batteries, level bombing attacks were costly. Even the use of super heavy bombs like the 12,000lb (5,433kg) 'Tall Boy' deep-penetration munitions was indecisive because they were unguided. Special targets called for special measures.

The Navy had begun considering the use of four-engine heavy bombers as a terminal-crash drone, and another as the control plane, during 1943. At that time, Commodore Smith contemplated an additional STAG equipped with eighteen PB4Ys to be employed in this manner. Such an aircraft could carry as much as 16,000lb (7,258kg) of explosives on a 1,500-mile (2,414km) one-way mission (although the controller would be at a round-trip range). The distance allowed the aircraft to be launched from mainland bases (Alaska, China), thus not encumbering ongoing naval air operations in-theater. The drones were to use 'sniffers' for attacking high-value targets at night and in bad weather, suggesting the use of radar for controller guidance. It was recognized that a nolo take-off of such aircraft presented additional complexities, so a human pilot for the early phase of the mission would be necessary, the man parachuting from the aircraft over some safe area before the drone was directed on remotely. Smith's proposal was not taken up because BuAer did not favor expanding the drone program at that time, and there were then no surplus of heavy bombers given the high demand and great losses in Europe.

A study of the heavy bomber drone at the Naval Air Modification Unit (NAMU), in Philadelphia, was finally approved by the CNO in March 1944. They were to use a B-24 already at NAMU for radar testing. The heart of the conversion was remote control of the Minneapolis Honeywell C-1 three-axis autopilot.* This eliminated the need to develop a separate

* The most common autopilot in American heavy aircraft, the C-1 featured altitude hold, a wing-leveler for heading hold, and a bank angle command for turning. Setting up the autopilot was 'touchy' and it needed repeated attention during a long-duration flight. It also required the hydraulic pressure source to remain operable.

stabilization system for the bomber. Introduced was the additional feature of turning to a preselected compass heading. It also had a television transmitter looking out from the nose for forward vision, and another for repeat-back of the compass heading (via small mirrors and a prism to permit the illuminated magnetic compass dial to be captured as an insert in the TV image), as well as a radio altimeter, radar beacon, throttle and elevator trim servomotors, an ordnance control board for arming (a solenoid for pulling pins in inertia switches), and the option of detonating the explosive load remotely rather than on impact. All this gear amounted to some 500lb (228kg). A total ten radio channels in the FM band were available for such functions as climb/dive, turn, speed control, activating radar altimeter, and explosives arming and detonation. When the radio command signal was interrupted the aircraft automatically leveled off. Between 18,800 and 19,300lb (8,528 and 8,754kg) of Torpex explosives could be loaded depending on distribution of the 335 charge boxes, and sand bags were also stacked inside to bring the gross weight to the maximum 63,000-65,000lb (28,576-29,483kg) for the highest impact kinetic energy.

Captain Temple, in the CNO's office, held a conference with Army and NDRC representatives in April 1944. Study results provided on 15 April concluded that many heavy bomber conversions might be available for drone operations later that year, with production reaching full stride, as a shorter and potentially more effective means to the end than building BQ aircraft. However, the senior Army attendee, General Hugh McClelland, responded later saying that his service did not believe the difficulties in establishing and operating such drones offered sufficient advantage over conventional use of bombers, and did not favor diversion of the airplanes. Temple also had to confess that such operations stretched the agreement on division of roles and responsibilities between the services. On 27 May 1944 the CNO called for a halt to the study.

A month later matters were different. The Germans launched their V-1 campaign against Britain in June despite heavy bombing of the launch sites. The V-2 ballistic missiles did not begin falling on London until September, but their launch sites were already being targeted. As the barrage continued, the heavily defended launchers remained difficult objectives to destroy by level bombing, despite thousands of tons of ordnance expended. The effort had already cost many bombers and aircrew. National leadership on both sides of the Atlantic decreed the launch sites the highest-priority target aside from immediate needs of the battlefield. The bomber drones, guided directly into the target, might turn the trick and relieve the tremendous strain on the island nation. At that time the B-17s were being produced at a rate of about twelve per day and the B-24s about thirty per day, with hundreds flying formation missions. This provided a steady pool of outdated and 'war-weary' models for conversion at a rate of perhaps twenty to twenty-five per month in the European Theater of Operations (ETO). However, only five to ten drones could be operated in a target area at a time owing to radio interference. Perhaps as many as sixty-five drones would be necessary to destroy all the identified targets.

On 24 June NAMU was ordered to undertake an all-out, three-shifts-per-day effort to create a PB4Y drone option as Project Anvil. The aircraft was stripped of all non-essential gear, aluminum shapes replacing turrets. The essentials of the drone equipment were installed and flight tested. The final design of the explosive load had 374 Torpex charges in 63lb (29kg) boxes, adding 20,570lb (9,330kg) in addition to a 600lb (272kg) TNT demolition charge plus 3,070lb (1,393kg) of related equipment for a gross of 65,000lb (29,483kg). This required the interior to be shored up with lumber to ensure suitable stiffness. The copilot seat was removed to provide an egress path for the pilot through the nose gear well, where the doors were also removed.

The concept of operations for the PB4Y drone was that the pilot would set the autopilot, ensure a good hand-off to the controller, then bail out of the aircraft at 2,000 feet (610 meters) altitude to be rescued from the English Channel by motor launch. For both the PB4Y and B-17, the parachute exit presented a specific hazard because the airspeed of the bail-out was quite high (approximately 180mph [290km/h]) and from a constrained exit area. One Lockheed PV-1 control plane followed behind at up to 1 mile (1.6km) as the drone was leveled off at 300 feet (91 meters) above the sea using the radio altimeter. The second PV-1 was 8-10 miles (13-16km) behind and following the drone's beacon with the onboard radar. This had the TV receiver, under a black hood, and the controller gear in the passenger compartment. The controller used the same stick and telephone dial equipment as the TDRs. When 5 miles (8km) from the target, the controller would line up the drone for the approach and, within 10 miles (16km), engage the TV. This PV-1 would then turn away as the second plane took control for the final run-in from a safe distance. Fighter escort was provided but would also serve to shoot down the drone should it go rogue.

It was only 1 July that BuAer reported that the drone (PB4Y-1 32271, a new airframe) and controllers (PV-1 33426 and 33429) would be ready to deploy to Europe on the 3rd. A Special Air Unit (SAU-1) was formed from a core of STAG-3 (recently decommissioned) and NAMU personnel. The eleven officers and sixteen men were led by Commander James A. Smith, formerly commanding STAG-3. An advantage of the PV-1s and PB4Y-1 was that they could self-deploy, flying the much-traveled route via Iceland on about 6-7 July together with two R4D transports. The two PV-1s, however, were grounded for three weeks in Greenland by weather. Once on site at the Army air base in England, the USAAF and Navy teams cooperated only reluctantly with little exchange of knowledge and experience. The USN personnel also had to adjust to the many unique procedures for operating in an intense air war zone.

In England the Eighth Air Force was ordered on 24 June to carry out the project, designated 'Aphrodite'. The Army's in-theater effort was under the operational command of Lieutenant Colonel Jim Forrest. They already had a design for the drone conceived locally that was much more rudimentary than the Navy system and did not benefit from the deep experience and knowledge of Wright Field personnel. This was sketched out by Major Henry 'Jim' Rand. Control was entirely visual, without TV. By using two sets of Azon bomb stability and control elements, the 'double-Azon' gave azimuth (roll left or right) and range (full down elevator) control. The latter required good judgment of distance to the target at an altitude of 300 feet for impact at the expected range from sending the down command. A radar altimeter was coupled to the autopilot for flight at 300 feet without controller action. Some of the components were difficult to come by and the addition of radio altimeters was seen as vital yet a 'long pole', radar beacons also being desired but not essential. This design was first test-flown from England in late June 1944.

While the double-Azon was cobbled together in England, Wright Field was engaged to rapidly assemble a more refined design. Its remote control systems had been matured, and their application to bombers with autopilots was quite feasible. Apart from the BQ-3, transports (C-47) and old bombers (B-18 and B-23) were considered in January 1944. The immediate need employing heavy bombers was first considered at a meeting on 12 April 1944 between the senior European air combat leadership and Wright Field development staff.[11] In March twelve kits with Block III TV for such conversion had already been requested, developed for testing by order of General Arnold. All resources, valued at some $100,000, were to be those already on hand, negating the need for outside procurement. The gear added an average $10,000 to the drone cost, and for the control plane $6,000. In June this effort had been reemphasized under the 'War Weary' or 'Willies' project (MX-541), five control kits added (a P-38J 'Droop Snoot' to get one of them), with the B-17 and B-24 identified as the intended drones.[12]

Carrying up to 4,000lb (1,814 kg) of bombs, the P-38 could be an effective bomber. Twenty-three P-38Js were modified in Belfast with an extended 'Droop Snoot' nose enclosing a bombardier and Norden bombsight. It was felt that these could also serve as fast bomber drone control platforms.
Air Force Test Center

The Wright Field design attempted to integrate the remote control with the C-1 autopilot for the first time. A Block III TV camera and transmitter were adopted for terminal guidance, the camera pointing through the bombardier's flat bombsight window to show the fight path ahead. There was an option of another camera in the cockpit to monitor specific instruments.* The radio altimeter was not initially part of the design; the USAAF was only then experimenting with the device on its AT-11 surrogate drone. However, the ETO team working double-Azon incorporated it readily and the Wright Field team soon came to the solution with the radio altimeter as part of Automatic Control Equipment (ACE). A late addition was a liquid smoke tank (a reworked P-47 centerline 75-gallon drop tank) mounted under the belly to aid visual tracking, also assisted by painting the top of the wings white or yellow.

The ACE B-17 drone design was as sophisticated as the Anvil PB4Ys and naturally more refined than the double-Azon lash-up. Signals included turn left/right, climb/dive, assume wings level, descend to preset radar altitude, maintain constant heading, smoke on/off, radio beacon on/off, and TV on/off. An amplifier could boost signal strength if enemy jamming became evident. They had direct throttle control as well as the magnetic compass repeat-back in the TV image. All such commands, of course, required separate radio channels. The radio beacon could be tracked by the radio compass aboard the control plane to give the bearing. The AN/APX-14 Black Maria S-band radar beacon, to be tracked via an H2X X-band airborne radar, was another late addition, helping to keep track of the drone even if

* The resolution of these early television cameras and displays would have permitted the reading of only a few instruments at close range.

The B-17 center console and glareshield shows some of the modification used to convert the bomber to a BQ-7 Castor bomb drone. Switches and indicator lights have been added to the glareshield, and actuation units installed above the console to drive controls via the light-colored pushrods, such as the rod on the starboard side going aft to the throttles. Plenty remains for the pilots to do before bailing out, as only a fraction of the normal engine controls were manipulated remotely. *National Archives*

it became lost in clouds. Assisting in this was the Rebecca transponder that emitted a signal permitting the control aircraft, equipped with the Eureka receiver, to determine the range and bearing to the drone. There was also a desire to permit greater bank angle during remote-control maneuvering.

It was 8 June before Materiel Division formally directed procurement of the twelve sets of remote control gear (plus three spares) for use on B-17F or G (BQ-7, initially BQB-17) and B-24D or J (BQ-8, initially BQB-24) drones, and five kits for the control planes (plus two spares) employing the same types; CQ-4, initially CQB-17 being a B-17G; CQ-5, initially CQB-24, a B-24; and CQ-6, a Lockheed P-38 or CQP-38, plus spares.[13] Designated Project Castor on 19 June, the work was granted top priority the same day, European theater commands expressing an urgent need for the capability.* The goal was assets en route to theater by 1 August. Requirements were stated as the Block III television system, 20,000lb (9,072kg) of explosives, a range of 100-600 miles (161-966km), dependent on the fuel and explosive load, a ceiling beyond 25,000 feet (7,620 meters), and the ability to dive under stabilized control at 15-45 degrees.[14]

Wright Field succeeded in assembling fifteen Castor M (missile) sets with three spares, and seven Castor C (control) with two spares. On 12 July a B-17G and B-24J were sent to

*'Castor' thereafter came to refer, perhaps incorrectly, to all remote-controlled airplanes.

modification centers at St Paul, Minnesota, and Cheyenne, Wyoming, for conversion to control planes in support of stateside testing. Flight-testing of converted bombers as drones and control planes was soon under way at Eglin. This immediately showed that diving from high altitude would be impractical given the natural longitudinal stability of the bomber, the C-1 servo motor not providing sufficient force. A normal let-down from around 2,000 feet (610 meters) proved more practical, for a feasible terminal dive from 300 feet (cutting the ignition was also advised later). In September and October two B-24Ds were converted to BQ-8 drones and two to CQ-5 control ships for testing at Eglin. At that time they still did not include altitude control or smoke-dispensing gear. There are no indications that these machines were deployed.[15]

A few kits were dispatched to the theater on 12 July, with the rest of those requested to follow by 1 August. On 15 July essential personnel (five officers and three civilians) departed for the UK to put the project into operation, arriving on the 18th. The on-site team was led by Colonel Leon Hoffman with the technical effort directed by Lieutenant Colonel Dale Anderson and civilian Peter R. Murray. The team began converting the first two bombers on the 23rd and flight-testing commenced on the last day of July. Refinements for operation were made and training conducted throughout most of August.

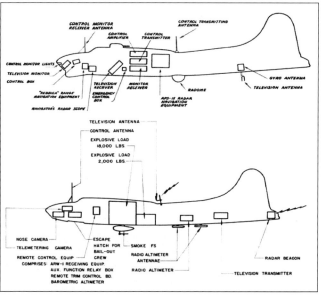

These drawings from period documents illustrate the major points of the 'Aphrodite' modifications to the B-17, both the control ship and the drone. Not all the features were present in all examples, these representing the nearly final and complete configurations. The B-24 option was evaluated in the States but not deployed. *United States Air Force*

Because of equipment shortages, most of the ships had to use the earlier TV kit from the GB-8 (Block I). Additional sources for some of the rarer items were being sought, and many dozens of addition kits were on order should the program increase in scope. However, final acquisition of some last gear was holding up the system from going into action, and it looked like it might be September before all would be in readiness. However, missions were launched purely visually while the TV gear was en route.

Examination was made of the use of the earlier A-4 or A-5 autopilots, of which there was a large surplus. These were found on medium bombers (A-20, B-25, B-26) that were then considered for drone conversion, and some B-24 models that also had the A-5. This was shelved after an assessment found undesirable aspects of the intended design and the fact that the C-1 application was already advanced and personnel were familiar with it.

All conversions for combat were performed in the UK. At Honington air depot all armament and non-essential equipment (especially guns, turrets and armor) was removed for a saving of 5,000lb (2,268kg). The aircraft was then flown to Burtonwood for structural beef-up and electrical work. At Woodbridge some 18,425lb (8,357kg) of nitrostarch explosives (335 boxes) was packed into the B-17 and rigged for detonation. Shoring and other components brought the gross for the explosive load to 21,105lb (9,573kg). The load distribution placed the CG unusually high in the aircraft, increasing the risk of it rolling over in a turn. Substituting Torpex, half as powerful again as nitrostarch, the bomber carried 18,425lb (8,357kg) of explosives together with 6,000lb (2,722kg) of fuel. Some of the bombers were packed with jellied gasoline (napalm) in cans in the hope that it would penetrate openings into underground facilities made by the explosive-laden ships, and suffocate the occupants. (The napalm concept was not flown except for one airplane with a mix of explosives that included 171 incendiary bombs distributed throughout plus 830 gallons [3,142 liters] of napalm in bomb bay auxiliary fuel tanks.) Expectation was that the drone would need to strike within yards of the hardened targets to destroy them. With 1,000 gallons (3,785 liters) of fuel and a full explosives load, the gross reached 63,000lb (28,576kg) for a range of 350 miles (563km). The Army converted a dozen B-17s as BQ-7s by September, and an eventual total of about twenty-five.* Experience showed that 700-900 man-hours were required to convert a bomber to either the drone or control configuration.

The USAF bomber drone effort focused on the B-17F and G. Each Flying Fortress was stripped of all guns and turrets as well as all other non-essential gear, to lighten it for the one-way BQ-7 mission, then modified for ease of pilot egress, addition of remote control gear and television (when available), then the explosives. This 'war weary' B-17F (42-30066) has been so stripped in preparation for the drone modification, but little else is visible. *United States Air Force*

*Although official sources indicate that only the bomber available by mid-August included ACE, combat accounts suggest that all the BQ-7s had this equipment. The smoke tank was also unavailable until September.

Control would be effective at a distance of 20 miles (32km). The control planes were expected to be Lockheed DB-34 Venturas (British models). Alternatively, they could be another B-17 (one expected for navigation pathfinding, in any event) or a B-24, with a P-38 'Droop Snoot' available if rapid egress from the area was anticipated. Under conditions of good visibility, a distinctive target could be acquired on the TV screen at 7-10 miles (11-16km). Plans evolved to fly four BQ-7s against a target (at least one with the Block III TV), a CQ-4 for each, flying at 20,000 feet (6,096 meters), while the drone went in at 300 feet. For the final dive, the ACE was turned off and the 'dump' command (full down elevator) sent. A second control plane for each drone was added for redundancy. Light liaison airplanes worked to locate the airmen after they parachuted to earth. The flight was typically accompanied by another B-17 as observer. A P-38 'Droop Snoot' commonly came along for photography, P-38s or P-47s flown by senior commanders zipping around the formation, and a squadron or two of fighters providing escort and to shoot down the drone if it went rogue. Several reconnaissance aircraft conducted post-strike photography. Prior reconnaissance flights over the entire route of the flight verified no stray emissions on the control frequency bands, and some of the control planes had onboard indicators for such interference. It was found that an RAF automatic landing system operated on one of the vital frequencies, so it was arranged that this be switched off during drone operations. Diversionary bombing raids were also flown at approximately the same time as some drone missions.

Once off, the explosives-filled drone was not to be returned to a landing but instead dumped into the North Sea if it would not steer properly. If fired on by friendly flak the men were to promptly bail out; the forward bottom hatch was to be removed for easy egress. Two pilots were required to get the B-17 off and set up for drone flight. A safety pilot flew the airplane off, retracted the undercarriage, synchronized the engines, trimmed the aircraft for 175mph (282km/h), set 300 feet (91 meters) on the radio altimeter, ensured a good hand-off to the controller, armed the explosives, then bailed out. Another man (initially an autopilot specialist and later another pilot) set up the autopilot before bailing out ahead of the pilot. Their backpack parachutes were deployed by static line while they had a back-up chest-pack chute.

A proposed mission was to hit the German battleship *Tirpitz*, holed up in a Norwegian fjord, with a drone carrying British hydrobombs. This weapon would detonate at a preset depth to burst the vessel's hull. However, the long bombs could not be loaded into the B-17 in the conventional manner, up through the bomb bay. The solution required major 'surgery' in removing the top decking of the fuselage and lowering in the bombs from above. Reassembly left the top of the flight deck off with just a windscreen in what was dubbed a 'roadster' configuration. An unarmed example was prepared and test flown to the great delight of the pilots. However, in the end the British refused to permit the bomb-laden airplane to leave the ground, and another solution finished off the *Tirpitz*.

By August, the Air Forces were looking to stateside conversion of 500 new bombers into drones and 100 control ships (plus 10 percent spares for each). These plans had been

Major 'surgery' saw the top of a BQ-7 removed to fit a super-heavy bomb, then reassembled with just a 'roadster' windscreen. The BQ-7 required two pilots to get it off and set it up for remote control flight, so it is assumed that one pilot was to bail out from the top to be replaced by the second man, or the second departed from the crew entrance hatch below. This configuration as armed (note the white paint smeared on the upper surfaces) never flew. *National Museum of the United States Air Force*

reduced by 17 October 1944 to preparing only kits at 275 each for the BQ-7 and BQ-8, plus fifty-five control kits for each, the P-38 'Droop Snoot' being set aside. These were to be supplied to the ETO at about 50-150 per month. Materiel Division was looking beyond the immediate configuration of the war-weary bomber drones to extending its effectiveness. This included the addition of the radar beacon for possible blind operations, the smoke dispenser, radio altimeter, automatic take-off capability, and telemetry of drone systems to support more extensive operations, requiring such instruments as manifold pressures, airspeed, altimeter and rate-of-climb indicators.*

A radar beacon installation had already been devised by MIT for the Castor drones, which would permit the flight to be followed and the drone possibly controlled to take it over a target visible on the radar PPI. This would permit a night operation (less vulnerable to AAA and fighters) and one at any time during the winter months in Europe, marked by frequent cloud cover.

*The limited insight into the drone system from the control plane meant that problems could not be diagnosed, much less corrected. The complex heavy bombers, especially the war-weary examples turned into drones, offered a considerable risk of system maladjustment that further reduced probability of mission success.

Tests of such operation at Eglin showed an average error of 450 feet (137 meters) at a range of 35 miles (56km), but the operational forces expected the weapon to fall within an area of 3-4 square miles (8-10km²), such as a city. Control from the ground was also considered, eliminating an airborne controller who was also subject to weather limitations. However, the range would be reduced to 75-100 miles (121-161km) and flight beyond that would have to be via dead reckoning with final dive by timer mechanism, but also not subject to enemy jamming of control signals. It was envisioned that up to twenty-five bombers per month could be flown on such terror missions. Attempts to use an infrared seeker also yielded very poor accuracy. Tests of all these techniques were under way at Eglin. Although the AAF gave this project its highest priority, the British government was opposed to this course as it could bring additional retribution down on London.

By early 1945 fighters were being assessed as potential drones, benefiting from their higher airspeed and assisting ground forces by hitting more tactical targets. The remote control gear amounted to 200lb (91kg), about that of a pilot with a parachute, and the range appeared to be 85 miles (137km) at 5,000 feet (1,524 meters), or at most 130 miles (209km). On 28 February 1945 procurement and conversions were suspended while the effort entered a restudy period, although work on remote-controlled fighters in support of tactical operations continued. As most of these aircraft were 'tail draggers' (such as the Republic P-47 Thunderbolt) and pilot bail-out presented an unacceptably high risk, catapulting was considered for the single-engine machines while the twin-engine, tricycle-gear P-38 could be flown off, as the Navy had demonstrated.[16] However, the development of launching from a catapult rail appeared to be long, and the war was concluded before this work progressed much further.

Big bang

The Army and Navy 'Aphrodite' programs came together nearly simultaneously. The USN team would operate under Eighth Air Force purview, as the USAAF dominated American air operations in Europe. Initially operating from Honington, the teams moved on 16 July to Fersfield, where all missions were launched. This airbase, just north of London, was approximately 350 miles (563km) from the targets in northern France. These were initially V-1 launch sites under the codename 'Crossbow' and V-2 sites as 'Noball'.

The USAAF had ten double-Azon BQ-7s converted on 10 July, nine stuffed with nitrostarch and the last with napalm. A B-17 and three B-24s were prepared as the control ships. Plans were that a pair of drones, taking off 5 minutes apart for an initial attack, would be followed by another pair to be guided by the same airborne task force making two trips across the water. The team scrubbed multiple missions waiting for favorable weather. The first two BQ-7 missions were flown on 4 August with four drones (B-17Fs 42-30342, 42-3461 and 41-24639, and B-17G 42-39835). Loaded well beyond their specified maximum gross weight, the bombers required the entire runway to stagger into the air; none of the training flights had employed fully loaded aircraft.

Aircraft 835 (the only one with the rare TV gear) stalled and spun in due to some equipment failure at hand-off, killing the pilot who was just egressing. Aircraft 342 would not respond to dive commands from the primary or secondary control ship because the ACE would not disengage; it was deliberately positioned to detonate above enemy AAA positions when hit. Aircraft 461 struck 1,500 feet (457 meters) short of the target due to a misjudgment of the distance remaining. The last (639) was downed by AAA, impacting about 500 feet (152 meters) short of the target with a defective altitude control. It was suspected that the C-1 was still struggling with full down elevator as airspeed built up in the dive, the forces eventually overcoming the servo and the bomber leveling out.

Of the seven jumpers, five had been injured, with two hospitalized. One man had a failure of both his main and back-up parachutes, having to force the silk out of the chest pack by hand. The hatch opening was subsequently enlarged and a spoiler added ahead of it. There was concern that the static lines left behind trailing out of the hatch were whipping about and damaging the drone antennae, like the radio altimeter that had experienced difficulty. The solution was the attachment of the line to a wire running on the bottom of the bomber to the tail; after the line had been pulled free of the jumper it would naturally slide aft and away from the antennae.

Only the B-17 drone, BQ-7, was used in combat, the B-17F and G being exclusively converted (the G model is shown here). All gun turrets would have been removed. Although intended to employ 'war-weary' airframes, much effort was made to ensure that they would operate reliably once packed with more than 10 tons of explosives and sent up to be flown remotely. *National Archives*

Only two drones (B-17F 42-30212 and B-17G 42-31394) were dispatched on the 6th to reduce the strain on resources and better deal with potential problems. Some changes in explosives distribution were made after the first day to reduce the CG vertical displacement and substitute the more powerful Torpex for some. The BQ-7 was to crack the target's concrete casing while the second followed with the mix of explosives, napalm and incendiaries. However, the results were no better. The first BQ-7 suddenly gave an opposite roll to a turn command, rolling over and crashing into the sea. Control of the second was lost despite both controllers making an attempt (with a confused hand-off). Although the fighters were ordered in to shoot down the rogue, it was finally directed into a crash just off the coast under spurious control after ominously circling an English town. Two of the four jumpers were injured, one losing an arm. The effort reverted to training while the Wright Field design was brought into line. In the meantime, attention turned to the more mature Navy system.

Anvil flight tests for the fully loaded PB4Y-1 began on 30 July. Control was possible up to a distance of 70 miles (113km). The team was soon ready for combat, but waited for favorable weather. On 12 August the PB4Y-1 was flown off en route to the target. Soon after the point where the radio control link was initially exercised the bomber unexpectedly exploded, killing the two pilots. No cause was found, but it was decided to use only mechanical fusing of the explosives, such as the USAAF was doing, and remove the electrical fusing via remote control.

Having brought another full kit for drone conversion, a second PB4Y-1 (63954) was converted within five days. Although a war-weary bird, the PB4Y had reconditioned engines installed, the tires were replaced with new, and all control cables replaced. Another change was to use one control plane to fly the drone to the target area and another, further back out of AAA range, for terminal guidance, such as was the Air Forces practice. Also, the aircraft would be flown by only a single pilot directly to the sea before hand-off, reducing the hazard to civilians under the flight path. After flight-testing it was ready for action, but the intended 'Crossbow' and 'Noball' targets had been overrun by Allied forces (and found to have been abandoned months before), so another was identified. The island of Heligoland had a sub pen cut into the cliffs and had proven impervious to all prior bombing missions.

The Navy's drone conversion used its PB4Y-1 patrol bomber variant of the B-24. As with the B-17, all the guns and turrets would be removed and replaced with sheet metal close-outs. The first example was a new airframe while the second was a 'war-weary' airframe. *National Archives*

After again waiting for suitable weather, the mission was launched on 3 September. All went well initially, with the officer departing from the aircraft, which then flew dutifully at 300 feet over the North Sea for nearly 3 hours. The one issue that arose was the failure of the VHF communications radios aboard the lead PV-1, and this led to both controllers sending commands. Control was compromised, then the TV was knocked out by AAA just before impact, prompting the controllers to send the dive command. The poor TV image had led to mistakenly aiming at the breakwaters of a nearby island, where it impacted ineffectually.

The cancellation of the USN assault drone effort on 8 September by Admiral King also fell on the UK detachment, which had only revealed continued limitations of the technology (albeit in a makeshift arrangement). With the war undecided and the 'war-wearies' yet to prove their worth, this was a bitter disappointment for those involved. On 20 September the CNO offered the USAAF resources from the Navy's cancelled assault drone program in the form of 200 surplus drone kits and thirty-five control plane kits, these including 200 Block III television kits, in addition to numerous drones (SNB, SNV, TDR) for training, and highly qualified individuals to support it. On 13 October the Army replied that it would welcome the equipment but not the personnel. It is doubtful whether any of these resources (other than perhaps the TV gear) were actually transferred or played a role in Army operations before the end of the war.

The next series of missions, with the Wright Field Castor equipment, were to be single-drone missions rather than two to four at once, B-17Gs serving as controllers. The design benefited from the addition of TV not only for the view forward from the drone but also inside the cockpit, showing the altimeter and compass to permit flight at lower altitudes and to increase survivability. The radar beacon and smoke tank were also added.

The first such mission, on 11 September, was B-17F 42-30180, weighing 63,163lb (28,650kg) when dispatched against the sub pens at Heligoland, 320 miles (515km) away. One of the airmen was killed when his parachute static line wrapped around him on egress (likely due to improper attachment of the line by the officer); he broke his spine and his chute did not open. The airplane was struck by AAA and likely suffered an engine failure that caused it to veer off and impact the cliff about 250 feet (113 meters) from the target.

Two drones were launched on the 14th to hit an oil refinery in Hemmingstadt, Germany, 376 miles (605 km) distant. For the first B-17F (42-30363), the TV did not deliver a clear image so the bomber was directed visually and overflew the target by 1,000 feet (305 meters). The control ship overflew the next BQ-7 (B-17F 42-30827) and the controller lost sight of his charge in haze during the 360-degree turn. The radio beacon having not been installed and the smoke proving faulty, no one could find the BQ-7. With the TV screen showing only water, the decision was made to dump the aircraft into the sea, where it went down unobserved.

From that point the attacks continued with diminishing high-level interest and with changes of command amidst dropping morale. The aircrew were given parachute training, but otherwise the operations were the same save for greatly deteriorating weather conditions. Operations had made clear that the then current equipment provided only a rudimentary capability with a high probability of error and failure given the weather, the climb and descent from a cruise altitude, the long duration flights, tracking the aircraft, and the required accuracy of impact. It was concluded that the missions should be launched from the Continent to avoid the weather over the North Sea. The weapon was then seen as best used en masse against industrial targets rather than one or two aircraft hitting a specific facility, although the limitation of radio frequencies presented a complication. Ground control via radar with a city-sized target was considered desirable because the weather was grounding most other bombing methods. This approach was given top priority on 14 October, the radar beacon added at this point. The addition of throttle control, monitored by the camera, which also showed the altimeter, permitted a more complex mission profile such as flight at 10,000 feet (3,048 meters) en route followed by descent to 300 feet (91 meters) for ingress to the target. (Higher altitudes were not possible without the additional complication of remotely controlling the engine superchargers.) To increase the probability of success, aircraft in top form were to be used instead of the 'wearies'.

Project Castor became 'Weary Willie' in October. Control planes became 'Mothers', drones controlled from 'Mothers' became 'Babies', and those controlled from a ground station 'Orphans'. On 28 November designations were altered again to 'Abusive' with 'Bluefish' control ships, 'Corticated' drones controlled from the air, and 'Cottongrass' drones controlled from the ground. Cottongrass Phase 1 was a directed missile with the aircraft set on a preset heading and barometric altitude until a timer ran out, after which the ignition was cut and the aircraft 'dumped' over the area target. Phase 2 used the same dead reckoning navigation but followed the course of the missile via a radar beacon return displayed on a plotting board. Corticated Phase 1 involved visual tracking of the drone until transitioning to the Block III TV for terminal guidance, but also included repeat-back of the compass heading in the image and the autopilot used either radio or barometric altitude for height control. Phase 2 added the Black Maria radar beacon for flight-following on a PPI display aboard the 'Mother' superimposed on the radar picture of the ground. Alternatively, a radio range and bearing could be determined from the 'Mother' and the drone directed to a target by navigational computation. Phase 3 added a telemetry TV image of selected instruments aboard the drone.

Operations continued as weather permitted based on the previous Castor hardware and methodology. The first 'Abusive' mission was launched from England on 15 October 1944 with a B-17F drone (42-30039) flown to Heligoland after the AAA sites were bombed. Weather was so poor that the flight had to circle for 45 minutes before attacking. Struggling with an inoperative ACE, the half-mile (0.8km) visibility made the TV almost useless. The drone was flown visually as well as possible until shot down a quarter of a mile (0.40km) offshore. Another attempt the same day (B-17G 42-37743) functioned perfectly and, despite the foul weather, made a good run-in with poor visibility but succeeding only in devastating a 2.5-acre area of buildings.

Taken from gun camera footage to document the 15 October mission, these frames show the drone with control planes on each wing while the parachute of one of the crewmen is visible below. The second picture shows the drone with smoke on and light-colored upper wing surfaces to aid visual tracking. The third view is the explosion of the drone just short of the cliffs at Heligoland, after being hit by AAA. *United States Air Force*

A B-17F (42-3438) directed at Heligoland on 30 October suffered from a faulty altitude hold feature and the descent command was inoperative. Again, low ceiling and visibility meant that the target could not be found visually. The drone was placed on a compass course towards Berlin and abandoned; it came down in neutral Sweden. The same day a B-17F (42-30066) drone experienced ACE and other unclear failures that rendered it only erratically controllable. Managing to get it on a heading into the North Sea, it was allowed to fly off into oblivion.

A 5 December mission of a B-17G (42-39824) against Herford, Germany, 336 miles (541km) away, had good control but poor Block operation, and was shot down by AAA after failing to find its primary target and en route to a secondary. Another attempt the same day (B-17F 42-30353) ended with a belly-landing in a marsh after the wings and carburetors iced up during let-down through the clouds. Attempts to destroy the drone failed due to the weather and a later inability to locate it. It had to be concluded that the remote control gear was compromised.[17] Two missions on 1 January (B-17G 42-30178 and B-17F 42-30237) against a thermal plant in Oldenburg, Germany, found that neither had operable smoke. One lacked the TV while the other's Block III failed. The first struck about 2 miles (3km) from the target despite the 'dump' command being sent at the proper time. The second came down in a residential area during a turn about 5 miles (8km) from the objective, likely due to an ACE failure.

With one robot airplane remaining and weather prohibitive, the 'Abusive' missions were suspended in late February 1945. Apart from some gratifyingly enormous explosions, the results were underwhelming at nineteen failures in nineteen attempts, with four servicemen dead and two badly injured.

Refinement of the drone bomber design had continued, including testing at Eglin. Plans were afoot in early 1945 for the radar-controlled phase ('Willie Orphan') with Major Rand as project officer. However, the British resisted suggestions of flying dozens of the drones against German population centers, either from their soil or the Continent, fearing retribution in kind. On 12 April 1945 further acquisition of the associated equipment was suspended.

After the collapse of Germany, attention turned to supporting ground forces in the struggle against Japan. Flying drones and glide bombs against point targets close to the line of advance, such as caves and bunkers, was assessed. Ground control via ships off the Japanese coast ('Cottongrass') or ashore flying the drones via line-of-sight into caves (Project 'Hermit') was considered. The concept was to take control of the aircraft flown in from as far as 1,500 miles (2,400km) away, then dive the aircraft into the target visually. The pilot might remain aboard until near the target area. Alternatively, an area target might be struck based on beacon indication relative to a geo-location on a radar screen aboard the control plane. This was not well regarded given the distances from likely ground stations and the low potential effect, offering nothing above bombing through overcast of an area target already possible via a bomber formation's onboard radar. Also examined was the use of the drones as decoys, controlled by B-29s, to draw away Japanese fighters from an area to be bombed by B-29s, or to deposit chaff ('window' or 'rope'). However, flight of the drones over 1,400 miles (2,250km) was seen as problematic given the experience in the ETO. Thus the American Second World War drone effort slowed through to the end of combat.

CHAPTER TWELVE

Moving On

Out in front

THE AMERICANS played catch-up, despite exceptional efforts, throughout most of the war. Before 1939 the military air capabilities of the nation ranked fifth in the world when assessing numbers and capabilities or modernization. Then, from the beginning of the conflict and during the two years that the combatants were exhausting themselves, the US built up a tremendous production capacity for existing warplanes while developing improved models or new and innovative designs. America was able to bring prodigious manpower and raw materials resources to bear with none of the bombing and little of the supply-line hazards all others suffered, as well as much less of the poor leadership and self-delusion endured by the Axis. The determined American efforts were definitely telling by the summer of 1944, with superior numbers and generally superior capabilities from more modern warplanes facilitating air superiority. The industry had grown to unimagined levels, employing over a million people and producing thousands of aircraft per month. This capacity made possible attention to special types and the development of new modes of delivering military capabilities.

All warring nations made their best materiel choices based on national policy and expectations of enemy reactions. This engendered unavoidable waste. As the most prolific manufacturer of aviation equipment, the USA was a leader in over-producing in most areas and expending effort on programs that contributed little if anything to the war. The combination of innovation, second-tier priority, and lengthened development all worked against the special types. Although, as usual, the Americans out-produced everyone else combined and fielded outstanding

The C-47C project (XC-47C 42-5671 is seen here on 12 June 1943) demonstrated American rapid design and modification capability in meeting an immediate need – or at least as rapidly as safe and effective aviation development and fabrication would permit. In this case the urgency of the need had eased by the time kits had been produced, and had essentially evaporated by the time of capacity deployment. Such are the fortunes of war, although few nations could have responded as did the United States. *National Archives*

weapons, the special types' contributions was a decidedly mixed bag. General Arnold expressed this approach as awarding contracts wherever there appeared the possibility of accelerating victory and saving American lives, money being secondary to that goal. He said, "Many, many thousands of contracts were let for all conceivable types of equipment – experimental and production. Some proved to be a failure; most were successful... My motives were guided purely and singly by a desire to win the war in the shortest possible space of time."[1]

Even in peacetime there are generally more weapons system development programs than can reasonably be carried to production. This ensures some measure of competition and the ability to terminate struggling efforts while rewarding those that are shown by performance to be the most successful in meeting requirements. Thus it is in war, although in the frantic year following Pearl Harbor this was stretched a bit too far given available resources, virtually guaranteeing that some would falter badly. The more evident proclivity in the special types was to accelerate the few programs to extents unlikely to be achieved. While in some cases this may have simply served as a 'stretch goal', the stress on the dedicated organizations as well as the external support agencies and suppliers was risky. Yet, in a war where new innovations and tactics appeared at a steady pace, pressing for new capabilities as hard as possible rather than long-studied choices and acquisition schedules appeared warranted.

The enemy successes via technological advances were an example that permitted traditionalism and organizational inertia to be overcome and projects launched that sought similar gains. Helicopters and unmanned airplanes were certainly radical concepts that met with much resistance before the US was drawn into the war, yet progressed remarkably afterwards. Although the services were sometimes seduced by the lure of the next more advanced weapon system, in general the Americans resisted the 'wonder weapons' that attracted the hard-pressed Axis nations, especially Germany. While such enemy undertakings yielded fascinating designs, most were equally fantastical and a waste of resources. This led many post-war observers to conclude that Germany led in all fields of aeronautics, was more daring and innovative, and with manufacturing excellence to match. This is a misleading conclusion.

The special types could drive none of the principal elements of aircraft performance such as propulsion and avionics (a term not then coined). They also benefited little from such aeronautical focus as resolving high-speed flight challenges, and were sometimes directed to be built of lesser materials such as wood so as not to impact on more urgent combat airplane production. Additionally, many of the designs were assigned to manufacturers with limited experience so as not to burden the main airframers, despite the new or unusual character of some of these products. This led to many instances of poor contractor performance with late deliveries and marginal quality. However, in some cases the limited attention of the overstretched service program managers, difficulty in recruiting essential engineering and shop personnel, and lower priority for resources were large contributors to disappointing outcomes. Yet the advanced nature of the projects themselves reflected a departure from pre-war conservatism with boldness in the face of enemy successes. Only in the final year of the war, with the outcome fairly certain, were some efforts focused on positioning for post-war systems.

Floatplanes – an era closes

Catapult launch and crane-recovery of floatplanes from surface combatants had always been a manpower-intensive and high-resource aspect of naval aviation. These were complex and hazardous activities requiring carefully choreographed procedures with deck, bridge and flight crew working in concert using only hand and flag signals. If all was not done properly or immediate action taken if something went wrong, loss of the aircraft and crew was a distinct possibility. Rapid aircraft wear and occasional loss was part of such operations. If swamped, the machine was usually only good for a few parts before being 'deep sixed' – used for target practice until disappearing beneath the waves. All this was costly in peacetime. Additionally, the convertible airplanes were not optimal for their shore-based missions.

The risks to the aircraft in floatplane operations from cruisers and battleships were great. Most of the vessels lacked hangars (and the non-folding wing OS2U would not fit anyway) and wartime exigencies sometimes demanded that they remain in the path of weather. Seen on 6 June 1945, this vessel was battered by a typhoon that destroyed one Kingfisher and severely damaged the other.
National Museum of Naval Aviation

The US built more floatplanes during the war than all other combatants combined. Most of them were the outstanding if uninspiring Kingfisher and the worthless SO3C. Save for the utility Duck, all were designed for catapult launch as against the large, twin-float, sea-launched types common with Japan and Germany. Always of small quantities compared with deck-launched types, American's growing number of aircraft carriers and the ability to establish land bases with astonishing speed steadily reduced the importance of the floatplanes. The same progress rendered the Army efforts at creating floatplane variants of landplanes for special missions moot. However, the experience was valuable in exercising the rapid design and modification capabilities that proved valuable in other endeavors.

The pinnacle of achievement was the SC-1, marking perhaps one of the very few (only Navy) new American types that commenced development after Pearl Harbor and actually saw combat, albeit via very limited exposure. However, following the Japanese example, it sought a true fighter-on-floats that only complicated the scout-observation mission and mistakenly added the useless and hazardous turbosupercharger. The other experimental floatplane models are remarkable for the bold vision behind them as a nation strove to meet combat demands with an aircraft industry still building to peak capacity of ingenuity, rapid prototyping, and manufacturing output. In typical American fashion, the country built to excess if not waste under the pressures of the conflict, with a mix from the excellent to the dismal. Such is the nature of aircraft development and production under the pressures of total war.

The end of the conflict brought a rapid and dramatic draw-down in combat forces. Excess ships were mothballed and aircraft either stored or scrapped. The final SC was delivered in October 1946. The Seahawk proved the last single-float shipboard aircraft ever acquired or operated by the Navy, serving four years beyond the Second World War. The rapid evolution of aviation during the war had rendered the floatplanes and their mission obsolete. The scout mission was met by shore-based patrol aircraft and carrier-based radar-equipped twins, while ship radar provided coverage for groups of vessels in a particular area. Soon helicopters began to appear on small-deck vessels to take over the observation role. Although the first few generations of rotorcraft came nowhere near the performance of the wartime floatplanes, they demanded fewer resources and deficiencies were suitably compensated for by other assets.

Photo recce bump

The United States moved quickly to establish the aerial photography capabilities indicated essential by the shifting nature of the world war, and as those already engaged had demonstrated. The Americans got by with modified fighters and bombers to perform the photography mission, just like all the other combatants. Those created stateside were well-engineered and reasonably effective. The more than 1,300 P-38 conversions as F-4s and F-5s made up approximately 13 percent of the type's production, indicating the importance placed on the mission. For all other 'foto' ships, the numbers were a much smaller fraction for the AAF, and insignificant for the USN.

The move to dedicated platforms in the Army was driven by the ranges and threats found in the Asia-Pacific theaters. While projects for the new aircraft were kicked off, they were too late to yield results during the war. This was partially owing to the choice of powerplants just coming to maturity, together with the necessary duration of aircraft development and production. (The different timescales of aircraft and aero engine development and maturation was the bane of many aviation projects.) In the end, the US forces made do with their imperfect solutions.

Despite late efforts to develop dedicated photography platforms, the United States got through the war quite adequately with converted fighters and bombers serving the photo recce role – the same as all other combatants. The standout workhorse of 'foto' ships was the F-5, derived from the Lockheed P-38 Lightning. The proud ground crew of this F-5A are seen in rather rough and dusty North African conditions, yet from which successful photo missions were launched. Following the war the new high-speed, high-flying types were set aside as too costly, and more converted fighters and bombers were adapted. *National Archives*

Post-war the XF-11 and XF-12 were found too costly to produce. All such recip prop jobs soon fading in the post-war era, where jets were clearly the wave of the future. Yet to meet the mission the immediate solution was modification of prop-driven bombers derived from the war. The adaptation of existing types continued with very few exceptions.

Tactical transports – too little, too late

Twin-engine medium transports made up less than 10 percent of the military aircraft produced by the US during the war. In the production schedules for 1942-43, these were 82 percent of the total transports manufactured, of which 77 percent was the C-47 and associated models.[2] The importance of this airplane and its tactical airlift mission grew with the expansion of airborne teams, the need for rapid replenishment of advancing forces, and the evident waste of glider assault. Increasing the efficiency of such operations with a purpose-built tactical transport was a reasonable undertaking. But efforts to develop such aircraft were frustrated by low priority and the initial decision to go with wood as the principal structural material.

Everyone consistently underestimated the time and resources required to develop suitable military aircraft of all types, immediately before and during the war. Few if any projects came in on time and cost. While shifting resource allocation and limitations were in part responsible, it was also due to the shallow experience from the lean pre-war years of fiscal straits. For the wooden transport, there was a misbegotten perception that it should be a fairly simple affair, as evidenced by occasionally foregoing the X-prefix prototypes for service test examples. The underappreciated pioneering challenges warranted extensive laboratory testing and an experimental airplane to assist in developing design criteria, validating construction methods, and

gaining operating experience. Even Curtiss, with a large and experienced engineering and production staff, struggled to create a wooden transport of even low performance under the pressures of war, given the application of the new and revised construction methodology. Any belief that such machines could be built more cheaply than a metallic airplane was also proven to be misbegotten. Late realization of these realities and discovery that aluminum supply would likely not be constrained was the cause of a change of course to metal designs, but too late for any numbers to enter fleet service.

The duplication of similar projects appeared acceptable initially, but these came to compete for scare material and manpower resources. The results were among the least successful and most costly shortfalls of American aircraft development of the war. Thus the C-47 soldiered on and the armed forces made do with great success while suitable aircraft emerged only in time for the next war. All this just emphasizes how damn hard it is to develop a successful airplane.

Experience was rapidly gained and Americans were soon shoulder-to-shoulder with all others in the industry. There was never a lack of bold vision and innovation, as evidenced by the tactical transport prototypes emerging during the war with advanced features and capabilities matching or exceeding anything elsewhere. The Americans were able to exploit these advances with true tactical airlifters that followed the war, but without the ill-starred resorting to wood and other constraints. Additionally, a lesson drawn from many wartime programs was to draft requirements based on a defined need before drawing up specifications and seeking an enthusiastic contractor. However, while combat needs evolved with the war with changing doctrine, it was felt in the early years that no time could be lost. In the case of the airlifter, this was unsuccessful as the operators rejected the aircraft despite clever design features.

More than 9,000 C-47s were built during the war and their utility was proven far beyond the commercial origins of the design. For US and Allied forces alike, they were vital transport resources. Their role in tactical missions such as glider tow, paratroop delivery and airdrop of vital supplies was a telling contribution to victory. *San Diego Air & Space Museum*

A captured Arado Ar 232B (V7) is photographed at RAE Farnborough during British evaluation following the German surrender. This four-engine machine had a rear loading ramp and cargo door, and good landing performance by virtue of the full-span Fowler flaps. The most unusual feature was the ability to partially collapse the main gear to settle on the multiple wheels beneath the fuselage, facilitating movement on uneven or soft ground. *Jay Miller Collection*

Long-range transport shortfall

Like most other special types, it was a struggle to produce strategic transports fast enough and in sufficient quantity. The military got by initially with mobilized airliners and shorter-range aircraft flying long distances via hazardous routing until industry was able to respond by 1943. Use of converted bombers and flying boats in the interim was a fortuitous melding of the tremendous industrial output of the United States producing thousands of such aircraft. This bought time for long-range airliner designs to be militarized and placed into high-rate production. The efforts yielded only the C-54 in any useful numbers, barely meeting minimal demand. This shortfall, while partially the fault of shifting requirements by the military, was also attributable to intentional balancing of combat and support aircraft production from an industry stretched to the limit. The resulting multiple models slowed the only effort that bore fruit – the Skymaster – and caused the C-69 to miss the war.

At the beginning of the conflict transoceanic flight was rare and costly, but by 1944 C-54s were making twenty round trips a day across the North Atlantic, as well as departures every 37 minutes across the Pacific by July 1945. A Skymaster was departing every 30 minutes on such long-range flights. The airplane had an exemplary safety record, with the ATC suffering only three losses in 79,642 ocean crossings during the war. The NATS flew 450,000 R5D hours with only one loss.[3] The airplane was 'vanilla' and boring – just what was needed at the time.

The American output in this area, while meager by the measure of the country's overall war production, was still head and shoulders above all other combatants combined. Foreign air arms took a similar approach to the Americans in adapting existing commercial transports while converting bombers as transports. Only the Germans undertook dedicated long-range transport development, albeit as further evolution of pre-war civil designs. These at least contributed something, while the Americans' advanced designs did not see service. The development of true long-range military cargo aircraft by the US had little hope of providing anything in the span of the conflict, but the War Department was duty bound to try given the public and political pressures. Efforts like the HK-1 were poorly conceived and wasteful. A post-war assessment concluded that 'the technical side of the war cannot be waged from day to day in a manner to accord with public opinion.'[4]

All the strategic airlifters were hamstrung by an excess of perfectionism and persistent efforts to make them suitable as post-war airliners. While it was correct to rate these programs lower in priority than combat types, there were clearly too many running and too many 'cooks in the kitchen'. The numerous direction changes in the C-69 were especially egregious. While its outstanding engineering and construction placed the United States in an excellent position for post-war air travel, they were only a burden on the war industries.

A lovely airplane, the C-69 (43-10315 shown) is symbolic of the well-considered decisions that delayed such strategic airlifters for so long that they contributed nothing to the war. The C-69 was pummeled by swings in choices of gross weight and freight/passenger options, that stretched out development and the move to production. Only a handful were completed during the war, and then as strictly personnel transports. *National Archives*

The Junkers Ju 290 is an example of a long-range heavy aircraft derived from pre-war commercial airliners. An outstanding design, it was built in small numbers and employed primarily for maritime patrol. Like most large British and German transports, the Ju 290 was dated and utilitarian, yet was actually produced and effective whereas many comparable American designs lagged due to shifting priorities and requirements. *Jay Miller Collection*

Rotorcraft taken together

The power required for a helicopter to turn a rotor and generate sufficient lift for hover and suitable forward flight is very inefficient compared with an airplane that can carry more and go faster or further with the same engine and fuel. Factors such as sonic blade tip speeds and retreating blade stall make for a theoretical helicopter speed limit speed of about 200mph (322km/h). None of the Second World War helicopters were equipped for instrument flight. Rain had to be avoided because blades impacting rain drops could quickly damage the fabric covering and imbalance the rotor to a hazardous extent. Likewise, icing was a very grave danger. It was soon learned that blades and hub elements wore rapidly and required careful attention, with those of the first generation of helicopters requiring replacement at 50 to 100 hours. Engines (drawn from those used on airplanes) were essentially run at full power during an entire flight, so also wore more quickly than for airplane applications. Although comparatively inefficient, the ability to take off and land almost anywhere, as well as hover and translate, made the helicopter a worthy pursuit for militaries and civil operators alike.

Second World War American rotorcraft development and production exceeded all other nations put together. All major helicopter layout and control types were being explored through research and prototypes. These numbered twelve major military programs with all but two flown during the span of the war, three taken to full production, and two to pilot production. Some 628 rotorcraft were manufactured, and eighty-six delivered to Great Britain. These were small quantities compared to even the liaison airplanes built in their thousands, but helicopters remained a new and unfamiliar battlefield asset that was reasonably approached with caution. The official projects were backed up by many more privately funded efforts. All was achieved in the span of just five years from a point at which only one truly practical helicopter had flown. The contribution to Army combat operations was minor thanks to the early end of the war; only a handful of Army helicopters, in two models, were deployed to combat zones. The Navy-developed helicopters remained test and evaluation assets throughout the war, an operational squadron not being formed until 1946.

The Germans built two models of helicopter in very small numbers. All manner of tests and operations were undertaken, including sling loads, operations from shipboard decks for

Germany was the leader in helicopter development just prior to the war, but put only two types into production during the conflict, of which fewer than three dozen entered service. This reflected some neglect as well as the effectiveness of Allied bombing. The Fa 223 shown here at the end of the war was the largest helicopter produced up until that time, and was not eclipsed in the United States until well after the close of hostilities. *National Archives*

While Germany had a head start in military rotorcraft development, the United States quickly closed the gap. In five years the nation went from having witnessed successful one-off helicopters to having multiple types of various configurations in development, test and production. The three types to see production are represented here. From left to right they are a Sikorsky XR-5, a XR-6A and a YR-4B, all developed for the Air Forces (photographed at Wright Field) but operated by all services. *National Archives*

anti-submarine action, rescue, relief, etc. These helicopters were practical and as reliable as could be expected from warplanes during the period. Essentially, everything the Americans achieved the Germans had done first, although independently. The record does not suggest that more extensive military missions and cross-country flying were performed by the Germans than the Allies. In the end,

helicopters contributed insignificantly in combat for any country and affected the course of the war not at all. However, the victor was positioned to exploit the lessons and resources after the conflict in preparing for the next and for commercial applications. The United States become the primary breeding ground for numerous helicopter aspirants and flying prototypes as a new industry took off.

Germany's small force of helicopters was compelled to perform some challenging combat support missions in the last year of the war as the entire country became a war zone and the situation ever more desperate. However, America also conducted many combat support missions and rescue operations with the handful of R-4s and R-6s that made it into theaters. Large-scale training by the Army and Navy/USCG was also undertaken, as suggested by these eleven R-4Bs on a USAAF flight training apron. *National Museum of the United States Air Force*

The Americans exceeded all other nations combined in helicopter production, as they did for almost any type of war aircraft. This saw nearly 400 Sikorsky R-6As manufactured by Nash-Kelvinator in Detroit, as seen here during 1945. This is a remarkable achievement given the start from zero just a few years earlier. *Author's collection*

Drones in hindsight

American drones were but one element in a plethora of winged guided and unguided munitions programs pursued by both the Navy and Army during the Second World War. As with almost all such wartime weapon development efforts, very few reached combat and none with any decided impact. The drones had the appearance of a shorter path to long-range guided bombs, but development proved prolonged, especially as experimental targeting systems were introduced. For the Navy TD program, it was the result of choosing, by necessity, a small firm with shallow aviation experience to take on a mammoth program, then burdening it with change requests and advanced models while struggling to obtain resources. Combat introduction of the TDR-1 was then late, coming at a time when suitable targets had diminished sharply.

The multiple guided missile efforts can be criticized for hasty movement to production of questionable weapons in addition to dropping promising projects (the drones among them) with the lure of the next advanced weapon. There was also no small resistance to unmanned aircraft within the development establishments in the States. Once the weapon showed promise in developmental trials there would usually be a surge of enthusiasm, but this would dissipate in the interim between test and fielding. Initiated in a period of near-static combat where aircraft production had yet to reach the mammoth quantities seen later in the war, by the time the weapons reached the field they did not fit the operational strategy and tactics of the theater, which

were being met in a very successful if costly manner by conventional manned aircraft. For the few weapons that were deployed, combat results were poor owing to modest accuracy, low reliability of the electronics prompting a high rate of system failures, and the need for favorable weather. The heavy bomber drones were just too complex to be operated reliably via a few radio channels. The weapons simply did not hold sufficient promise and instead showed mostly the cumbersome nature of their immature, albeit pioneering, design.

The time required for development, production, training and deployment to a combat status was consistently underestimated by both services. Competition for resources by duplicative programs did not help. A late lesson was learned about establishing an operational requirement, conducting operational testing away from actual combat, and thus making informed and measured moves to production. Commanders consumed with the demands of combat were understandably loath to divert attention and resources, as well as risk lives, for experimental deployment of new and unfamiliar weapons. Initiated early in the war, when their chances of success were difficult to judge but the need for such weapons as drones was great, the rationale for such projects was almost unassailable. By mid-1944 such could no longer be said. One took risks during war, even in weapon systems development, and the potential of guided weapons appeared to substantiate any haste, expense and duplication. In this case, there was little to show for the effort apart from a basis for supporting future wars.

The early introduction of aircraft before they had undergone many operationally representative trials, and in a piecemeal fashion, was evident in other instances such as night fighters. The assault drones were simply a step too far as an operational concept. When they were introduced they produced results comparable to conventional arms, so did not appear worth the effort of adopting them on a large scale. (The use of drone bombers can be set aside as an emergency measure with an understood modest chance of success.) Some of the more exotic guidance means like radar and infrared simply had not stepped far enough from the laboratory to be employed.

The demand for combat trials was a bit excessive. Without the crucible of a war, weapons are developed and placed into production on the basis of realistic trial. The pressures of total war required dramatic shortening of schedules and processes. The first pressurized high-altitude bomber, the B-29, was deployed without combat trial, as was the atomic bomb. Yet a radically new weapon such as the drone did require very realistic operational testing, and performing this at the earliest opportunity while preparing for large-scale production was entirely reasonable. The 100 TDNs should have permitted this as they were all expended in testing and training without the need to burden combat forces engaged in an ongoing total war. The deployment of the guided torpedo (GT-1), glide bomb (GB-1), and Bat missile as add-ons to existing squadrons were consistent with ongoing operations, so not terribly disruptive. Yet the results demonstrated that development trials had failed to identify clear deficiencies. The deployment of an entire drone task force was another matter entirely.

One is tempted to consider the Navy TD program as having held more promise than it displayed in combat. The advocates of the system argued that the intent was to target vessels in the open ocean, for which TV resolution would be suitable, and Block III television would have provided superior performance. With a demonstrated 50 percent success against a static ship of medium size and near-ideal lighting conditions, success against even a capital ship maneuvering at high speed under combat conditions (which might include a smoke screen or running close to shore) appeared slim. In any event, this was not required at that stage of the war. Although the advocates argued that the land targets were a poor test of the drone's potential compared with anti-ship attacks, most naval aviation had come to focus on ground attack as the Japanese air and sea assets were catastrophically reduced. An inability to operate effectively against such targets did not support their case, which had never overtly claimed it was solely an anti-ship weapon. Additionally, night operations were impossible, but few manned platforms conducted night missions either. This first combat experience with a surface-to-surface guided missile was certainly significant, but in the circumstances of the war at that stage, it had little to recommend it over vastly more numerous and flexible manned aircraft.

Could the TDR and TD3R have done a better job against the priority European targets that the B-17 drones consistently failed to destroy, as some have suggested? This is doubtful as they all used essentially the same technology that was demonstrated both in Europe and the Pacific to be immature and significantly limited. Strenuous effort in both theaters had yielded mixed results, at best, with drones and other guided weapons. Weather and range would have been an even greater impediment. The move to employ the B-17 drones as area terror weapons was a misguided waste and only demonstrated the failure to generate a weapon of suitable accuracy.

This photo shows shore catapult trials of TDR-1 27858 at Mustin Field, Philadelphia – a capability that was not entertained beyond the aircraft development and test community. The machine has been fitted with constant-speed metal propellers and a radar antenna above the spine (not an ideal location) while carrying the very heavy torpedo. It is clear in this photo that the main gear wheels lack brakes. *National Museum of Naval Aviation*

The 'high-performance' airplane drones were too little, too late. The speed of the TD3R-1 seen here (XTD3R-1 33921) was too small a step above the TDN and TDR to truly add any significant value, especially as the payload capacity was unchanged. By the time the program was cancelled, the TD3R production effort had floundered and was unlikely to meet any combat demands during the span of the war. *National Archives*

The guided missiles eventually represented less costly and more quickly manufactured alternatives to the drones. By August 1944 it appeared that the JB-2 could be in production quickly at $3,000-4,000 each, with demonstrated performance as the V-1, while the Navy assault drones were $150,000 a piece.[5] Once the missiles had progressed to a stage of similar development, the drones' few advantages paled and were judged impractical by comparison, then cancelled. The Luftwaffe's successful introduction of guided air-to-surface munitions during late summer 1943 was the impetus to redouble efforts, although only the drone held any potential for 'long range' and the ability to be turned away from the target and recovered if the conditions for success were not optimal. In terms of radio control, flight stability and targeting technology, it suffered the same limitations as the missiles, including effective range from the mother plane. The Navy drones had progressed further towards operation, so were deployed just as these decisions were being made. The V-1 attacks on England that began in June 1944 demonstrated that the jet-propelled, high-speed missiles under development were the path to the future and could answer the range need. This is why the JB-2 was pursued with such vigor. Even if employed earlier in the war, the consequences would have remained nil other than as a terror weapon. The guidance and targeting limitations of the JB-2 just pointed anew to the need for precision, purpose-built weapons benefiting from continued evolution of the technology. This yielded superior results only many years after the war.

The drone work met or exceeded in scope, technical excellence and achievement the similar efforts by Germany, albeit initially a year behind this adversary. The Americans clearly led in the development of guidance systems. The much lauded V-1 and V-2 were directed, not guided, weapons meant to hit large area targets. Their other guided munitions had direct American counterparts, although combat employment was constrained to tests and very limited combat trials that proved largely disappointing. Because of their circumstances after 1943, the Germans were more prone to pursue a large number of advanced weapons and introduce them into combat piecemeal while still in pilot production as the war came to the missiles. Deploying American complex technical assets to distant theaters was a much more involved affair.

Poised for advancement

Disregarding combat capability, even special types development programs flourished in the final year of the war. Quality as well as quantity generally exceeded enemy and Allied efforts alike. Unlike other weapons, the British had little to contribute to development of the special types. Yet what was achieved was remarkable by any standards of development and production time, and pace of technological advancement.

By the second half of 1944 the course of the war was clear and victory almost certain. The weapons at hand and persistence alone would decide the outcome, although the Allies had to be prepared for any unexpected turn of events. The considerable resources 'in the pipeline' appeared adequate. Consequently,

The German V-1 'Buzz Bomb' was reverse-engineered as the JB-2 in late summer 1944 for a decided leap forward in powered missile progress. The same rail launch was employed but a superior targeting system added. This advancement emphatically showed that the propeller-powered airplane drones had been a stop-gap that had quickly outlived any combat value. *National Archives*

many of the more radical programs began to be cancelled or substantially reduced in scope. Within weeks of VJ-Day the axe had fallen on most of the remaining efforts. Just a few continued as research projects or to sustain post-war defense, but at much slower pace. The missile programs were particularly seen as the wave of the future, and thus continued to be funded.

The inspiration, technical excellence and work ethic that propelled the United States from a position of inferiority before the war to world dominance in aeronautics by the end of the conflict were sustained after the war. The wartime successes created an expectation for post-war aeronautical progress for which few but the US could reach in a broad way,

as it alone emerged whole and wealthy from the devastating conflict. The nation's airpower was the largest, best equipped and most powerful in the world. The foresight that allowed such momentous progress on helicopters and drones was carried forward as the world dealt with the aftermath of the momentous conflict and as the Cold War dawned. The excellence of the aircraft industry, no matter that it was reduced by cuts following the war, stood ready to respond, albeit at a more reasoned peacetime pace of development and procurement. Even for special types, the US remained the stand-out world leader for decades as it continued to sustain a large, world-spanning military.

Another wartime system that proved indicative of future trends was the small radio controlled drone targets. Inexpensive and easy to operate, the Radioplane TDD (Army OQ-2A) is shown during a demonstration at NAS Barbers Point, Hawaii, on 4 June 1945. Similarity to today is striking (though drones are currently most commonly used for reconnaissance and surveillance) with the small airplane on the launch catapult, the operator with control box beyond and ground crew standing apart from officers who are engaged in introducing the operation to civilian visitors. *National Archives*

Glossary

Air-cooled engine   A piston engine employing the passing air to cool the cylinders and other components. This requires a properly formed cowling and baffling encircling the engine, and usually cowl flaps to regulate the flow of air while reducing cooling drag.

Airfoil   A wing cross-section shape determining lift characteristics.

Angle-of-Attack   The angle between the wing's mean chord line and the incident airflow.

Anti-ice   A system aboard an aircraft that works to prevent atmospheric moisture from freezing on the exterior in flight, which could compromise safety. During the Second World War these were heated surfaces like windscreens and leading edges, the latter usually from heated air passed locally within the structure, and alcohol or glycol fluid emitted to be spread across a surface by the passing airflow or, for the propeller, radial acceleration.

Aspect ratio   The square of the wingspan divided by the area of the wing. A high-aspect-ratio wing is comparatively long and narrow.

Catapult   A means of launching an airplane off an aircraft carrier deck, usually by a bridle between the aircraft and a shuttle in a slot along the deck. The shuttle is propelled by a hydraulic or gas piston below deck to accelerate the aircraft to take-off velocity.

Center of gravity (CG)   The point at which an aircraft would balance if suspended from that point, or the center of gravitational attraction acting on the mass of the vehicle. A CG too far forward or too far aft of limits could make an airplane uncontrollable. The CG position is measured as a percentage of the mean aerodynamic chord (MAC) of the wing.

Chord   The width of a wing or the line between the leading and trailing edges, usually referred to as chord length, or a mean chord for a tapered wing.

Collective   The control that adjusts the incidence angle of each rotor blade collectively regardless of its position around the spinning disc. This causes the rotorcraft to rise or descend and permits hover if the rpm is maintained by the engine turning the rotor shaft. Engine rpm and collective pitch are largely synchronized automatically.

Combustion heater   A device that burns the aircraft fuel to provide heated air for cabin comfort or anti-ice features.

Contra-rotating propeller   Also known as a dual-rotation propeller or 'contraprop', this employs two propellers, front to back, turning in opposite directions on the coaxial power shafts to eliminate torque effects.

Counter-rotating propeller   Propellers on opposite sides of the aircraft (as in a twin-engine installation) that rotate in opposite directions to eliminate torque effects.

Cyclic   A mechanism that changes the pitch of the rotor blades with relation to their position around the disc to counter the asymmetrical lift distribution created during forward flight. This articulation permits intentional asymmetrical lift creation to generate forward thrust as well as forces in any axis for translation, roll and pitch. It can also refer to the control stick in the rotorcraft cockpit.

De-icing   The systems aboard an aircraft that work to shed accreted ice from the exterior in flight. During the Second World War these were usually pneumatically inflated leading edge rudder boots or thermal heating.

Dive brakes   Flaps or other deployed surfaces intended to slow the aircraft in a steep descent.

Drag   The resistance of the air to the passage of an aircraft through it. It is made up of induced drag from the creation of lift, and profile drag that includes skin friction drag, the overall frontal area offered to the incident air, cooling drag from air passing through a cowling and engine baffling, and other elements.

Drift-meter | Common in aircraft with dedicated navigators, this was a vertically mounted telescope with visible lines in the reticle that could be rotated to align with the flow of observed objects. This then yielded a drift angle for correction by the pilot or determination of ground speed.

Dual-rotation propeller | See Contra-rotating propeller

Feathering | Turning propeller blades edgewise to the line of flight to stop rotation and reduce drag when an engine has stopped.

Flaps | Articulated portions of a wing trailing edge that enhance lift at the expense of drag, and are usually employed on approach to allow a reduced landing speed. The split flap is a lower portion of the trailing edge simply hinged to rotate down. Fowler flaps slide aft and down, usually creating a slot between the wing mainplane and flap surfaces through which air accelerates, as well as adding to effective wing area for more lift enhancement at low airspeeds. Double-slotted flaps have a vane fixed ahead of the leading edge of the main flap surface. When extended, a slot is formed between the vane and the cove in addition to the slot between the vane and main flap surface.

Flutter | An unstable oscillation of a portion of the aircraft or control surface that can grow in amplitude to catastrophic levels. The instability is induced by unsteady air loads interacting with elastic deformation of the structure or control surface rotation at similar frequencies (resonance).

Hardpoint | A strengthened structural portion within the bottom surface of a wing or fuselage with fittings for the carriage of weapon or fuel tank mounts.

Ground effect | The phenomenon is evident within approximately one rotor diameter above the ground as a cushion of air that is created, enhancing rotor lift and thus reducing the power required to hover. Airplanes also encounter the same lift-enhancement effect upon landing.

Ground resonance | On-gear instability at certain rotor speeds that could make the rotorcraft oscillate dangerously and risk an overturn.

Inline engine | A reciprocating engine in which the pistons are arranged in one or more longitudinal lines parallel to the center power shaft. An upright or inverted V-arrangement is typical.

Intercooler | One or more heat exchangers cooling the air passing to a supercharger to increase density.

Laminar flow | A boundary layer of air adjacent to a surface in an air stream with an even pressure distribution as opposed to turbulent, and possessing less skin friction drag. A laminar-flow wing is one with an airfoil designed to maintain laminar flow for more of the chord length than typical airfoils.

Lend-Lease | A US government policy by which weapons and other materiel assistance was purchased by the United States and provided as a form of loan to nations fighting or arming to fight the Axis powers.

Load factor | A measure of acceleration in the vertical axis of an aircraft defined as units of gravitational pull on the surface of the earth (1g). This is a primary criterion for structural design to ensure that the airframe can withstand maneuvering airloads and inertia, plus a factor or safety.

Pressurization | A system that pumps compressed air into the sealed cockpit to maintain pressure at a safe 'cabin altitude' as the aircraft climbs into the rarefied air at high altitude.

Propeller reversing | The ability to reverse the pitch on a constant-speed propeller (variable pitch) to reverse the thrust for slowing on landing or backing the aircraft on the surface.

Propeller synchronization | The process of ensuring a similar rpm for each propeller on a multi-engine aircraft to prevent an annoying rhythmic noise.

Radial engine | Denoted by an R prefix, this is a reciprocating engine in which the pistons are arranged radially about the center power shaft. One or two rows of these radially grouped cylinders are typical.

Radio or Radar altimeter	A device for measuring height above the ground or sea by reflected electromagnetic waves, permitting safer night flying at low altitude.
Rigid rotor	A rotor lacking flapping and lead-lag hinges.
Rotor articulation	A horizontal pin permitting blade flapping up and down, and a vertical hinge for fore and aft (lead and lag) motion. These motions under the lift and drag forces work to equalize the lift across the disc and prevent forces beyond the power of the flight control to counter while also relieving blade bending stresses.
Rotor brake	A handle and mechanism serving to a stop after landing.
Slat	A segment of a wing leading edge that slides forward to increase wing camber (inflection) to add lift. This usually creates a slot between the surface and the wing mainplane through which air is accelerated to energize flow downstream and delay stall.
Slot	A narrow spanwise opening between the lower and upper surface of a wing allowing the high-pressure air below to accelerate up and over the top of the wing to energize the airflow and delay stall.
Specification ('Spec')	An agreement between a manufacturer and the government as to the characteristics of an aircraft yet to be designed and built.
Spin	An out-of-control condition produced by the stall of one wing coupled with high yaw angle. The result is a descending flight path with the aircraft rotating about a vertical axis.
Stall	The turbulation and separation of air on a wing or other surface due to high angle-of-attack and adverse pressure gradients within the boundary layer that causes an enormous loss of lift.
Static line	An anchor cable stretched along the length of a transport aircraft cabin near the ceiling to which paratroopers attach their parachute static lines. Upon jumping from the airplane, the line is pulled from the parachute pack to deploy the chute, then remains attached to the cable to be retrieved after all jumpers have departed from the aircraft.
Supercharger	A device commonly possessing a spinning compressor impeller, usually driven off the engine accessory gearcase, through which the fuel-air mixture from the carburetor is ported before passing into the intake manifold. This 'boost' helps maintain intake pressure nearer sea level even with the lower air density at altitude for sustained high engine power output.
Swashplate	The most common rotor articulation technique used during the Second World War with the stick tilting a nonmoving plate through which the rotor shaft passes. This, in turn, tilts a moving plate above, on bearings, that is attached to each blade via rods. This causes each blade to undergo cyclic changes in pitch as the rotating plate passes over the tilted non-rotating plate. Owing to flapping hinges, this actually tilts the disc and its lifting force, with the fuselage following this motion to a large extent due to the CG being below the rotor and seeking to remain under the center of lift.
Torque	The moment (lateral displacement tendency) created by a propeller, especially at high power on take-off and low speed on landing. This is a combination of mechanical effects from turning the heavy prop and asymmetrical pressure distribution on the propeller disk, as well as the asymmetrical airflow effects on the aircraft elements aft of the propeller.
Translational lift	Forward flight or 'translation' adding to the lift generated by the rotor spin alone. This is especially advantageous for the initial climb after lift-off.
Turbosupercharger	A turbine spun by engine exhaust gases that, in turn, spins a compressor to 'charge' air taken in via a ram air duct. This air is then passed to the carburetor or supercharger.
Wind tunnel	A fabricated tunnel in which fans cause air motion through a test section in which a model of an aircraft or part thereof is mounted for data collection. In a full-scale wind tunnel, the test section is large enough to mount the entire aircraft and operate it remotely.

Acronyms and Abbreviations

AAA	anti-aircraft artillery	MIT	Massachusetts Institute of Technology
AAF	Army Air Forces	mod	modification
AoA	Angle of Attack	mph	statute miles per hour
APP	auxiliary power plant	mpm	meters per minute
APU	auxiliary power unit	N	Newton(s)
ASR	Air-Sea Rescue	NACA	National Advisory Committee for Aeronautics
ASW	anti-submarine warfare	NAF	Naval Aircraft Factory
ATC	Air Transport Command	NAMC	Naval Air Material Center
aux	auxiliary	NAMU	Naval Air Modification Unit
BuAer	Bureau of Aeronautics	NAS	Naval Air Station
BuNo	Bureau Number	NATS	Naval Air Transport Service
CAA	Civil Aeronautics Authority	NDRC	National Defense Research Committee
cal	caliber	No, No.	number
CBI	China-Burma-India Theater	NRL	Naval Research Laboratory
CCP	Control Plane Pilot	OSRD	Office of Scientific Research and Development
CG	center of gravity	P&W	Pratt & Whitney
CinC	Commander in Chief	PPI	Plan Position Indicator
CinCPac	Commander in Chief Pacific	PR	photo reconnaissance
cm	centimeter(s)	RAF	Royal Air Force
c/n	construction number	RC	radio control, radio controlled
CNO	Chief of Naval Operations	RCA	Radio Corporation of America
DC	direct current	rep	representative
D.C.	District of Columbia	rpg	rounds per gun
DCP	Drone Control Pilot	RN	Royal Navy
deg	degree(s)	rpm	revolutions per minute
ETO	European Theater of Operations	SAR	search and rescue
FM	Frequency Modulated	SATFOR	Special Air Task Forces
fpm	feet per minute	SAU	Special Air Unit
ft	foot, feet	sec	second(s)
gallon	US gallon	s/n	serial number
GFE	government-furnished equipment	spec	specification
GM	General Motors	STAGRON	Special Task Air Squadron
HF	high frequency	STAG	Special Task Air Group
hp	horsepower	SWOD	Special Weapons Ordnance Devices
Hz	Hertz	tech	technician
IFF	Identification Friend or Foe	TV	television
in	inch(es)	TWA	Transcontinental and Western Airlines
JATO	Jet-Assisted Take-Off	UK	United Kingdom
JCS	Joint Chiefs of Staff	US, USA	United States, United States of America
JPU	jet power unit	USAAC	United States Army Air Corps
kg	kilogram(s)	USAAF	United States Army Air Forces
km	kilometer(s)	USCG	United States Coast Guard
km/h	kilometers per hour	USMC	United States Marine Corps
kW	kilowatt(s)	USN	United States Navy
lab	laboratory	USS	United States Ship
lb	pound(s)	V	volts
lbf	pounds force	VHF	Very High Frequency
M	million, mega	VIP	Very Important Person
m	meter, meters	Wg Cdr	Wing Commander
MAC	mean aerodynamic chord	WPB	War Production Board
max	maximum	WWI	World War One
MG	machine gun	WWII	World War Two
MHz	megacycles, megahcrtz		

Endnotes

Chapter One

[1] These were sometimes called the 'V Division' for the heavier-than-air aircraft designation. They were formally VO for Heavier-than-Air and Observation, likewise VS for Scout, or VBCS for Cruiser/Battleship Scout.

[2] Historical Division Intelligence, Development of Transport Airplanes and Air Transport Equipment, Part IV, p279.

[3] Buchanan, p364.

[4] Licensed products of Spaniard Juan de la Cierva's design were spelled 'autogiro', as opposed to 'autogyro'. Autogiro, with a capital A, denoted those built directly by Cierva and his licensees. A gyroplane was a generic term for such craft. Gyrocopter is another proprietary name. The more generic autogyro is be used in this text.

Chapter Two

[1] From 1 November 1941 operational control of the US Coast Guard was transferred from the Treasury Department to the US Navy for rescue, coastal patrol, convoy escort, and anti-submarine warfare roles. For the duration of the war the USN procured aircraft for the Coast Guard.

[2] The Vought-Sikorsky Division of the United Aircraft Corporation resulted from the merger in April 1939 of the two historical aircraft design and manufacturing firms of Chance-Vought Corporation of Long Island City, New York, and Sikorsky Aviation Corporation of Stratford, Connecticut. This association would end on 1 January 1943 when they became Chance-Vought Aircraft and Sikorsky Aircraft.

[3] Adcock, *US Navy Floatplanes in Action*, p22.

[4] Adcock, *OS2U Kingfisher in Action*, p44.

[5] The record on the number of SO3Cs accepted by and delivered to the British is unclear. See Pearcy, *Lend-Lease Aircraft in World War II*, p153, and Green, p164.

[6] Cornwell, p1.

[7] Morley, *AAHS*, Summer 1992, pp109-10.

[8] Long, p3.

[9] Bowers, *'Fleet Ranger'*, is the principal source for the history of the XOSE-1, particularly the discussion of the early composite design approach.

Chapter Three

[1] Goodall, Ryan ST-M in Australia.

[2] Ibid.

[3] The curious aspect of this approach is that it was the strategy Japan adopted to help defend and communicate with its over-extended possessions in the early war years. Although it offered the Americans some rude surprises, the strategy ultimately failed.

[4] Francillon, *Grumman Aircraft Since 1929*, p200.

[5] Raines, pp291-92.

[6] Peperell, p44.

[7] Bowers, *Airpower*, September 1997, p34.

[8] Green, p173. This contradicts Bowers, *Of Wings and Things*, p182, which states that the modification was performed at Floyd Bennett Field in Brooklyn.

[9] The report that the aircraft struggled to get aloft from anything but the smoothest water is repeated in several sources, but no official document or authoritative individual is referenced. It is suspect because seaplanes are notoriously difficult to lift off from smooth water.

[10] Reports that the modification was intended to combat a compressibility effect known as Mach Tuck, or that test pilot Ralph Virden was killed when the modified booms failed in flight, are false. Virden died a year prior to the seaplane tests.

Chapter Four

[1] Numerous sources credit this as an order for 1,489 aircraft, likely based on a block of unused serials. However, 'Army Aircraft Characteristics', p52, gives the contracted number as 775, as substantiated by other specifically researched sources.

[2] Sharp and Bowyer, p375, discusses the British Production plans. Chilstrom and Leary, p186, reveals that the F-8 difficulties were likely due to an aft CG and an elevator trailing edge "bead" insisted upon by the Canadian factory test pilot. Both factors gave unsatisfactory handling from the American perspective. Stanley, p92, goes on to mention performance and serviceability shortfalls. In 1944, 28 were returned to Canada, 12 others having been written-off, and the program cancelled in September 1944.

[3] Futrell, pp14, 23, and 28.

[4] Ibid, p9.

[5] Ibid, p23.

[6] Historical Office, Case History of the F-7 Airplane, p1.

[7] Ibid, p3.

[8] Historical Section, Case History of Hughes D-2, D-5, F-11 Project, document summary, entry 62.

[9] Harding and Long, p18.

[10] Giles, 'Development of Special Photographic Mapping Airplane'.

[11] Craig, 'Military Characteristics of Aircraft'.

[12] Historical Division, Case History of XF-12 Airplane, documents summary entry 4, and Carroll, 'High Altitude Photographic Airplane'.

[13] Chidlaw, letter to Commanding General, Materiel Command, 12 June 1943.

[14] Boeing was then planning the B-29C with the fuel-injected R-3350 and reversible-pitch propellers as well as the B-29D with R-4360s. The photographic model would have eliminated all but the tail armament to lighten the airframe for improved performance. McCoy.

[15] The XP-58 was a twin-boom fighter with a convoluted history that would fly on 6 June 1944. It promised a cruise speed of more than 274mph (441km/h) at 25,000 feet (7,620 meters). It was designed with cabin pressurization and had a 38,400-foot (11,704-meter) ceiling. Claims by the Wright Field engineers that the P-58 would fly higher, faster and further than the proposed D-5 was ill-founded, and it certainly could not meet the spec. The design was very heavy and neglected at that stage of the war.

[16] In 1941 the USAAC's Materiel Division adopted an MX-__ code for designating development programs.

[17] Hughes had licensed the use of the Duramold process from Fairchild with the understanding that the California firm would apply it to large aircraft and Fairchild smaller machines. This therefore represented additional sunk costs that appeared to be wasted, in addition to design and construction experience that could no longer be exploited.

[18] This concept of processing film aboard the tight fighter-like airplane was eventually seen as impractical, although carried as an alternate crew complement throughout the project.

[19] Hughes drawings showed wingtip tanks of 600 gallons (2,271 liters), but it is unclear if these were part of the final design.

[20] Hughes pushed to recoup $3,650,000 of development costs on the precursor D-2. The company insisted that it could not embark on the F-11 development while suffering such a loss on the D-2. Although Arnold initially directed the charges be honored, this simply did not pass any casual examination, with the dispute continuing even beyond the contract signing, which included $3,313,338.19 for the D-2. For the contract to be approved, it took assurance from General Arnold to the Under Secretary of War on 17 July that the contract represented an urgent military necessity given that there was no other aircraft that met the requirement and no other manufacturer prepared to deliver such an aircraft. A committee was formed to review the D-2 charge. Considering how little that unsuccessful airplane contributed to the very different XF-11, the Air Forces made a compelling case in the negative. It took until November for the committee to assess the D-2's value at $1,906,826.13 and Hughes was apparently satisfied. In any event, the D-2/X-37 would not be accepted or evaluated by the Army because it was consumed in a mysterious hangar fire on 11 November 1944.

[21] Fleetwings was by then a division of Kaiser Cargo, with which Hughes was partnered on the giant HK-1 flying boat.

[22] Case History of Hughes D-2, D-5, F-11 Project, document summary entry 226, and Army Aircraft Characteristics, p39, also speaks of the F-11A. These were likely the production aircraft incorporating leading edge deicing and any other changes derived from flight testing.

[23] Northrup, 'High Altitude Photographic Aircraft Development'.

[24] Carroll, 'High Altitude Photographic Airplane'.

[25] Historical Division, Case History of XF-12 Airplane, p2.

[26] Morgensen, Mock-up Inspection of Republic XF-12 Airplane.

[27] Literature on the XF-12 mentions a retractable bombing/navigation radar radome. Although some drawings show an APQ-31 navigation radar in a shallow blister radome beneath the forward fuselage, this appears to have been associated with a notional electronic warfare ('Ferret') variant of the airplane. A radar operator station is shown in several drawings as well as being included in the mock-up, and there was a requirement for radar gear. Neither this nor the retractable radar appears to have been fitted to the prototypes.

[28] Historical Division, Case History of XF-12 Airplane, documents summary entry 28.

[29] Riley, Contract #33-038 ac-1079, XF-11 and F-11 Aircraft Conference at Washington, DC.

[30] 'Army Aircraft Characteristics' reflects the order for two XF-12s but notes one delivered, with another as a XF-12A. The XF-12 is noted as being equipped with Aeroproducts propellers and the XF-12A with Curtiss 15.7-foot (4.8-meter) props, the substitution bringing the ceiling down 1,000 feet (305 meters). Fahey acknowledges one XF-12 and zero for the XF-12A. If this was a formal designation, it was all but ignored. In late 1948 the new USAF considered a re-engined variant also tentatively labeled F-12A. The first test aircraft lacked missions systems while the second was fully equipped with cameras, but both were also referred to as XF-12 until the designation was altered to XR-12 in 1948.

[31] Gross, 'Immediate Development of a Long Range Photo Reconnaissance Aircraft'.

Chapter Five

[1] The author's book *American Military Gliders of World War II* gives a complete account of the glider development and employment, to include the few powered glider models.

[2] Anon, 'Military Characteristics of Aircraft', p1.

[3] Commanding General, AAF Materiel Command, Cancellation of C-76 Airplane Contracts, p2.

[4] St Clair Streett. These estimates are wildly optimistic and reflect either ignorance of aircraft development or intentional misstatements for the purpose of garnering immediate support.

[5] Martin, et al, p4.

[6] Research and Development Projects of the Engineering Division, p43. Although drawings of the design had lines suggesting a nose door or doors, none are mentioned in the meager literature available.

[7] Brandley, p198. When this occurred is uncertain, as General Echols reported on 29 July 1942 that it still had the steel tube understructure. Historical Office, Air Technical Services Command, Case History of C-76 Airplane, p74. Additionally, the authoritative 'Army Aircraft Characteristics', p30, describes the aircraft as steel tube and wood.

8 Historical Division Intelligence, Development of Transport Airplanes and Air Transport Equipment, Part V, p34.

9 Production Division to General Echols.

10 Research and Development Projects of the Engineering Division, p43.

10 Balmer and Davis, p49.

12 General Echols reported on 29 July 1942 that it still had the steel tube understructure. Historical Office, Air Technical Services Command, Case History of C-76 Airplane, p1, and Cook, 'Waco C-62 Transport Airplanes'.

13 Commanding General, AAF Materiel Command, Cancellation of C-76 Airplane Contracts, p2.

14 Branshaw, 'Production of the C-76 Airplane', p2.

15 Echols, Termination of Contracts for C-76 Airplanes.

16 Moffitt, p2.

17 Ibid, p6.

18 Anon, Case Study of C-76 Contract Termination, p12.

19 Hatcher, p1.

20 Belknap, et al, pp40 and 107.

21 Hatcher, pp3-5.

22 Warren, p1.

23 Brentnall.

24 Chidlaw, C-76 Airplane, p2.

25 Branshaw, pp1-2.

26 Wolfe/Chidlaw, p2, and Boyne, p64.

27 Chidlaw, p1.

28 Ibid.

29 Anon, 'Summary of Unsatisfactory Characteristics in the Model C-76 Airplane', p4.

30 Belknap.

31 Ibid.

32 Kemmer, p2.

33 Historical Office, Case History of C-76 Airplane, documents summary entry 54.

34 Andrade, p80.

35 Wolfe/Chidlaw, p1.

36 Wolfe/Chidlaw, pp1-2, and Wolfe/Sessums, p2.

37 Sessums, lecture, p6. This account is stated such as to suggest the first flight of the C-76 rather than of the sixth aircraft. However, aspects of the recalled events make it clear that it refers to the Louisville mishap airplane.

38 Fischel, p2.

39 Echols, 'C-76 Cargo and B-36 Bomber', p1.

40 Anon, 'Report on the C-76 Airplane', p12.

41 Boyne, p64.

42 Ibid.

43 Pole.

44 Sessums, lecture, pp6-7.

45 Anon, 'Report on the C-76 Airplane', pp12-13.

46 Resources Division.

47 Chief of Staff.

48 Cook, 'Allocation of C-76 Airplanes'.

49 Historical Office, Case History of C-76 Airplane, documents summary entry 104.

50 Tabular Summary, and Case History of C-76 Airplane, documents summary entry 106.

51 Wolfe/Chidlaw, pp1-2, Wolfe/Sessums, p2, and Sessums, Memorandum Report of Second Meeting on Standardization of Transports, p3.

52 'Army Aircraft Characteristics', p36.

53 Phillips, p120.

54 Sessums, Memorandum Report of Second Meeting on Standardization of Transports, p2, and 'Report on the C-76 Airplane', p2-3.

55 This is the technique described by Dr Watter in his Spring 1967 'The Budd RB-1' article, p61. The flight manual describes a fairly routine take-off, calling for 0-10-degree nose-down elevator until rotate and three-quarter flaps for hard surfaces and full (assumed to mean 35 degrees) for soft. The Jim Lesher summary states that Budd was struggling to meet some CAA requirement for 1,000 feet and that the technique involved partial flaps retracted immediately after unstick. The split flaps were by then anachronistic and it is curious that the designers did not go with at least slotted plain flaps, if not Fowler flaps, then featured on many other transports.

56 Lesher, p2.

57 Juptner, p195.

58 Bureau of Aeronautics, Airplane Characteristics & Performance, Model RB-1.

59 By late 1944 some airlines had been allowed to resume commercial operations, although only authorized wartime movements were permitted.

60 Kavelaars, H. C., 'The Air Transport Department of the Shell Company of Ecuador 1937-1950', Part 1, p103.

61 Commanding General, AAF Materiel Command, Cancellation of C-76 Airplane Contracts, p2.

62 Historical Division Intelligence, 'Development of Transport Airplanes and Air Transport Equipment', Part V, p38.

Chapter Six

1 Historical Division Intelligence, 'Development of Transport Airplanes and Air Transport Equipment', Part VI, p213.

2 Andrade records BuNos for 112 machines (90020/131) and says that only as far as 90059 were completed (forty machines). Pearcy records 90021/47, 90048, and 90112/131 as taken up by the RAF, or forty-eight airplanes. It is known that 90020 was retained for testing. Yet 90044 and 90049 were seen in USMC markings. This uncertainty remains unresolved.

3 Craven and Cate, Volume VI, p224, and Volume III, p277.

4 Ibid.

5 Ibid, p215.

[6] The Model 249 was a proposed bomber version of the Constellation, designated XB-30. It was not selected for preliminary design.

[7] Pilot's Flight Operating Instructions for Army Model C-69 Airplane, p21.

[8] Bowers, 'Stratofreighter', p38, and Historical Division Intelligence, 'Development of Transport Airplanes and Air Transport Equipment', Part VI, pp219-20.

[9] The fabric and tabs caused a problem during flight testing when, during a 340mph dive, ballooning of the fabric ahead of the elevator tabs disturbed the flow to an extent that the tabs oscillated and drove elevator motion that produced severe pitching and overloaded the outer wing panels. The panels broke away and the airplane had to be abandoned. The solution was doubling the number of ribs ahead of the elevator tabs. The age of fabric surfaces was nearing its end.

[10] The double-bubble canopy arrangement soon met with widespread panning by pilots who could not easily communicate and coordinate without making eye contact or easily pass items across the cockpit, requiring them to duck their heads down. A modification program would replace these with a conventional windscreen arrangement.

[11] Lockheed was definitely positioning itself for the post-war period with capabilities and resources via the Navy contract. The Constitution looked nothing like a military transport. Hammer, p111, describes one example of apparent excess. Lockheed included 340lb (154kg) wheel chocks that were lowered from the cargo compartment by davits and rolled with a tow bar into place between the forward and aft wheel pairs; the chocks' wheels then retracted, and the chocks expanded to span this width.

[12] The Consolidated XB-36 and XC-99 were initially built with two main gear tires, 9.2 feet (2.8 meters) in diameter and 3.8 feet (1.2 meters) wide weighing 1,475lb (669kg). While this permitted the undercarriage to fit within the wing when retracted, the surface contact pressure limited the airplane to just three reinforced runways in the continental United States. Furthermore, a single tire blowout on take-off or landing would likely have been catastrophic. Norton, *American Bomber Aircraft Development in World War II*, p174.

[13] Historical Division Intelligence, 'Development of Transport Airplanes and Air Transport Equipment', Part VI, pp219-20.

[14] Chamber and Chambers, pp53-54.

[15] Barton, pp146-48. This used compressed air with a system that automatically compensated for changes in atmospheric pressure. The supply bottles were automatically filled by compressors, although the supply would be sufficient for a flight without refill. A moisture absorption system prevented any water in the lines that might freeze.

[16] Barton, pp189 and 199. An 'iron bird' replicates all the control system elements, distances, masses and simulated airloads in a laboratory setting for test and refinement.

[17] As usual, Howard Hughes insisted on approving nearly everything personally and interested himself in the smallest details, sometimes to excess. He spent long periods before making a decision and was usually inaccessible. His penchant for working all hours of the night and weekends, and treating the business as a personal hobby shop, drove away many talented people. When he became exhausted he would disappear for weeks or months, leaving the program in limbo. The lack of government spec or close oversight clearly suited him, but also allowed him to indulge his idiosyncrasies to excess. Cutting out the military aeronautical development agencies to give Hughes an unimpeded chance at success also robbed the company of their insight. Kaiser and Hughes were of such different dispositions and working habits that they did not associate closely on the program.

[18] At the time, Loening explained that an aircraft generally becomes more efficient as it grows in size. Skin area, affecting drag, increases by the square of the size, while volume increases by the cube of the size, using some linear measure like span. This suggests that payload volume will be greater than drag as size goes up in a beneficial relationship. However, the increase in wing size to lift the larger airplane weighs more than the proportionally smaller wing. Where the size efficiency crossed a point in which wing overall weight and structural efficiency become prohibitive was a matter of debate, especially given the unknowns of a wooden structure.

[19] Howard Hughes's legendary secrecy and his increasingly bizarre behavior, together with the growing post-war controversy over the HK-1, meant that little reliable information such as empty weight has ever been made available. (It is known that, when the hull alone was moved decades later, it weighed 122,000lb – Wildenberg and Davies, p72.) The first flight with just 2,000 gallons (12,000lb) of fuel (Anon, 'Hughes' Jinxed Giant', p13) was conducted at 280,000lb gross with no mention of ballast (Barton, p218). Considering that the airplane lacked operational accoutrements adding to the operating weight, an excessive empty weight is suggested for an airplane intending to carry 75,600lb of fuel and 120,000lb of cargo.

[20] Here again, little reliable information is available as to the final expense of the H-4 development. Barton, p209, and Schwartz/Maguglin, p23, provide a figure of $7 million of private funding, while Francillon, Volume II, p102, gives the often-quoted $17 million.

[21] The repair is evident on the aircraft as now displayed.

Chapter Seven

[1] In the United States, the two most prominent Cierva autogiro licensees were under the supervision of the Autogiro Company of America. The Pitcairn Autogiro Company of Willow Grove (Pitcairn Field), Pennsylvania, was the creation of Harold F. Pitcairn. Brothers Ray W. Kellett and Roderick 'Rod' G. Kellett formed the Kellett Autogiro Corporation in Lansdowne, Pennsylvania.

[2] The G was for autoGiro. Later, R would be applied to autogyros and helicopters, denoting Rotorcraft.

[3] Charnov, p172.

[4] Summary of Rotary Wing Projects, p6. This source appears to combine modifications incorporated into both the YG-1C (which is not named) and the XR-2. It credits only 5 degrees of pitch enabling the jump take-off, but this is believed to confuse the added 5 degrees on top of the 4 degrees already adopted for accelerated take-off.

[5] Brooks, p237, and Charnov, p173. The serial number of the craft has not been found.

[6] Charnov, p173, and Summary of Rotary Wing Projects, p7.

[7] Myall, p11. Presumably the US Navy worked with the British on their commercial aircraft purchasing activities while Lend-Lease remained in the future.

[8] As a bit of disinformation, the British reported these lost at sea when the freighter carrying them was torpedoed, also carrying all spares to the ocean bottom.

[9] Jarrett, p181. Other sources speak of just one of the pair being assembled for evaluation (Witkowski, p69) or both being flown for trials until wrecked (Townson, p80).

[10] Autogyros never reached the stage of mass serial production, only 300 or so being manufactured in the US before the Second World War. They remained novelties that where challenging and costly to operate, and with a discouraging safety record.

[11] Summary of Rotary Wing Projects, p8.

[12] See Gregg, p14, for details of this program.

[13] R.C.W.B., Rotary Wing Aircraft Operated from Merchant Freighters, Routing and Record Sheet, comment dated 16 June 1942, on memorandum of the same name, reporting Arnold's telephone instructions.

Chapter Eight

[1] Gregory, pp91-2, describes a back-and-forth on performance specifics that he rightly says were far beyond reason given the immature state of rotorcraft technology, and thus not adopted. Yet some authors have repeated the figures as if they were within the specifications despite Gregory's statements to the contrary. These figures included a 1,000fpm (305mpm) rate of climb (Francillon, p49), a minimum top speed of 120mph (193km/h) and a desired 250mph (402km/h), the ability to clear a 50-foot (15.2-meter) obstacle straight up and down, a 1,200-1,800lb (544-816kg) useful load, and fuel for 3½ hours endurance. Any knowledgeable rotorcraft researcher or designer of the period would have scoffed at the absurdity of such numbers. What precisely went into the Circular Proposal and the Specifications has eluded research. However, it is said by many (Smith, p281, and Charnov, p166) to have strongly implied 'helicopter', with the vertical take-off over a 50-foot obstacle clearly mentioned as frustrating the autogyro advocates. Clearing a 50-foot obstacle on take-off, and landing over same, was and is a common airplane performance measure appearing in most aircraft specifications.

[2] All the Sikorsky experimental helicopters, XR-4A, XR-5A, and XR-6, would fall under project MX-245. However, the XR-6 was also identified as the MX-256.

[3] LePage, p159, clarifies where others had stated that he only borrowed the layout concept or that the agreement was never formally completed. The agreement was fully signed, negotiated because of the close similarity in the rotor design to the patents submitted in several countries by Platt and LePage. It is assumed that the terms of the license could not be fulfilled after Germany went to war, and were then informally nullified after the United States found itself at conflict with that nation. Jarrett, p182, discusses the James Weir G&J firm's development in the UK of its pre-war W.5 helicopter that also benefited from some association with Focke until broken off by the war. The pressure to meet warplane production goals meant that their helicopter was neglected. The author of this section of the book, Elfran ap Rees, goes on to state that 'essential design data was subsequently passed to the USA where, together with patented Cierva work, it was to contribute to the first successful US helicopter flights from 1940 onwards.' This would likely have benefited Platt-LePage most directly. Certainly such technical exchanges did occur between the countries once they became allies and divided development work for efficiency. An example is the highly secret radar technology. Any hand-off of helicopter design knowledge in 1940 could potentially have contributed to the XR-1 and XR-4 developments. However, no other source, official or otherwise, mentions such a transfer of data.

[4] LePage, p176, Gregory p93, Summary Report of Rotary Wing Projects, p1, and Francillon, p49. The PL-1 was under detail design and, with some parts fabricated, assessed as half complete at the time of the XR-1 contract award. The PL-2 must have been a subsequent intermediate design. There have been erroneous reports that one or more of these PL designs had already flown.

[5] Gregory, p 99. By this point available funding permitted more than one prototype on many programs. This was a wise choice given flight test risks.

[6] Pitcairn had patented many of his designs from nearly two decades of rotary-wing development and was receiving royalties from those employing such features as cyclic and collective rotor blade pitch control. For a time a plate was attached to each Sikorsky helicopter, listing thirty-eight patents licensed from the Autogiro Company of America. After the United States entered the war, Pitcairn formally declared in July 1943 that he would seek only a pittance in royalty payments for War Department uses of his patents for the duration of the war.

[7] Gregory, p113.

[8] Army Aircraft Characteristics, p82.

[9] Morris, p78.

[10] Propeller manufacturer Hamilton Standard's attempt at developing and manufacturing superior blades was unsuccessful. Spenser, *Whirlybirds*, pp48-49.

[11] Army Aircraft Characteristics, p82.

[12] Gregory, p176.

[13] Spenser, *Whirlybirds*, p45, details a British cable to United Aircraft exploring a 150-helicopter order, while Wolf, p39, mentions 240 without citing a source. Myall, p15, confesses that the record is unclear but does not suggest anything approaching these numbers. Such quantities explain the move to establish the Bridgeport plant for what ultimately ended up as a short run production.

[14] Army Aircraft Characteristics, p82.

[15] It is not clear if disassembly for transport was a USAAF requirement, but it is likely, given that self-deployment overseas was impractical and the machine with rotors installed could not easily be handled aboard ship or train. The same had been true for gliders, which were designed to be broken down and shipped in huge crates. However, flight inside a cargo airplane was likely not envisioned for the helicopters, and this may have been among the first instances of an aircraft transported via aircraft.

[16] Wagner, p28.

[17] There is also mention of R-4 casualty evacuations in the Philippines (Jarrett, p189) and a covert personnel insertion in the Balkans, but these are not corroborated by any other sources, official or otherwise.

[18] Spenser, *Whirlybirds*, p46.

[19] Summary of Rotary Wing Projects, p22.

[20] Boyne, p30.

[21] Gregory, p219. This is an example of a very rare dual-service aircraft program during the war and for decades after.

[22] This was a change from the radial engine (R) to a 'flat' engine with opposed (O) cylinder orientation.

[23] Gregory, p219.

[24] Boyne, pp25-26, and Summary of Rotary Wing Projects, p28. In Boyne's book, Ralph Alex, the R-6 project engineer, provides an insightful summary of the wartime Sikorsky rotorcraft work with these extraordinary details of R-6 production.

[25] Summary of Rotary Wing Projects, pp27 and 33, Army Aircraft Characteristics, p83, and Myall, p28. Ralph Alex in Boyne, p24, suggests that an O-435-powered XR-6 was never completed and all were XR-6As, the first XR-6 so redesignated. Army Aircraft Characteristics, p82, states that no XR-6s were delivered. Aircraft 43-47955 and the five originally designated XR-6As are externally identical, suggesting no difference in powerplant. Gregory is silent as to this history and refers only to the "XR-6", although being equally nonspecific for other models. Other records are confused on this subject. Again, the researcher must bow to the knowledge of Alex, who was intimate with the program throughout this period. Further muddling the picture, Army Aircraft Characteristics, p82, and Myall, p26, indicate that a contract was promulgated for 100 R-6Bs, with the engine change, but apparently set aside for the larger R-6A order, the machines being identical. However, Fahey, p36, and Summary of Rotary Wing Projects, p31, indicate that these were to have the original Lycoming engine, but this was reconsidered when the Franklin-powered machines performed so well.

[26] Boyne, p29. This, again, comes from the well-informed Ralph Alex, but is not substantiated by other sources. No serials for these 200 machines are recorded. Additionally, 200 helicopters added to the recognized 27 plus 193 plus 500 more would exceed the contracted total of 731, and even the original 900. The production of some 425 machines in the span of eight months is not inconceivable in light of other American aircraft production achievements and the relative simplicity of the helicopter compared to frontline fighters and bombers.

[27] Pearcy, p136, states that the order was reduced to forty, while Myall, pp18-19 and 24, provides the quoted figure; Myall is more specifically and thoroughly researched, so holds sway. Additionally, Pearcy's statement that one went on to Canada is not reflected in the details provided by Myall.

[28] Boyne, p26, and Wolf, p42.

[29] Initially the Army chose this seating arrangement, common with bombers and transports. It created an issue for Sikorsky, which placed a single collective between the seats such that the pilot in the port seat had to use his right hand to operate this lever whereas the left hand was commonly used for operating an airplane throttle quadrant. Soon, however, the helicopter operators and manufacturers would adopt the starboard seat as the standard helicopter pilot station.

[30] Army Aircraft Characteristics, p82, Boyne, p31, and Summary of Rotary Wing Projects, p32.

[31] Wolf, p36.

[32] See a notation on the drawing in Allen, *Wings*, p43.

[33] Army Aircraft Characteristics, p83. There is no indication of how these were to be mounted, or that they were ever flown.

[34] This became a common developmental challenge for rotorcraft, and still is today.

[35] Boyne, p29.

[36] Army Aircraft Characteristics, p83a, suggests that the maximum airspeed authorized did not exceed 80mph.

[37] Allen, *Air Enthusiast*, p29.

[38] This was quite unlike civil airplane work, which essentially ceased. It appears that since these machines consumed few resources and flew in small areas at low altitude, they escaped the general prohibition in the USA of private flying during the war and the difficulties in obtaining 'strategic resources' like engines (provided used examples were found).

[39] Perry, Report AU-126, p8. The nature of the Army contract with G & A is unclear, and only this report reveals a serial number for this first machine. However, records indicate that 44-90991 was for an assault glider, although that contract was cancelled. Fahey, p36, provides no serial for the 1944 aircraft, and photos show no military or even civil identification. This was done for some wartime programs in which the machine was considered merely a flying test rig.

[40] Smith, p313, and Summary of Rotary Wing Projects, pp38-39. A probable reason might have been to eliminate a competing helicopter that Congress might have insisted the service acquire, slowing and complicating more favored ongoing acquisitions. The Army stated that "the handling characteristics of the helicopter were sufficiently different from other helicopters to preclude operation by helicopter pilots without proper checking out."

[41] A dimension of 27.6 feet (8.4 meters) is found in Fahey, p36, and Kohn, *Armchair Aviator*, February 1973, p34.

[42] Summary of Rotary Wing Projects, p41.

[43] Ibid, p44.

[44] Army Aircraft Characteristics, p83, gives the capacity as four passengers or four litter patients, or six litters in an emergency. This appears to reflect the original requirement, whereas the six litters or ten troops was the specification to which the aircraft was built.

[45] Beard, *AAHS Journal,* Summer 2012, p131.

[46] Ibid, p132.

[47] The Navy created the new class designation H for the helicopter with subclass HN for training, HO for observation, and HR for transport.

[48] Beard, p134.

[49] Spenser, *Whirlybirds*, p411 photo.

[50] There are also reports of YR-4B 43-28247 as a HNS-1.

[51] Polmar, p139, and Summary of Rotary Wing Projects, p30.

[52] Andrade, p195.

[53] Polmar, p141, and Beard, *AAHS Journal*, Fall 2012, p166, report this as April 1945. However, Grossnick, p149, and Spenser, *Whirlybirds*, p403, say that it was in February and March.

[54] Beard, *AAHS Journal* Summer 2012, pp162-163.

[55] Spenser, *Whirlybirds*, pp395 and 408.

[56] Grossnick, pp138 and 142, and Spenser, *Whirlybirds*, p410.

[57] Claims that this was the largest helicopter in the world are incorrect when the resulting XHRP-1 is compared with the German Fa 223. During the war the Americans claimed numerous 'world records' and 'firsts' with ignorance of progress elsewhere given the wartime impediment to openness and communication. With the benefit of hindsight, most of these claims have to be judged as inaccurate.

[58] The company only obtained the engine after Stan Hiller made personal appeals to the War Production Board and following a favorable review of the design by NACA.

[59] An interesting side effort of the Hiller work was a 1944 Navy contract to build a small, unmanned helicopter to fly on a 300-foot (91-meter) tether and lift an antenna above a life raft. The single-rotor Sky Hook would be stored in a tube measuring 36 by 6 inches (300 by 50cm) and be launched by survivors in the raft to permit emergency radio transmissions. Powered by a 1.1hp (0.8kW) gasoline engine, the Sky Hook had a single rotor without an anti-torque device apart from vanes directing downwash opposite the body rotation. Thus some body rotation under the rotor was accepted. This was evaluated just after the war but set aside. Spenser, *Hiller*, p13.

[60] Francillon, pp8 and 69.

Chapter Nine

[1] The Navy initially bought two Stearman-Hammond-Y JH-1 (Y-1S) tricycle-gear light planes with pusher props and a high degree of natural stability. Reliance on such purpose-built machines was soon seen as unnecessary.

[2] Holloman, Memorandum Report on Status Report on Aerial Targets, p2, provides the 2 May 1939 date. Botzum, p11, states that the deciding successful demonstration occurred in November 1939, thus conflicting with the official report.

[3] The Army employed an A-_ designation for powered aerial target drones from 1940 to June 1941. This was altered to the subscale OQ-_ and optionally piloted PQ-_ in June 1941 to avoid confusion with Attack aircraft designations. Drone control aircraft were CQ-_.

[4] Mathews, *Cobra!*, p167.

[5] Lest and Carroll, Memorandum Report on Remote Controlled Aircraft, Power Driven (Man-Carrying) – MX-53/MX-264, p870.

[6] Ibid, p869.

[7] Long after the war, drones were employed as targets for fighter and airborne missile attack, but this was not seriously pursued during the conflict.

[8] The YB-40 was a B-17F converted as a bomber escort with many more guns and turrets. It did not enter production.

[9] An R prefix denotes a configuration restricted from combat use.

Chapter Ten

[1] The National Defense Research Committee was formed in the fall of 1940 and soon placed under the Office of Scientific Research and Development (OSRD) to mobilize the American scientific community to focus energies on research to support weapons development.

[2] The possibility of a missile or drone, remotely directed via beacon to a surface vessel represented by a radar-reflected blip on a radar screen, actually striking the target was low and not pursued.

[3] Norton, Chapter 13 (pp199-211), contains the fullest published account of the American bomb glider efforts during the war.

4 Craven and Cate, Volume VI, p255, The Development of Guided Missiles, Part II, p10.

5 Ibid.

6 In later years the use of wood would also be lauded as providing a reduced radar signature, thus promoting surprise in an attack. However, the wartime motivation to employ wood in this and many other military aircraft of modest performance or second-line status was purely to reduce the demand on metals production.

7 Trimble, *Wings for the Navy*, p261.

8 This is particularly remarkable given the specific drop conditions required for the standard Mk 13 torpedo at that point in the war, with pilots aboard naval attackers finding a successful shot most challenging. This led some to conclude that it was a lucky shot.

9 Fahrney, p374.

10 Bruins, p98.

11 Participant Jones, p22, claims the aircraft were catapulted off the deck. Wolf, 215, says this consisted of six fully loaded TDR-1s.

12 Jones, p8, would have the reader believe that Towers, together with his "cabal" of aviation officers, had a deep philosophical opposition if not personal loathing for the drones and missiles, and associated personnel, and actively schemed against their success in an unprofessional manner. The present account will make no effort to explore such assertions. However, it is instructive to note that the Army abandoned the same technology at about the same time for essentially the same reasons with no suggestion of conspiracy.

13 It is unclear whether the calculations were done balancing the drone program expenditures and resources (including aircrew) in destroying a target with the same for an existing carrier-based fighter wing or an Air Forces bomber formation doing the task.

14 Trimble, *Wings for the Navy*, p259, and Fahrney, p338, mention the requirement for catapult launch for the TDN-1. It is unclear if this was carried forward to the final design. The shipboard trials did not include catapulting the aircraft.

15 This implies that the propellers on either side of the fuselage turned in opposite directions, meaning that the engines would have to be of slightly different models of the same type. This feature would reduce directional trim demands from slightly different engine thrusts side-to-side, which would be difficult to deal with under remote control.

16 A series of photos scanned at the National Archives in College Park, Maryland, shows this event dated 10 August 1943. The other events described above are also shown in photographs from the same source.

17 Hall, pp64 and 140. This is as one would expect given the mission and nature of the aircraft. However, Hall goes on to describe some number of TDR-1s transported to the Pacific theater fully assembled on the deck of the USS *Marcus Island*.

18 Photos dated 14 January 1944 and located in the National Archives in College Park, Maryland, show the internal installation with a radar monitoring station, and the lowered radome.

19 Details of the TD2R and TD3R are especially lacking, and what little is available is muddled. Army Aircraft Characteristics, p75, provides the best information, presumably communicated by the Bureau of Aeronautics to ATSC. There the engineering characteristics and performance numbers are provided for the Interstate XBQ-5, identified as an airplane equipped with an O-805-2. Yet it then mentions the XBQ-6 as also possessing O-805-2s while the XBQ-6A had the R-975-13s, and states at the end that this was similar to the TD3R-1 without being clear which version, XBQ-6 or XBQ-6A, was being referenced. Given that both the TD2R and TD3R had the same basic airframe and performance requirements, but with modest differences in weight owing to different engines – the O-805 weighed 590lb (268kg), the R-975 675lb (306kg), the performance given for the XBQ-5/XTD2R-1 is likely representative of the XBQ-6A/XTD3R-1. Adding more confusion, the USAAF summary of the two programs – Anon, Progress Report of Army Air Forces, Pilotless Aircraft as Guided Missiles, Development Status and Availability, pp146 and 148 – gives the performance of the XBQ-5 as a range of 2,380 miles (3,830km) at 280mph (451km/h) with a maximum speed at 17,000 feet (5,182 meters) of 310mph (499km/h). For the XBQ-6 (again, unclear as to engine) it says 1,350 miles (2,173km) at 200mph (322km/h) at sea level. None of these figures match those in Army Aircraft Characteristics.

20 Swanborough and Bowers, *United States Navy Aircraft Since 1911*, p604, credits a dozen TD3R-1s having been built. This could not be substantiated.

21 Glines, p80, Rosendahl, p142, Shock II-52, and Wright, p160, contain tantalizing photos but few details of the Glimpy project. The website http://www.alternatehistory.com/discussion/showthread.php?t=209566 also contains a few tidbits of information. Curiously, Fahrney is silent on the project.

22 Glimpy is supposedly a contraction of 'Glomb' and 'Blimp' with a cute 'y' at the end. 'Glomb' was a contraction of Glider Bomb, which was another remote-controlled aircraft project. Although the Piper was not a glider, the name was probably satisfyingly amusing.

23 The Army appears to have contemplated acquiring more of the N2C2 drones because, according to Holloman, W670, they reserved the A-3 designation for such aircraft. However, Army Aircraft Characteristics, Production and Experimental, p79, shows no quantity for the A-3, delivered or ordered.

24 Jones, p16.

25 Bogert, Research and Development Projects of the Engineering Division, p840.

26 This base was on the edge of Muroc Lake, a vast expanse of normally dry lakebed surface found very advantageous for testing experimental aircraft. Its proximity to the southern California aviation manufacturers was fortuitous.

27 Cully and Parsch, MX-500 to MX-999 Listing.

28 Anon, Details of A.A.F. Guide Missiles Program, pp254-55, and Sims, 'Technical Instructions CTI-1102, Addendum No 1, Power Driven Controllable Bombs', p883.

29 Portion of document lacking pages with title of author(s), Air Force Historical Research Agency AFHRA microfilm reel (disk) A2083, frame 1328.

30 Anon, Progress Report of Army Air Forces, Pilotless Aircraft as Guided Missiles, Development Status and Availability, AFHRA disk A2083, frames 510-16.

31 Anon, The Development of Guided Missiles, p6.

32 There is confusion in the literature about when or if the specification moved from a 300lb to a 500lb bomb. The preponderance of evidence is that the GM drone was designed to carry a 300lb warhead. See, for example, Sims, Controllable Bomb, Power Driven, General Motors, Type A-1, p14. There is further confusion engendered by the word 'bomb', which suggests an aerial bomb casing nestled within the fuselage. While there was a standard 500lb bomb in the US inventory, there was not one of 300lb.

33 Werrell, AAHS, p286. It is logical that automaker GM would seek assistance from Cessna in designing an airplane. However, the USAAC had at first planned to place the contract with Cessna with the intention that GM would be the subcontractor. General Motors protested this arrangement and the service relented. The Development of Guided Missiles, Part II, p1.

34 Werrell, AAHS, p286, and LeVier, p95-96, provide a $500,000 figure with reference to the contract itself, while seemingly contradicting himself in the earlier *The Evolution of the Cruise Missile*, p28, with a $250,000 figure and apparent reference to a summary of controlled missiles. Yet the same reference from *The Evolution of the Cruise Missile*, p30, also provides the final program expenditure of $350,000. Consequently the $500,000 figure, which does appear excessive, is considered an error.

35 Ibid, pp286 and 289.

36 The A-1 designation was apparently a GM creation. The USAAC's formally designated A-1 was a Fleetwings target. The GM drone does not appear in the common reference sources. This may account for the more common 'GMA-1' found in official literature.

37 Fahrney, p776, and Werrell, p287. This is an astonishingly long take-off distance for a small airplane, especially as it all had to be on a track laid on even ground. One is tempted to believe that the information is erroneous. If true, it is not surprising that alternative launch methods were sought.

38 Wolf, p140.

39 The determination of which drone flew on which day is partially provided by the Fahrney and Werrell accounts, but also an examination of available photographs in which the aircraft number is painted in large digits on the vertical tail and wings. While Werrell, AAHS, gives a table (p292) with a partial list of aircraft numbers against flight dates, Fahrney uses phraseology that suggests ship numbers but is inconclusive and conflicts with Werrell's summary. Werrell states that the last A-1 to fly was ship number 9. Photos support that this craft was flown at Muroc and launched off the car, but one other A-1 was also flown under these circumstances. It is also evident that ship 12 was placed on tricycle gear, but one mysteriously numbered 16 is shown in a taxi run. The wings of 13 are shown being placed on another airframe with a tricycle undercarriage, suggesting a swap after the ground mishap. The record is therefore incomplete if not muddled, so the account in this book does not attempt to make these tie-ups.

40 Lewis, Ed, note regarding XBQ-2A contributed to Fleetwings XBQ-1 entry in http://www.aerostar.org/air/usa/sleetwings _xbq.htp dated 12/11/2012.

41 Reading between the lines, one has to conclude that the Fleetwings proposal for the drone capable of hauling the 4,000lb weapon was unsatisfactory, so the Air Corps turned to Fairchild. The company was already struggling to get the AT-14 program (initially XAT-13) up to speed given numerous USAAF design changes (which included recasting it again as the AT-21) and skilled labor shortages.

42 Army Aircraft Characteristics, p74, indicates that three BQ-3 aircraft were on contract, but Mitchell, p164, and a program summary, Anon, Progress Report of Army Air Forces, Pilotless Aircraft as Guided Missiles, Development Status and Availability, p139, are clear that only two were delivered. Perhaps the third was a static test article.

43 Army Aircraft Characteristics, p74. The return in December 1943 is corroborated by Anon, Progress Report of Army Air Forces, Pilotless Aircraft as Guided Missiles, Development Status and Availability, p148. A very specific note on the back of a photo at the National Museum of the United States Air Force, A1/(b)Q-4/pho/1, gives the details of "Destroyed due to cracked ribs", mentioning "Lt Anderson" as the pilot who most frequently flew the aircraft.

44 Army Aircraft Characteristics, p75, Chidlaw, Technical Instructions CTI-1102, and Sims, Technical Instructions CTI-1102 Addendum 1.

45 Lest and Carroll, Memorandum Report on Controllable Bombs, Power Driven, Ground Launched – MX-53, pp876-77 and 882.

Chapter Eleven

[1] Jones, p149.

[2] Hall, pp140 and 151.

[3] Ibid, p167, and Wolf, p216.

[4] Jones, p22. The literature only mentions SBD-3s and shows 6537. However, photos at the National Archives, College Park, Maryland, show control equipment being added to the cockpit of an airplane identified as SBD 36662, which is an SBD-5.

[5] Hallstead, p52. The National Archives photos show the command airplane modifications.

[6] Sakaida, p60.

[7] This suggests that the self-destruct system originally called for and tested on the TDN-1s was not incorporated into the TDR-1 design or its deployed configuration.

[8] Hall, p207.

[9] Hall, p164. The report of the STAG-1 operations attests to 16 knots at 30 degrees off the nose as about the safe limit of the system. This equates to 9 knots direct crosswind or quite a marginal capability for even a light airplane. Manual compensation for this by a remote pilot would be very challenging, but even this was not possible with the TDR-1 and the Cast system. This was a marked limitation of the weapon when compared with manned combat aircraft. Additionally, the loss of a TDR-1 on take-off when one engine was slow in power advanced again points to a limitation of the system. A multi-engine pilot would be trained to immediately retard all throttles and steer to maintain the centerline. The control pilot simply had too little system insight and interface capability.

[10] Sakaida, p60.

[11] Windsok.

[12] Wilson, Use of Airplane as Remotely Controlled Bomb, p956. The P-38J Lightning 'Droop Snoot' was a modification giving the fighter an extended nose with a bombardier station that offered suitable space for a remote-control operator station.

[13] Many references mention B-17Es and Fs, but more specific accounts of the aircraft actually converted to drones indicate that they were Fs and Gs.

[14] Historical Division, Case History of Controlled Missiles – Aircraft, Part II – Castor, frame 240.

[15] References to B-24Js being converted appear to be erroneous.

[16] The Development of Guided Missiles, Part I, pp2 and 17, and Craven and Cate, Volume VI, pp260-61.

[17] It was learned after the war that German soldiers had approached the airplane to capture the crew. Receiving no response from inside, they entered the bomber and tripped the explosives.

Chapter Twelve

[1] Case History of Hughes D-2, D-5, F-11 Project, document summary entry 258.

[2] Historical Division Intelligence, Development of Transport Airplanes and Air Transport Equipment, Part IV, p283.

[3] Taylor, p46.

[4] Barton, p219.

[5] Bruins, p105. This figure was likely arrived at by dividing all program costs by the small number of aircraft actually produced, whereas the JB-2 figures remained notional if not fantastic. However, the point is taken that a true missile would likely have a per-unit production cost much less than a multi-engine airplane.

The R-5D was conceived during the war but the first, produced via a modified A model, flew a few months after suspension of hostilities. It was another step towards the light helicopters that came in the postwar years with a widened cabin for two seated line-abreast and a single pilot forward. The port side had a sliding cabin door and an overhear rescue hoist (partially visible). *San Diego Air & Space Museum*

Bibliography

Books

Abel, Alan, Abel, Drina Welch and Matt, Paul *Piper's Golden Age* (Wind Canyon Books, Brawley, California, 2001)

Ahnstrom, D. N. *The Complete Book of Helicopters* (The World Publishing Company, New York, 1968)

Anderson, Fred *Northrop, An Aeronautical History* (Northrop Corporation, Los Angeles, California, 1976)

Andrade, John M. *U.S. Military Aircraft Designations and Serials 1909 to 1979* (Midland Counties Publications, Leicester, UK, 1997)

Armitage, Michael *Unmanned Aircraft*, Brassey's Air Power: Aircraft Weapon Systems and Technology Series, Volume 3 (Brassey's Defence Publishers, London, 1988)

Bach, Martin *Boeing 367/377 Stratocruiser, Stratofreighter, & Guppies* (NARA-Verlag, Allershausen, Germany, 1996)

Balmer, Joe and Davis, Ken *There Goes a Waco* (Little Otter Productions, Troy, Ohio, 1992)

Barton, Charles *Howard Hughes and His Flying Boat* (Aero Publishers, Inc, Fallbrook, California, 1982)

Berlin, Earl *Douglas C-124 Globemaster II*, Air Force Legends Number 206 (Steve Ginter, Simi Valley, California, 2006)

Botzum, Richard A. *50 Years of Target Drone Aircraft* (Northrop Corporation, Newbury Park, California, 1985)

Bowers, Peter M. *Boeing Aircraft Since 1916* (Naval Institute Press, Annapolis, Maryland, 1989)
Curtiss Aircraft 1907-1947 (Naval Institute Press, Annapolis, Maryland, 1987)

Bowman, Norman J. *The Handbook of Rockets and Guided Missiles* (Perastadion Press, Pennsylvania, 1963)

Boyne, Walter J, and Lopez, Donald D. (ed) *Vertical Flight, The Age of the Helicopter* (Smithsonian Institution Press, Washington, D.C., 1984)

Brandley, Raymond H. *Waco Airplanes, "Ask Any Pilot"*, Second Edition (Raymond Brandly, USA, 1988)

Brigman, Leonard (ed) *Jane's All the World's Aircraft, 1945-1946* (Sampson Low, Marston, and Company, Ltd., London, 1947) – also years 1946-47 and 1947-48.

Brooks, Peter W. *Cierva Autogiros, The Development of Rotary-Wing Flight* (Smithsonian Institution Press, Washington, D.C., 1988)

Buchanan, A. R. *The Navy's Air War, A Mission Completed* (Harper & Brothers Publishers, New York, date unknown)

Carey, Keith *The Helicopter, An Illustrated History* (Patrick Stephens, England, 1986)

Cassagneres, Ev *The New Ryan, Development and History of the Ryan ST and SC* (Flying Books International, Eagan, Minnesota, 1995)
The Spirit of Ryan (Tab Books, Inc, Blue Ridge Summit, Pennsylvania, 1982)

Chambers, Joseph R. and Chambers, Mark A. *Radical Wings & Wind Tunnels, Advanced Concepts Tested at NASA Langley* (Specialty Press, North Branch, Minnesota, 2008)

Charnov, Bruce H. *From Autogiro to Gyroplane, The Amazing Survival of an Aviation Technology* (Praeger, Westport, 2003)

Chilstrom, Ken and Leary, Penn, *Test Flying at Old Wright Field* (Westchester House Publishers, Omaha, Nebraska, 1995)

Coates, Steve *Helicopters of the Third Reich* (Ian Allan, Surrey, 2002)

Craven, Wesley F. and Cate, James L. (eds) *The Army Air Forces in World War II*, Volume III, *Europe: Argument to V-E Day January 1944 to May 1945* (The University of Chicago Press, Chicago, 1955)
The Army Air Forces in World War II, Volume VI, *Men and Planes* (The University of Chicago Press, Chicago, 1955)
The Army Air Forces in World War II, Volume VII, *Services Around the World* (US Government Printing Office, Washington, D.C., 1958)

Editors, *Airlift Tanker, History of U.S. Airlift and Tanker Forces* (Turner Publishing Company, Paducah, Kentucky, 1995)

Everett, H. R., *Unmanned Systems of World War I and II* (The MIT Press, Cambridge, Massachusetts, 2015)

Everett-Heath, John *Helicopters in Combat, The First Fifty Years* (Arms and Armour, London, 1993)

Floherty, John J. and McGrady, Mike *Whirling Wings, The Story of the Helicopter* (J. B. Lippincott Company, New York, 1961)

Francillon, Dr René J. *American Fighters of World War Two*, Volume One (Doubleday & Company Inc., Garden City, New York, 1971)
Grumman Aircraft Since 1929 (Naval Institute Press, Annapolis, Maryland, 1989)
Lockheed Aircraft Since 1913 (Naval Institute Press, Annapolis, Maryland, 1988)
McDonnell Douglas Aircraft Since 1920, Volume I (Putnam Aeronautical Books, London, 1988)
McDonnell Douglas Aircraft Since 1920, Volume II (Naval Institute Press, Annapolis, Maryland, 1990)

Francis, Devon *The Story of the Helicopter* (Coward-McCann, New York, 1946)

Friedman, Norman *US Naval Weapons* (Conway Maritime Press Ltd, London, 1983)

Gablehouse, Charles *Helicopters and Autogiros, A History of Rotating-wing and V/STOL Aviation* (J. P. Lippincott Company, New York, 1969)

Glines, Carroll V. *Those Legendary Piper Cubs, Their Role in War and Peace* (Schiffer Publishing, Atglen, Pennsylvania, 2005)

Green, William *War Planes of the Second World War*, Volume Six, *Floatplanes* (Doubleday and Company, New York, 1962)

Gregory, H. Franklin *Anything a Horse Can Do, The Story of the Helicopter* (Cornwall Press, New York, 1944) *The Helicopter, A Pictorial History* (A. S. Barnes and Company, New Jersey, 1976)

Grossnick, Roy A. *United States Naval Aviation 1910-1995* (Naval Historical Center, Department of the Navy, Washington, D.C., 1997)

Gunston, Bill *The Illustrated Encyclopedia of the World's Rockets and Missiles* (Crescent Books, New York, 1979) *World Encyclopedia of Aircraft Manufacturers* (Sutton Publishing, Gloucestershire, UK, 2nd Edition 2005)

Gunston, Bill and Batchelor, John *Helicopters 1900-1960* (Phoebus Publishing, London, 1977)

Hall, James J. *American Kamikaze* (J. Bryant Ltd, Titusville, Florida, 1984)

Harris, Franklin D. *Introduction to Autogyros, Helicopters, and other V/STOL Aircraft*, Volume I, *Overview and Autogyros* (May 2011); Volume II: *Helicopters* (October 2012) (National Aeronautics and Space Administration, Ames Research Center, Moffett Field, California)

Hickman, Ivan *Operation Pinball* (Motorbooks International, Osceola, Wisconsin, 1990)

Holder, Bill *Unmanned Air Vehicles, An Illustrated Study of UAVs* (Schiffer Publishing, Atglen, Pennsylvania, 2001)

Holder, Bill and Vadnais, Scott *The 'C' Planes, U.S. Cargo Aircraft 1925 to the Present* (Schiffer Publishing, Atglen, Pennsylvania, 1996)

Howeth, Capt Linwood S., USN *History of Communications-Electronics in the United States Navy* (United States Government Printing Office, Washington, D.C., 1963)

Jackson, Robert *The Dragonflies, The Story of Helicopters and Autogiros* (Arthur Barker Limited, London, 1971)

Jacobsen, Meyers K. *Convair B-36, A Comprehensive History of America's 'Big Stick'* (Schiffer Publishing, North Branch, Minnesota, 1997)

Jarrett, Philip (ed) *Aircraft of the Second World War: The Development of the Warplane 1939-45* (Putnam Aeronautical Books, London, 1997)

Jenkins, Dennis R. *Convair B-36 'Peacemaker'* (WarbirdTech Series, Volume 24) (Specialty Press, North Branch, Minnesota, 2001) *Magnesium Overcast, The Story of the Convair B-36* (Specialty Press, North Branch, Minnesota, 2001)

Johnsen, Frederick A. *Bell P-39/P-63 Airacobra & Kingcobra* (WarbirdTech, Volume 17) (Specialty Press, North Branch, Minnesota, 1998)

Jones, Robert F. and Jones, Stephen E. *National Security Disasters: Their Causes and Prevention*, 2nd Edition (Communications Concepts, Cape Canaveral, Florida, 1996)

Juptner, Joseph P. *U.S. Civil Aircraft Series*, Volume Eight, (ATC 801-ATC 800) (TAB Books, Blue Ridge Summit, Pennsylvania, 1994)

Kranzhoff, Jörg Armin *Arado Ar 232 'Tatzelworkm'* (Schiffer Publishing, Atglen, Pennsylvania, 2012) *Arado, History of an Aircraft Company* (Schiffer Publishing, Atglen, Pennsylvania, 1997)

Lambermont, Paul and Pitie, Anthony *Helicopters and Autogyros of the World* (A. S. Barnes and Company, New York, 1970)

Larkins, William T. *U.S. Navy Aircraft 1921-1942, U.S. Marine Corps Aircraft 1914-1959* (Orion Books, New York, 1988)

LeMay, Curtis and Yenne, Bill *Superfortress, The Boeing B-29 and American Airpower in World War II* (Westholme, Yardley, Pennsylvania, 2007)

LePage, Wynn Laurence *Growing Up With Aviation* (Dorrance & Company, Pennsylvania, 1981)

LeVier, Tony and Guenther, John, *Pilot* (Bantam Books, New York, December 1990)

Long, Jack *Curtiss SC-1/2Seahawk*, Naval Fighters No Thirty-Eight (Steve Ginter, Simi Valley, California, 2004)

Love, Terry M. *L-Birds, American Combat Liaison Aircraft of World War II* (Flying Books International, New Brighton, Minnesota, 2001)

Lloyd, Alwyn T., *Fairchild C-82 Packet and C-119 Flying Boxcar* (Midland Publishing, England, 2005)

Machat, Mike *World's Fastest Four-Engine Piston-Powered Aircraft, Story of the Republic XF-12 Rainbow* (Specialty Press, North Branch Minnesota, 2011)

Marrett, George J. *Howard Hughes, Aviator* (Naval Institute Press, Annapolis, Maryland, 2004)

Matthews, Birch *Cobra!, Bell Aircraft Corporation 1934-1946* (Schiffer Publishing Ltd., Atglen, Pennsylvania, 1996)

McDaid, Hugh and Oliver, David *Robot Warriors, Top Secret History of Pilotless Aircraft* (Welcome Rain, New York, 1997)

Smart Weapons, Top Secret History of Remote Controlled Airborne Weapons (Welcome Rain, New York, 1997)

Mitchell, Kent A *Fairchild Aircraft 1926-1987* (Narkiewicz/Thompson, Santa Ana, California, 1997)

Mondey, David *American Aircraft of World War II* (Chancellor Press, London, 2000)

Mondey, David (ed) *The Complete Illustrated Encyclopedia of the World's Aircraft* (Chartwell Books, Secaucus, New Jersey, 1978)

Moran, Gerard P. *Aeroplanes Vought 1917-1977* (Historical Aviation Album, Temple City, California, 1977)

Morris, Charles Lester *Pioneering the Helicopter* (McGraw-Hill Book Company, New York, 1945)

Munson, Kenneth *The Pocket Encyclopedia of World Aircraft in Colour, Helicopters and Other Rotorcraft Since 1907* (Blandford Press, London, 1975)

Myall, Eric *The Hoverfly File* (Air-Britain, Kent, UK, 1997)

Myhra, David *Arado Ar 232, The Luftwaffe's Combat Zone Transport Aircraft in World War II* (Schiffer Publishing, Atglen, Pennsylvania, 2002)

Neufeld, William *Slingshot Warbirds, World War II U.S. Navy Scout-Observation Airmen* (McFarland & Company, Jefferson, North Carolina, 2003)

Newcome, Laurence R. *Unmanned Aviation, A Brief History of Unmanned Aerial Vehicles* (American Institute of Aeronautics and Astronautics, Reston, Virginia, 2004)

Nicolaou, Stéphane *Flying Boats & Seaplanes, A History from 1905* (MBI Publishing, Osceola, Wisconsin, 1998)

Norton, Bill *American Military Gliders of World War II* (Schiffer Publishing, Atglen, Pennsylvania, 2012) *American Bomber Aircraft Development in World War II* (Midland Publishing, Surrey, UK, 2012)

Nowarra, Heinz J. *German Helicopters 1928-1945* (Schiffer Publishing, Pennsylvania, 1990)

O'Leary, Michael *Lockheed P-38 Lightning, Production Line to Frontline 3* (Osprey Publishing Ltd, Oxford, UK, 1999)

Olsen, Jack *Aphrodite: Desperate Mission* (G. P. Putnam's Sons, New York, 1970)

Ord-Hume, Arthur W. J. G. *Autogiro, Rotary-wings Before the Helicopter* (Mushroom Model Publications, United Kingdom, 2009)

Pace, Steve *Boeing B-29 Superfortress* (The Crowood Press, Ramsbury, Marlborough, Wiltshire, UK, 2003)

Pape, Garry R., Campbell, John M. and Campbell, Donna *Northrop P-61 Black Widow* (Schiffer Publishing Ltd, Atglen, Pennsylvania, 1995)

Paton, Steven C. (publisher) *Yesterday, Today, Tomorrow, Fifty Years of Fairchild Aircraft* (Fairchild Hiller Corporation, not dated)

Pawle, Gerald *Secret Weapons of World War II* (Ballantine Books, New York, 1968)

Pearcy, Arthur *A History of U.S. Coast Guard Aviation* (Airlife Publishing, Shrewsbury, UK, 1989) *Lend-Lease Aircraft in World War II* (Motorbooks International, Osceola, Wisconsin, 1996)

Pelletier, A. J. *Beech Aircraft and Their Predecessors* (Naval Institute Press, Annapolis, Maryland, 1995)

Penn, Test Flying at *Old Wright Field* (Westchester House Publishers, Omaha, Nebraska, 1995)" and "Everett, H. R., *Unmanned Systems of World War I and II* (The MIT Press, Cambridge, Massachusetts, 2015)

Peperell, Roger W. *Piper Aircraft, The Development and History of Piper Designs* (Air-Britain, London, UK, 1996)

Phillips, Edward H. *Cessna, A Master's Expression* (Flying Books, Eagan, Minnesota, 1996)

Polmar, Norman *Historic Naval Aircraft, From the Pages of Naval History Magazine* (Potomac Books, Dulles, Virginia, 2006)

Raines, Edgar F. Jr. *Eyes of Artillery, The Origins of Modern U.S. Army Aviation in World War II* (Army Historical Series, Center of Military History, United States Army, Washington, D.C., 2000)

Rosendahl, Charles E. *United States Navy Airships in World War II* (Atlantic Productions and Airship International Press, 2007)

Ross, Frank Jr. *Guided Missiles: Rockets and Torpedoes* (Lothrop, Lee & Shepard Company, New York, 1951) *Flying Windmills, The Story of the Helicopter* (Museum Press, London, 1956)

Rubenstein, Murray and Goldman, Richard M. *To Join with the Eagles, Curtiss-Wright Aircraft 1903-1965* (Doubleday & Company, Garden City, New York, 1974)

Sakaida, Henry *The Siege of Rabaul* (Phalanx Publishing, St Paul, Minnesota, 1996)

Scutts, Jerry *Lockheed P-38 Lightning* (The Crowood Press Ltd, Wiltshire, UK, 2006)

Shapiro, Jacob *The Helicopter* (Frederick Muller, London, 1957)

Sharp, C. Martin and Bowyer, Michael J. F. *Mosquito* (Crécy Books, Bristol, UK, 1995)

Shock, James R. *U.S. Navy Pressure Airships 1915-1962* (M & T Printers, Florida, 1994)

Sikorsky, Igor I. *The Story of the Winged-S* (Dodd, Mead and Company, New York, 1967)

Sikorsky Aircraft, *Straight Up* (Penshurst Press, UK, 1984)

Simpson, Rod *Airlife's Helicopters & Rotorcraft* (Airlife Publishing, London, 1998)

Smith, Frank Kingston *Legacy or Wings, The Harold F. Pitcairn Story* (T-D Associated, Pennsylvania, 1981)

Smith, Peter C. *Curtiss SB2C Helldiver* (The Crowood Press, Wiltshire, UK, 1998)

Spenser, Jay P. *Vertical Challenge, The Hiller Aircraft Story* (1st Books Library, Bloomington, Indiana, 2003) *Whirlybirds, A History of the U.S. Helicopter Pioneers* (University of Washington Press, Seattle, 1998)

Stanley, Roy M., *World War II Photo Intelligence* (Charles Scribner's Sons, New York, 1981)

Stoff, Joshua *The Thunder Factory: An Illustrated History of the Republic Aviation Corporation* (Motorbooks International, Osceola, Wisconsin, 1990)

Swanborough, Gordon and Bowers, Peter M. *United States Military Aircraft Since 1909* (Putnam Aeronautical Books, London, 1989) *United States Navy Aircraft Since 1911* (Putnam Aeronautical Books, London, 1976)

Taylor, John W. R. *Images of America, Sikorsky* (Tempus Publishing, Gloucestershire, UK, 1998)

Thomason, Tommy H. *The Forgotten Bell HSL, U.S. Navy's First All-Weather Anti-Submarine Warfare Helicopter*, Naval Fighters No Seventy (Steve Ginter, Simi Valley, California, 2005)

Thompson, Warren E. *Northrop P-61 Black Widow* (WarbirdTech Volume 15) (Specialty Press, North Branch, Minnesota, 1997)

Townson, George *Autogiro, The Story of 'the Windmill Plane'* (Autogiro, Trenton, 1985)

Trimble, William F. *High Frontier, A History of Aeronautics in Pennsylvania* (University of Pittsburgh Press, Pittsburgh, Pennsylvania, 1982) *Wings for the Navy: A History of the Naval Aircraft Factory, 1917-1956* (Naval Institute Press, Annapolis Maryland, 1990)

Underwood, John W. *The Stinsons* (Heritage Press, Glendale, California, 1982)

Wagner, Ray *American Combat Planes of the 20th Century* (Jack Bacon & Company, Reno, Nevada, 2004)

Wagner, Van R. D. *Any Place, Any Time, Any Where: The 1st Air Commandos in World War II* (Schiffer Publishing, Pennsylvania, 1998)

Wegg, John *General Dynamics Aircraft and Their Predecessors* (Naval Institute Press, Annapolis, Maryland, 1990)

Werrell, Kenneth P. *The Evolution of the Cruise Missile* (Air University Press, Maxwell Air Force Base, Alabama, September 1985)

White, Graham *Allied Aircraft Piston Engines of World War II* (Society of Automotive Engineers, Inc, Warrendale, Pennsylvania, 1995)
R-4360, Pratt & Whitney's Major Miracle (Specialty Press, North Branch, Minnesota, 2006)

Wildenberg, Thomas and Davies, R. E. G. *Howard Hughes, An Airman, His Aircraft, and His Great Flights* (Paladwr Press, McLean, Virginia, 2006)

Witkowski, Ryszard *Allied Rotorcraft of the WW2 Period* (Stratus, Poland, 2010)
Rotorcraft of the Third Reich (Stratus, Poland, 2007)

Wolf, William *Boeing B-29 Superfortress, The Ultimate Look: From Drawing Board to VJ-Day* (Schiffer Publishing, Atglen, Pennsylvania, 2005)
U.S. Aerial Armament in World War II, The Ultimate Look, Volume 3, *Air-Launched Rockets, Mines, Torpedoes, Guided Missiles, and Secret Weapons* (Schiffer Publishing, Pennsylvania, 2010)

Wragg, David *Helicopters at War, A Pictorial History* (St Martin's Press, New York, 1983)

Yenne, Bill *Attack of the Drones, A History of Unmanned Aerial Combat* (Zenith Press, St Paul, Minnesota, 2004)
Birds of Prey, Predators, Reapers and America's Newest UAVs in Combat (Specialty Press, North Branch, Minnesota, 2010)
Seaplanes of the World, A Timeless Collection from Aviation's Golden Age (First Glance Books, Cobb, California, 1997)
Secret Gadgets and Strange Gizmos (Zenith Press, St Paul, Minnesota, 2005)

Zaloga, Steve J. *Unmanned Aerial Vehicles, Robotic Air Warfare 1919-2007*, New Vanguard 144 (Osprey Publishing, Oxford, United Kingdom, 2008)

Monographs

Adcock, Al, 'OS2U Kingfisher in Action', Aircraft No 119 (Squadron/Signal Publications, Carrollton, Texas, 1991)

'TBD Devastator in Action', Aircraft No 97 (Squadron/Signal Publications, Carrollton, Texas, 2005)

'US Liaison Aircraft in Action', Aircraft No 195 (Squadron/Signal Publications, Carrollton, Texas, 2006)

'U.S. Navy Floatplanes in Action, Aircraft No 203 (Squadron/Signal Publications, Carrollton, Texas, 2006)

Anderson, Holmes G. 'The Lockheed Constellation', Profile No 120 (Profile Publications, Surrey, UK, 1966)

Andrews, Harold 'The Curtiss SB2C-1 Helldiver', Profile No. 124 (Profile Publications, Leatherhead, Surrey, UK, 1966)

Bell, Dana 'OS2U Kingfisher', Aircraft Pictorial No 3 (Classic Warships Publishing, Tucson, Arizona, 2010)

Dann, Richard S. 'F4F Wildcat in Action', Aircraft No 191 (Squadron/Signal Publications, Carrollton, Texas, 2004)

Davis, Larry 'C-47 Skytrain in Action', Aircraft No 149 (Squadron/Signal Publications, Carrollton, Texas, 1995)

Doll, Tom 'SB2U Vindicator in Action', Aircraft No 122 (Squadron/Signal Publications, Carrollton, Texas, 1992)

Doll, Thomas E. and Jackson, Berkely R. 'Vought-Sikorsky OS2U Kingfisher', Aircraft Profile 251 (Profile Publications, Berkshire, UK, June 1972)

Fahey, James C. 'U.S. Army Aircraft, 1908-1946' (Ships and Aircraft, New York, 1946)

Ginter, Steve 'Douglas TBD-1 Devastator', Naval Fighters No 71 (Steve Ginter, Simi Valley, California, 2006)

'Grumman JF/J2F Duck', Naval Fighters No 84 (Steve Ginter, Simi Valley, California, 2009)

'Lockheed R6O/R6V Constitution', Naval Fighters No 83 (Steve Ginter, Simi Valley, California, 2009)

"The Reluctant Dragon", The Curtiss SO3C Seagull/Seamew', Naval Fighters No 38 (Steve Ginter, Simi Valley, California, 1999)

Harding, Stephen and Long, James I. 'Dominator, The Story of the Consolidated B-32 Bomber' (Pictorial Histories Publishing Company, Missoula, Montana, 1983)

Hatfield, D. D. 'Howard Hughes H-4 "Hercules", Aircraft Series, Hatfield History of Aeronautics (Aviation History Library, Northrop Institute of Technology, Historical Airplanes, Los Angeles, California, 1972)

House, Kirk W. 'Images of America, Curtiss-Wright' (Arcadia Publishing, Charleston, South Carolina, 2007)

Jackson, B. R. and Doll, T. E. 'Douglas TBD-1 "Devastator", Aero Series Vol 23 (Aero Publishing, Fallbrook, California, 1973)

Jones, Lloyd S. 'Fax-File Volume 1' (Aerolus Publishing, Vista, California, 1987)

'Fax-File No 12' (Pacific Aero Press, Vista, California)

Kinzey, Bert 'F4F Wildcat, In Detail & Scale', Volume 65 (Squadron/Signal Publications, Carrollton, Texas, 2000)

'P-38 Lightning, Part 1, In Detail & Scale', Volume 57 (Squadron/Signal Publications, Carrollton, Texas, 1998)

'SB2C Helldiver, In Detail & Scale', Volume 52 (Squadron/Signal Publications, Carrollton, Texas, 1997)

Larkins, William T. 'The Curtiss SOC Seagull', Profile 194 (Profile Publications, Surrey, UK, undated)

Lloyd, Alwyn T. 'B-17 Flying Fortress, Part 3, More Derivatives, In Detail & Scale', Volume 20 (Tab Books, Blue Ridge Summit, Pennsylvania, 1986)

Love, Terry 'C-46 Commando in Action', Aircraft No 188 (Squadron/Signal Publications, Carrollton, Texas, 2003)

Maloney, Edward T. 'Lockheed P-38 "Lightning", Aero Series Volume 19 (Aero Publishing, Fallbrook, California, 1968)

Mayborn, Mitch 'The Ryan PT/ST Series', Profile 158 (Profile Publications, Surrey, UK, undated)

McDowell, Ernie 'P-39 Airacobra in Action', Aircraft No 43 (Squadron/Signal Publications, Carrollton, Texas, 1980)

Mesko, Jim 'A-20 Havoc in Action', Aircraft No 144 (Squadron/Signal Publications, Carrollton, Texas, 1994)

Nowarra, Heinz J. 'German Helicopters 1929-1945' (Schiffer Publishing, Pennsylvania, 1990)

Stern, Robert 'SB2C Helldiver in Action', Aircraft No 54 (Squadron/Signal Publications, Carrollton, Texas, 1982)

Schwartz, Milton L. and Maguglin, Robert O. 'The Howard Hughes Flying Boat' (Wrather Corporation, Rosebud Books, The Knapp Press, United States, 1983)

Weber, Le Roy 'The P-38J – M Lockheed Lightning', Profile No 106 (Profile Publications Ltd, Leatherhead, Surrey, UK, 1966)

Woodring, Frank and Suanne 'Images of America, Fairchild Aircraft' (Arcadia Publishing, Charleston, South Carolina, 2005)

Periodicals

Allen, Francis, 'Ambitious "Eggbeater"', *Air Enthusiast*, May/June 2004, pp26-30

Allen, Francis, 'Kellett's Whirling Eggbeater', *Wings*, August 1990, pp34-45

Allen II, Francis J., 'Ugly Duckling', *Wings*, August 2003, pp14-27

Allen II, Francis J., 'A Duck Without Feathers', *Air Enthusiast*, No 23, December 1983-March 1984, pp46-55 and 77-78

Anon, 'American Aircraft Bombs 1917-1974', *Replica in Scale*, Spring/Summer 1974, Vol 2 No 3 & 4, pp126-49

Anon, 'Grumman (G-36) F4F-3S', *Air International*, April 1981, p206

Anon, 'The Howard Hughes Legend', Part 3 'The Final Chapter', *Take Off*, Part 39, 1988, pp1078-85

Anon, 'Hughes Flying Boat', *Air Classics*, February 1981, pp41-53

Anon, 'Hughes' Jinxed Giant', *Wings*, December 1982, pp10-15

Anon, 'The Immortal DC-3', Part 2 'War and Peace', *Take Off*, No 53, Vol 5, 1989, pp1480-87

Anon, 'A Page from History, OS2U Kingfisher', *Approach*, March 1972, pp?

Anon, 'The Curtiss "Caravan"', *Aero Digest*, date unknown, pp186 and 187

Anon, 'The Howard Hughes Legend (Part 2): In Peace and War', *Take Off*, Vol 4 Part 38, 1988, pp1052-59

Anon, 'The Lockheed Constitution', *The Aeroplane*, 6 September 1946, p287

Anon, 'Monoplane "Duck"', *Air Enthusiast*, November 1971, p262

Anon, 'More on the Norwegian Northrop N-3PB', *Small Air Forces Observer*, No 23 April 1982, pp87 and 91

Anon, 'Navy's Helicopter For Land or Sea Has Twin Rotors', *Popular Mechanics Magazine*, November 1945, p49

Anon, 'The Noon Balloon', The Official Newsletter of the Naval Airship Association, Inc, No 81, Spring 2009, p10; discussion of the Glimpy project by three individuals, no specific article

Anon, 'OSE', *Naval Aviation News*, April 1976, pp20-21

Anon, 'Pilotless Aircraft', *Naval Aviation News*, January 1946, pp19-21

Anon, 'Radio Robots', *Naval Aviation News*, July 1951, pp1-5

Anon, 'A Remarkable Republic', *Air Enthusiast International*, February 1974, pp84-85

Anon, 'Short-Hop Helicopter', *Popular Science*, April 1946, p104

Anon, 'The Sikorsky Story (Part 2): Whirlybirds', *Take Off*, Vol 10 Part 113, 1990, p3160-67

Anon, 'US Navy Inter-War Floatplanes', *Take Off*, No 101, Vol 9, 1990, pp2832-36

Anon, no title (short mention of XR-1A testing), *Popular Science*, October 1944, p78

Antone, Jay, 'Interstate Drone', *Air Classics*, Vol 43 No 6, June 2007, pp52-53

Barr, Louis, 'The Lockheed Constellation: A History, Part I', *AAHS Journal*, Vol 28, Nos 3/4, Fall/Winter 1983, pp190-205

Barton, Charles, 'XF-11: The Plane That Almost Killed Howard Hughes', *Air Classics*, April 1983, pp62-71 and 80-82

Beard, Tom, "Number Two": Helicopter Pioneer Stewart Ross Graham', *AAHS Journal*, Vol 57 No 2, pp127-139, Summer 2012
'Number Two;' Helicopter Pioneer Stewart Ross Graham, Part II', *AAHS Journal*, Vol 57 No 3, pp162-175, Fall 2012

Berry, P., 'Interstate TDR-1', *Air Pictorial*, September 1967, pp328-29

Berry, Peter, 'Budd RB-1 Conestoga' (letter), *AAHS Journal*, Vol 41, No 2, Summer 1996, p158

Bodie, Warren, 'Sky Bolt IV', *Wings*, August 1976, pp8-28 and 66
Sky Bolt, Conclusion', *Wings*, August 1978, pp10-53 and 62-63

Bonner, Kit, 'Cowboy in the Clouds', *FlyPast*, No 172, November 1995, pp89-90
'Army Seaplanes Pt. II', *Airpower*, September 1997, pp9-11 and 34-41
'Constellation! Pt. I The Airliners', *Wings*, October 1990, pp8-21 and 46, and 48-55
'Constellation! Pt. II', *Airpower*, November 1990, pp10-23 and 42-55
'Dog of War Pt. II', *Wings*, February 1996, pp8-45
Of Wings & Things, Volume 1:1972-1979 (Reprints from *The Flyer*, Flyer Media, Lakewood, Washington, 2000)
'The DC-3 in Uniform, Army Production Models – C-47s, C-53s and C-117s', *Wings*, February 1981, pp8-19 and 40-48
'Sea Scouts', *Wings*, February 1985, pp32-52
'Bomb Ten, Scout Five, Spot One!', *Wings*, February 1988, pp10-23 and 39-51 and 55
'Fleet Ranger', *Airpower*, July 1993, pp10-21 and 52-55
'King of the Deep Pt I', *Airpower*, January 1990, pp10-19 and 50-55
'King of the Deep Pt. II', *Wings*, February 1990, pp10-19 and 50-55
'Ryan S-T, The Sportplane That Went to War', *Wings*, April 1987, pp38-54
'Stratofreighter, Pt I', *Airpower*, July 1999, pp18-49
'Streamlining, Pt II', *Airpower*, November 1991, pp10-25 and 34-43

Boyne, Walter J., 'Airplanes – Great, and Not So Great', *Aviation Quarterly*, Vol 3, No 1, First Quarter 1977, pp15-45 'Super Bomber', *Wings*, October 1973, pp10-39 'C-76 'The Basketcase Bummer', *Airpower*, May 1974, pp60-65
'The Most Elusive Hughes … The D-2/F-11 Recon. Bomber', *Wings*, June 1977, pp44-55

Brazelton, David, 'The Curtiss SOC Seagull', *AAHS Journal*, Vol 3, No 3, July-September 1958, pp167-71

Chana, Bill, 'The XC-99', *AAHS Journal*, Vol 46, No 4, Winter 2001, pp319-20

Christy, Joe, 'Commando Extraordinaire', *Airpower,* May 1973, pp22-35 and 67

Daniels, C.M., 'Skymaster', *Airpower*, January 1974, pp46-60
'Winged Workhorse', *Airpower*, July 1973, pp8-19

Dean, Jack, 'Eyes of the Fleet', *Airpower*, July 1997, pp44-55
'Grumman's Seabirds', *Wings*, August 1994, pp8-31 and 48-55
'Old Shaky', *Wings*, February 1992, pp44-53

Donald, David, 'All the Fours, The Republic XF-12', *Wings of Fame*, Vol 3, 1996, pp26-33
'Lockheed P-38 Lightning "Fork-tailed Devil"', *International Air Power Review*, Vol 14, 2004, pp124-155

Editors, 'The Annals of Sugar Baker Two Uncle', *Air Enthusiast Quarterly*, No 8, October 1978-January 1979, pp1-8 and 74-79

Editors, 'Commando, A Dove from Curtiss-Wright', *Air Enthusiast*, No 34, September-December 1987, pp25-42

Erickson, Frank A., 'The First Coast Guard Helicopters', *Proceedings*, July 1981, pp62-66

Fahrney, Delmar S., 'Guided Missiles (U.S. Navy the Pioneer)', *AAHS Journal*, Vol 27, No 1, Spring 1982, pp15-28
'The Birth of Guided Missiles', *Proceedings*, United States Naval Institute, Vol 106/12/934, December 1980, pp54-60

Friederichsen, Roland C., 'The Story of a Patrol Plane Pilot 1942-1954', *AAHS Journal*, Vol 57, No 3, Fall 19201292, pp190-209

Francillon, René, '"Connies" in Uniform, Lockheed's Constellation/Super Constellation Military Variants', *Wings of Fame*, Volume 20, 2000, pp112-139

Gregg, E. Stuart, 'Jump Ship', *Air & Space*, March 2001, pp14-15

Griffin, Larry, 'Grumman's Immortal Duck', *Historical Aviation Album*, Vol VI, 1969, pp37-47

Hagedorn, Dan, letter regarding RB-1, *AAHS Journal*, Vol 59, No 1, Spring 2014, p73-74

Halcomb, Mal, 'Vertical Lift', *Airpower*, March 1990, pp10-21 and 38-45

Hallion, Richard P, 'The Republic XF-12/RC-2 Rainbow, Twilight of the Piston-Powered Airplane', *Aviation Quarterly*, Vol 3, No 1, First Quarter 1977, pp62-86

Hallstead, William F., 'The U.S. Navy's Kamikazes', *Aviation History*, January 2004, pp50-56 and 79

Hammer, L. M., 'Lockheed XR6O-1 Constitution', *AAHS Journal*, Vol 43, No 2, Summer 1998, pp110-12

Hendrix, Lin, 'The Republic XR-12 Rainbow', *AAHS Journal*, Vol 21, No 4, Winter 1976, pp282-85

'Hughes' Twin Boomer', *Aeroplane Monthly*, October 1984, pp512-516

Heslop, Nancy Caravan, 'A Story of the Budd RB-1 Conestoga', *AAHS Journal*, Vol 58, No 4, Winter 2013, pp275-85

Historical Division Intelligence, T-2, 'Development of Transport Airplanes and Air Transport Equipment', Air Technical Services Command, Wright Field, April 1946, reprinted in *AAHS Journal*, Part III, Vol 45, No 3, Fall 2000, pp162-75; Part IV, Vol 45, No 4, Winter 2000, pp276-93; Part V, Vol 46, No 1, Spring 2001, pp32-39; Part VI, Vol 46, No 3, Fall 2001, pp208-23

Jesse, William, 'Budd's Covered Wagon, The RB-1 Conestoga', *Air Enthusiast*, No 69, May-June 1997, pp73-75
'Last Waterbird, Edo XOSE-1 – The U.S. Navy's Last Floatplane', *Air Enthusiast*, No 86, March/April 2000, p70

Kavelaars, H. C., 'The Air Transport Department of the Shell Company of Ecuador 1937-1950', Part 1, *AAHS Journal*, Vol 31, No 2, Summer 1986, pp92-105

Kuhn, Leo J., 'Early Workhorse Helicopter', *Armchair Aviator*, Vol 2, No 6, July 1973, p37-40
'Conestoga', *Armchair Aviator*, Vol 1, No 3 December 1972, pp38-40
'The Culver V', *Armchair Aviator*, Vol 2, No 3, March-April 1973, pp11-14
'Firestone's Helicopter', *Armchair Aviator*, Vol 2, No 2, February 1973, pp33-34
'Igor Sikorsky's Triumph', *Armchair Aviator*, Vol 1, No 2, November 1972, pp39-42
'Last 'Last Chance' for the Autogiro', *Armchair Aviator*, Vol 1, No 3, December 1972, pp35-37

'Vigilant', *Armchair Aviator*, Vol 1, No 3, December 1972, pp41-45
'Firestone XR-9 (GA-45)', *World War II Journal*, No 15, p64

Larson, George A, 'The XC-99 – Convair's Very Heavy Transport', *AAHS Journal*, Vol 46, No 3, Fall 2001, pp162-69

Lawrence, Thomas H., 'The Sikorsky R-4 Helicopter', *Advanced Materials & Processes*, August 2003, pp57-59

Lowe, Thomas E., 'Rare Interstate Bomber Flies Again', *AAHS Journal*, Vol 22, No 4, Winter 1977, pp308-11

Machat, Mike, 'Bring in the Choppers!', *Wings*, October 2003, pp14-27
'Somewhere, Under the Rainbow', *Wings*, April 1994, pp8-19 and 50-55

Marrett, George, 'Flights into the Future', *Wings*, December 2005, pp16-27
'The Mystery Ship', *Wings*, February 2005, pp44-55

Marson, Peter J., 'Constellation, Lockheed's "Queen of the Skies"', *Air Enthusiast*, No 14, December 1980-March 1981, pp29-42 and 76-78

Marthason, A., 'The Republic Rainbow', *The Aeroplane*, Part I, 6 December 1946, pp686-91; Part II, 13 December 1946, pp718-22

McCarthy, Dan, 'The Desert Bound Amphibian', *Air Classics*, Vol 9, No 12, December 1973, pp40-47

McCullough, Anson, 'Load 'Em Up!', *Airpower*, November 1996, pp8-33

McKee, Angus, 'Helicopter Rescue!', *Air Classics Quarterly Review*, Vol 5, No 4, Winter 1978, pp58-61

Mitchell, Kent A., 'Armand J. Thieblot, Aircraft Designer', *AAHS Journal*, Vol 48, No 1, Spring 2003, pp28-35
'The Fairchild C-82 Packet', *AAHS Journal*, Vol 44, No 1, Spring 1999, pp2-15
'The Saga of the Fairchild AT-21', *AAHS Journal*, Vol 32, No 3, Fall 1987, p171

Mizrahi, Joe, 'Production Wars', *Wings*, October 1991, pp28-47 and 50-53

Morely, Richard A., 'The Ohio-Curtiss Airplane Connection, Curtiss-Wright Division in Columbus 1940-1950', *AAHS Journal*, Vol 36, No 3, Fall 1991, pp184-199
'The Ohio-Curtiss Airplane Connection, An Addendum', *AAHS Journal*, Vol 37, No 2, Summer 1992, pp104-11

Morfis, Gus, 'The Northrop N-3PB, Norway's Patrol Bomber', *Small Air Forces Observer*, No 17, October 1980, pp13 and 15

Mormillo, Frank B., 'Defenceless Warrior, Culver's PQ-14 Drone', *Air Enthusiast*, No 93, May/June 2001, pp6-7

Noles, James L. Jr., 'Old Slow & Ugly', *Air & Space*, March 2005, pp66-73

O'Leary, Michael, 'Flying the Circuit with the Flying Tigers', *Air Classics*, Vol 9, No 11, November 1973, pp26-33

Olmsted, Merle, 'Helicopter Rescue in the Early Years', *AAHS Journal*, Vol 21, No 2, Summer 1976, pp112-17

Owen, Steve, letter regarding RB-1, *AAHS Journal*, Vol 59, No 1, Spring 2014, p73

Pape, Garry R., Campbell, John M. and Campbell, Donna 'The Airplane Designs of Hughes Aircraft Company', *AAHS Journal*, Vol 55, No 3, Fall 2010, pp182-95.
'Framing and Flying the Constitution', *Airpower*, March 1977, pp10-17 and 64-67

Peck, James L. H., 'Who is Yehudi?', *Popular Science*, December 1945, pp93-96 and 224

Premselaar, Joel, ''Launch Aircraft!'' The Story of WWII Battleship and Cruiser Seaplane Operations', *Airpower*, November 2004, pp44-55

Ragnarsson, Ragnar J., 'Phantom of the Fjords, Northrop's N-3PB Flying Viking!', *Wings*, February 1981, pp24-39 and 50-51

Redman, Rod, 'Airborne Robots, How the Navy Developed Drones & Missiles', *Sea Classics*, January 2005, pp?

Rhodes, H. N., 'The Death of Joseph P. Kennedy Jr.', *AAHS Journal*, Vol 53, No 1, Spring 2008, pp69-70

Riviere, Pierre and Beauchamp, Gerry, 'Autogyros at War', *Air Classics Quarterly Review*, Vol 3, No 4, Winter 1976, pp92-97

Rodina, Matthew, 'Columbia XJL', *AAHS Journal*, Vol 29, No 2, Summer 1984, pp136-40

Roos, Frederick W., 'Curtiss-Wright St Louis', *AAHS Journal*, Vol 35, No 4, Winter 1990, pp293-305
'Make Me in St Louis', *Airpower*, July 1992, pp36-55

Schoeni, Art, 'Mayday! Mayday!', *Aeroplane Monthly*, November 1979, pp570-77

Scott, Neal T. and Vivell, Earl, 'General Motors Aerial Torpedo', *AAHS Journal*, Vol 13, No 1, Spring 1968, p65

Scutts, Jerry, 'Vought Kingfisher', *Air International*, January 1996, pp50-53

Smith, Frank Kingston, 'Mr Pitcairn's Autogiros', *Airpower*, March 1983, pp28-49

Spark, Nick, 'Command Break: The Battle Over America's Secret WWII Cruise Missile', *Proceedings*, United State Naval Institute, February 2005, pp?
'The Secret Weapons of World War II', *Wings*, Vol 34, No 10, October 2004, pp40-56

Spenser, Jay, 'Flying Bull's Eye', *Wings*, Vol 12, No 3, June 1982, pp30-33

Stringfellow, Curtis K. 'When the Army Flew Connies!', *Air Classics*, August 1990, pp14-24

Taylor, H. A., 'Skymaster Story … The Fourth Douglas Commercial', *Air Enthusiast*, No 15, 1981, pp38-48 and 78-80

Thompson, Warren, 'The First F-15', *Wings*, August 1988, pp10-17 and 54-55
'Northrop P-61 Black Widow', *Wings of Fame*, Vol 15, 1999, pp36-101
'The Reporter Reported', *Air Enthusiast*, No 30, March-June 1986, pp27-33

Vincent, David, 'Kangaroo Kingfisher, The Vought OS2U-3 in Australian Service', *Air Enthusiast*, No 77, September/October 1998, pp54-62

Wagg, Robert J. 'Kingcobra, America's Great Giveaway Fighter', *Airpower*, September 1973, pp16-23 and 58-61

Wallace, J. J., 'Use of Wood in Aircraft Design and Construction – Part I', *Aero Digest*, pp190-91, 284, 288 and 290

Watter, Michael, 'The Budd RB-1', *AAHS Journal*, Vol 12, No 1, Spring 1961, pp54-61

Werrell, Kenneth P, 'The Forgotten Missile: The Kettering-General Motors A-1', *AAHS Journal*, Vol 30, No 4, Winter 1985, pp284-293

Westell, Freeman, 'Fast Freight', *Airpower*, May 1998, pp40-55 'Japan's Forlorn Floatplane Flotilla', *Airpower*, July 2000, pp46-55

Wildenberg, Thomas, 'A Visionary Ahead of His Time: Howard Hughes and the U.S. Air Force', Part II 'The Hughes D-2 and the XF-11', *Air Power History*, Spring 2008, pp16-27

Williams, Nicholas M., 'Bug-Eyed Monster: The Douglas Model 415A, the First Globemaster and DC-7', *Air Enthusiast*, No 60, November-December 1995, pp40-53
'Globemaster, The Douglas C-74', *AAHS Journal*, Vol 25, No 2, Summer 1980, pp82-103

Wixey, Ken, 'Commando', *FlyPast*, March 1990, pp27-30
''Flying Fuel Cans'', Vought's SB2U Vindicator', *Air Enthusiast*, No 86, March/April 2000, pp62-69

Wolf, William, 'America's First Helicopters', *AAHS Journal*, Vol 33, No 1, Spring 1988, pp26-43

Wood, J. P, 'Three Curtiss Scouts', published for the International Plastic Modelers Society (IPMS), USA National Convention, San Francisco, California, 1977

Wright, Jay E., 'Whazzit?', *AAHS Journal*, Vol 39, No 2, Summer 1994, p160

Manuals

Constitution, Erection and Maintenance Instructions, Navy Model XR6O-1 Airplane (Lockheed Aircraft Corporation, Burbank, California, 1 June 1948, revised 15 May 1949)

Familiarization and Inspection Manual for the C-54A (Material Center, Wright Field, Dayton, Ohio, undated)

Handbook Flight Operating Instructions for USAF Series H-5A, D and E Navy Model HO2S-1 Helicopters, AN 01-230HB-1, 29 May 1951

Handbook Flight Operating Instructions, USAF Series C-74 Aircraft, AN-01-40NT-1, 20 December 1946, revised 26 February 1952

Handbook Flight Operating Instructions, USAF Series C-82A, T.O. No 1C-82A-1, 27 August 1947, revised 1 March 1954

Handbook Flight Operating Instructions for USAF XC-99 Airplane, 31 March 1949

Hughes Flying Boat Manual (Hughes Tool Company Aircraft Division, undated)

Pilot's Flight Operating Instructions for Army Model C-54A and Navy Model R5D-1 Airplanes, AN 01-40NM-1, 25 June 1944, revised 15 March 1945

Pilot's Flight Operating Instructions for Army Model C-69 Airplane, AN 01-75CJ-1, 20 January 1945, revised 15 July 1945

Pilot's Flight Operating Instructions for Army Model C-93 Navy Model RB-1 Airplanes, AN 01-185CA-1, 15 February 1944

Pilot's Handbook for Army Model R-6A Navy Model HOS-1, Helicopters, AN 01-230HC-1, 5 July 1945, revised 20 December 1945

Pilot's Flight Operating Instructions for Helicopters Army Model R-5A Navy Model HO2S-1, AN 01-230HB-1, 5 September 1945

Pilot's Handbook, Flight Operating Instructions for XF-11 Airplane, Report No HAC-01-197-SP, undated

Pilot's Handbook for Navy Model R6O-1 Airplanes, NAVAER 01-75CLA-501, 1 July 1949, revised 1 May 1950

Pilot Training Manual for the C-47 Skytrain, AAF Manual 51-129-2 (Headquarters, Army Air Forces, 15 August 1945)

Pilot Training Manual for the C-46 Commando, AAF Manual 50-16 (Headquarters, Army Air Forces, undated)

Pilot Training Manual for the C-54 Skymaster, AAF Manual 50-14 (Headquarters, Army Air Forces, undated)

Pilot Operating Instructions, C-47 Airplane, Technical Order No 01-40NC-1 (Headquarters, Army Air Forces, revised 25 November 1942)

Reports

AAF Historical Office, Headquarters, Army Air Forces, Evolution of the Liaison-Type Airplane 1917-1944 (Army Air Forces Historical Studies: No 44, April 1946)

Air Research and Development Command, United States Air Force, Air Force Developmental Aircraft, April 1957

AMC Historical Division, Historical Data on Aircraft Developed But Not Produced, 1945-Present, Cargos: History of the XC-99 Airplane, March 1957

Anon, Army Aircraft Characteristics, Production and Experimental, Report No TSEST – A2, ATSC (Wright Field, Ohio, United States Army, 1 April 1946)

Anon, Case Study of C-76 Contract Termination, 14 December 1943

Anon, The Development of Guided Missiles (Historical Division, Intelligence, Air Materiel Command, Wright Field, June 1946)

Anon, Progress Report of Army Air Forces, Pilotless Aircraft as Guided Missiles, Development Status and Availability, AAF PAR-AB (Handbook of Guided Missiles) Report Number AAF-MD-E 98 (HQ Air Technical Service Command, Wright Field, Dayton, Ohio, 2 August 1945, revised through 1 January 1946)

Anon, Report on the C-76 Airplane, Draft, 2 August 1943

Anon, Research and Development Projects of the Engineering Division, Fourth Edition, 1 January 1944

Anon, Summary of Power Driven Weapons Developed by Special Weapons Branch, Equipment Laboratory, MX-53, 20 November 1943, within Appendix B pp902-09 of The Development of Guided Missiles (Historical Division, Intelligence, Air Materiel Command, Wright Field, June 1946)

Belknap, Kothe and Pesta, Actual Weight and Balance Report for Airplane #5 Model C-76 Serial No 2-86917 Factory No 7567 Contract No AC-27018, Report No 27-W3 (Curtiss-Wright Corporation, Airplane Division, Engineering Department, St Louis, 19 July 1943)

Bogert, H. Z., Colonel, Air Corps, Chief, Technical Staff, Engineering Division, Research and Development Projects of the Engineering Division, Fourth Edition, 1 January 1944

Finley, H. B., Detail Weight Statement – Preliminary Model XR-9, AU-115 (G & A Aircraft, 11 August 1944)

Detail Weight Statement – Preliminary Model XR-9, AU-117 (G & A Aircraft, 11 August 1944)

Preliminary Group Weight Statement Model XR-9, AU-117 (G & A Aircraft, 19 October 1944)

XR-9 Weight and Balance Status, AU-120-W (G & A Aircraft, 19 October 1944)

XR-9 Weight and Balance Status, AU-126-W (G & A Aircraft, 19 January 1945)

XR-9 Weight and Balance Status, AU-132-W (G & A Aircraft, 20 February 1945)

XR-9 Weight and Balance Status, AU-135-W (G & A Aircraft, 20 March 1945)

Fischel, Capt J. R. and Miller, W. B, Aircraft Laboratory, Memorandum Report 'Investigation of Crash of C-76 Airplane (A.F. Serial No 42-86918) Near Louisville, Kentucky, ENG-51/0359-17', 20 May 1943

Futrell, Robert F., Command of Observation Aviation: A Study of Control of Tactical Airpower (USAF Historical Studies, No 24, USAF Historical Division, Maxwell AFB, Alabama, September 1956)

Historical Division, Intelligence, T-2, Air Materiel Command, Wright Field, Case History of Controlled Missiles – Aircraft, Part II – Castor, 24 July 1945, document fragment on microfilm reel A2083 (as digitized) from the Air Force Historical Research Agency, frames 230-72

Historical Division, Intelligence, T-2, Air Technical Services Command, Wright Field, Case History of XF-12 Airplane, January 1946

Historical Office, Air Technical Services Command, Case History of C-76 Airplane, Wright Field, October 1944

Historical Office, Air Technical Services Command, Case History of the F-7 Airplane, Wright Field, August 1945

Historical Division, Intelligence, T-2, Air Materiel Command, Wright Field, Case History of Hughes D-2, D-5, F-11 Project, August 1946

Historical Division, Intelligence, T-2, Air Materiel Command, Wright Field, Case History of XF-12 Airplane, January 1946

Kemmer, Col Paul M. and Fischel, Capt J. R., Aircraft Laboratory, Materiel Command, Memorandum Report on Conference on C-76 Airplane at Curtiss-Wright Plant, Louisville, Kentucky, ENG-51/C359-21, 18 June 1943

Knighton, Capt James D., Fischel, Capt J. R., and Kemmer, Col Paul M., Engineering Division, Aircraft Laboratory, Memorandum Report on Investigation of Production Materials Used on C-76 Airplanes, ENG-51-C359-10 Addendum 16, 19 August 1943

Lest, Capt Jack, Bogert, Col H. Z., and Carroll, Brig Gen F. O., Air Corps, Memorandum Report on Remote Controlled Aircraft, Power Driven (Man-Carrying) – MX-53/MX-264, Serial No ENG-M-50-810, Engineering Division, Materiel Division, 5 February 1943, within Appendix B, pp869-74 of The Development of Guided Missiles (Historical Division, Intelligence, Air Materiel Command, Wright Field, June 1946)

Air Corps, Memorandum Report on Controllable Bombs, Power Driven, Ground Launched – MX-53, Serial No ENG-M-50-820 Engineering Division, Materiel Division, 1 March 1943, within Appendix B, pp 876-82 of The Development of Guided Missiles (Historical Division, Intelligence, Air Materiel Command, Wright Field, June 1946)

Perry, J. P, July Progress Report XR-9 Helicopter, AU-107 (G & A Aircraft, July 1944)

August Progress Report XR-9 Helicopter, AU-110 (G & A Aircraft, August 1944)

September Progress Report XR-9 Helicopter and Appendix, AU-115 (G & A Aircraft, September 1944)

Appendix to September Progress Report XR-9 Helicopter, AU-115-A (G & A Aircraft, September 1944)

October Progress Report XR-9 Helicopter and Appendix, AU-120 (G & A Aircraft, October 1944)

November Progress Report XR-9 Helicopter and Appendix, AU-124 (G & A Aircraft, November 1944)

December Progress Report XR-9 Helicopter and Appendix, AU-126 (G & A Aircraft, December 1944)

Proctor, Maj Phimister B., Materiel Division, 'Memorandum Report on Investigation of Inspection Policies and Procedures, C-76 Airplane, Curtiss-Wright Corp, Louisville, Ky., and Subcontractors, INSP-M-3A-(255)', 16 July 1943

Reisert, Thomas D., Tests of 1/17-Scale Model of the XBDR-1 Airplane in the NACA Gust Tunnel, National Advisory Committee for Aeronautics Memorandum Report L-539, 3 February 1944

Resources Division, teletype to Commanding General, Materiel Command, 12 July 1943

Rotary Wing Branch (TSEOA-5) Aircraft Projects Section, Engineering Division, Summary of Rotary Wing Projects of Aircraft Projects Section (By Model), Air Materiel Command, February 1947

Sessums, Col J. W. Jr., Chief, roduction Branch, Materiel Division, Memorandum Report of Second Meeting on Standardization of Transports, Held April 20, 1943 in Room 4E 993, Pentagon Building, Arlington, Virginia

Stewart, C. E., Basic Weight Data, Edward G. Budd Manufacturing Company RB-1 Conestoga (C-93), 14 June 1944

Stewart, Col S. R., Holloman, Col G. Y., and Carroll, Brig Gen F. O., Air Corps, Engineering Division, Air Technical Services Command, Memorandum Report on Special Weapons Development Program, Serial No TSEPL-3-673-37-I, Engineering Division, Materiel Division, 28 February 1945, within Appendix B, pp1028-33 of The Development of Guided Missiles (Historical Division, Intelligence, Air Materiel Command, Wright Field, June 1946)

Correspondence

Anon, 'Military Characteristics of Aircraft', to Chief of Army Air Forces, 21 August 1941

Anon, Office of the Commanding General, Materiel Center, Inter-Office Memorandum to Chief, Production Division, 'Summary of Unsatisfactory Characteristics in the Model C-76 Airplane', 13 May 1943

Author's name illegible, Colonel, Air Corps, Acting Chief Development Engineering Branch, Materiel Division, 'Use of Airplane as Remotely Controlled Bomb', to Commanding General, Materiel Division, Wright Field, 25 March 1944, within Appendix B, p954 of The Development of Guided Missiles (Historical Division, Intelligence, Air Materiel Command, Wright Field, June 1946)

Author's name illegible, Colonel, Air Corps, Chief, Production Engineering Section, Materiel Division, Wight Field, 'Castor Project Status Report – B-17 and B-24 Airplanes', 5 August 1944, within Appendix B, pp957-58 of The Development of Guided Missiles (Historical Division, Intelligence, Air Materiel Command, Wright Field, June 1946)

Beaman, Maj Bartlett, Chief, Evaluation Unit, Air Corps, 'Autogiros', correspondence to Colonel Taylor, 22 November 1941, Henry Harley Arnold file frame 776

Bogert, Col H. Z., Air Corps, Acting Chief, Engineering Division, Materiel Division, Wight Field, 'Expedited Development of Altitude Control Device for Castor Aircraft and Other Guided Missiles', to Acting General, AAF Materiel Command, 31 July 1944, within Appendix B, pp218-20 of The Development of Guided Missiles (Historical Division, Intelligence, Air Materiel Command, Wright Field, June 1946)

Branshaw, Maj Gen Charles E., Commanding Materiel Center, to Commanding General, Army Air Forces, Assistant Chief of Air Staff, Materiel, Maintenance and Distribution, 'Production of the C-76 Airplane', 18 July 1943

Brentnall, Col S.R., Chief, Production Engineering Section, 'Re. Flight at St Louis on C-76 Airplanes', 4 March 1943

Air Corps, Assistant Chief, Materiel Division, Washington, D.C., 'Project Willie and Effect on CTI 1747 and Addendum', to Director, AAF Air Technical Services Command, Wright Field, 17 October 1944, within Appendix B, pp962-64 of The Development of Guided Missiles (Historical Division, Intelligence, Air Materiel Command, Wright Field, June 1946)

Carroll. Lt Col F. O., Air Corps, Chief, Experimental Engineering Section, 'Controlled Bomb Project', Experimental Engineering Section, Wright Field, to Chief, Materiel Division, Washington, D.C., 17 January 1942, within Appendix B, pp529-30 of The Development of Guided Missiles (Historical Division, Intelligence, Air Lt Col Materiel Command, Wright Field, June 1946)

Carroll, Col F. O., Air Corps, Chief, Experimental Engineering Section, 'Directive from Joint Chiefs of Staff Reference Report on Controlled Missile Projects, 1st Endorsement', Experimental Engineering Section, Wright Field, to Commanding General, AAF Materiel Command, Washington, D.C., 19 May 1942, within Appendix B, pp255-61 of The Development of Guided Missiles (Historical Division, Intelligence, Air Materiel Command, Wright Field, June 1946)

Carroll, Brig Gen F. O., Chief, Engineering Division, inter-office memorandum to Chief, Aircraft Laboratory, Wright Field, 'High Altitude Photographic Airplane', 30 June 1943

Chidlaw, B. W., Brig Gen, Materiel Command, Washington, D.C., 'Technical Instructions CTI-1102, Power Driven Controllable Bombs', letter to Technical Executive, Materiel Center, Wright Field, 16 February 1943, within Appendix B, p875 of The Development of Guided Missiles (Historical Division, Intelligence, Air Materiel Command, Wright Field, June 1946)

Chief, Materiel Division, letter to Commanding General, Materiel Command, 12 June 1943

Chief, Production Division, Materiel Division, memorandum for General Meyers, 'C-76 Airplane', 10 April 1943

Chief, Materiel Division, 'Memorandum for Record To Record a Conference Held in General Arnold's Office on Friday, July 23, 1943, Regarding Discontinuance of the Curtiss C-76 Transport Program', 23 July 1943

Chief, Materiel Division, teletype to Commanding General, Materiel Command, Wright Field, 19 May 1943

Chief of Staff, teletype to Assistant Chief of Air Staff, Materiel, Maintenance, and Distribution, 29 July 1943

Clayton, W. L., memorandum to Martin, Thomas O., Chambers, Reed M. and Harding, Barclay, 'Need for Special Planes for Latin America', 18 July 1941

Commanding General, AAF Materiel Command to Commanding General, Army Air Forces, Assistant Chief of Air Staff, Materiel, Maintenance, and Distribution, 'Cancellation of C-76 Airplane Contracts', 28 May 1943

Cook, Lt Col Orval R., Assistant Chief Production Engineering Section, Inter-Office Memorandum to Chief, Material Division, 'Waco C-62 Transport Airplanes', 5 March 1942

Cook, Lt Col Orval R., Chief, Production Division, Materiel Command, Inter-Office Memorandum to Commanding General, Materiel Command, 'Delivery of Model C-76 Airplanes', 22 June 1943

Chief, Production Division, to Commanding General, Air Service Command, 'Allocation of C-76 Airplanes', 18 September 1943

Cornwell, D. S., 'SO3C Model Airplanes – Utilization of, Planning Directive 94-A-43', Navy Department, Washington, 15 December 1943

Coupland, Col R. C., GSC, Acting Assistant Chief of the Air Staff, A-4, 'Rotary Wing Aircraft Operated from Merchant Freighters', Memorandum for the Chief, Bureau of Aeronautics, Navy Department, 18 June 1942, Henry Harley Arnold file frames 771-73

Craig, Brig Gen H. A., Assistant Chief of Air Staff, Operations, Commitments and Requirements, letter to Assistant Chief of Air Staff, Materiel, Maintenance and Distribution, 'Military Characteristics of Aircraft', 15 October 1943

Echols, Maj Gen O. P, Assistant Chief of Air Staff, Materiel, Maintenance and Distribution, Memorandum to General Chidlaw, Materiel Division, 'C-76 Cargo and B-36 Bomber', 19 June 1943

Assistant Chief of Air Staff, Materiel, Maintenance and Distribution, letter to The Air Judge Advocate, 'Termination of Contracts for C-76 Airplanes', 24 August 1943

Everett, Bart, email of 21 January 2014 quoting Maurice Schecter

Gardner, Col Grandison, Air Corps, letter regarding missiles to Lieutenant-General H. H. Arnold, Commanding General, Army Air Forces, Washington, D.C., 24 April 1942, within Appendix B, pp750-53 of The Development of Guided Missiles (Historical Division, Intelligence, Air Materiel Command, Wright Field, June 1946)

Giles, Maj Gen M. Barney W., Acting Chief of Air Staff, letter to Assistant Chief of Air Staff, Materiel, Maintenance and Distribution, 'Development of Special Photographic Mapping Airplane', 26 May 1943

Gross, Brig Gen Melvin E., Routing and Record Sheet, 'Immediate Development of a Long Range Photo Reconnaissance Aircraft', 30 November 1944

Hatcher, Lt Col G. A., Chief, Training and Transport Branch, Materiel Center Inter-Office Memorandum to Chief, Production Division, 'Summary of Unsatisfactory Characteristics in Model C-76 Airplane', 13 May 1943

Hatcher, Lt Col George A., Chief, Training and Transport Branch, Inter-Desk Correspondence to Cook, Col Orval R., Chief, Production Division, 'Curtiss-Wright C-76 Airplane', 23 July 1943

Haugen, Col Victor R., Air Corps, letter regarding Chief, Aircraft Projects Section, Services Engineering Division, Air Technical Services Command, 'Use of Fighter Aircraft as Pilotless Guided Missiles', to TSEAL-2, Chief, Aircraft Laboratory, 3 April 1945, within Appendix B. pp774-75 of The Development of Guided Missiles (Historical Division, Intelligence, Air Materiel Command, Wright Field, June 1946)

Hodgson, Richard, 'Radar Phase of the Willie Orphan Program', to Major-General H. S. Vandenberg, Commanding General, 9th Air Force, 2 February 1945

Holloman, Capt G. V., Air Corps, 'Engineering Section Memorandum Report on Status Report on Aerial Targets, Power Driven', Serial No I-54-1410, 26 June 1939, W668-673, within Appendix W, ppW668-673 of The Development of Guided Missiles (Historical Division, Intelligence, Air Materiel Command, Wright Field, June 1946)

Lovett, Robert A., Assistant Secretary of War for Air, letter to Clayton, W. L., 'Need for Special Planes for Latin America', 8 August 1941

Maxwell, Col Alfred R., Air Corps, Headquarters, United States Strategic Air Forces in Europe, 'Implementation of "WILLIE ORPHAN" Project', 17 January 1945

McCoy, Col Jerald W., Chief, Reconnaissance Branch, Memorandum for Chief, Requirements Division, 'Development of Special Photographic Mapping Airplanes', 30 June 1944

Moffitt, Henry K., Curtiss-Wright Corporation, letter to Commanding General, Army Air Forces, Materiel Center, Wright Field, 'Contract W535 ao-27018, C-76 Airplanes, Delivery', 30 September 1942

Morgensen, J. O., Engineering Division Memorandum Report No ENG-50-1071, Mock-up Inspection of Republic XF-12 Airplane, 11 August 1944

Northrup, Col George O., Chief, Photographic Requirements Section, Memorandum for Assistant Chief of Air Staff, Operations, Commitments and Requirements, 'High Altitude Photographic Aircraft Development', 25 June 1943

Ofer, Capt J. H., Air Corps, 'TI-2003, Addendum No 19, Use of Fighter Aircraft as Pilotless Guided Missiles', to Commanding General, Army Air Forces, Washington, D.C., 16 March 1945, within Appendix B, pp972-73 of The Development of Guided Missiles (Historical Division, Intelligence, Air Materiel Command, Wright Field, June 1946)

Partridge, Maj Gen E. E., US Army, Commanding 3rd Air Division, 'Report on Aphrodite Project', to Commanding General, Eighth Air Force, 20 January 1945

Pole, Col George W. Jr., Chief, Inspection Section, letter to Major General Branshaw, Commanding General, Materiel Command, 'Curtiss-Wright Contract for C-76 Airplane at Louisville, Kentucky', 12 July 1943

Production Division, teletype to General Echols, 18 May 1943

R.C.W.B., Secy/A.S., 'Rotary Wing Aircraft Operated from Merchant Freighters', Routing and Record Sheet, Headquarters Army Air Forces, comment dated 16 June 1942, Henry Harley Arnold file frame 767

Riley, Maj D. E., 'Contract #33-038 ac-1079, XF-11 and F-11 Aircraft Conference at Washington, D.C.', 10 August 1944

Roth, Col M. S., Engineering Division, Materiel Center, 'Memorandum Report on Conference Relative to Engineering Matters on C-76 Airplanes, ENG-50-889', 14 June 1943

R.R.G., 'Rotary Wing Aircraft Operated from Merchant Freighters', Memorandum for Colonel Chidlaw, 14 June 1942, Henry Harley Arnold file frames 768-70

Sims, Col T. A., Air Corps, Deputy, Chief of Staff, 'Technical Instructions CTI-1102, Addendum No 1, Power Driven Controllable Bombs', to Engineering Division, Wright Field, 3 July 1943, within Appendix B, pp883-84 of The Development of Guided Missiles (Historical Division, Intelligence, Air Materiel Command, Wright Field, June 1946)

Air Corps, Deputy, Chief of Staff, 'Controllable Bomb, Power Driven, General Motors, Type A-1', to Commanding General, Army Air Forces, Washington, D.C., 24 August 1943, within Appendix B, pp888-901 of The Development of Guided Missiles (Historical Division, Intelligence, Air Materiel Command, Wright Field, June 1946)

Air Corps, Chief of Administration, Air Technical Services Command, Wright Field, 'War Weary Aircraft as Guided Missiles', to Commanding General, Army Air Forces, Washington, D.C., 12 April 1945, within Appendix B, pp69-70 of The Development of Guided Missiles (Historical Division, Intelligence, Air Materiel Command, Wright Field, June 1946)

Air Corps, Chief of Administration, Air Technical Services Command, Wright Field, Technical Instruction Serial No TI-2003, Addendum No 19, 'Use of Fighter Aircraft as Pilotless Guided Missiles', to Commanding General, Army Air Forces, Washington, D.C., 22 February 1945, within Appendix B, pp212-13 of The Development of Guided Missiles (Historical Division, Intelligence, Air Materiel Command, Wright Field, June 1946)

Smith, Brig Gen C. R., Chief of Staff, Headquarters, Air Transport Command, to Assistant Chief Air Staff, Operations, Commitments and Requirements, 'C-76 Aircraft', 21 July 1943

Spaatz, Brig Gen Carl, Air Staff, Memorandum for General Arnold, 'Troop-carrying Transport Airplanes', 2 August 1941

St Clair Streett, memorandum for Lovett, R. A., 2 August 1941

Vanaman, Lt Col Arthur W., Secretary, Air Staff, 'Military Characteristics of Airplanes', 11 September 1941

Warren, E. A., Manager of Military Contracts, Curtiss-Wright Corporation, letter to Commanding General, Army Air Forces, Materiel Center, Wright Field, 'Army Flight Testing of the C-76 Airplane – Contract 27018', 1 March 1943

Wieber, C. W., 'SO3C Model Airplanes – Disposition of, Aviation Planning Directive 15-A-44', Navy Department, Washington, 4 February 1944

Wilson, Col P. C., Air Corps, Acting Chief Development Engineering Branch, Materiel Division, 'Use of Airplane as Remotely Controlled Bomb', to Commanding General, Army Air Forces, Washington, D.C., 8 June 1944, within Appendix B, p956 of The Development of Guided Missiles (Historical Division, Intelligence, Air Materiel Command, Wright Field, June 1946)

Air Corps, Acting Chief Development Engineering Branch, Materiel Division, 'Expedited Development of Altitude Control Device for Castor Aircraft and Other Guided Missiles', to Commanding General, Materiel Command, Wright Field, 10 July 1944, within Appendix B, pp785-86 of The Development of Guided Missiles (Historical Division, Intelligence, Air Materiel Command, Wright Field, June 1946)

Wilson, Brig Gen Donald, US Army, Assistant Chief of Air Staff, Operations, Commitments & Requirements, 'Status of Weary Willie Orphans Project', to General Arnold, 22 December 1944, within Appendix B, p71 of The Development of Guided Missiles (Historical Division, Intelligence, Air Materiel Command, Wright Field, June 1946)

Windsok, Capt G. H., Air Corps, for Brigadier General Carroll, Chief, Experimental Engineering Division, 'Use of Airplane as Remotely Controlled Bomb', to Commanding General, Army Air Forces, Washington, D.C., 12 April 1944, within Appendix B, p955 of The Development of Guided Missiles (Historical Division, Intelligence, Air Materiel Command, Wright Field, June 1946)

Wolfe, Brig Gen K. B., Chief, Production Division, 'Telephone conversation between Brig Gen B. W. Chidlaw and Brig Gen K. B. Wolfe, Subject Re. Cargo Planes', 12 May 1943

Chief, Production Division, 'Telephone conversation between Col J. W. Sessums Jr. and Brig Gen. K. B. Wolfe, 'Subject Re. Cargo Planes, Meeting in Washington Wednesday, with General Meyers', 12 May 1943

Lectures

Sessums, Col J. W., Air Materiel Command, 'Design and Engineering Problems of Aircraft Production', 14 May 1946, presentation at the Industrial College of the Air Force, downloaded from https://digitalndulibrary.ndu.edu/cdm4/results.php?CISOOP1=all&CISOBOX1=sessums&CISOROOT=all&CISOFIELD1=CISOSEARCHALL&CISORESTMP=results.php&CISOVIEWTMP=item_viewer.php&CISOSUPPRESS=1

Other

Anon, 'AAF Announces C-97, Newest and Largest Cargo Airplane', press release, Air Technical Services Command, Wright Field, Dayton, Ohio, 12 January 1945

Anon, The AMA History Program Presents: Biography of Reginald Denny, American Model Aeronautics, undated

Anon, Details of AAF Guide Missiles Program, within Appendix B, pp221-54 (15 April 1944), pp243-71 (1 July 1944), pp 802-15 (2 September 1944) and pp1501-23 (3 October 1944) of The Development of Guided Missiles (Historical Division, Intelligence, Air Materiel Command, Wright Field, June 1946)

Anon, 'Detail of AAF Guided Missiles Program, Special Projects, 1. Castor – Use of Airplanes as Remotely Controlled Bomb', 1 July 1944, within Appendix B, p544 of The Development of Guided Missiles (Historical Division, Intelligence, Air Materiel Command, Wright Field, June 1946)

Anon, Kellett Aircraft Corporation, September 1952, unpublished summary of company and product history found in Department of Special Collections, The University of Texas at Dallas

Bruins, Berend Derk, 'US Naval Bombardment Missiles, 1940-1958: A Study of the Weapons Innovation Process' (Columbia University, 1981, Doctoral Dissertation)

Bureau of Aeronautics, Navy Department, Airplane Characteristics & Performance, Model RB-1, 1 September 1944

Dronen, Gordon, letter dated 20 May 2002 to the San Diego Aerospace Museum providing details of the Navy TDD experience based on the author's personal involvement during the Second World War

Fahrney, RAdm Delmar S., USN (Ret), 'The History of Pilotless Aircraft and Guided Missiles', unpublished manuscript prepared for US Navy Bureau of Aeronautics, undated but likely 1958

Henry Harley Arnold file. Microfilm Reel 28167 provided on CD Rom from the Archives Branch of the Albert F. Simpson Historical Research Center, Air Force Case History Files, Air Force Historical Research Agency, Maxwell AFB, Alabama, collection of correspondence and other documents

Kellett XR-10, 1/72 scale model kit, LF Models, 72100

Lesher, Jim, 'RB-1 Conestoga', summary found in files of the National Museum of the Naval Aviation, undated

Navy Department, 'Radio-Controlled Hellcat First Standard Military Plane to Fly Without Pilot', press release, 12 October 1945

Platt LePage XR-1/XR-1A, 1/72 scale model kit, Anigrand Craftswork, #AA-2062

McDonnell XHJD-1 Whirlaway, 1/72 scale model kit, Anigrand Craftswork, #AA-2024

Signor, Philip W., 'Cruise Missiles for the U.S. Navy: An Exemplar of Innovation in a Military Organization' (Naval War College, Newport, Rhode Island, June 1994)

This Stinson L-5 Sentinel (over The Philippine Islands in July 1945) is emblematic of the light airplanes originally acquired for Observation but redesignated Liaison while also performing some photography close to the front. The leading edge slots and trailing edge flaps on the wings are evident, supporting slow flight and also, along with the large tires, the ability to land and takeoff in short distances on some unprepared surfaces. These inexpensive and easy to maintain airplanes had nearly the performance of autogyros without the difficulties and so that 'species' of rotorcraft faded away. *National Archives*

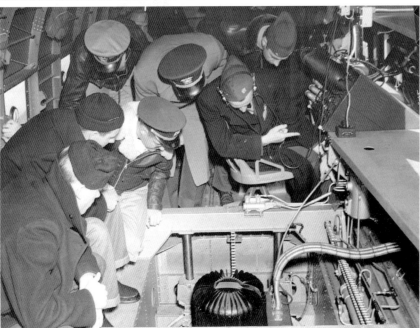

Websites

Aero Files: http://www.aerofiles.com
Aero Web: http://www.aero-web.org
alternatehistory.com/discussion/showthread.php?t=209566
Anon, 'The JRB-1', Naval Encounters, downloaded from beechrestorations.files.wordpress.com/2012/06/naval-encounters.pdf
Aviation History: http://www.aviation-history.com
Avistar: http://www.avistar.org
Bruning, Al, 'World War II Louisville, Kentucky', *Louisville Cultural History Examiner*, 8 June 2010, http://www.examiner.com/cultural-history-in-louisville/world-war-ii-louisville-kentucky
Designations of US Air Force Projects, Cully, George and Parsch, Andreas: http://orbat.com/site/andreas/U_S_ per cent20Air per cent20Force per cent20Projects.htm
Helicopters: http://www.helis.com
Hiller: http://www.hiller.org
http://en.wikipedia.org/wiki/C-76_Caravan
National Museum of the United States Air Force: www.nationalmuseum.af.mil
Military Television Equipment Built by RCA: http://www.qsl.net/w2vtm/mil_television_history.html
MX-1 to MX-499 Listing, Cully, George and Parsch, Andreas: http://www.designation-system.net/usmilav/mx/1-499.html and also /500-999
Piasecki: http://www.piasecki.com/helicopters
Platt-LePage Aircraft Company Archives, http://www.plattlepageaircraft.com
Ryan ST-M in Australia, Geoff Goodall, 28 September 2013, http://www.goodall.com.au/australian-aviation/ryan-stm/ryan-stm.htm
Sikorsky Archives: http://www.sikorskyarchives.com
Smithsonian Institution: http://airandspace.si.edu
Stag One: http://stagone.org
Unicopters: http://www.unicopter.com
US Military Rockets and Missiles: www.designation-system.net/dusrm/app1/, 2006
Vectors: http://www.vectorsite.net/twcruz_1.html
Wikipedia: http://en.wikipedia.org/wiki

Left: The Navy's drone control gear (Roger) was also placed aboard a modified R4D-5 (a C-47A) for flight test and training. Operated by VJ-6 at Clinton, Oklahoma, it was photographed here on 4 January 1944 and displays fine workmanship. The drone monitor and control station is clear while the top of the lowered radar fairing (extending out the bottom of the aircraft) is being examined by the distinguished visitors. *National Archives*

Opposite top: Test pilot Jack Reeder flies the Bendix Model K helicopter in 1945, likely at NACA Langley where he was employed. Martin Jensen designed the co-axial rotor aircraft of 25-ft diameter which first flew in June 1945. Powered by a 100hp Continental C-100, the tiny ship grossed just 1,200lb. *NASA*

Bottom: Light airplane optionally-piloted drone production amounted to thousands over five years. The most prolific was Culver Airplane Company of Wichita, Kansas, with the PQ-8 and PQ-14 airplanes, the PQ-14 line shown here on 12 July 1944. The small wooden aircraft (30-foot span) is diminished by the P-38 looming over them at the end of the line. *San Diego Air & Space Museum*

AMERICAN AIRCRAFT DEVELOPMENT OF WWII

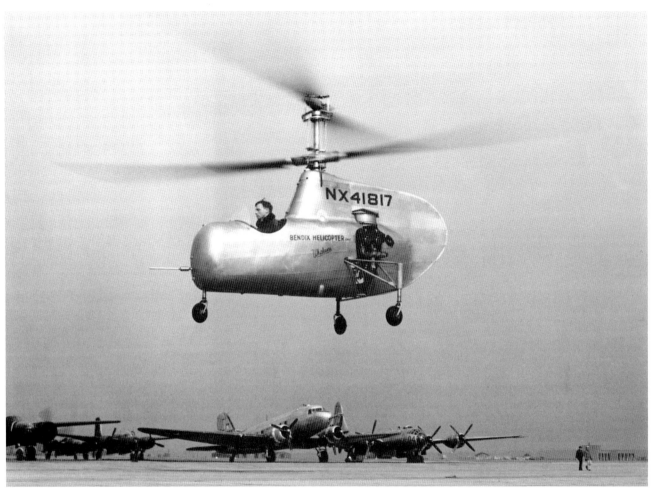

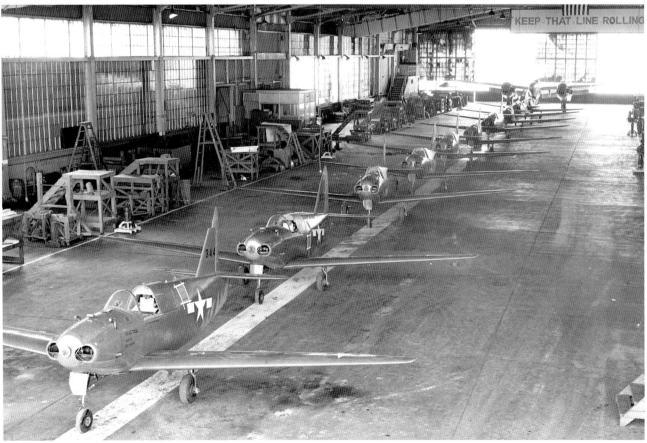

Index

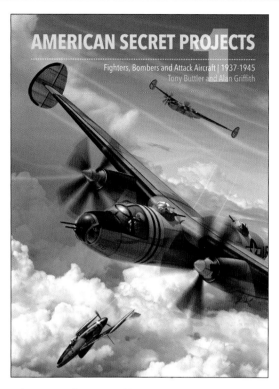

American Secret Projects -1

Fighters, Bombers and Attack Aircraft 1937-1945

Tony Buttler and Alan Griffith

With all that has been written about the United States' combat aircraft of WWII, it is astounding how little has been published about the dozens of aircraft designs that were rejected before reaching production. By December 7, 1941 almost all the major American combat aircraft of WWII had been designed, selected and in many cases were under production - everything from the P-40 fighter to the huge B-36 'Peacemaker'. Even so, the war years to 1945 saw a dizzying array of new aircraft designs and types being proposed. For example, between 1942 and 1944 Boeing alone submitted no fewer than eight multi-engine, intercontinental bomber designs for consideration by the USAAF - every one of which had a wingspan of over 200ft; one had a span of a whopping 277ft! The Navy competition that resulted in the F7F Tigercat carrier fighter received more than a dozen different design submissions from at least half a dozen manufacturers. Then there are the virtually unknown Vought 'flying flapjack' series of designs, including one fighter and one attack aircraft for the USAAF.

In researching American Secret Projects - 1, internationally-renowned aviation authors Tony Buttler and Alan Griffith have uncovered hundreds of previously classified files to provide specifications, histories, artist illustrations and 3-view drawings - many redrawn for clarity from the original factory submissions specifically for this book. The result is an unparalleled and fascinating record of the creative genius of American aircraft designers, from material which has lain hidden and forgotten for over 70 years.

American Secret Projects - 1 is filled not only with aircraft that most historians, aircraft enthusiasts and modellers have never heard of, but many more that no-one but their designers could ever have dreamt up.

ISBN: 978 190653 7487
Binding: Hardback
Dimensions: 280mm x 210mm
Pages: 192
Photos/Illus: Over 300
Price: £27.50

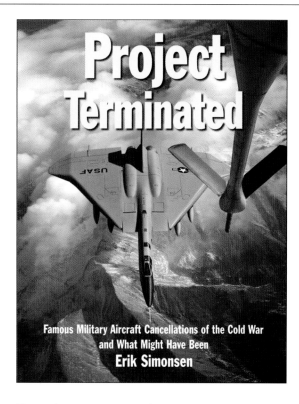

Project Terminated

Famous Military Aircraft Cancellations of the Cold War and What Might Have Been

Eric Simonsen

Aerospace history is a fascinating subject. However, what is genuinely intriguing is an examination of those twists of fate, sometimes referred to as, 'what might have been'.

New aeronautical designs are often developed in response to a particular need for which the government may ask industry for input. Yet, in the many attempts to achieve a viable product, even the competition winners do not always survive, and are subsequently cancelled for poor performance, not meeting schedule milestones, budgetary pressures or political intrigue.

Each aircraft requires very different thinking in aerodynamics, materials, manufacturing techniques, training and logistics and where some of these advances were long contemplated by designers such as Jack Northrop and the YB-49, others, such as the Boeing X-20 Dyna-Soar were radically new, forced by the rapid advance of science and welfare.

Imposing their will upon the instincts and the experience of their military subordinates in such diverse programs as the North American Rockwell XB-70, Boeing X-20, Lockheed F-12B, Rockwell B-1A, Avro CF-105 Arrow, BAC TSR.2 and the Northrop F-29, politicians often seal the fate of promising contenders.

Project Terminated provides a succinct, accurate assessment of the development of these aircraft, analysing technical and political challenges and their solutions. Combined with the concept of how these remarkable aircraft would have appeared in operational use, and illustrated throughout with over 250 photographs and drawings, *Project Terminated* provides an enticing look at both the past and the future.

ISBN: 9 780859 791731
Binding: Hardback
Dimensions: 290mm x 216mm
Pages: 224
Photos/Illus: 200 colour and 25 b/w photos
Price: £23.95 $39.95